SandCastle
Let's Go!

LET'S GO
BY
RV

ANDERS HANSON

Consulting Editor, Diane Craig, M.A./Reading Specialist

ABDO Publishing Company

Published by ABDO Publishing Company, 8000 West 78th Street, Edina, MN 55439.

Copyright © 2008 by Abdo Consulting Group, Inc. International copyrights reserved in all countries. No part of this book may be reproduced in any form without written permission from the publisher. SandCastle™ is a trademark and logo of ABDO Publishing Company.

Printed in the United States.

Editor: Pam Price
Curriculum Coordinator: Nancy Tuminelly
Cover and Interior Design and Production: Mighty Media
Photo Credits: Corbis Images, iStockphoto/Marcin Balcerzak, JupiterImages Corporation, Shutterstock, Winnebago Industries

Library of Congress Cataloging-in-Publication Data

Hanson, Anders, 1980-

    Let's go by RV / Anders Hanson.
      p. cm. -- (Let's go!)
    ISBN 978-1-59928-902-1
    1. Recreational vehicles--Juvenile literature. 2. Recreational vehicle living--Juvenile literature. 3. Vacations--Juvenile literature. I. Title.

    TL298.H36 2008
    796.7'9--dc22

                                                2007013890

SandCastle™ Level: Transitional

SandCastle™ books are created by a team of professional educators, reading specialists, and content developers around five essential components—phonemic awareness, phonics, vocabulary, text comprehension, and fluency—to assist young readers as they develop reading skills and increase their general knowledge. All books are written, reviewed, and leveled for guided reading, early intervention reading, and Accelerated Reader® programs for use in shared, guided, and independent reading and writing activities to support a balanced approach to literacy instruction. The SandCastle™ series has four levels that correspond to early literacy development. The levels are provided to help teachers and parents select appropriate books for young readers.

Emerging Readers
(no flags)

Beginning Readers
(1 flag)

Transitional Readers
(2 flags)

Fluent Readers
(3 flags)

SandCastle™ would like to hear from you. Please send us your comments or questions.

sandcastle@abdopublishing.com

RV stands for recreational vehicle. RVs are like homes you can take with you on vacation.

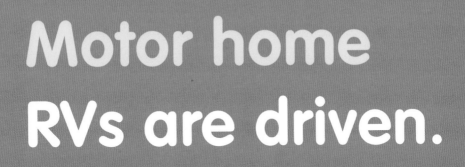

Motor home RVs are driven.

Travel trailer RVs are towed.

Most RVs have a kitchen and a place to eat.

RVs have at least one bed.

The Jones family has a pop-up RV. It is also called a folding camper.

Jenny and
Tim went to
Yellowstone
National Park
in their RV.

Leah and her family take their RV to the lake each summer. They like to play card games.

Marcy and her parents wait by their RV for the rain to stop. The awning keeps them dry.

HAVE YOU BEEN IN AN RV?

WHERE DID YOU GO?

TYPES OF RVS

conversion vehicle

folding camper

motor home

travel trailer

truck camper

Nearly 8 million U.S. families own recreational vehicles.

There are more than 16,000 campgrounds in the United States where you can camp in an RV.

Many RV parks offer Internet and wireless Internet services.

GLOSSARY

awning – a rooflike structure, usually canvas, that provides protection.

folding camper – a trailer with canvas walls that pop up or unfold when the trailer is opened.

travel trailer – a motor home that is pulled by a car or a truck.

vacation – time off from school or work, often spent traveling, relaxing, and having fun.

To see a complete list of SandCastle™ books and other nonfiction titles from ABDO Publishing Company, visit **www.abdopublishing.com**.

8000 West 78th Street, Edina, MN 55439 • 800-800-1312 • 952-831-1632 fax

The Rise and Fall of Culture History

R. Lee Lyman
Michael J. O'Brien
University of Missouri–Columbia
Columbia, Missouri

and

Robert C. Dunnell
University of Washington
Seattle, Washington

PLENUM PRESS • NEW YORK AND LONDON

Library of Congress Cataloging-in-Publication Data

The rise and fall of culture history / R. Lee Lyman,
   Michael J. O'Brien, and Robert C. Dunnell.
         p.   cm.
      Includes bibliographical references and index.
      ISBN 0-306-45537-4 (hardbound). -- ISBN 0-306-45538-2 (pbk.)
      1. Archaeology--United States--History--20th century.
   2. Archaeology--North America--History--20th century.   3. Indians of
   North America--Antiquities.   4. Archaeology--Classification.
   5. Antiquities--Classification.   I. Lyman, R. Lee.   II. O'Brien,
   Michael J. (Michael John), 1950-   . III. Dunnell, Robert C., 1942-
   .
   CC101.U6R57   1997
   930.1--dc21   97-14507
                                                                 CIP

Cover illustration from J. A. Ford, Figure 3 of "On the Concept of Types: The Type Concept Revisited," in *American Anthropologist* 56: 42–54. © American Anthropological Association.

ISBN 0-306-45537-4 (Hardbound)
ISBN 0-306-45538-2 (Paperback)

© 1997 Plenum Press, New York
A Division of Plenum Publishing Corporation
233 Spring Street, New York, N. Y. 10013

http://www.plenum.com

Printed in the United States of America

Preface

Over forty years ago Gordon R. Willey (1953b:361) stated that "[t]he objectives of archeology . . . are approached by the study and manipulation of three basic factors: form, space, and time." A few years later, Albert C. Spaulding (1960b:439) repeated this thought using different words: "[A]rchaeology can be defined minimally as the study of the interrelationship of form, temporal locus, and spatial locus exhibited by artifacts. In other words, archaeologists are always concerned with these interrelationships, whatever broader interests they may have, and these interrelationships are the special business of archaeology."

Many of the means Americanist archaeologists use to examine formal variation in artifacts and the distribution of that variation across space and through time were formulated early in the twentieth century. The analytical tenets, or principles, underlying the various methods and techniques were formalized and axiomatized in later years such that by the 1930s they constituted the first formal paradigm for Americanist archaeology—a paradigm commonly termed *culture history*. This paradigm began with a very specific goal—to document the history of the development of prehistoric cultures in the Americas. Although it fell from favor in the 1960s, many of its central tenets were carried over to newer paradigms and thus continue to be fundamental within Americanist archaeology.

With Willey's and Spaulding's conceptions as our guide, we elsewhere reprinted (Lyman et al. 1997) what we view as the benchmark papers of culture history, in which the fundamental principles of the paradigm were established. We compiled and reprinted the papers because it is our strong impression that many archaeologists today tend to overlook the central tenets of the discipline—tenets that underpin virtually everything we do. Moreover, contemporary knowledge of our discipline's past often appears to be derived from secondary sources that often impart orientations and characteristics that the original authors would not recognize. Thus, we find ourselves in strong agreement with Bohannan and Glazer (1988:xv), who note that ignorance of a discipline's past can result in "unnecessary originality" while detailed knowledge of it can "give one a great many good ideas, for the past never says things quite the way the present needs them said."

To place those benchmark papers in a comprehensible context, we provided a brief overview of how the elements of time, space, and form, in various guises, came to assume center stage in Americanist archaeology after the beginning of the twentieth century (Lyman et al. 1997). Our discussion was necessarily abbreviated, and while we noted how and why the culture history paradigm took the form that it did, we did not go into great detail. It is our purpose in this volume to do just that. Our essay is written from a critical viewpoint and seeks not only to document the history of the culture history paradigm but also to demonstrate why that paradigm flourished for a time and why it was ultimately set aside by a large segment of the discipline. The structure of our essay is partly chronological and partly topical. In most cases it is impossible to separate a discussion of time from discussions of space and form, and hence a mixed chronological and topical structure appeared to represent the best means of organizing the discussion in coherent fashion.

The number of Americanist archaeologists who contributed to the development of the culture history paradigm is large. There are, to be sure, some figures who were more central than others to that development, and it is, of course, the former's work to which we devote much of our attention. The story is an intriguing one, and not just because one might construe the first few decades of the twentieth century as the "good old days" of Americanist archaeology, when every newly found site or excavated trench revealed previously unknown kinds of artifacts or promised to fill a gaping hole in knowledge. Sometimes the history of Americanist archaeology during that period is so characterized either directly or indirectly (e.g., Givens 1992; Lyon 1996; Woodbury 1973). To be sure, it was an exciting time for precisely these kinds of reasons (see especially Elliott 1995), but with the benefit of hindsight, it was also an incredibly intellectually stimulating time. Some histories have tried to capture that feeling and discuss the implications thereof (e.g., Trigger 1989), whereas others have chronicled the names of the excavators, the names of the sites excavated, the dates of excavation, and some of the analytical innovations that resulted (e.g., Fitting 1973; Willey and Sabloff 1974, 1980, 1993). We seek to do more than that here.

The intellectual history of the culture history paradigm is informative as to the status of the discipline today. Not only can the origins of certain innovative analytical techniques be traced, but the reasons for their innovation can be determined. Why was there a stratigraphic revolution in the 1910s? Or, was there really such a revolution? Why are there so many ways to seriate artifact collections, and where did these various techniques come from? What theoretical notions, if any, underlay their development? What is a component, a focus, a phase, a tradition, a horizon, and do such units have a role to play in the discipline today? If so, what kind of role? Did Folsom evolve from Clovis, did Mississippian evolve from Woodland, or were these the result of migrations of different groups of people? Why would we think that any of these scenarios might be correct or incorrect, and how might we go about choosing one over another? In short, how and why do we know what we think we know about the prehistory of the Americas in so far as that prehistory is reflected along the dimensions of time, space, and form? Producing an answer to that question is the major goal of this volume. The answer hinges on understanding how and why the culture history paradigm developed the way it did.

We thank Eliot Werner of Plenum Press for his continued interest in this project and Mary Curioli and Herman Makler of Plenum, who helped us get the manuscript in publishable shape. We also thank the American Anthropological Association for permission to use Figure 3 from James A. Ford, "On the Concept of Types: The Type Concept Revisited," *American Anthropologist* 56: 42–54 on the cover of the book. Dan Glover tracked down numerous references and redrafted all the figures, and Jennifer Smith Glover proofread the manuscript. Correspondence with Jon L. Gibson, William G. Haag, and especially James B. Griffin helped tremendously when it came to some of the fine details. Comments on a draft by several anonymous reviewers, and especially the very sharp eyes of E. J. O'Brien, are appreciated.

Contents

Tables and Figures

1

Introduction

The first major paradigm of Americanist archaeology[1] was one generally known as *culture history* (e.g., Binford 1965, 1968a; Caldwell 1959; Dunnell 1978; Flannery 1967; see Kidder 1932:2 for an early use of this term). It was within the context of this paradigm, between about 1910 and 1960, that many of the central tenets of Americanist archaeology were first developed and applied. Most Americanist archaeologists would agree that much of what we think we know about human prehistory has significant ties to the culture history paradigm. At the very least, none could successfully dispute the fact that most textbooks produced by American-trained archaeologists—whether those books concern how to do archaeology (e.g., Sharer and Ashmore 1993; Thomas 1989) or the results of doing archaeological research (e.g., Fagan 1991; Jennings 1989)—have at their core various organizational and interpretive elements that were developed by culture historians.

The fundamental principles of the culture history paradigm were so ingrained in Americanist thought that archaeologists, whether they realized it or not, carried many of them over to the so-called new archaeology of the 1960s (Meltzer 1979). Those principles are still so ingrained in our thinking that we often fail to realize that we use them day in and day out as we go about our research and teaching. Many modern presentations of these principles (e.g., Browman and Givens 1996) are variously superficial or derived from secondary or tertiary sources, and they seldom do justice to the original thoughts, often garbling them to such a degree that they would be unrecognizable to their originators. It therefore is critical to read the original discussions to ensure a firm and accurate understanding of what the original authors meant and, equally important, to place those discussions within their proper historical contexts. It is for these reasons that we reprinted what we view as the benchmark articles of the culture history paradigm in a companion volume to this one (Lyman et al. 1997).

In that companion volume, we provide a short overview of the development of the culture history paradigm and touch on why it eventually fell from favor among Americanist archaeologists. We concluded that its fall was tied to its inability to attain the goals it set out for itself. Here, we explore that conclusion by reviewing the history and development of the paradigm in detail. Americanist archaeology's attempts to be "scientific" did not, as some have suggested, originate with the new, or processual, archaeology of the 1960s and 1970s. Early-twentieth-century Americanists expressed precisely the same desire (see Dunnell 1992 for a review). How they attempted to fulfill that desire is an interesting, integral, and critical part of our discipline's history. Importantly, because those attempts still influence Americanist archaeology almost a century later, it is reasonable to ask whether earlier culture historians attained their goal, and, if not, how and why they failed. To examine this issue, we need to establish a framework for analyzing the writings of culture historians and the methods and principles they developed.

Reference to biological evolution—or at least to evolutionary metaphors—as a source of explanations for culture history was fairly common during the early twentieth century (e.g., Kidder 1915; Kidder and Kidder 1917; Kroeber 1931a; Nelson 1919a). Further, some of the early members of the paradigm—a few of whom were originally trained as biologists—attempted to incorporate various notions of biological evolution into their archaeological research (e.g., Colton 1939; Gladwin and Gladwin 1934). At least one of the founding members of the paradigm explicitly noted that the "ultimate goal" of culture history was to solve "the problems of cultural evolution" (Kidder 1932:8). Because the culture history paradigm ultimately sought to document and explain the historical development of cultures in various areas—a development that often was referred to as *cultural evolution*—we adopt a particular framework in the following chapters that allows us to examine whether the principles and methods of culture history were up to the task.

We chose modern evolutionary theory as the source of our analytical framework because it allows us to contrast two views of reality that play as important a role in archaeology as they do in biology. As we will see, one emphasizes differences, the other differences *and* change (e.g., Gould 1986; Mayr 1982). Culture historians, as we noted above, were interested in both; problematically, many of the methods and units they devised to monitor difference and change were derived from the wrong view of reality. This was, in effect, one major weakness of culture history as it was conceived, though this fundamental flaw has rarely been noted. Conversely, some of the methods and units that were appropriate for one task were co-opted for tasks for which they were ill suited. This flaw has also been overlooked.

Science and Kinds of Science

Science is, simply, a way of understanding and explaining how and why the world works the way it does. Common sense is another way of knowing and explaining phenomena, but it is markedly different from science (Dunnell 1982). Science uses "performance standards" (Dunnell 1978, 1982) to establish the correctness of a conclusion. That is, does a conclusion actually account for the phenomena it is supposed to? Use of this method to establish correctness allows conclusions to be integrated into a systematic body of knowledge. Theory specifies (1) the kinds of phenomena to be examined; (2) how phenomena are to be structured and measured for examination; and (3) how those phenomena should interrelate, interact, and respond to one another given particular contingencies. Theory thus provides the basis for explanation. Common sense may appear to serve well in the place of theory, but its liabilities include the facts that it is subconscious, ethnocentric, and contingency bound (Kluckhohn 1939b), and it embodies no developed concept of time. It entails an essentialist view of the world and of all the things in it (see below).

Scientific inquiry consists of three significant parameters (Lewontin 1974; see also Dunnell 1982): (1) dynamic sufficiency, (2) empirical sufficiency, and (3) tolerance limits. A discipline is scientific if its theory is dynamically sufficient—that is, if its theory contains the proper elements in the proper structure to generate scientifically acceptable explanations. A scientifically acceptable explanation is one that works well in an empirical context; hence, an empirically sufficient theory is one that has elements or units that are directly measurable in the phenomenological world. Units or elements that are not measurable render empirical testing impossible. Finally, the fact that models of things always differ from the things themselves results in the requirement of tolerance limits—that is, how closely must our models mirror the things they were set up to model? As Lewontin (1974:8) so eloquently put it,

> the problem of theory building is a constant interaction between constructing laws and finding an appropriate set of descriptive state variables [units or elements] such that laws can be constructed. We cannot go out and describe the world any old way we please and then sit back and demand that an explanatory and predictive theory be built on that description. . . . [T]here is a process of trial and synthesis going on . . . in which both state descriptions and laws are being fitted together.

A few years earlier Hull (1970:32) said virtually the same thing:

> The two processes of constructing classifications and of discovering scientific laws and formulating scientific theories must be carried on together. Neither can outstrip the other very far without engendering mutually injurious effects. The idea that an extensive and elaborate classification can be considered in isolation from all scientific theories and then transformed only later into a theoretically significant classification is purely illusory.

We need, then, units of measurement of sorts that are relevant to our theory and that allow us to monitor the empirical manifestations of the processes included in that theory. This relates to an issue familiar to all Americanist archaeologists, variously known as classification or typological-unit construction. It has been recognized for some time by evolutionary biologists that there are two basic kinds of units one might construct (e.g., Mayr 1959) and that those units derive from two completely different views of reality, but explicit recognition of this dichotomy for archaeology has come about only recently (e.g., Dunnell 1982; O'Brien and Holland 1990), though a few foreshadowings appeared earlier (Osgood 1951).

Essentialism and Materialism

A historical science, as a direct result of its materialist metaphysic, can monitor *change* in phenomena; ahistorical science, because it employs an essentialist metaphysic, can only measure *difference* (Hull 1965; Mayr 1959; Sober 1980). An essentialist metaphysic presumes the existence of discoverable, discrete kinds of things. Things are of the same kind because of shared essential properties—their "essences"—and these essential properties dictate whether a specimen is of kind A or kind B. The essential properties define an ideal, or archetype, "to which actual objects [are] imperfect approximations"; nonessential variation between specimens is "annoying distraction" (Lewontin 1974:5). Chemical elements are essentialistic units, the properties of which are known. Individual atoms within each class are so like all the other atoms in that class that they escape the "imperfect approximation" label, being instead clones of each other. Given the theory that we have regarding how and why atoms interact, coupled with the fact that all atoms within a class not only are alike but will behave the same way, we are able to *predict* future outcomes of atomic interaction regardless of where or when the interactions occur. Importantly, prediction is possible only because the units are real.

Because of our own limited span of existence (witness the debates over catastrophism and uniformitarianism during the nineteenth and twentieth centuries) and because we typically call on common sense in our everyday endeavors, the essentialist metaphysic is manifest within human thinking. Regardless, it is inappropriate for the study of change over time precisely because it denies change. Specimens grouped within natural, essentialist kinds must always be the same—they must share essential properties—regardless of their position in time and space. Thus, change is impossible; only the difference between different kinds, or types, can be measured. For this reason, essentialism often is referred to as *typological thinking* (Mayr 1959, 1988). As Mayr (1959:2) notes, "Since there is no gradation between types, gradual evolution is basically a logical impossibility for the typologist. Evolution, if it occurs at all, has to proceed in steps or jumps." This gives studies of change undertaken within the essentialist metaphysic their transformational character. A specimen of kind A is kind A in this time and place, but in another time and place it somehow has been transformed into kind B. "Genuine change, according to essentialism, is possible only through the saltational origin of new essences" (Mayr 1982:38–39).

The materialist metaphysic holds that phenomena cannot exist as bounded, discrete entities because they "are always in the process of becoming" something else (Dunnell 1982:8). Variation between and among specimens "is the cornerstone of [Darwinian evolutionary] theory" (Lewontin 1974:5). "All [things] are composed of unique features and can be described collectively only in statistical terms. Individuals . . . form populations of which we can determine an arithmetic mean and the statistics of variation. Averages are merely statistical abstractions, only the individuals of which the populations are composed have reality" (Mayr 1959:2). In sum, then, "For the [essentialist-thinking] typologist, the type is real and the variation an illusion, while for the [materialist-thinking] populationist, the type (average) is an abstraction and only the variation is real" (Mayr 1959:2). But if only *variation* is real, how do we study it? The answer is, by constructing a set of units that allow *properties* of phenomena to be measured. We use the term measurement to denote the assignment of a symbol—letter, number, word—to an observation made on a phenomenon according to a set of rules. The rule set includes specification of a scale (e.g., Stevens 1946) and the relation between the symbols and the scale.

The analyst selects attributes relevant to some problem, and it is those attributes and their combinations that result in the sorting of specimens into internally homogeneous, externally heterogeneous piles. Observation and recording of the attributes of specimens comprises measurement. Importantly, specimens that share attributes or properties—those that end up together in one of the analyst's piles—do not necessarily (and need not) have an essence (Mayr 1987:155). They have been grouped together because they hold attributes *selected by the analyst* in common, not because of some inherent, shared quality. Thus, from the materialist view, change is rendered as alterations in the frequencies of analytical kinds. Essentialism and materialism demand, then, different kinds of units.

Units

Theory is the final arbiter of which attributes out of the almost infinite number that could be selected are actually chosen by the analyst. Selected attributes must be relevant to solving a particular problem—not any or all problems, but only the one under investigation. Theory also specifies the kinds of units to be measured. We might decide that the color of a stone tool probably is not related to the function of that tool, whereas the angle of the working edge probably is; thus if we are interested in functional variation in stone tools, we choose as our attributes edge angles, traces of use wear, and other attributes that theoretically are causally related to the property of analytical interest. Note that we did not say that color is definitely *not* related to function; rather, our theory of function precludes color from consideration.

Because *we* decide on the attributes to be recorded, they are *ideational*; they are not real in the sense that they can be seen or picked up and held. An edge angle—itself an ideational unit with various empirical manifestations—is measured, using a goniometer, in ideational units known as degrees. Ideational units are tools to measure or characterize real objects. An inch and a centimeter are used to measure length, just as a gram and an ounce are used to measure and record weight. Inches, centimeters, grams, and ounces do not exist empirically; they are units used as analytical tools to measure properties *of* empirical units. A pencil is an empirical unit that can be placed in a set of things that are all six inches long *if* the attribute distinguishing the set specifies that the things within it must be six inches long to be included; our theory, of course, tells us what length is and how it differs from width, color, and so on.

Attribute combinations specify the kinds of phenomena we should measure or record for each specimen and how we should arrange and group specimens displaying the combinations. The term *class* denotes an ideational unit that has been explicitly defined in terms of its characteristic attributes; that is, a class is a definition that specifies the necessary and sufficient conditions—*significata*—that must be displayed by a specimen in order for it to be considered a member or an example of the class (Dunnell 1971b).

Ideational units can be used merely to characterize or describe a property or a thing, or they may be *theoretical*. The distinction is important. We may choose to characterize something on the basis of its color and to specify several colors (red, black, blue, yellow), but that attribute may have nothing to do with the concept of interest—say, function. In light of a theoretical (causal) relation between function and edge angle of stone tools, we would be well advised to specify ideational units defined as sets of edge angles such, as 1–30°, 31–60°, 61–90°, and the like, and then to measure the edge angle of specimens. Given their theoretical relation to the property of interest, our ideational units—classes of edge angle—would also be theoretical units. In short, a theoretical unit is an ideational unit that has explanatory significance *because of its theoretical relevance.*

A real, phenomenological thing that has an objective existence is an *empirical unit.* Such units can be made up of one thing or of multiple things. When multiple things are included, the empirical unit is termed a *group,* which is an aggregate, or set, of objects that are either physically or conceptually associated as a unit (Dunnell 1971b). Specimens identified as members of a class constitute the *denotata* of that class. A group is not a set of denotata unless the included specimens have been identified as members of a class: "The denotata of a class constitute a special kind of group, one with an explicit meaning" (Dunnell 1970:307). Because they are ideational, classes of phenomena have *distributions* in time and space displayed by their empirical members; because they are empirical, groups have *locations* in time and space.

An *intensional definition*[2] comprises the necessary and sufficient conditions for membership, that is, the explicitly listed distinctive features that a phenomenon must display to be a class member. Thus, a class can be an intensionally defined unit; its significata are explicit (without reference to real, empirical specimens) and can be derived from theory. Thus our three classes of edge angles derive from a theory of stone tool function that indicates that acute edge angles are necessary for cutting, middle-range edge angles are necessary for whittling, and obtuse angles are necessary for scraping.

A class may also be extensionally defined. An *extensional definition* comprises the necessary and sufficient conditions for membership in a unit and is derived by enumerating selected attributes shared by the unit's members (Dunnell 1971b). Thus, the significata of extensionally defined classes are seldom theoretically informed in an explicit manner. Many well-known types of artifacts, based as they are on intuitively grouped specimens, have been extensionally defined, which makes these units historical accidents that are dependent entirely on the specimens originally examined. Discussions of the inductively—that is, extensionally—derived neck-width definitions of western American projectile points as characterizing the differences between arrow points and dart points (e.g., Corliss 1980; Thomas 1978) are excellent examples.

Using intensionally defined classes derived from theory is required if one desires to study change—examining alterations in the frequencies of classes of variants represented by empirical specimens through time and explaining those alterations based on contingencies that theory informs us are relevant to them. Explanation of frequency changes in nontheoretical, extensionally defined units is improbable because the unit definitions are potentially modifiable every time a new specimen is found, thus creating all sorts of potential problems if one seeks to measure change.

We use the terms *type* and *category* synonymously for units of unspecified kind; they may be classes (ideational), or they may be groups (phenomenological). We note this is not always the meaning given to "type" by those whose work we cite. We use the term *classification* in a general sense to denote the construction or modification of units of whatever kind.

Specimens and the Problem of Analogs versus Homologs

Specimens—the real things we study—have limited life spans. This applies equally to human-produced objects within their systemic contexts (*sensu* Schiffer 1972) and to living organisms of every sort. Yet both still exist today, whether it be an artifact in archaeological context or a fossil in geological context. It is, of course, the life history of an artifact specimen that interests archaeologists. What was an artifact's function in the systemic context? Why was it made the way it was? Why was it made when and where it was? The point is that a specimen has a life history. It also has a postmortem history, but this is the subject of taphonomy and related fields (e.g., Lyman 1994; Schiffer 1987). Presuming that we can strip away the attributes of a specimen's postmortem history, the attributes of an artifact's life history are the major subject of archaeological study.

In biological terms, artifacts also have ontogenetic histories. Raw materials are procured, a tool is made, it is used, it is resharpened or recycled and used again, and it is discarded or lost. An artifact changes form, just as an organism does. Similarly, a population of specimens may change membership through time (artifacts are discarded, lost, and replaced) and thus change composition. How are such changes to be measured? Because classes are ideational, they cannot change or transform (an inch is always an inch, a gram is always a gram). The study of change through time and of variation across the spatial dimension must, therefore, involve the study of change and variation in the *frequency of representation* of various classes of phenomena. This is the heart of the materialist metaphysic. Most scientists would agree that units of measurement cannot change through time or vary across space, else change or variation within the set of phenomena being monitored may be either missed or spuriously detected. Keeping one's ideational units separate from empirical units that they are meant to measure is critical to any study of change.

Two other concepts must be explicit if our analysis of the culture history paradigm is to shed light on its strengths and weaknesses, its successes and failures. Given that culture historians were and are interested in the history, development, and evolution of cultures, they, like (and probably as a result of) their anthropological colleagues, were well aware of historical processes such as invention, innovation, diffusion, and migration, and they sometimes sought parallels for those processes within the biological realm (see Bray 1973 for a review of such parallels during the heyday of processual archaeology). Kroeber (1931a:151) made an important observation in this regard: "The fundamentally different evidential value of homologous and analogous similarities for determination of historical relationship, that is, genuine systematic or genetic relationship, has long been an axiom in biological science. The distinction has been much less clearly made in anthropology, and rarely explicitly, but holds with equal force." Kroeber (1931a:151) went on to imply that a "true homology" denoted "genetic unity," arguing that

> There are cases in which it is not a simple matter to decide whether the totality of traits points to a true [genetic, homologous] relationship or to secondary [analogous, functional] convergence. . . . Yet few biologists would doubt that sufficiently intensive analysis of structure will ultimately solve such problems of descent. . . . There seems no reason why on the whole the same cautious optimism should not prevail in the field of culture; why homologies should not be positively distinguishable from analogies when analysis of the whole of the phenomena in question has become truly intensive. That such analysis has often been lacking but judgments have nevertheless been rendered, does not invalidate the positive reliability of the method. (Kroeber 1931a:152–153)[3]

Kroeber was suggesting that there are two forms of similarity—one homologous and the other analogous. The former results from shared or common genetic (in biology) ancestry; the latter results from functional convergence, such as when two genetically unrelated populations of organisms reach a similar adaptive solution. How are the two distinguished? Kroeber (1931a:151) suggested that "Where similarities are specific and structural and not merely superficial . . . has long been the accepted method in evolutionary and systematic biology." The wings of eagles and those of crows are structurally as well as superficially similar; this is homologous similarity. The wings of eagles and those of bats are superficially, but not structurally, similar; this is analogous similarity.

Today, evolutionary biologists have a much more detailed and thorough knowledge both of analogous and homologous similarity and of the value of each to understanding phylogenetic relationships among organisms (e.g., Eggleton and Vane-Wright 1994; Smith 1994; Sober 1988). *Primitive traits* are features displayed by a modern organism and its genetic ancestors; our own pentadactyly (possession of five digits) is a primitive mammalian trait. *Derived traits* are features displayed by modern organisms that differ from features displayed by their ancestors (see Forey [1990] for a concise and understandable summary). The single digit of a horse is a trait derived from the primitive mammalian condition. Many paleobiologists and biologists believe that only by studying derived traits that are shared by different (daughter) species can we determine phylogenetic—in this sense, ancestor-descendant—relationships. This approach demands that analogous similarities be distinguished from homologous ones. Features shared by two organisms may be primitive or derived, but only derived homologous features shared by two organisms denote their common ancestry.

Culture historians were aware of the distinction between analogous and homologous similarity, and they tended to focus on the latter. Early in this century, culture historians spoke of *styles* of artifacts as denoting historical relationships. Stylistic similarity in this sense denotes homologous similarity: "[I]t is the result of direct cultural transmission once chance similarity in a context of limited possibilities is excluded" (Dunnell 1978:199). That is, styles are forms that have no detectable selective value; they confer no adaptive advantage to those who possess them (Dunnell 1978; O'Brien and Holland 1990, 1992; O'Brien et al. 1994). The difference between a red car and a blue car is stylistic, given a selective environment not focusing on color. As Kroeber (1919:239) indicated in an early definition, different styles "do not vary in purpose." The difference between a car with a four-cylinder engine and one with an eight-cylinder engine is functional if the selective environment favors the individual who uses less gasoline driving around town. Because styles change independently of changes in selective environments, one can define classes of styles—historical classes—that allow the measurement of time; further, because stylistic similarity results from transmission, styles can be used to measure interaction between spatially separate groups of people.

Studies of artifact styles were the forte of culture historians, though, as we discuss throughout the book, explanations for the behavior of particular styles were founded on common sense rather than on theory. Further, determination of what was thought to constitute *style* was not theoretically informed but rather based on trial and error. Those artifact forms that allowed one to successfully measure time and space became known as *styles* in the 1920s. But at the same time, styles were variously thought to correlate with distinct ethnic groups or cultures. This conflation of the essentialist and materialist metaphysics—built into the culture history paradigm from the start—would, ultimately, lead to its downfall, as culture historians of the 1950s attempted with increasing effort to attain the implied goal of Philip Phillips's (1955:246–247) famous statement that "New World archaeology is anthropology or it is nothing."

An Abstract

We argue in the following pages that the culture history paradigm came rather close to developing an evolutionary (in a Darwinian sense) archaeology, but it failed to do so for several reasons. Although culture historians occasionally approximated a materialist metaphysic, they more generally adopted an essentialist one. The paradigm grew up around an ad hoc consensus concerning some empirical generalizations that, in the absence of theory, were incapable of serving as explanations. The essentialist metaphysic produced a commonsense understanding of the archaeological record in which interpretations were expressed in simple English words that (sometimes) had agreed-upon meanings. There was no attempt—such as occurred in biology in the 1930s and 1940s—to develop a uniquely archaeological theory of change. While the programmatic literature of the paradigm extolled the virtues of an evolution-like approach to the archaeological record, what was done in practice did not involve evolution in any sort of Darwinian sense; instead, it used what has been termed *cultural evolution,* a decidedly non-Darwinian form of evolution (Dunnell 1980; Freeman 1974; Rindos 1985; see also the papers in Rambo and Gillogly 1991). The failure on both fronts—to develop an explanatory theory of change and to produce historical descriptions of change explainable in other than commonsense terms—left the door wide open for the "new archaeology" to walk through in the early 1960s. As it turns out, however, archaeology yet again chose the wrong door. (We touch on this point in Chapter 8.)

Our discussion in the following pages is organized somewhat by topic and somewhat by time of publication. We have found it particularly difficult to follow one or the other strictly—a result of the way in which the culture history paradigm itself developed. In a very real sense, efforts on the part of culture historians to contend with the temporal, spatial, and formal dimensions (Spaulding 1960b; Willey 1953b) of the archaeological record were simultaneous as opposed to simply sequential. Discovery or invention of a way to deal with one often entailed implications for dealing with one or both of the other dimensions. But as well, once techniques for measuring time with form were developed, most efforts became focused on measuring form in such a manner as to allow the measurement of time. Before time was measured with form, the focus was on measuring space with form. But always lurking in the background was the notion that cultural products were the subject of analysis, and thus cultures were the proper subject of study. This creates quite a confusing situation for anyone interested in following individual trains of thought.

By the middle of the twentieth century, much of the formalization of procedure that was going to be attained had already occurred, and interests turned to interpretation of the cultures that were thought to be represented in the archaeological record. Thus the ultimate source of interpretations of the record was cultural anthropology, with a large dose of common sense thrown in. The notion that archaeological manifestations could be linked to cultures had been around for decades, but it wasn't until the 1940s that it got kicked into high gear. To understand the roots of this notion we need to review, albeit quickly, what was happening in Americanist archaeology prior to the beginning of the twentieth century and how that intellectual climate produced what came to be known as culture history.

Notes

1. We use the term *Americanist* archaeology (as opposed to *American* archaeology) to emphasize archaeology undertaken by American-trained archaeologists, regardless of where in the world their research area is located.
2. Not to be confused with *intentional*. Intensional as used here, in the logical sense, refers to the properties connoted by a term.
3. A decade later, Kroeber (1943:108) noted that anthropology was still "backward" with regard to distinguishing between these two kinds of similarities among culture traits.

2

Before Culture History

Most histories of Americanist archaeology suggest that culture history first emerged as a recognizable paradigm in the second decade of the twentieth century (e.g., Strong 1952; Trigger 1989; Willey and Sabloff 1993). To understand why it appeared when it did and why it had the look it did at the time, we need to understand the intellectual climate from which the paradigm emerged. We have chosen to begin rather early in the history of Americanist archaeology and to review the status of each of the three dimensions—time, space, and form—that eventually united to create the focal point of culture history.

Americanist archaeology (using the latter word loosely) up to the late nineteenth century was not a very scholarly discipline. There were no professional archaeologists, no established field methods, no educational programs, and few data (Willey and Sabloff 1993:35; see also Patterson 1991). There were, however, a few bright spots on this otherwise bleak landscape, one of which was Thomas Jefferson's 1784 excavation of a trench through one of the earthen mounds on his property in Virginia. He subsequently made notes on the stratigraphic relation of layers of earth and human bones in the mound and remarked on the chronological implications of the layering:

> At the bottom [of the mound], that is, on the level of the circumjacent plane, I found bones; above these a few stones . . . then a large interval of earth, then a stratum of bones, and so on. At one end of the section were four strata of bones plainly distinguishable; at the other, three; the strata of one part not ranging with those in another. . . . Appearances certainly indicate that [the mound] has derived both origin and growth from the accustomary collection of bones, and deposition of them together; that the first collection had been deposited on the common surface of the earth, a few stones put over it, and then a covering of earth, that the second had been laid on this, had covered more or less of it in proportion to the number of bones, and was then also covered with earth; and so on. (Jefferson 1801:141–142)

13

Jefferson's work was later said to have anticipated modern archaeological methods by a century and to have been undertaken "to resolve an archaeological problem" (Lehmann-Hartleben 1943:163), but it had no visible impact on Americanist archaeology. As Sir Mortimer Wheeler (1954:59) later observed, "Unfortunately, this seed of a new scientific skill fell upon infertile soil. For a century after Jefferson, mass-excavation remained the rule of the day." It was seventy-five years later, and then in Great Britain, that Jefferson's approach was reinvented with effect, having been used sporadically in Europe since the late eighteenth century (Lehmann-Hartleben 1943; Van Riper 1993). The excavation of Brixham Cave by prominent British geologists and paleontologists in 1858 focused explicitly on stratigraphic context. That work was based on J. J. A. Worsaae's principle of association, first proposed in 1843. Rowe (1962c:131) indicated this principle was stated as follows: "with regard to the burials themselves, we know that they regularly contain not only the bones of the dead but also many of their weapons, implements and ornaments which were buried beside them in antiquity. Here, therefore, we can in general expect to find together those things which were originally used together at one time." Using this principle—which came to mean that objects found within the same stratum tend to be the same age—the excavations at Brixham Cave resulted not only in the recognition that human antiquity was deeper than indicated by biblical history but also in archaeology becoming a legitimate scholarly pursuit in the Old World (Grayson 1983; Van Riper 1993).

Americanist archaeology, such as it was, was influenced by the Brixham Cave discoveries (Meltzer 1983). If ancient people were to be recognized by their association with extinct fauna, then surely such an association might be found in the New World. But in North America, "there were no deeply stratified alluvial valleys or caves with human artifacts or remains mixed indiscriminately with Pleistocene-aged fauna. As a consequence, the definition of an American Paleolithic age became of necessity based on typological analogues" (Meltzer 1983:7). The basic idea was that American Paleolithic artifacts, like those of Europe, would be crude and primitive in appearance—a notion that resurfaced a century later (Ascher and Ascher 1965). Thus, "In accordance with the unilinear theory of evolution then in vogue, the early American archaeologists searched for the same periods of culture which had been discovered in the Old World" (Rouse, in Taylor 1954:572). The resulting argument over the Trenton, New Jersey, gravels between Charles C. Abbott (1877, 1888), G. Frederick Wright (1888, 1892), and their supporters, who argued the artifacts were ancient, and William Henry Holmes (1892, 1897) and his fellow Bureau of American Ethnology colleagues, who argued the Trenton specimens were variously unfinished and/or rejected tools of potentially young age, culminated at the end of the nineteenth century in a stalemate (Meltzer 1983, 1991).

The Trenton artifacts would play another significant but seldom remarked role in the development of the culture history paradigm in 1914–1916, but at the end of the nineteenth century these collections had two apparent influences on Americanist archaeological thought. First, the European model of artifact evolution could not be reliably applied to the American archaeological record. Second, there was no clear evidence of an extensive time depth to human occupation of the Americas. Together, these two interpretations resulted in the discipline initially tending to focus more on the spatial dimension and formal variation within that dimension and less on the temporal dimension. As well, these interpretations meant that a uniquely Americanist set of archaeological methods and explanatory models would have to be developed if the study of culture change were to become a viable subject of inquiry. As anthropologist Franz Boas (1902:1) noted, "In the study of American archaeology we are compelled to apply methods somewhat different from those used in the archaeology of the Old World." The problem in the late nineteenth century was one of how to classify artifacts such that the resulting groups of specimens would make some kind of sense, and it is to this dimension that we turn first.

Classification and the Formal Dimension

As more artifacts and more variant forms of artifacts came to light, it became increasingly difficult to keep track of where particular kinds of artifacts came from and for individual investigators to communicate with one another about the particular forms in their respective collections. The history of artifact classification is, therefore, critically important to the foundation of modern Americanist archaeology (see also Dunnell [1986b], whose analysis we borrow heavily from and expand in certain respects here).

The development of archaeological classification in the second half of the nineteenth century marked the emergence of archaeology as a distinct area of inquiry. Classification theoretically serves two functions—to structure observations so that they can be explained and to provide a set of terminological conventions that allows communication—though as we will see, in Americanist archaeology it more often has served the latter rather than the former function. In the United States, early classification systems were developed solely as a way to enhance communication between researchers who had multiple specimens they wanted to describe (see Dunnell's [1986b:156–159] discussion of Rau 1876 and Wilson 1899). The

"Report of the Committee on Archeological Nomenclature" by John H. Wright, J. D. McGuire, Frederick W. Hodge, Warren K. Moorehead, and Charles Peabody (1909[†]),[1] which had been commissioned by the American Anthropological Association, exemplified this kind of approach—one that would, in some quarters, persist for several decades (e.g., Black and Weer 1936).

Since the intent of the persons devising the classification schemes was to standardize terminology, most of the systems were based on readily perceived differences and similarities between specimens. This meant that form received the lion's share of attention. Despite the best efforts of the classifiers, form and function often were conflated. Certainly this was the case with the system devised by the Wright committee. Despite the statement that "it has been the particular aim of the Committee to avoid or to get rid of those classes and names that are based on uses assumed but not universally proved for certain specimens" (Wright et al. 1909:114), many of the committee's unit names, such as vessels, knives, and projectile points, have functional connotations in English.

Piles of more or less similar-looking specimens that late-nineteenth- and early-twentieth-century classifiers were forever creating lacked any archaeological meaning: "In an effort to make categorization more systematic and scientific, these early workers had arbitrarily focused on formal criteria that lacked any archaeological or ethnographic rationale" (Dunnell 1986b:159). Further, variation in artifact form within each pile—and to some extent between piles—of specimens had no perceived explanatory value and was simply conceived as noise resulting from different levels of skill in manufacturing or from raw-material quality. As Rau (1876:159) observed, "A classification of the arrowheads with regard to their chronological development is not attempted, and hardly deemed necessary. North American Indians of the same tribe (as, for instance, the Pai-Utes of Southern Utah) arm their arrows with stone points of different forms, the shape of the arrowhead being a matter of individual taste or convenience."

Even ethnic, or spatially based, classifications were often disparaged because particular forms were found in widely separated areas (e.g., Fowke 1896)—an issue we treat in the following section. The problem was that common sense dictated the choice of attributes; thus groups of artifacts were largely ad hoc and only accidentally had chronological or ethnic meaning (Dunnell 1986b:159). The perceived shallow time depth of the American archaeological record—the "short chronology"—probably contributed to the feeling that it was futile to search for chronologically meaningful artifact types, though S. T. Walker (1883) and a few others had earlier shown that such types could be found.

In the late nineteenth century, classification systems for pottery lagged behind those developed for stone artifacts because most classifications used shape, and ceramic specimens more often than not were represented by sherds rather than by intact vessels. One bright spot was Bureau of (American) Ethnology prehistorian William Henry Holmes, who worried about how to explain variation in vessel form. He "was embued with anthropological evolutionism, particularly the cultural evolutionism of Lewis Henry Morgan, [and] like many of his colleagues, employed the Morgan stages of humanity (i.e., savagery, barbarism, etc.) as if they were matters of fact" (Meltzer and Dunnell 1992:xxviii [e.g., Holmes 1888:196]), but he was "ambivalent about [the] precise direction and form" of such progressive evolution (Meltzer and Dunnell 1992:xxxvi). Time was not of paramount interest for Holmes or for virtually anyone else who embraced the short chronology. Further, his knowledge of the archaeological record prompted him to doubt the possibility of documenting evolutionary progress prehistorically. His chronological controls were stratigraphic, and thus he "frequently found it difficult to see the evident change [in artifact forms] as progressive. Consequently, he was forced to seek other (e.g., racial, environmental, and diffusionist) explanations for the differences" (Meltzer and Dunnell 1992:xxxvii). Holmes's seminal papers on pottery classification (e.g., Holmes 1886a, 1886b, 1886c, 1903) were focused on establishing ceramic groups that were internally consistent, and they actually served as a reinforcement or justification for emerging notions of culture areas (e.g., Mason 1896).

In the early years of the twentieth century, archaeologists came to appreciate a spatial element in the formal variation of artifacts, particularly pottery; they suspected a chronological component demonstrable with stratigraphy in a few places, but such was not yet generally detectable or was thought to be of minimal significance. As a result, classification remained ad hoc, local, and addressed only the issues of communication and simplification of description. Attempts to formalize classification procedures "did not provide any guidance in the *selection* of definitive attributes" (Dunnell 1986b:165). Simply put, there was no theory to guide classification efforts.

Space

Difference in geographic location was obvious, but of what significance was the difference? What came to be known as the culture-area concept had its roots in the culture classification work of Otis T. Mason (1896, 1905), in Cyrus Thomas's (1894) regional groupings of mound forms, and in Holmes's (e.g., 1886a, 1886b) focus on regional variation in pottery.

Mason (1905:427) apparently was influenced by C. Hart Merriam, first director of the U.S. Biological Survey, for he indicated that "Within the American continent N. of Mexico there were ethnic environments which set bounds for the tribes and modified their industrial, esthetic, social, intellectual, and religious lives. . . . The climate zones which Merriam has worked out for the U.S. Department of Agriculture in regard to their animal and vegetal life correspond in a measure with the areas of linguistic families as delimited on Powell's map" (see also Mason 1896:642). Merriam's (1892, 1898) concept of life zones has since largely fallen from favor (Hoffmeister 1964), but the correspondence between such zones and the distribution of language families apparently guided Mason (1905:427) to distinguish twelve "ethnic environments."

As A. L. Kroeber noted in "The Culture-Area and Age–Area Concepts of Clark Wissler" (Kroeber 1931b[†]), Wissler did much to popularize the culture-area concept among Americanist anthropologists (e.g., Wissler 1914, 1916a, 1917a, 1923, 1924). Murdock (1948:294) indicated that Kroeber agreed with Wissler's age–area concept and suggested that Wissler was heavily influenced by Franz Boas and Livingston Farrand and that he developed the notion "in the endeavor to find a more satisfactory system for the classification of ethnological specimens [at the American Museum of Natural History] than was provided by the previous classification according to linguistic stocks." The influence of this concept on archaeology extended from the 1880s into the early twentieth century, as shown in Holmes's paper "Areas of American Culture Characterization Tentatively Outlined as an Aid in the Study of Antiquities" (Holmes 1914[†]).

Holmes (1914:413) suspected that the distribution of "antiquities" would reveal geographic (ethnic) distributions similar to those identified ethnographically. This proposition, of course, assumed that cultural areas, however defined, were static entities through time. Hence, they were essentialist units, an assumption fostered by the perceived short chronology that dominated Americanist archaeological thinking at the time and of which Holmes was a leading proponent. By the 1930s, the assumption that these were static entities was rejected by leading scholars (e.g., Kroeber 1939:1–2; McKern 1934, 1937, 1939:302–303; see also Quimby 1954), though their essentialist nature as units remained. The concept served as an organizational device in many later archaeological texts (e.g., Fagan 1991; Jennings 1989; Martin, Quimby, and Collier, 1947; Willey 1966).

How was the temporal dimension to be integrated with the spatial dimension? Ethnologists had long attempted to derive methods for measuring time from culture traits (see review in Sapir 1916), defined by Wissler (1923:50) as a "unit of observation . . . a unit of tribal culture." He implied that a trait could be an attribute of an object, an attribute combination represented by a discrete object, or an attribute combination represented by what some archaeologists call a feature. Kroeber (1940:29) was only slightly more explicit when he noted that if a trait was "ambiguous," it could "usually be broken down into two or more traits, which can then be successfully described as present or absent." Taylor (1948:96) merely stated that a trait was "a unit of culture." Ehrich (1950:471) emphasized the "fallacy [of] regarding the trait as the smallest cultural unit. . . . [I]f we regard the cultural trait as a cultural molecule we find that it too can be atomized, and that different culture traits have different degrees of complexity." But Ehrich (1950:471) went on to state that "Each artifact should be considered as representative of a trait," clearly precluding the possibility that an attribute of an artifact might be conceived of as a trait. The lack of any explicit definition of what a culture trait is implies that such atheoretical and largely empirical units are simply used to measure similarities and differences.

One result of the focus on culture traits was the formulation of the age–area concept. This concept made three interrelated assumptions: (1) Culture traits will disperse in all directions from the point of origin—like the "ripples" (Murdock 1948:294) emanating from a rain drop that hits a puddle; (2) all culture traits will disperse at the same rate—again, like ripples; and (3) the larger the geographic area over which a culture trait is found, the older that trait is. Thus, mapping the geographic distribution of culture traits evidenced by archaeological remains should indicate something of their history. The age–area concept was supported in some quarters of anthropology and archaeology (e.g., Kroeber 1931a, 1931b) because an identical concept existed in biology (e.g., Willis 1922), though it was by no means completely accepted within that discipline (Gleason 1923).

Criticisms of the age–area concept, such as that contained in Julian H. Steward's "Diffusion and Independent Invention: A Critique of Logic" (Steward 1929[†]) (see also Wallis 1925, 1945; Woods 1934), were swift and sure. The concept did not recognize independent invention or convergence—processes that everyone agreed took place even if their relative importance might be disputed. The age–area concept explained similarities in different cultures as the result of homologous similarities and ignored analogous similarities. This did not, however, dissuade Wissler (1919) or others from retaining the notion of culture areas, no doubt because of the loose parallels perceived between cultural evolution and biological evolution.

Kroeber (1931a) later argued that culture traits were analogous to species of organisms and that cultures, which comprise suites of traits, were analogous to faunas and floras, which comprise suites of animal and plant species, respectively. For Kroeber (1931a:149), although a "culture complex is 'polyphyletic' [and] a genus is, almost by definition, monophyletic . . .

the analogy does at least refer to the fact that culture elements [traits] like species represent the smallest units of material which the historical anthropologist and biologist respectively have to deal with." Therefore, data on the geographic distribution of culture traits, as with data on plant and animal taxa, allow "inferences as to the origin and areal history of the group" because the "Age and Area principle seems the same in biology and cultural anthropology" (Kroeber 1931a:150).

Kroeber, however, recognized the obfuscating factor of independent invention—analogous similarity—and noted that anthropologists had too often not sufficiently tested their diffusionary explanations: "The fundamentally different evidential value of homologous and analogous similarities for determination of historical relationship, that is, genuine systematic or genetic relationship, has long been an axiom in biological science. The distinction has been much less clearly made in anthropology, and rarely explicitly, but holds with equal force" (Kroeber 1931a:151). Lewis Binford (1968a:8) repeated this criticism over three decades later: "How can archeologists distinguish between homologous and analogous cultural similarities?"[2] Part of the problem, of course, resided early this century in the lack of a method for measuring time. Insofar as the archaeological record is two dimensional—that is, it consists of forms distributed in space—temporal and spatial variation cannot be distinguished observationally. Rather, they must be distinguished analytically. As we discuss below, the solution to the problem of how to measure time with form came close on the heels of the popularization of the culture-area and age–area concepts and the study of trait distributions.

Time

American archaeological publications from the last half of the nineteenth century tended to be descriptive works, some of them certainly of epic proportion (e.g., Bandelier 1892; Cushing 1886; Holmes 1886a, 1886b; Squier and Davis 1848; Thomas 1894), though a few theoretical statements also appeared (e.g., Holmes 1886c). A significant event of the period was the professional resolution of the mound-builder controversy (Thomas 1894). All these studies served both to awaken serious interest in archaeological remains and to form the foundation for the emergence of a distinctively Americanist archaeology (Dunnell 1986a). Interest in the archaeological record as simply another curious part of the record of the earth's natural history would fade only with the development of archaeological methods. How could the age of artifacts be measured, and what did those artifacts signify about the humans who had made and used them?

The principles of stratigraphic analysis were not archaeological, but they did provide a way to tell time. And given the history of Americanist archaeology, it is not surprising that the first archaeological applications of stratigraphic principles were either by natural historians or by those with parallel interests rather than by professional archaeologists (of which, as we noted earlier, there were none). For example, physician Jeffries Wyman, who served as the first curator of the Peabody Museum (Harvard), examined shell mounds in New England, observing "A section through the heap at its thickest part showed that it belonged to two different periods, indicated by two distinct layers of shells" that were separated by "a layer of dark vegetable mould, mixed with earth and gravel" (Wyman 1868:564). These observations prompted Wyman to suggest that a sequence of two occupations separated by a period of abandonment was represented by the strata. A few years later, Wyman (1875:11) indicated that the absence of artifacts of Euroamerican manufacture from shell mounds in Florida suggested that the mounds dated "before the white man landed on the shores of Florida." But Wyman (1875:81) also lamented that "No satisfactory data have been found for determining, with any degree of accuracy, the age of the shell heaps." He recognized the value of dendrochronology for assessing the age of the mounds, although rather than count the rings, which he recognized as annual formations, he calculated the average number of rings per inch of trunk diameter and "upon this all our estimates [of age] are based" (Wyman 1875:83).

More or less at the same time Wyman was working in Florida, William Healey Dall, a conchologist and "a naturalist in the full meaning of the term" (Merriam 1927:346), was excavating shell mounds in the Aleutian Islands (Dall 1877). He not only recognized distinct strata in the mounds, but excavated them in such a manner that he was, apparently, able to record the stratigraphic provenience of many of the artifacts he recovered. He also was able to characterize, on the basis of food remains and artifacts, three temporal periods—an early hunting period, a middle fishing period, and a late littoral period. He referred to these not only as temporal units. but also as evolutionary stages. Willey and Sabloff (1993:62) suggest Dall's work "had no impact at all on other archaeologists of the time," perhaps because of the "remoteness of the Aleutians" and because he did no follow-up excavations. More likely, it was because he was unable to overcome the general consensus that (1) there was a very shallow time depth to the occupation of North America and, more importantly, (2) pre-A.D. 1500 cultures—so far as they were known—were quite similar to historically documented ones (Meltzer 1983).

S. T. Walker did not excavate any shell mounds in Florida, but he closely examined the stratigraphy of those that had been exposed by construction-related activities. Importantly, he noted a three-stage sequence in the development of pottery. He characterized the earliest pottery "style" (Walker 1883:679) as large, rude, heavy, and destitute of ornament. Middle-period pottery had thinner walls and some modification of the surface. Late-period pottery was thinner because of the "employment of better materials" and was "beautifully ornamented." Perhaps, then, an artifact's form—for pottery, at least—could be used to tell time, but as with those by Wyman and Dall, Walker's report had no apparent impact on Americanist archaeology.

Charles Peabody of Phillips Academy in Andover, Massachusetts, excavated Edwards Mound in Coahoma County, Mississippi, in 1901–1902 (Peabody 1904). He noted that the stratigraphy indicated there were two periods of mound construction and use, and he reported differences between the artifacts and burials associated with the two periods. In 1903, Peabody and Warren K. Moorehead excavated Jacobs Cavern in McDonald County, Missouri, using what was at the time a sophisticated excavation strategy. They laid out the cave floor in a series of 1-m-square units and then removed the deposits "in order, front to back, using the lines of stakes as coordinates to determine the position of any objects found. The linear distances of 1 m. were numbered from northwest to southeast in Arabic numerals from 1 to 21, and lettered from southwest to northeast from A to Q" (Peabody and Moorehead 1904:13). Three vertical levels were recognized in the deposit, though it is clear from reading their account that Peabody and Moorehead did not pay much attention to separating artifacts by level as they excavated.

They did, however, develop a fairly elaborate (for the time) typological scheme to categorize stone artifacts from the site, using a mix of metric, morphological, and functional variables to create the categories. For example, they first separated pieces that were over 5 cm long from those that were under 5 cm, then placed them into one of five categories—pieces without stems, pieces with stems, shouldered knives, perforators, and pieces of doubtful form—the first three of which contained subcategories. Peabody and Moorehead concluded that the crudeness of the stone tools and the paucity of arrow points and pottery indicated that Jacobs Cavern was occupied by a group or groups of people who had preceded what they termed "the so-called 'mound builders'" (Peabody and Moorehead 1904:27). They attributed the six bundle burials that were found in an ash level to a group that had occupied the cave after the group responsible for the ash deposit but before the Osage had assumed control of the region during the historical period.

On one hand, Peabody and Moorehead had no way of estimating when occupation of Jacobs Cavern might have begun except to note that no bones of extinct animals were found. On the other hand, they laid the foundation for a later piece of what we might term unfortunate work that was used to provide evidence of the cave's occupation by Pleistocene-age groups (O'Brien 1996b). They noticed that all of the stalagmites in the cavern had their points of origin on the surface of a clay-and-limestone deposit and that the stalagmites had grown up through the overlying ash deposit as a result of continued water seepage through the fissure-ridden overhang. They concluded their report by stating that "The evidence from the quantity of the ashes, the types of implements, the stalagmitic deposits, is toward the assumption of a very early and protracted occupancy of Jacobs Cavern by man" (Peabody and Moorehead 1904:29).

Measuring Time Stratigraphically?

At the turn of the century, Boas (1902:1) indicated that "[i]t seems probable that the remains found in most of the archaeological sites of America were left by a people similar in culture to the present Indians." This is a critically important statement, for it indicates why Americanist archaeologists did what they did between about 1900 and 1915. The usual perception of historians is that there was a "stratigraphic revolution" in the mid-teens (e.g., Browman and Givens 1996; Strong 1952; Taylor 1948, 1954; Willey 1968; Willey and Sabloff 1974). This is somewhat a matter of semantics, for the materials reviewed in the previous section suggest that time *was* being measured using stratigraphy prior to this time. What is critical, then, is to understand precisely what is meant by the term "stratigraphic excavation."

Browman and Givens (1996:81) distinguish between "post facto stratigraphic observation" and "actual stratigraphic excavation." They equate the former with the identification of "archaeological strata . . . in the walls of trenches excavated as single [vertical] units" and the latter with the identification of "archaeological strata [that are] microstrata of geological units" and the employment of those strata as "data recovery units" (Browman and Givens 1996:80). A straightforward way to make strata visible is to expose them by excavation. Then, one might excavate the strata horizontally *one at a time*. But simply because one does *not* excavate strata back one at a time does not indicate an absence of stratigraphic excavation, if what is meant by this term is the use of discrete and distinct depositional (or merely vertical) units as artifact-recovery units.

If stratigraphic excavation is taken to mean the *identification of archaeological strata and the collection of artifacts from discrete depositional units,* clearly archaeologists were doing just that prior to 1912. But there is something missing from this definition—the *measurement of time* that results from analyzing such a collection. After adding this criterion to the above definition of stratigraphic excavation, the relevant issue becomes not whether archaeologists excavated in or collected artifacts from discrete vertical units prior to 1912 but whether Americanist archaeologists sought to measure time via stratigraphic excavation. Were Americanist archaeologists early this century—those working prior to the 1915–1916 "stratigraphic revolution"—even interested in time?

Peabody (1904, 1908, 1910, 1913; Peabody and Moorehead 1904) regularly used a horizontal grid to guide his excavation, and he consistently recorded the vertical and horizontal provenience of artifacts, burials, and features. Peabody was well aware that more deeply buried materials were older than materials located near the surface, and, given the way he excavated, he generally knew which strata produced which artifacts. However, he seldom spoke of temporal differences as measured by the relations of the vertical positions from which his artifacts were collected. For all intents and purposes, he was not particularly interested in questions of chronology.

Mark R. Harrington (1909a, 1909b) not only made post facto stratigraphic observations, he employed stratigraphic excavation, as defined above, in New York in 1900–1901. He first excavated several trenches in a rock shelter, noting there were three strata, the middle one containing no artifacts. He indicated which artifacts came from which stratum and presented two drawings of "vertical sections" of the stratigraphy (Harrington 1909b:126–129). He then wrote the following:

> When the [excavations had] been completed, it was thought that everything of value had been found and removed from the cave; but on further deliberation, taking into consideration the darkness of the cave and the blackness and stickiness of the cave dirt, it was thought best to sift the entire contents. The results were surprising. The earth had all been carefully trowelled over, then thrown with a shovel so that it could be watched—but a great number of things had been overlooked, as the subsequent sifting showed. Of course all data as to depth and position have been lost, yet the specimens are valuable as having come from the cave. (Harrington 1909b:128)

Harrington was well aware of the temporal significance of superposed strata and the provenience of artifacts in those strata, and during his excavation he used strata—depositional units—as artifact collection units. He did not, however, discuss the cultural or temporal differences between his two superposed collections, except to note that the stratigraphically uppermost level contained pottery while the lowermost did not. While his excavation results could have readily been used to *measure* time, he chose not to use them in this fashion.

Harrington's (1924a:235) description of how he excavated a site in New York in 1902 is the most revealing statement we have encountered concerning whether Americanist archaeologists were excavating stratigraphically prior to 1912. He indicated that after digging "test holes [to determine] the depth and richness of the deposit[, he chose the parts of the site that] warranted more thorough excavation." He then exposed a vertical face "at the edge of the [site] deposit." This vertical face was extended down through the "village layer" or "the accumulated refuse of the Indian Village," which included various depositional units such as layers of shellfish, ash, and black sediment. The face extended into the sterile stratum beneath the village layer. A "trench of this kind was carried forward by carefully digging down the front with a trowel, searching the soil for relics, then, with a shovel, throwing the loose earth thus accumulated back out of the way into the part already dug over, so as to expose a new front." Once a trench was completed, "another trench was run parallel and adjacent to the first on its richest side, and so on, until the investigator was satisfied that he had covered the entire deposit, or at least as much as his purpose required" (Harrington 1924a:235). As a result, Harrington noted that different artifacts came from different strata. For example, in the deepest stratum he found "stemmed arrow points and crude crumbling pottery of a somewhat more archaic character than most of the specimens" recovered from higher strata (Harrington 1924a:245). He also noted that the archaic artifacts were stratigraphically "below the village layer" (Harrington 1924a:283).

Harrington's (1924a) discussion underscores the fact that although Americanists did not excavate strata (or arbitrary levels) one at a time prior to 1912, many of them did employ strata as artifact-recovery units. It also underscores the fact that it actually matters little how the sediment is removed from the hole one is digging, *as long as the stratigraphic proveniences of the artifacts are known and recorded.* Harrington's (1924a) work also meets our further criterion—that artifacts from such proveniences are used to measure the passage of time. Harrington's excavation technique was much like Peabody's, hence we term it the "Harrington–Peabody technique." Many of the early twentieth century reports we have read describe nearly identical excavation procedures.

Peabody and Harrington were not the only archaeologists employing strata as collection units during the pre-1912 period, nor were they the only ones to note that superposed artifacts and/or deposits measured time. Almost everyone made this assumption. Skinner (1917), for example, mentioned individuals who made post facto stratigraphic observations and inferred chronology in 1893 and 1900. Will and Spinden (1906) used the Harrington–Peabody technique in 1905 and also made post facto chronological observations on the basis of superposition. Pepper (1916), working in 1904, made post facto chronological observations on the basis of super-position, as did Schrabisch (1909). Some individuals under the influence of Boas (e.g., Aitken 1917, 1918; Haeberlin 1917, 1919; Hewett 1916), and others who do not seem to have been influenced by him (e.g., De Booy 1913; Fewkes 1914; Hawkes and Linton 1916, 1917; Heye 1916; Mills 1916)—many of whom used the Harrington–Peabody technique—were making stratigraphic observations for chronological purposes between 1910 and 1915. But the point is that none of these archaeologists was overly concerned with chronological matters, even though the artifacts they collected were known to fall in *different time periods,* given their provenience in *different strata.* The question is, why weren't they concerned?

Working in 1914, Fred H. Sterns (1915:121) observed that "the proof of [cultural] sequences must be grounded on stratigraphic evidence, and stratified sites have been very rare [in North America]. Hence such a site has a high scarcity value and warrants special study even though it be otherwise of minor importance." Similar observations were frequent in the middle of the second decade (e.g., Sapir 1916; Spinden 1915). But Sterns, like many of his contemporaries, did not devote much time to chronological matters. They did not because many of them, like Sterns (1915:125), observed "An important fact arguing against any great difference in time between the upper and lower ash-beds is that the pottery and the flint and bone implements found in these two sets of fireplaces show absolutely no difference in type." This is simply a rewording of Boas's (1902) earlier statement that there were no significant differences between historically documented cultures and prehistoric ones, a statement based on the shallow time depth then ascribed to the American archaeological record. And, simply put, this is why no one consistently or rigorously asked chronological questions, despite the fact that many archaeologists collected artifacts from distinct depositional units.

Our conclusion that everyone knew superposed artifacts marked the passage of time but no one bothered to ask chronological questions is exemplified by the work of Frederic B. Loomis and D. B. Young, who excavated a shell mound in Maine in 1909. They chose that particular mound because it "has never been disturbed by previous excavation" (Loomis and Young 1912:18)—a statement that leads us to suspect they were well aware of the importance of vertical provenience. Their excavation method was the Harrington–Peabody technique: "the heap was [plotted] in sections five feet wide, and as each section was worked, every find (of a tooth, tool, bit of pottery, etc.) was recorded, both as to its horizontal position and vertical depth. . . . [Vertical s]ections of the heap were plotted from time to time" (Loomis and Young 1912:19). They noted that in some strata

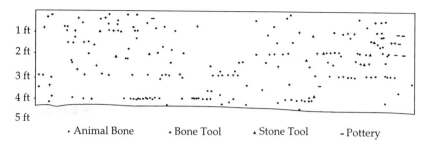

Figure 2.1. Diagram of a cross-sectional excavation of a shell midden in Maine made by Frederic Loomis and D. Young in 1909. Note the different symbols used for different material classes appearing in the sectional face (after Loomis and Young 1912).

the shells were very much broken up, apparently due to tramping and building fires on them. Where the shells were but little broken, and free from ashes, they would seem to indicate rapid accumulation, and offered but little in the line of finds. . . . Where the layers were made of ashes and finely broken shells, the period of accumulation was longer and agreeing with that, the numbers of articles found in these layers was also greater." (Loomis and Young 1912:19–20)

Clearly, they collected artifacts and faunal remains from particular depositional units just as Harrington (1909b, 1924a) had done eight or nine years earlier.

Loomis and Young's (1912:21) sectional diagram (Figure 2.1) shows "the depth at which each find was made in [two five-foot-wide trenches] and the relative abundance and relationship of the different articles." As Leslie Spier (1915:346) observed, this diagram "would be improved by the addition of lines indicating the position of the several [stratigraphic] layers, that [the artifacts'] relation to the strata . . . might be made clear." This is a predictable comment from someone interested in chronology and site formation processes, but Loomis and Young had no such interests. They knew time was measured by superposition, but they were not asking questions that demanded chronological control and thus did not use stratigraphic excavation to address such questions.

In an important admission, Wissler (1909:xiii) indicated that interest in rock shelters in the northeastern United States was "partly due to the obvious analogies to European caves, but chiefly to their *apparent presentation of chronological cultural differences* respecting the use of pottery" (emphasis added). Wissler was here referring to Harrington's (1909b) excavations in which pottery was present in shallow strata but absent from deep strata. Importantly, the addition of pottery signified a cultural change of the epochal or qualitative—essentialist—sort. Minor temporal changes in culture—such as shifts in the *kind* of pottery—were, at the time, of little importance.

Measuring Time with Form?

Friedrich Max Uhle used stratigraphic principles to a minor extent during fieldwork in Peru (Uhle 1903; see Willey and Sabloff 1993:79). Rowe (1954:20) indicated that Uhle used stratified collections—that is, superposition—to confirm the chronology of pottery styles he had developed based on other criteria such as historic documentation. It is Uhle's work in the San Francisco Bay area, however, which was published in "The Emeryville Shellmound" (Uhle 1907[†]), that is best known to archaeologists, because it was there that he apparently excavated parts of the mound in stratigraphic fashion. Aided by paleontologist John C. Merriam (Woodbury 1960a), Uhle geared his excavations to "obtain a view of all the strata contained in the mound" (Uhle 1907:8) because, given a suspected occupation of several centuries, he believed that "cultural differences should be indicated in the successive strata" (Uhle 1907:36). Although he excavated "stratum by stratum," Uhle noted that "the dividing lines [between] the various strata (I to VII) were chosen arbitrarily from the several visible lines of structure" (Uhle 1907:8). Those strata then were tied to lower strata (VIII to X) by excavating a separate trench that contained the missing strata. Uhle (1907:15) indicated that "The lines of stratification mark clearly the gradual development of the strata of the mound." He was able to note the stratigraphic provenience of burials, to examine variation in the artifact assemblages associated with each stratum, and to estimate the age of the deposits.

Uhle's work was summarily dismissed by Kroeber (1909:15), who stated that "An independent examination of the material on which [Uhle's opinion of distinct progression and development of civilization having taken place during the growth of the deposit] is reared, tends to [negate] rather than to confirm it." Kroeber (1909:15) noted that "finely worked objects" occurred in shallow stratigraphic contexts and that "rough stone fragments predominate in [the] low layers," but most artifact types were found throughout the stratigraphic sequence. This indicated to him that while there was "some gradual elaboration and refinement of technical processes . . . it was a change of degree only, and one in no way to be compared even for a moment with a transition as fundamental as that from palaeolithic to neolithic" (Kroeber 1909:16; see also Rowe 1975:158).

Over a decade later, Kroeber (1923b:140) lamented that archaeological evidence of cultural change and time depth in California was hindered by

(1) "the absence of pottery from the greater portion of the state"; (2) the "little evidence of stratification" in the state's sites; and (3) the minimal attention archaeological research had paid to "depth, position, or colloca-tion" of artifacts. He noted that he saw no evidence of major cultural change in Nels Nelson's materials from the Ellis Landing shell midden on the edge of San Francisco Bay (Nelson 1910), and he reiterated his earlier assessment of Uhle's Emeryville work: There were few artifacts (a lament he was to express regularly regarding the shell middens of California [e.g., Kroeber 1925b, 1936]); they showed no "marked cultural changes"; change was in "quality and finish . . . rather than [in the introduction of] new types"; and "the principal types . . . occur in all strata" (Kroeber 1923b:141). For Kroeber (1909:15), these observations indicated that the "same modes of life . . . were followed in the periods represented by the earliest and the latest strata."

Kroeber (e.g., 1909:39, 41) knew full well the value of data regarding the stratigraphic context of artifacts; such data were an "urgent need" if one was to acquire "information as to cultural and chronological relations." Thus, he did not discount the value of Uhle's stratigraphic method; rather, he questioned the significance of the chronological indications of cultural change Uhle documented. Part of the problem was the small sample of artifacts at Uhle's disposal (see also Kroeber 1925b, 1936), a problem that plagues archaeology in various guises even today. The major problem, how-ever, lay in Kroeber's conceptions of culture history. Being Boas's student, it is not surprising that Kroeber elaborated on his mentor's (Boas 1902) earlier comment regarding the culture history of the Americas:

> The civilization revealed by [archaeology] is in its essentials the same as that found in the same region by the more recent explorer and settler. . . . [N]either archaeology nor ethnology has yet been able to discover either the presence or absence of any important cultural features in one period that are not respectively present or absent in the other. . . . [A]rchaeology at no point gives any evidence of significant changes in culture. . . . [D]if-ferences between the past and present are only differences in detail, in-volving nothing more than a *passing change of fashion* in manufacture or in manipulation of the same process. (Kroeber 1909:3–5; emphasis added)

Rowe (1962a:399-400) argued that in 1909 Kroeber was visualizing "cultural change in terms of major shifts in technology and subsistence, any changes of less moment [such as what Uhle documented] were insig-nificant." Uhle seems to have favored a gradualistic, nonessentialist form of cultural evolution, whereas Kroeber favored an essentialist form such as that represented by Europe's Paleolithic–Neolithic–Bronze Age–Iron Age sequence—a point that is very clear in his later analyses of Uhle's South

American pottery collections. The essentialist viewpoint of change was typical around the turn of the century. For example, "[Bureau of American Ethnology] archaeologists did not consider cultural change on a scale less than the Paleolithic–Neolithic change to be significant. Variation in archaeological material was generally ascribed to inter-tribal (e.g., spatial or functional) variation (e.g., Holmes 1919:77)" (Meltzer 1985:255). Change through time was, therefore, marked by major differences in materials. Kroeber (1935:545) and his contemporaries thus rationalized these marked differences in terms of common sense and referred to "historical impulses" to account for these seemingly abrupt changes.

Kroeber, like his mentor (see Boas 1896), generally accepted some notion of progressive evolution—that culture would evolve from a low, or primitive, stage to a higher and more complex stage. Kroeber (1923b:141) described the upper strata of the Emeryville and Ellis Landing shell middens as the "richest culturally." This view, in conjunction with the perceived shallow time depth of North America's human past, simply would not allow the detection of the epochal changes (read essentialist differences) Kroeber sought; the few thousand years granted to human antiquity on the coast of California—and everywhere else in the Americas—rendered "any evidence of radical change" or "notable development" unlikely (Kroeber 1909:16). Kroeber was, however, within a very few years, to have a significant change of heart brought about by access to collections of a kind of artifact—pottery—that in 1909 he saw as having the potential to measure temporal change in cultures (recall his lament in 1923 [Kroeber 1923b:140] that the California shell middens contained little pottery).

Summary

In taking stock of the discipline just prior to the so-called stratigraphic revolution, Roland B. Dixon (1913:551) pointed out various apparent instances of cultural change, but he also indicated that many of these were little more than "increasing perfection of the products of a uniform culture"—a reiteration of Boas's and Kroeber's point. Even when archaeological cultures seemed to Dixon to be significantly different, he could only presume that they represented an essentialist-like series of "successive cultures" (Dixon 1913:553) rather than samples of a materialist-like continuum of change. He thus suggested that the successions were the result of "numerous and far-reaching ethnic movements, resulting in a stratification of cultures, such that later have dispossessed and overlain earlier" (Dixon 1913:559). His view was of the essentialist sort: Materialist cultural evolution was precluded, and all difference observed in the archaeological record was explained in commonsense, ethnological terms as ethnic difference.

Commentators remarking on Dixon's paper noted things such as "There is always danger of mistaking analogy [convergence] for genealogy [homology]. There is likewise danger of misconstruing the phenomena of parallelism and of convergence" (MacCurdy, in Dixon 1913:569). Further, "Chronology is at the root of the matter, being the nerve electrifying the dead body of history. It should be incumbent upon the American archaeologist to establish a chronological basis of the pre-columbian cultures" (Laufer, in Dixon 1913:577). Again, the clear challenge was to establish temporal control so that one could begin to sort out analogous from homologous similarities. That challenge would be met in admirable fashion shortly after Dixon's remarks were published, but it would not be as a result of archaeologists starting to excavate stratigraphically; as we have argued here, that was already being done. What had to happen, rather, was a change in how formal variation in artifacts was studied.

Notes

1. Items reprinted in our companion volume (Lyman et al. 1997) are indicated by [†]. All references are to the original pagination.
2. Biologists themselves confess that identifying homologous features is not a straightforward endeavor (e.g., Bock 1977:882–890; Simpson 1975:16–17).

3

The Birth of Culture History

As discussed in the preceding chapter, strata were used on a regular basis as artifact collection units during the late nineteenth and early twentieth centuries, but only occasionally were superposed artifact assemblages used to measure the passage of time and thus to discuss culture change. Such change was discounted as insignificant by Boas, Kroeber, and other leading figures in the discipline. What led to the shift in thinking and the eventual emergence of the culture history paradigm? Histories of Americanist archaeology (e.g., Browman and Givens 1996; Strong 1952; Taylor 1954; Willey and Sabloff 1993:97) typically refer to a "stratigraphic revolution" that took place in the teens, but, as we explain below, the revolution resided elsewhere.

The units of observation favored by most anthropologists and archaeologists at the turn of the century involved "culture traits." Wissler (1923:50–51) noted that "we must *discover* the nature and characteristics of [these units]" (emphasis added), resulting in the ambiguity noted in Chapter 2 regarding the appropriate scale of a culture trait. Most culture traits being discussed prior to the midteens were rather general units such as pottery or basketry or substantial architecture. The revolution resided in a shift in scale from study of the presence or absence of such general traits to the study of shifting frequencies of particular variants of traits that came to be variously known as types or styles. This shift in scale, and in metaphysic from essentialism to materialism, allowed archaeologists to measure the passage of time using that decades-old strategy of stratigraphic excavation. Importantly, that strategy initially served as a way to confirm, rather than to discover, the passage of time as indicated by shifting frequencies of types.

We review below the work of several individuals who made significant contributions to the birth of culture history. The discussion is arranged by individual in order to track the reasoning that lay behind the work. It will become apparent that there really was no stratigraphic revolution in the sense usually implied; rather, superposed artifact collections were used to confirm what had been suspected for several years—that there were chronological differences among artifact (usually pottery) variants. Along the way, we discuss the origins of the shift in metaphysic that resulted in the birth of the culture history paradigm.

Franz Boas and Manuel Gamio

Late in the first decade of the twentieth century, Zelia Nuttall, honorary assistant in Mexican archaeology at the Peabody Museum (Harvard), was sufficiently familiar with the archaeological record of the Valley of Mexico to suspect that different kinds of clay figurines and pottery represented temporally distinct cultures (Nuttall 1926; see also Mason 1943; Vaillant 1935a, 1935b). She therefore asked workmen to collect artifacts from under the Pedregal lava flow—artifacts that clearly "antedated any Aztec remains" (Nuttall 1926:246), which had been found above the lava flow. At about the same time, Manuel Gamio (1909) "recognized [what he believed was] a succession of various styles of figurines and pottery" in the same area (Vaillant 1935a:289). How could the suspected chronological relations of these various materials be validated empirically?

As is well documented by Browman and Givens (1996:88–89), Boas sought to use stratigraphy to address chronological questions and to train Americanist anthropologists in its value. Boas (e.g., 1900:387–388) was aware of the temporal significance of superposed archaeological materials. Given our reading of the late-nineteenth-century literature and the fact that most Americanists knew well that superposed artifacts denoted the passage of time, we suspect that all Boas was really trying to do was to integrate archaeology with anthropology and to flesh out the results of one with the results of the other (e.g., Boas 1902). On the advice of Boas, Gamio (1913) excavated several deep trenches at the site of Atzcapotzalco in Mexico City (Figure 3.1) in 1911–1912, primarily to test the validity of the suspected sequence of Mexican pre-Columbian cultures then known as Tipo del Cerro (Archaic), Teotihuacán, and Aztec. His published stratigraphic profile is shown in Figure 3.2. This profile is significant because it indicates that his arbitrary levels were of varying thickness, though it seems his rule was to excavate in 25-cm-thick levels (Adams 1960; Gamio 1959). Some of Gamio's contemporaries excavated in arbitrary levels of uniform thickness because they were worried that different sediment volumes would produce different abundances of sherds.

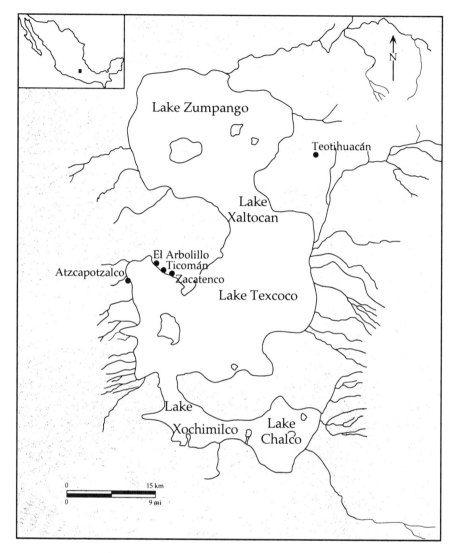

Figure 3.1. Map of the Valley of Mexico showing the locations of sites mentioned in the text. The shoreline is approximate as of 1521.

Boas (1936:139) later took credit for his role in Gamio's work, noting that work to be, with the exception of Dall's (1877) earlier investigations, "the first stratigraphic work in North America." Rouse (1967:155) suggested that Boas "seems to have been the first to seriate refuse deposits.

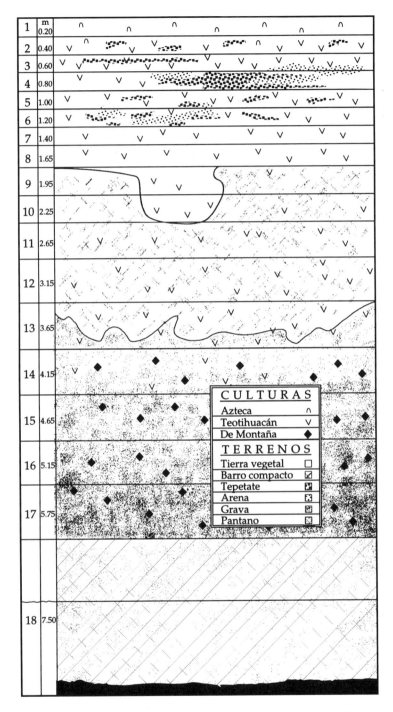

Figure 3.2. Manuel Gamio's stratigraphic profile at Atzcapotzalco in Mexico City. Note the varied thicknesses of the arbitrary levels and the vertical distribution of different artifact forms, which Gamio assigned to one of three cultures (inverted ∪, ∨, and diamond symbols) (after Gamio 1913).

In 1910 [he] arranged [sherds from the surface of sites in the Valley of Mexico] in three successive groups." Rouse also indicated that it was this sequence that Gamio tested using superposition. Boas did not engage in seriation in any modern sense, nor did he so claim (Boas 1936). Rouse reached his conclusion because to him the term "seriation" meant any dating method operating on artifacts. Boas (1912, 1913) was never clear about the source of the chronological suspicions he and his contemporaries held. But importantly, in his "Archaeological Investigations in the Valley of Mexico by the International School, 1911–12," Boas (1913:179[†]) indicated that Gamio's excavations were not the only ones geared toward working out the chronological sequence; excavations by a "Miss [Isabel] Ramírez Castañeda" also helped establish that sequence, though her work is seldom mentioned in later literature (Mason [1943:60] is a rare exception).

Gamio (1913) identified the superposed relations of the three types of remains. From a historical perspective what is important is that Gamio's approach to the chronological problem concerned a suspected local sequence and the fact that superposition was used to confirm rather than to create that sequence—points that we will come back to later. Also important here is the fact that Gamio's excavation showed that the ceramic types occupied nearly unique stratigraphic positions with minimal overlap. This is similar to earlier discussions of superposed artifact collections in which different kinds of artifacts were shown to occupy different strata (e.g., Boas 1900; Harrington 1909b). That Gamio followed the essentialist metaphysic of many of his contemporaries, such as Boas (e.g., 1900, 1905), and believed that the distinct styles of pottery making up the sequence represented distinct cultures is evident in his discussion (Gamio 1913). Gamio (1917; see also Gamio 1924) later suggested that the waxing and waning of a type indicated the growth and decline of a population, thereby maintaining his distinction of discrete cultural populations and his essentialist view. Gamio's metaphysic was, then, quite a different notion than that held, at least initially, by Nelson, Kidder, Kroeber, and Spier, the other major contributors to the so-called stratigraphic revolution. Because of this, and because of the fact that virtually everyone knew superposed strata marked the passage of time and many used those units as collections units, we find the work of the latter four individuals to be of much greater significance to the birth of culture history than Gamio's work.

Nels C. Nelson

In 1906, Nels Nelson, a student of Kroeber's at the University of California, excavated the Ellis Landing shell midden near San Francisco Bay

(Nelson 1910). He apparently was influenced by Uhle's slightly earlier work at Emeryville because he made an effort at Ellis Landing to record observations on stratigraphic positioning and site structure (Woodbury 1960a). For example, Nelson (1910:374) reported that "there are no well-defined strata of raw and calcined materials such as marked the upper part of the Emeryville mound [and] bedding planes [are] readily distinguishable only at some few points." Nelson (1910:372) also discussed his use of an excavation technique that sounds much like the Harrington–Peabody technique. In addition, when working below the water table, Nelson clearly excavated stratigraphically. "Under the circumstances, the dirt could not be carefully looked over at the time of removal from the [vertical] shaft [excavated beneath the water table], and was therefore laid out on the surface *according to horizons* [strata] and later thoroughly examined" (Nelson 1910:373; emphasis added). This most definitely was stratigraphic excavation in that strata were employed as artifact collection units. But Nelson, being well aware of Kroeber's (1909) earlier salvo across Uhle's (1907) bow, simply did not ask chronological questions at Ellis Landing, despite his estimate that the shell mound had formed over some 3500 years (Nelson 1910:371). Kroeber was his advisor, and Nelson's work at Ellis Landing served as part of his master's thesis.

Nelson was hired by Clark Wissler at the American Museum of Natural History and began working in the Galisteo Basin near Santa Fe, New Mexico, in 1911–1912, returning to the region in 1914–1915 (Nelson 1913, 1914, 1915, 1916, 1917a). His first report (Nelson 1913:63), while a popular account, documents that he was there for a very specific reason:

> It is felt that many problems relating to the origin and distribution of peoples and to cultural traits now observable in the Southwest cannot be solved in their entirety by the examination of present-day conditions or even by consulting Spanish documentary history, which though it takes us back nearly four hundred years and is reasonably accurate, shows us little more than the last phase of development within this most interesting ethnographic division of the United States. By a tolerably exhaustive study of the thousands of ruins and other archaeological features characteristic of the region, we may hope in time to gain not only an idea of prehistoric conditions but perhaps also an adequate explanation of the *origin, the antiquity and the course of development* leading up to a better understanding of the present status of aboriginal life in the region. (Nelson 1913:63; emphasis added)

Looking back a few years later, Nelson (1919c:133) remarked that "there was always a set problem to be solved, but it was purely a local one." In regards to Nelson's work Wissler (1915:395) indicated that the "plan was to take up the historical problem in the Southwest to determine if possible the relations between the prehistoric and historic peoples." Toward that end, the area chosen, apparently by Wissler, was what "seemed most likely to have been the chief *center* of Pueblo culture as we now know it" (Wissler 1915:397; emphasis added). This is an important point to which we will return.

Nelson's (1914:111–112) formal report of the first two seasons of excavation mentions only a few chronological observations: "The surviving artifacts [recovered from the various sites sampled] were of the same types, with nevertheless a local and also a *stratigraphic variation* in general finish and decoration of the pottery. . . . the execution of glazed ornamentation on pottery seems to have degenerated in late prehistoric times, but the artists continued to use the glaze of older days" (emphasis added). In a later popular report written while in the field, Nelson (1915) did not mention chronological issues, although an accompanying article by his supervisor (Wissler 1915:398) indicated that "The net result of [Nelson's] work has been to make clear the chronological relations of the various ruins in the vicinity, which in turn enables us to determine their historic relation to the living peoples. . . . [T]he way is now clear to a chronological classification of many groups of ruins." What happened between about 1913 and 1915?

In his formal report on his later excavations, Nelson (1916:162) stated that by the beginning of the 1914 season he suspected he knew the chronological order of five types of pottery. Apparently, Nelson's initial efforts in 1914 to locate an undisturbed stratigraphic section so that he might study the chronology of ruins and pottery styles were thwarted (Nelson 1916). Late in the 1914 field season, however, he found such a section at Pueblo San Cristóbal (Figure 3.3). Nelson had visited the stratigraphic excavations of Otto Obermaier and Henri Breuil in Spain in 1913 and had seen "levels marked off on the walls" of the excavations and participated in excavating Castillo Cave; this experience, according to Nelson, served as his "chief inspiration" for his excavations at Pueblo San Cristóbal (Nelson, in Woodbury 1960b:98). We believe that Nelson's particular technique of excavation came from Europe, but certainly not the notion that superposed collections marked the passage of time; the latter was a notion that had been around for decades within Americanist archaeology.

Nelson excavated San Cristóbal in arbitrary 1-foot-thick levels rather than in natural stratigraphic units. He kept sherds from each level separate and identified (typed) and counted them by level. The results of Nelson's chronological investigations were mentioned without detail in a January 1915 publication (Anonymous 1915) and also discussed with minimal detail by Nelson in December 1915 at the International Congress of Americanists (Nelson 1917a). The heart of the matter is found in his publication "Chronology of

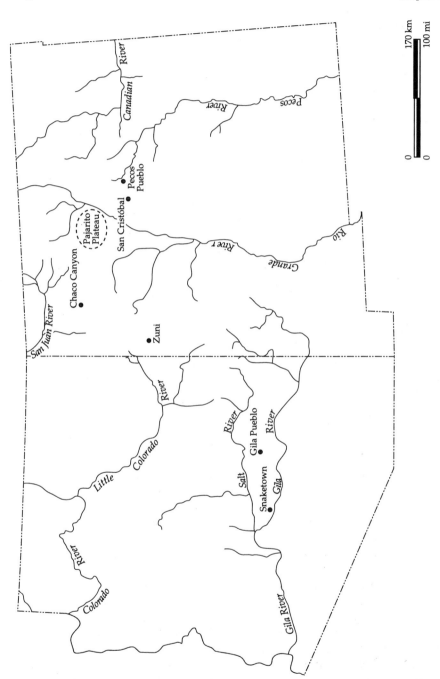

Figure 3.3. Map of Arizona and New Mexico showing locations of sites mentioned in the text.

the Tano Ruins, New Mexico" (Nelson 1916[†]). There, Nelson presented the absolute abundances of each of five types of pottery from each of his ten 1-foot-thick levels, and in an accompanying table he adjusted observed sherd frequencies to account for different excavation volumes—both rather innovative procedures for the time.[1] His adjustment of observed frequencies, however, clearly is unnecessary if the relative, or proportional, abundances of the artifacts are calculated. No less an individual than A. V. Kidder also presumed that different excavation volumes compromised the usefulness of artifact frequency data, writing with regard to using strata as artifact collections units that "This method derogates from the absolute statistical value of the material, as the cuts, not being of exactly equal thickness, are not strictly comparable statistically" (Kidder and Kidder 1917:340).

The reason prehistorians assumed that type frequencies must be adjusted to account for different excavation volumes is unclear. Perhaps they were attempting to make the clearly relative time scale of superposition more absolute, as implied in Kroeber's (1919:259) assessment of Nelson's excavation: "Each foot of debris may be taken as representing an approximately equal duration of deposition, as indicated by the fairly steady number of sherds of all types found at each depth." This comment was offered by Kroeber when mentioning Wissler's (1916b:194–195) discussion of Nelson's data. Rates of pottery deposition would influence absolute abundances of sherds, but only if the rate of sediment deposition remained constant throughout the sequence. Clearly, not all of the relevant variables were being considered by Nelson, Kroeber, and Wissler, as they were not by James A. Ford (1935b) two decades later. Kidwell (1986) provides a useful discussion of some of these considerations in a paleobiological context.

Nelson (1916:167) interpreted the absolute abundances of some of his pottery types as approximating "normal frequency curves" (Figure 3.4). Such a pattern was to be "expected," Nelson (1916:167) suggested, because a pottery style had come "slowly into vogue, attained a maximum and [then went through] a gradual decline . . . to extinction." Thus Nelson rationalized such frequency distributions as the waxing and waning of an item's popularity. With explicit reference to Nelson's work, Wissler (1916b:194) indicated that "we do not know the particular causes that give us this [unimodal frequency] form of curve," but like Nelson, Wissler believed they "represent in the main the rise and decline of a culture trait."

In a retrospective look at Nelson's work, Leslie Spier (1931:279–280) also referred to the frequency distributions as "normal frequency distributions." This is not surprising given Spier's apparent role in the birth of culture history. There was no explanatory theory to account for such frequency distributions. Instead, the observed distributions were accounted for by common sense. This notion that the frequency of a culture trait was a

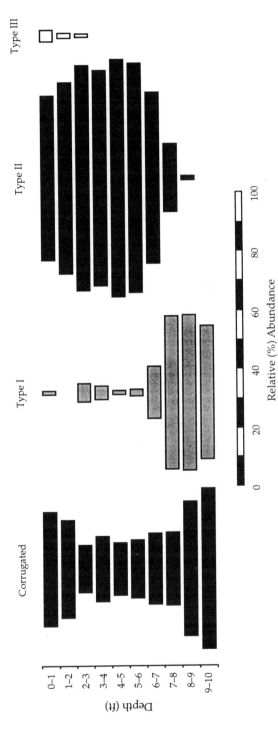

Figure 3.4. Nels Nelson's pottery data from Pueblo San Cristóbal, New Mexico, in seriated form. Note that Nelson believed, correctly, that the frequency of corrugated ware was not a good indicator of age. Note also the essentially monotonic frequency distribution of his types I–III (after Nelson 1916).

measure of its popularity—what we refer to as the *popularity principle*—was to become a central tenet of culture history. The conceptual baggage it entailed was eventually to influence heavily any effort to write such history.

It is the stratigraphic context of the pottery, not the potential conceptual or methodological implications of sherd frequencies for culture history, that is remembered by historians (e.g., Browman and Givens 1996; Taylor 1954; Willey and Sabloff 1993; Woodbury 1960a, 1960b). In his retrospective look at Nelson's work, Spier, Nelson's former colleague at the American Museum, stated that Nelson's use of superposition was "the first exposition of a refined method for determining exactly the time sequence of archaeological materials in a primitive area" (Spier 1931:275), though in our view this is somewhat of an overstatement; clearly Dall (1877), Uhle (1907), Harrington (1909b) and others had accomplished more or less the same thing. Wissler (1917b) referred to Nelson's work as "the new archaeology," but since Wissler (1915) had "initiated" Nelson's work in the Galisteo Basin (Nelson 1948:246), perhaps this is not such a surprising statement. Given that collecting artifacts from distinct vertical proveniences was not new, what *was* so new about Nelson's approach to chronological questions, and what was the source of that new approach?

A New Metaphysic

Nelson (1916:162) stated explicitly that when he went back to San Cristóbal in the Galisteo Basin of New Mexico in 1914, he sought to test a suspected local sequence of four pottery types: "By the opening of the [1914] season, it was reasonably certain, both from internal evidence and from various general considerations, what was the chronological order of the four apparent pottery types, but tangible proof was still wanting." He knew or suspected the relative chronological positions of pottery types, but only by excavating at San Cristóbal was he able to establish their relative chronological positions (Nelson 1916:163–166); all previous superpositional indications of chronology were "incomplete and fragmentary, each showing merely the time relations of two successive pottery types at some place or other in the total series of four or five types" (Nelson 1916:163). We note that Nelson's use of the word "merely" demonstrates that he viewed the temporal implications of superposed pottery types as nothing out of the ordinary. Thus, as noted by Willey and Sabloff (1974:94), Nelson never claimed that his stratigraphic excavation was particularly new, innovative, or revolutionary. It may well have. been, as he clearly peeled back each vertical unit as a distinct unit rather than using the more typical Harrington–Peabody technique, but the resulting vertical-provenience information was essentially the same. More importantly, Nelson also did not claim that his *analytical technique* was new, innovative, or revolutionary.

The important innovation found in Nelson's (1916) work is his demonstration that pottery types altered in absolute frequency through time in a pattern that he characterized as "very nearly normal frequency curves [that reflected the fact that] a style of pottery . . . came slowly into vogue, attained a maximum and began a gradual decline" (Nelson 1916:167). He was able to measure culture change not by using the then-typical qualitative differences in artifact assemblages such as the presence or absence of pottery—a culture trait—as had been done by Harrington (1909b) and Wissler (1909), but rather by documenting—in revolutionary fashion—the changing *frequencies of pottery types*. Stratigraphic provenience confirmed that those frequencies in fact measured the passage of time. Wissler (1916b:195–196) suggested that such frequency changes in "specific styles in ceramic art [represented] stylistic pulsations." These represented, as Kroeber (1909:5) had noted a few years earlier, "passing change of fashion." The question thus becomes less one of wondering where Nelson got the idea to collect artifacts from vertically discrete units—many of his predecessors had done that—but rather wondering where he got the idea to study the frequencies of particular artifact types. We believe it was a collaborative effort, and here the roles of Wissler and, particularly, of Spier are critical.

Spier (1916, 1918b) excavated near Trenton, New Jersey, in 1914 and 1915 to yet again examine the archaeological significance of the Trenton Argillite Culture, as new claims for its significance to American prehistory had recently appeared (Volk 1911). He used the Harrington–Peabody excavation technique at the site: "trenching proceeded by scraping the breast or face of the trench with a trowel. The depth below the plane of contact of [the uppermost] black and [middle] yellow soils . . . and the lateral position of each [artifact] specimen was noted before it was removed" (Spier 1918b:180). He did not ask chronological questions but rather was concerned with determining how the materials had been deposited. Spier (1916, 1918b) showed not only that the materials consistently occupied a particular vertical position within the rather thick yellow stratum but that those materials also consistently displayed a particular absolute-frequency distribution when plotted vertically within that stratum. He termed it a "typical frequency distribution" (Spier 1916:186, 1918b:185) that reflected a "normally variable series" (Spier 1918b:192).

Wissler (1916b:197) and Spier (1918b) interpreted the absolute-frequency distribution as evidence of redeposition—an interpretation supported by a similar distribution of nonartifactual pebbles. Further, Wissler (1916b) showed that when summed (by Spier), Loomis and Young's (1912) cultural materials from their Maine shell midden displayed no such normal frequency distribution, nor did Nelson's (1916) pottery from San Cristóbal. The normal frequency distributions exhibited by Nelson's sherds occurred only for "specific styles in ceramic art and [were] not the typical distribution for the ceramic art of San Cristobal *as a whole*" (Wissler 1916b:195; emphasis added). That is, only sherds of particular "styles" (types) displayed a normal distribution, not sherds as a whole or as a culture trait. The Trenton artifacts, all made of stone, were a "culture trait" as a whole just as sherds were (Wissler 1916b:196). Spier (1918b:201) indicated that the particular types of pottery from San Cristóbal and Pecos pueblos gave "distributions of the normal type. . . . But these are not comparable to the Trenton series since they represent fluctuations in single cultural traits—stylistic pulsations—which attain their maxima at the expense of other similar traits."

Spier (1918b:180) began plotting the absolute frequencies of Trenton artifacts late in 1914 or early in 1915, just as Nelson was coming out of the field, having recently completed the excavation of the 10-foot-deep column at San Cristóbal in 1-foot levels. Wissler wanted to show that the argillite materials were naturally deposited in order to perpetuate the museum's long-standing position that the artifacts were not Pleistocene in age (see Meltzer 1983), a position that was at odds with that of other institutions such as the Peabody Museum (Harvard), which had long sponsored Volk's work at Trenton. It likely was Spier and Wissler who gave Nelson the idea of plotting the absolute frequencies of artifact types vertically. The evidence for this includes the fact that Spier, Nelson, and Wissler all worked at the American Museum, the coincidence in timing of the Trenton and San Cristóbal analyses, Wissler's use of Nelson's data, and the use of absolute frequencies of specimens in all of these seminal analyses. In later analyses, Spier (1917a, 1917b, 1918a, 1919) used percentages of artifact types, and Nelson (1920) alluded to the fact that he would have done so himself had his samples from a site excavated later been adequate. As noted earlier, Nelson (1916:166) adjusted the absolute frequencies of his pottery to account for different excavation volumes. He did this because it brought his sherd frequencies in line with both Spier's (1918b) Trenton data and with Wissler's (1916b:195) evidence showing that the Trenton materials were secondarily deposited. To have converted his absolute frequencies to relative frequencies would have negated the necessity of adjusting for different excavated volumes, but it also would have made Nelson's data incomparable with the Trenton data.

Thus, Nelson's data helped Spier and Wissler, but how did Nelson's data help *him*? Nelson had found superposed remains before the critical 1914 field season in the Southwest, but he noted that in such cases "there is often no appreciable [chronological] differentiation of remains" (Nelson

1916:163). When he found evidence of chronological differentiation, it was between types at the ends of a continuum of several pottery types, and thus he lamented that such instances were *"merely* clean-cut superpositions showing *nothing but time relations"* (Nelson 1916:163; emphasis added). The data referred to, then, provided an essentialist-like perspective of culture history. However, when two types in the continuum were found stratigraphically mixed together, "one *gradually replacing* the other[, this] was the evidence wanted, because it accounted for the otherwise unknown time that separated the merely superposed occurrences of types and from the point of view of the merely physical relationships of contiguity, *connected them"* (Nelson 1916:163; emphasis added). The data from San Cristóbal, then, provided a materialist-like perspective of culture history.

The preceding is important because it reveals that Nelson was thinking about culture change in terms that simply did not mesh with the thinking of Boas, Gamio, or Kroeber. While many of his colleagues thought in essentialist terms, Nelson was thinking in materialist terms. Thus, in one sense, Nelson replaced, at least in his own mind, the then-prevalent notion that culture change could be modeled as a flight of stairs, each step representing a static evolutionary stage and each change in elevation representing a rather abrupt transformation from one stage to the next—or in Nelson's case prior to 1914 from one type to another with no overlap—with a model that viewed culture change as a gradually ascending ramp (e.g., Nelson 1919a, 1919b, 1919c, 1932), albeit a ramp that moved through progressively more advanced stages. Plotting frequencies of types against time (rendered as geologically vertical space) would illustrate the gradual cultural evolution Nelson sought and eventually allow one to document the relative ages of the cultural stages (e.g., Nelson 1937). This was not only a revolution in analytical method, it was a revolution in metaphysic. It was decidedly *not* a revolution in excavation strategy.

Alfred V. Kidder

A. V. Kidder (1915:461) noted that a December 1914 (actually Anonymous 1915) announcement indicated Nelson's excavation had revealed a deposit "so stratified that the relative ages of [four distinct types of pottery] could be ascertained," but he also lamented that "What the wares were has not yet been announced." Based on his dissertation research on the Pajarito Plateau (Figure 3.3), Kidder (1915:452) suspected what the sequence of pottery wares, or types, was, but he stated that "as yet no stratified finds have given us absolutely conclusive proof of this." His early suspicions regarding temporal sequence were founded on (1) the association of certain pottery types with "nearly obliterated ruins of obviously greater age than any others in the region" (Kidder 1915:452–453); (2) the geographic distribution of certain pottery styles (the age–area concept [Kidder 1931:4]); and (3) suspicions regarding the evolutionary progression of pottery styles and technologies (Kidder 1915:453–456). He concluded his early foray into the prehistory of the Southwest by noting the necessity of finding stratified sites in order to draw "reliable developmental or historical conclusions" (Kidder 1915:461). Superposed collections would, thus, serve to *confirm* a suspected local sequence rather than to create one.

In a paper presented in December 1915 (Kidder 1917b), Kidder was more concerned with mapping the spatial distribution of cultures and mentioned only in passing that stratigraphy indicated the cultural sequence he discussed therein—Basketmaker to Slab-house to Kiva—to be in correct chronological order. Questions such as which cultural manifestations—and Kidder believed there were several "sub-cultures" (Kidder 1917b:110)—developed in place, which evolved into something new, and which were intrusive to the area could not be answered through reference to stratigraphy alone. In Kidder's view, spatial as well as chronological data were necessary. Thus it seems that Kidder was well aware of the chronological value of superposed sets of artifacts, but his major interests initially were elsewhere, particularly on the horizontal distribution of artifact forms (e.g., Kidder 1931:4, 6–7).

Kidder (1916:120) reported that Pecos Pueblo, New Mexico (Figure 3.3), was chosen for study because historical documents indicated that it had been occupied from 1540 until 1840 and that surface finds included "practically all types of prehistoric wares known to occur in the upper Rio Grande district." Occupation was thus believed to have been continuous and from "very early times." No other site then known in New Mexico and "available for excavation" seemed to have that attribute:

> [I] hoped that remains [at Pecos] would there be found so stratified as to make clear the development of the various Pueblo arts and to enable students to place in their proper chronological order numerous New Mexican ruins whose culture has long been known but whose relation to one another has been entirely problematical. This hope was strengthened by the fact that Mr. N. C. Nelson . . . had recently discovered very important stratified remains at San Christobal a few miles to the west. (Kidder 1916:120)

Similar deposits at Pecos would allow comparative analyses and the extension of Nelson's chronology—which ended at 1680 when San Cristóbal was abandoned—into the middle of the nineteenth century (Kidder 1916:120).

Early in his excavations, Kidder (1916:122) recognized that pottery types in the lower levels of his trenches were "markedly different from [those] at the top and that there were several distinct types between," and his summary chart (Kidder 1924) (Figure 3.5) arranged them in terms of their vertical distribution (see also Kidder 1916, 1931, 1936b; Kidder and Kidder 1917). Not all excavations at Pecos were undertaken with close attention to superpositional relations. Rather, such relations were observed by "tests made at different points as the [excavation] advanced. The tests consisted of the collection of all the sherds in a given column of debris, the fragments from each layer being placed in a separate paper bag bearing the numbers of the test and of the layer" (Kidder 1916:122). During the first year's field season—the summer of 1915—those tests employed arbitrary levels that were 1-foot to 1.5-feet thick, but when it was apparent that the arbitrary levels split strata, "a new bag was started," which apparently meant that Kidder paid attention to the stratigraphic provenience of the artifacts found within his arbitrary levels. Kidder (1936b:xix) referred to the "stratigraphic excavations at Pecos in 1915." Based on the literature of that time (e.g., Kidder 1916), he was excavating in arbitrary levels, though he at least occasionally collected artifacts from distinct depositional units. He indicated that while he was proposing a chronology "based on technological and artistic grounds" (e.g., Kidder 1917a), Nelson "was attacking the same problem on the much sounder basis of stratigraphy, a method which had not been used, save sporadically, in southwestern archaeology. . . . Its importance cannot be overlooked" (Kidder 1936b:xix).

Kidder was careful to place his tests only in areas that appeared to be undisturbed, abandoning tests "when it became clear that a grave shaft had disturbed the original deposition of the refuse" (Kidder 1916:122). By the second field season (1916), Kidder was generally excavating in natural stratigraphic levels (Kidder and Kidder 1917:340). In some excavated blocks the vertical units "averaged 2 feet 3 inches in thickness"; in others the average was "about 1 foot 8 inches in thickness"; in others "1 foot 6 inches"; and in still others 7 inches (Kidder and Kidder 1917:341). Kidder and Kidder (1917:340) explained the reasoning behind the use of such an excavation technique:

> The Pecos tests were not divided into exactly equal cuts, as was done by Mr. Nelson, but were laid out in nearly equal divisions based on sand, ash, or other strata which indicated actual levels of deposition during the formation of the mound. This was necessitated by the fact that the Pecos deposits were for the most part laid down on sloping or irregular surfaces, and cuts made on arbitrarily chosen plane levels would have resulted in the splitting or cross-cutting of strata.

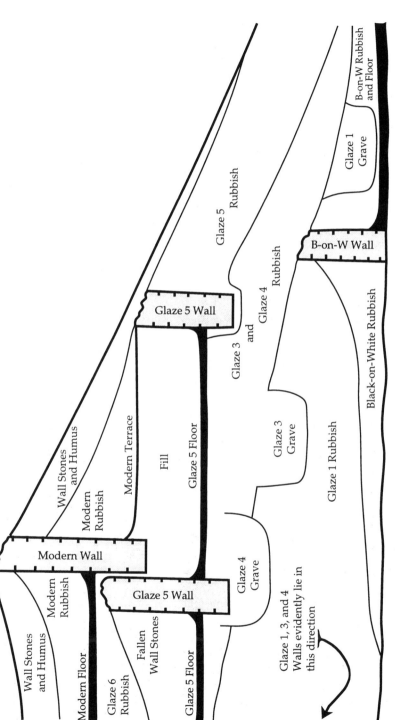

Figure 3.5. A. V. Kidder's summary diagram of the stratigraphic relations of pottery types at Pecos Pueblo (after Kidder 1924).

In a detailed discussion of his excavation methods written well after the completion of his fieldwork, Kidder (1931:9) indicated that when strata were particularly evident in vertical exposures at Pecos, (1) "a column, its size determined by the extent of the deposit, was isolated by exposing two, three, or even all four of its sides by trenching from surface to bottom. A horizontal base line was established toward the center of this column, for measuring purposes"; (2) the vertical faces of the columns "were then carefully scraped to a vertical face to reveal every line and band in the column, and the limits of each cut to be made were fixed along such lines by placing pegs at frequent intervals to guide the workmen, who were instructed to cut each layer precisely down to the row of pegs"; (3) a stratigraphic profile was then drawn to show the "position and thickness of each layer. In dividing the column into layers care was taken to follow a natural division . . . rather than an arbitrary line. The resultant layers were not always of equal volume . . . but they did represent the actual structure of the column"; and (4) excavation of the column proceeded "layer by layer, working from the surface downward. . . . All objects found in a layer were of course kept apart [and] labeled with the cut [vertical layer] number they represented, for later study. . . . The strata alone determined the number of cuts made" (Kidder 1931:9–10).

Kidder, then, unlike his predecessors Nelson and Gamio, both of whom used arbitrary levels, excavated portions of Pecos after the first field season in natural stratigraphic layers. It is clear that Nelson excavated San Cristóbal in arbitrary 1-foot levels, but it also is clear that he knew well the hazards of doing so if one was interested in questions of chronology. A few years after his work in New Mexico, Nelson (1918:86) reported on his 1917 investigation of a shell mound in Florida: "In ordinary geological formations of a stratified nature a given fossil specimen—barring accidental intrusions—is accepted as being at least as old as the formation itself; and under certain conditions depth is an index to age. . . . But unless we take strict account of the order of deposition, the depth at which a given artifact occurs may signify little or nothing." His illustrations of the sloping strata he dealt with underscored this point.

Kidder was a student of Egyptologist George Reisner, who in turn had been a student of W. M. Flinders Petrie (Browman and Givens 1996; Stiebing 1993:82), the person responsible for popularizing stratigraphic excavation in Egypt. Interestingly, Kidder's 1931 discussion of the Pecos excavation method quoted above had a footnote appended stating that "Most of this paragraph was prepared by Mr. [Charles Avery] Amsden" (Kidder 1931:10). Kidder (1931:14) indicated that "During the excavations . . . Mr. Amsden was an invaluable collaborator." The paragraph on excavation technique attributed to Amsden is found in his contribution to Kidder's first report on the pottery of Pecos (Amsden 1931:27). Amsden made other significant contributions to the Pecos work that we discuss below.

Kidder's biographers (e.g., Givens 1992:50; Willey 1988:307; Woodbury 1973:43) and historians of archaeology (e.g., Willey and Sabloff 1993:103–105) have suggested or implied that Nelson influenced Kidder relative to the latter's paying attention to superpositional relations of artifacts. Woodbury (1960a:401) indicated Kidder visited Nelson's excavations and "began stratigraphic excavations during the first field season at Pecos in 1915" (see Kidder 1916). Taylor (1954:564) suggested "it was Nelson's theoretical principles and direct suggestion that led Kidder to . . . excavate . . . Pecos." However, it probably is more accurate to suggest that it was Kidder who perfected the technique of stratigraphic excavation and modified Nelson's technique to focus on natural stratigraphic units as a result of his educational background (Wauchope 1965:151).

Although Kidder is remembered for peeling back individual strata and collecting artifacts from each unit, he made two other seldom remarked but nonetheless important contributions to the birth of culture history. Recall that Nelson (1916:167) described frequency distributions as "very nearly normal frequency curves" and suggested that such distributions were to "be expected." Kidder mimicked Nelson's analytical technique but modified it in the process. Kidder not only listed the absolute frequencies of pottery types against their vertical provenience in tabular form—the mimicking part—but he also graphed the changes in relative frequencies of his pottery types against his excavation levels (Kidder and Kidder 1917[†]) using a broken-stick graph—the innovative part.

We have redrawn one of the Kidders' graphs in Figure 3.6. When they inspected those graphs, Kidder and Kidder (1917:341) noted that many—but not all—types displayed "approximately normal frequency curves." They echoed Nelson and Wissler and interpreted such curves as "indicating that each [type] had a natural rise, vogue, and decline" (Kidder and Kidder 1917:349). While the graphs implied a materialist metaphysic, the included interpretive statements were not theoretically informed explanations; they were merely commonsensical interpretations of observations that were expressed in words everyone could comprehend. In this case, the words constituted the *popularity principle.* Similar observations on the ordering of frequencies of material were, at the same time, being made without the aid of superposition (see discussion of Kroeber and Spier below), and they resulted in the development of a new and important archaeological method founded in the materialist metaphysic. Thus, one of Kidder's less often noted contributions to culture history involved the perfection of an analytical technique in line with the materialist metaphysic. This analytical technique came to be known later as "ceramic stratigraphy" (Willey 1938,

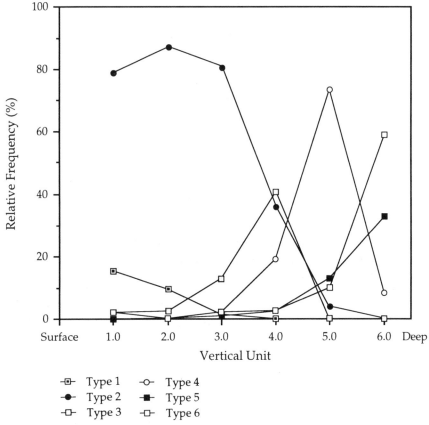

Figure 3.6. An example of M. Kidder and A. V. Kidder's (1917) percentage-stratigraphy graphics (after Kidder and Kidder 1917).

1939), or "percentage stratigraphy" (Ford 1962; Willey 1939:142). We use the latter term here because it underscores the fact that frequencies of types were tabulated (and sometimes graphed) rather than merely presence or absence data being reported.

Kidder's other seldom-noted contribution was of a decidedly different sort. Kidder (1931:7) later claimed to have "attempted a seriation, on comparative grounds, of the material available" in 1914–15, and he cited his own work (Kidder 1915) as demonstration. This claim is repeated by Givens (1992:44). Similarly, Browman and Givens (1996:86) state that Kidder presented a pottery seriation in his dissertation. We have not examined Kidder's dissertation, but in the report to which Kidder (1931:7) referred

(Kidder 1915) and which was extracted from his dissertation, there is no evidence that he seriated sherds in the same manner that Kroeber (1916a, 1916b) and Spier (1917a, 1917b) did (see below). Kidder (1915, 1917a[†]) performed what Rowe (1961:327) later characterized as "ordering by continuity of features and variation in themes." This is precisely what John Evans (1850, 1875; see also Pitt-Rivers 1875b) had done in England sixty-five years earlier, and it differed markedly from Kroeber's and Spier's seriation technique (Rowe's [1961:327] "ordering by type frequency"), a patently American invention. Kidder probably learned the technique he used from Reisner, who, as noted above, had worked in Egypt (Browman and Givens 1996:86). This was where Rowe's "ordering by continuity of features and variation in themes" was used by Petrie (e.g., 1899) (Givens 1992:51). Kidder probably was also influenced in his thinking about the technique he used by art historian George Chase, "a specialist in the study of classical Greek ceramics" (Givens 1992:25).

Kidder's (1915) original pottery sequence was based on his suspicions regarding the evolution of various design and technological features (Figure 3.7). In a brief but important (and seldom cited) paper published in 1917

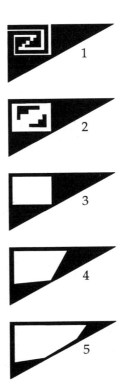

Figure 3.7. A. V. Kidder's illustration of the evolution of a ceramic design. The designs are numbered in chronological sequence; "1" is earliest and "5" is latest (after Kidder 1917a).

(Kidder 1917a), he demonstrated how such an evolutionary and thus temporal sequence—what he termed a "series" (Kidder 1917a:370)—could be worked out. Importantly, in that paper he cautioned that "The only safe method for the working out of developments in decorative art is to build up one's sequences from chronologically sequent material, and so let one's theories form themselves from the sequences" (Kidder 1917a:369). The chronological sequence was determined, in 1917, by study of superposed collections. Two or three years earlier, the sequence suspected on the basis of Kidder's method was to be confirmed, not created, by stratigraphic excavation (Kidder 1915). While others, such as Wissler (e.g., 1916c), were hinting at just such a technique for measuring time in the American archaeological record, this other contribution of Kidder's is less often noted than is his use of percentage stratigraphy, probably because such a seriation technique was used informally by many culture historians (e.g., Uhle 1903).

The term *phyletic seriation* is a reasonable one for labeling Kidder's seriations. It is different from Rowe's (1961[†]) "similiary seriation" and Rouse's (1967) "developmental seriation." For Rowe, there are several kinds of similiary seriation, including what he termed "evolutionary seriation," which involves arranging artifacts in a sequence according to some rule of development. Rouse proposed the term "developmental seriation" in an attempt to avoid the connotation of evolution according to a rule, but we fear that the term "developmental" might connote just such a rule. While Kidder no doubt had a rule in mind—progressive cultural evolution in the sense of Morgan (1877)—he also knew that the chronological implications of such a seriation had to be tested and thus no doubt knew that any notion of progress would simultaneously be tested. His seriations were, therefore, very much phyletic in an ancestor–descendant sense. The term "phylogenetic" might be used here instead of "phyletic," but there are at least two reasons not to use the former. First, phylogenetic denotes branching, whereas phyletic merely denotes a line of descent (Mayr 1969). Second, the former term, given its form, entails the notion of genetic descent, whereas the latter term does not, given its form. By the 1940s, culture historians expressed displeasure with any genetic connotation in archaeological terminology. Our use of the term phyletic is a compromise, then, and we note that it can entail linear, branching, or reticulate descent.

It is important to emphasize that neither Kidder nor anyone else working at the time had the slightest notion of what a materialist metaphysic entailed or of how it might differ from an essentialist metaphysic. If they had, we would not be writing this essay, because Americanist archaeology would not have entered the snare it set for itself by conflating the two. Since no one recognized the difference, there occurred the somewhat ironic situation that the materialist methods of percentage stratigraphy and seriation employed to bring temporal order to archaeological assemblages were simultaneously co-opted to address issues that were clearly formed under an essentialist perspective. We return to this important topic a bit later.

Alfred L. Kroeber

Rarely is the origin of a major innovation in science clear. Ambiguities feed the history of science. Not only are matters usually clouded by competing versions of similar age, but initial presentations tend to be post hoc functional accounts that lack discussion of the conditions and reasoning that led to the innovation. Not so with frequency seriation. A. L. Kroeber (1916b), in his remarkable paper "Zuñi Potsherds," gives a discursive account of precisely how he came up with the idea of frequency seriation. His discussion also makes it quite clear that earlier explorations of similar ideas (e.g., Evans 1850, 1875; Petrie 1899; Pitt-Rivers 1875a; Uhle 1903) played absolutely no role in the development of the method, as is often claimed or implied (e.g., Browman and Givens 1996; Praetzellis 1993:76; Willey and Sabloff 1993:109–110).

To the ultimate benefit of the discipline, Kroeber volunteered to help the American Museum with its research in the Southwest during the summer of 1915 (Wissler 1915:397). While walking across the countryside around Zuñi Pueblo in New Mexico (Figure 3.3), Kroeber (1916a, 1916b) began collecting sherds from the surfaces of more than a dozen prehistoric sites. He noticed that some collections tended to be dominated by "red, black, and patterned potsherds," whereas other collections were dominated by white sherds (Kroeber 1916b:8). He concluded, "There could be no doubt that here, within a half-hour's radius of the largest inhabited pueblo [Zuñi], were prehistoric remains of two types and two periods, as distinct as oil and water. The *condition of the sites* indicated the black and red ware ruins as the more recent" (Kroeber 1916b:9; emphasis added). Based on historical evidence and on the condition of the sites, Kroeber (1916b:9–10), like Kidder, concluded that concerning "the type and period of white ware and the type and period of black and of red ware, the latter is the more recent [belonging] in part to the time of early American history; the former is wholly prehistoric." Thus, Kroeber had two lines of evidence to indicate that he was dealing with temporal differences in the kinds of pottery he found: (1) historical data that indicated that "Several of the ruins were inhabited in Spanish times" (Kroeber 1916a:43), whereas other ruins were said by his informants to have been inhabited "long ago" (Kroeber 1916b:9); and (2) "Type A [historic] ruins normally include standing walls, and loose rock abounds. All Type B [prehistoric] sites are low or flat, without walls or rock, and . . . it seems more likely that this condition is due to the decay of age, or to the carrying away of the broken rock to serve as material in the nearby constructions of later ages" (Kroeber 1916a:43).

Various lines of evidence, including historical data (e.g., Sapir 1916), tree rings and the diameters of trees (e.g., Wyman 1875), and stratigraphic positioning (e.g., Dall 1877), had been used to help measure time prior to Kroeber's work. The condition or extent of decay had also been used by individuals investigating chronological aspects of the archaeological record. For example, Kidder (1915), as we have seen, used the deterioration of pueblos as an indication of relative age. Differences in pottery associated with the two kinds of ruins—historically documented and not deteriorated, and deteriorated and not historically documented—were thus also *potential* chronological indicators.

Kroeber (1916b:8) "attempted to pick up all sherds visible in certain spots [of each site], rather than range over the whole site and stoop only for the attractive ones." He did not excavate: "I have not turned a spadeful of earth in the Zuñi country. But the outlines of a thousand years' civilizational changes which the surface reveals are so clear, that there is no question of the wealth of knowledge that the ground holds for the critical but not over timid excavator" (Kroeber 1916b:14). But he was cautious. Kroeber (1916b:20, 21) believed that for his proposed chronological classification, "The final proof is in the spade," and he lamented that "in the present chaos of knowledge who can say which of these differences [in frequencies of sherd types] are due to age and which to locality and environment?" Thus, just as for his contemporaries, superposed collections were the as-yet-unavailable confirmational proof of the chronology suspected on the basis of variations in type frequencies.

Kroeber (1916a, 1916b) arranged his surface collections to derive not just a two-period sequence but a five-period (actually six, if one includes modern Zuñi pottery) cultural sequence—what he referred to as "shorter epochs" (Kroeber 1916a:44). The more familiar and more often referenced "Zuñi Potsherds" paper (Kroeber 1916b) contains all the relevant data, but Kroeber's "Zuñi Culture Sequences" (Kroeber 1916a[†]) contains a summary of the data (Kroeber's table 5) in seriated form that is adequate to illustrate the innovative nature of his analysis. The innovative aspect of Kroeber's work has, however, sometimes been overlooked. Rowe (1962a:400) stated that "Kroeber's seriation of Zuñi sites on the basis of surface collections was not the first successful seriation in North America; A. V. Kidder [1915] had published a seriation of the pottery of the Pajarito Plateau the previous year." Kidder arranged pottery on the basis of an assumed "universal rule of cultural or stylistic development" (Rowe 1961:326) and thus performed what Rouse (1967) later termed a *developmental se-riation.* Kroeber arranged assemblages of pottery on the basis of the simi-larity of frequencies of the various pottery types in the collections, performing what Rowe (1961) termed a *similiary seriation* and what we would term a *frequency seriation* (Dunnell 1970). Kroeber's was the first seriation of the latter kind; the former had been around since Thomsen's Three Age System (e.g., Evans 1850; Petrie 1899; Pitt-Rivers 1875a) and involved an essentialist metaphysic known as the typological method. In a postscript added to his manuscript prior to publication, Kroeber (1916b:36–37) mentioned Kidder's (1915) publication but made no mention of Kid-der's arrangement, though he noted how Kidder's sequence aligned with his own.

Kroeber's frequency seriation began with corrugated ware as the oldest and most frequent type. Sites—actually, the collections of pottery from in-dividual sites—were arranged so that the relative abundance of that type decreased monotonically, with two exceptions (so this is a rather clean so-lution in the summary table). The basis for this arrangement was Kroeber's (1916b:15) impression that corrugated ware, given its rare association with modern pottery types and its regular association with decayed ruins, de-creased in frequency as time passed; this allowed him to arrange "the sites in order accordingly." The observations of others (e.g., Morris 1917) lent some credibility to Kroeber's suspicions.

The relative abundance of Kroeber's "Three Color" type increased monotonically once it appeared in the sequence and was most abundant in the modern Zuñi assemblage. Frequencies of his "Black on Red" type merely tagged along and fluctuated in abundance, but his "Any Red" and "Black" types tended to decrease monotonically. Kroeber (1916b:16–18) in-itially distinguished ten pottery types but lumped five of them into two types (and ignored two others) for purposes of his seriation (Table 3.1). Ultimately, he used the relative frequencies of only three types to seriate his Period A sites and presented only the summed site frequencies for the other two types (lumped from the original five). Kroeber's seriated "Black" type included not only his original "Black" type but also his original "Cor-rugated Black" type; his seriated "Corrugated" type included both his origi-nal "Corrugated White" type and his original "Corrugated Black" type. Thus, his "Corrugated Black" type was tallied twice in the seriated types. Similarly, his original "Black on Red" type was tallied separately as well as with his "Any Red" type, and his original "Three Color" type was tallied separately as well as with his "Any Red" type. Kroeber (1916b:20) justified this lumping by noting that variations in the frequencies appeared to be a result of sampling error. Such lumping indicates clearly that Kroeber con-ceived of his types as theoretical units rather than as empirical ones; that

Table 3.1. A. L. Kroeber's Pottery Types from Sites around Zuñi Pueblo, New Mexico

Original types[a]	Original types[b]	Seriated types[c]
Black, dark gray, dull, without slip	Black	Black
Red on one or both sides	Red	Any Red
White or whitish on one or both sides	White	Not seriated
Corrugated black or dark	Corrugated Black	Black, and also Corrugated
Corrugated white or light	Corrugated White	Corrugated
Black pattern on white	Black on White	Not seriated
Black pattern on red	Black on Red	Black on Red, and also Any Red
Red pattern on white	Red on White	Any Red
White pattern on red	White on Red	Any Red
Three colors—black and red on white	Three Colors	Three Colors, and also Any Red

[a]From Kroeber's (1916b) tables 1 and 2.
[b]From Kroeber's (1916b) table 3.
[c]From Kroeber's (1916b) table 5.

is, they were not discovered but were, rather, created by the analyst. They were theoretical units that allowed—if properly constructed—measurement of differences in time. But there was no theoretical warrant for such an inference. Rather, the basis of the arrangement was the observed association of different pottery types with ruins inferred to be of different ages.

Kroeber's (1916a:44) chronologically sensitive pottery types indicated that his short "epochs . . . shade[d] into one another," and there was "no gap or marked break between periods A and B," his two main periods. On the one hand, Puebloan culture change was a flowing stream. The two major periods might have originally been "as distinct as oil and water" (Kroeber 1916b:9)—an essentialist notion—but they had originally been distinguished on the basis of criteria (e.g., degree of deterioration of associated ruins) other than those used in the seriation. Kroeber (1916b:15) believed that the two major periods "can normally be distinguished without the least uncertainty, and the separateness of the two is fundamental, [but] nevertheless they do not represent two different migrations, nationalities, or waves of culture, but rather a steady and continuous development on the soil." This was a clear expression of the materialist metaphysic. On the other hand, his referral to his minor periods as "epochs" and his referral to migrations, nationalities, and waves of culture suggests that he, like his mentor Boas, leaned strongly toward the essentialist camp.

How did Kroeber, then, come up with his early, middle, and late epochs? His divisions appear to have been founded on the magnitude of differences in the relative abundance of corrugated ware. Within each of his periods the average difference in the relative abundance of corrugated ware between assemblages is 5.2%; the average difference in the relative abundance of corrugated ware between adjacent assemblages assigned to different short periods is 13.5%. The range of differences between assemblages within the same period is 0–15%, and the range between adjacent assemblages of different periods is 3–28%. Thus, Kroeber may have, without being explicit, maximized within-group homogeneity and between-group heterogeneity. Otherwise, his periods seem arbitrary. That he believed "however the present classification be altered in detail or supplemented by wider considerations, in essentials it will stand" (Kroeber 1916b:20) suggests he could not escape the implicit rationale for his ordering—the *popularity principle* that was being discussed by Nelson (1916) and Wissler (1916b) at the same time that Kroeber was at Zuñi. But recall, too, that Kroeber (1916b:20) indicated "The final proof is in the spade."

Leslie Spier

Kroeber's desired proof was provided by Spier, though he took a circuitous route to obtain it. In his paper "An Outline for a Chronology of Zuñi Ruins," Spier (1917a:253[†]) expressed concern that Kroeber's surface samples might not be random in the statistical sense, but he believed that samples taken from Nelson's (1916) successive arbitrary levels were random because the horizontal location of the 3 × 6-ft horizontal block Nelson excavated was "chosen at random [and thus the sample of sherds] may be assumed representative" (Spier 1931:277). However, Nelson's block had *not* been chosen at random. Rather, Nelson (1916:162–163) stated explicitly that he had figured out the basic sequence without a "complete [stratigraphic] section" and that the sections he had examined were variously "incomplete and fragmentary, each showing merely the time relations of two successive pottery types at some place or other in the total series of four or five types." He wanted a complete section to confirm the sequence suspected on the basis of two partial sections—one with the most recent pottery type on top, the other with the apparently earliest pottery on the bottom—a section that "connected" the two partial sections (Nelson 1916:163). The way to relate those two incomplete sequences was "found at Pueblo San Cristobal," where in 1914 Nelson (1916:164, 165) very purposefully selected "A visibly stratified section of the refuse exposure showing no evidence of disturbance." The absence of visible disturbance, of course, was critical; Nelson knew well the hazards of using chronologically "mixed" deposits for measuring time from artifact styles. Thus, his selected block was chosen quite purposefully, not, as Spier (1931:277) suggested, "at random." Whether the ceramic sherds included in that selected block constituted a random and representative sample of all sherds within the site is, in fact, unknown, though Spier's (1931) assumption that they did is not unreasonable.

Wedding Kroeber's proportional frequencies with Nelson's super-posed levels was, Spier (1917a:253) suggested, a method that "is strikingly direct and entirely eliminates the error of selection, but it is only applicable to refuse heaps of considerable depth." (This was, as we have seen, precisely what Kidder and Kidder [1917] had done in perfecting the per-centage-stratigraphy technique.) Spier's sites often were shallow, but those that were deep provided tests of the chronological implications of his seriated surface collections. Spier (1917b:281), like everyone else at the time, believed that of the methods then in use for measuring time—stratigraphically superposed artifact collections, Kroeber's frequency se-riations, and Kidder's phyletic seriations—"the advantages rest with the first."

Based on Nelson's, Kroeber's, Kidder's, and some of his own strati-graphic work, Spier (1917b) knew the basic ceramic sequence: "It seems reasonable to believe that we are dealing with no other phenomenon than the several phases of a single pottery art" (Spier 1917a:281). But how was he going to deal with the surface collections? Citing his own superposi-tional data and Kroeber's (implied popularity) principle of ordering cor-rugated ware from having a high relative abundance early and being absent late in the temporal sequence, Spier (1917a:281) used "fluctuations in this type for a first grouping, a preliminary seriation of the data from superficial [i.e., surface] samples," arguing that "It might prove fertile then to arrange these data according to their percentages of corrugated ware in sequence from lowest to highest" (Spier 1917a:281–282). He never questioned the basis of this (popularity) "principle for the seriation of the data," but rather indicated the principle was "to be subjected to the method of proof of concurrent variations" (Spier 1917a:281). The latter statement, however, referred only to the correctness of the resulting ar-rangement rather than to the notion that the arrangement represented the passage of time.

After noting that the seriation based on the frequency of corrugated ware resulted in the recognition that painted wares apparently preceded glazed wares in time—all inferential and implicitly founded on the popu-larity principle—Spier elaborated on his method of proof: "The test of such a seriation as an historical series will lie in the observed seriation of the accompanying wares; for, when a group of three or more distinct, but mu-tually dependent, values are ranked according to some postulated sequence for one, and the other values are found to present serially concurrent variations, it may be concluded that the result is not fortuitous" (Spier 1917a:282). By demanding that at least three types be used, Spier revealed his awareness of the problem of closed arrays. If only two types are used, and one decreases in relative abundance, then the other must increase in relative abundance because the sum of the two must always equal 100%. Not so if three types are used, because while their abundances must sum to 100%, a monotonic increase in one type demands only that (1) one of the other types decrease monotonically, or (2) one of the other two types first decrease and then the third decrease, or (3) both of the other two types decrease. Smooth—in the sense of consistent increase or consistent decrease—nonfluctuating frequencies of all three types would suggest all three were measuring the same thing, which, for Kroeber and Spier, was inferred to be the passage of time. The implicit rationale for the inference was, of course, the popularity principle.

After arranging his collections on the basis of consistent frequency change in one type, Spier then determined if the other types included in his seriation consistently increased or decreased in the arrangement of assemblages. He clearly had some experience with statistical methods (Spier 1916), and in the case of the Zuñi potsherds he applied that experience. He used a form of simple least-squares regression—he regressed the independent variable against the dependent variable after subtracting the mean observed value of the latter from the observed value for each case—to determine if the other types included in his seriation displayed approximately monotonic frequency distributions (Spier 1917a:283, 285).[2] He then noted the direction, not the degree, of the slopes of the lines defined by the regression analysis and finally indicated that what we would today term residuals "are as often positive as negative" and thus "the variations [between observed values and values predicted by the regression] appear to be accidental and that the [regression line] curves represent the [frequency] distributions rather well" (Spier 1917a:283, 285). He considered this to be "the usual test for fit" (Spier 1917a:285), which it was, and is, in statistics, despite its seminal character in archaeology, and indicated that it suggested the seriation was valid "but not certain." That is, the arrangement was good, but whether it represented the passage of time was unclear. He tested the latter proposition using superposition, and thus just as those who preceded him by a year or two, his stratigraphic excavations were used to confirm rather than to create a chronological sequence.

Spier (1917a:300–305) also undertook an analysis that would become a standard part of culture-historical procedure: He produced four maps of various time-sensitive cultural traits—in this case, pottery types—in order to map movements of human populations. There was no theoretical warrant for such an inference; the fact that his types tended to measure time did not ensure that they would also measure ethnicity. Common sense informed by ethnography seems to have served as the rationale for his implied correlation of one or several distinct pottery types with a particular ethnic group or people and his resulting inferences of population distributions. This was an essentialist notion. Its conflation with the materialist notion of change being reflected by shifts in the frequencies of types would be commonplace throughout the tenure of culture history. Spier's particular procedure and inferences, as we discuss later, were to be repeated many times in many places in subsequent decades (see Hughes 1992 for a recent analysis of such efforts).

Spier (1917a:293) found some of his frequency seriations to be corroborated by Kidder's (e.g., 1916) stratified sequences and others by his own excavations. He also noted that "parallel development" might invalidate his sequence (Spier 1917a:305). In his summary, Spier (1917a:326) suggested that there was "no reason to doubt that samples of potsherds collected from successive levels of the ash heaps present us with valid chronological indices," and he argued that he had demonstrated "that it is possible to collect surface samples approximating in [chronological representativeness] those from refuse heaps." Of course, he knew which way time was going in his frequency seriation based on superposition of the stratified sequences and on the general nature of the frequency distribution of particular kinds of pottery that resulted from the work of Nelson, Kidder, and others. His test of concomitant variation in types used in the seriation, along with regression analysis and analysis of residuals, was innovative. Importantly, he also indicated that "When the ruins are ranked according to the pottery scheme, a parallel sequence of architectural types was found" (Spier 1917a:328). This finding was probably more important than even Spier realized, as seriations of multiple artifact kinds thought to represent the passage of time can serve as solid tests of the chronological significance of one another (Dunnell 1970, 1981).

Truly, Spier's (1917a:328) work was, as he said, "an exposition of archaeological method." In his review of Spier's (1917a, 1917b) work, Kidder (1919:301) stated that

> Mr. Spier's presentation and statistical handling of his material are essentially sound. His ranking of sites on the basis of their percentages of wares (which [Nelson's] stratigraphical work had shown to be chronologically significant) is a new and valuable contribution to method. . . . Good method can only lead to good results; Mr. Spier's conclusions are thoroughly satisfactory. His work will stand as the basis for all future archaeological study of the Little Colorado drainage. . . . [It is] fundamental.

The Aftermath

Just as he had been impressed with Nelson's work (Wissler 1917b), Wissler (1919, 1921) was impressed with the work of Kroeber and Spier. He noted that their studies had been geared, in part, to "seek the relation" of then-occupied Zuñi Pueblo to the "many adjacent ruins," which required "developing a method by which the relative age of these ruins can be determined and correlated with Zuñi itself" (Wissler 1919:iii, vi; see also Wissler 1915). Kroeber had laid a foundation that was later tested and refined by Spier. Wissler (1919:vi) noted that the ruins "fall into eight successive periods, each of which seems to be an outgrowth of the others. The most definite index to this chronology is found in pottery forms and decoration, as is the case in many other parts of the world." The importance here, of course, is in the shift in scale from studying the presence or absence of culture *traits* to studying the shifts in frequencies of *variants* of traits or types, a critical point overlooked by most historians.

Wissler (1919:vi) did not, however, ignore the spatial dimension: "obviously Zuñi did not work out its career in absolute isolation, for its growth was a mere part of the whole Pueblo development." Citing the work of Nelson (1916) in the Rio Grande district, Earl H. Morris (e.g., 1917) in the San Juan Valley, and Kidder (e.g., 1916) at Pecos, Wissler argued that "the general outline of culture history for the Southwest now stands revealed." Wissler (1919:vi) reprinted Nelson's (1919b) diagram (see Figure 3.8) summarizing the temporal–spatial relations of various cultural units of the Southwest, suggesting that it was "based upon the well-known facts of culture distribution, and the observed tendencies for marginal cultures to present the more archaic forms and thus stand as indices of the older culture level. As has been pointed out by many students of culture, once the center of a culture has been located, its earlier forms can be inferred from the surviving marginal traits."

Wissler (1923:60) later published a simplified version of Nelson's figure, again integrating the temporal, formal, and spatial dimensions in order to substantiate his position that the study of the distribution of culture traits within culture areas by using the age–area concept was valid. The important point is that Nelson (1919b), using the age–area notion, integrated the temporal distribution with the spatial distribution of artifact forms and wrote a history of Southwestern cultures. This was no small accomplishment, but only the chronology was verifiable empirically.

As Wissler (1915) had noted earlier, the suspected culture center had been chosen by him and this was where he sent Nelson, Kroeber, and Spier to work. All of these originators of the culture history paradigm failed to

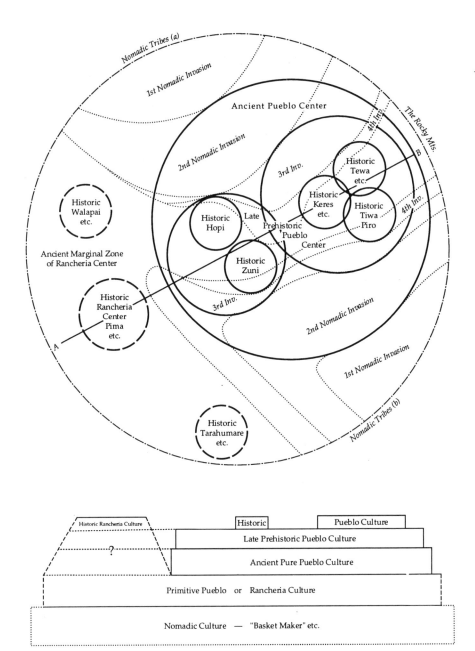

Figure 3.8. Nels Nelson's summary diagram of the time–space distribution of cultural forms in the Southwest. This diagram was reprinted by Wissler (1919:iv) in his introduction to Kroeber's (1916b) and Spier's (1917a) papers (after Nelson 1919b).

realize that had they worked anywhere else, they would have concluded that that other place was the culture center. This is so because the pottery types they used were extensionally derived. Given such units, it would appear that as one moved away from the original location, the units would begin to smear and blend with surrounding materials, later referred to as typological creep. They would only appear to be pure in the area from which the type definitions first were extracted from the particular sherds available. This perception fit with the notion of culture history as a braided stream, and the two reinforced one another.

Within two years, 1916 and 1917, Nelson and Kroeber, followed quickly by Spier and Kidder, showed beyond any doubt that culture change could be analytically detected by examination of shifts in artifact-type frequencies, and they confirmed that such shifts in fact were temporal by using superposition. One would suspect, then, that they might well have pursued this truly innovative way of approaching the archaeological record—a way founded in the materialist metaphysic—in their later work. They did not, and why they did not is important. Curiously, Kidder did not replicate his initial effort at assessing pottery chronology and development based on type frequencies in his later reports on Pecos (Kidder 1924, 1931, 1932, 1936a, 1936b). Willey and Sabloff (1974:95) and Givens (1992:67-68) imply that Kidder (1931) used percentage stratigraphy in later work, but in fact the application they refer to was done by Charles Amsden (1931:17–72). In most of his later work, Kidder used particular pottery types as index fossils, thus abandoning percentage stratigraphy and following the precedent he had set initially (e.g., Kidder 1915, 1917a). We explore why Kidder followed this course in Chapter 4.

It has been suggested that after his work in the Southwest, Nelson "conducted similar excavations at Mammoth Cave [Kentucky] (Nelson 1917b) and in Florida (Mitchem 1990)" (Browman and Givens 1996:84), but inspection of the published record clearly indicates that this suggestion is wrong. Nelson worked in Kentucky in 1916 (Nelson 1917b) and in Florida in 1917 (Nelson 1918). In the former, he excavated in both Mammoth Cave and a small rock shelter several miles away. He dug one "small pit" in the latter and made no mention of vertical provenience; his only comment concerning stratification was that there was an upper surficial "covering of earth" beneath which was "another stratum [that] averaged five inches in thickness and in about the middle of it there was a thin streak of ashes and charcoal" (Nelson 1917b:41). Clearly, this was postexcavation stratigraphic observation.

He excavated a number of trenches in deposits in Mammoth Cave (Nelson 1917b:47–53) but provided only minimal discussion of how he excavated. Thus his several drawings of stratigraphic profiles appear to be

based on postexcavation observations. He did make two revealing comments, however. He noted that upon its initial exposure in a trench, he
could not determine if a particular depositional unit "was a primary or a
secondary deposit—i.e., whether it lay as the aborigines had left it or [if
it] had been moved by modern man from some place in the [cave] interior.
But after working the vertical breast back for a few feet stratification duly
appeared" (Nelson 1917b:48). This sounds like Nelson was using the Harrington–Peabody excavation technique, and this suspicion is strengthened
by another of Nelson's comments. After providing a summary table of the
artifacts recovered from individual trenches, Nelson (1917b:57) stated that
"The approximate volume of refuse handled has been added [to the table]
for the benefit of those who may desire to figure percentages, etc. Approximate data are also at hand for the different depths at which artifacts
were obtained, but as there appears to be nothing especially significant
about the figures and their publication would require a much more extended table they have been omitted."

Did Nelson excavate stratigraphically in Kentucky? It depends on how
you define such excavation. In Mammoth Cave, his strata were decidedly
not units of artifact collection in the sense that each stratum was excavated
separately from every other one by peeling back first one and then another. He did, however, note which strata produced which artifacts. Regardless, if he excavated in vertical units, of either the arbitrary or the
natural depositional sort, it was not made explicit. That did not stop him
from making chronological inferences. Given that pottery was found in
the small rock shelter but not in Mammoth Cave, Nelson (1917b:44) suggested that the two sites represented two "different stage[s] of culture"
and that in Mammoth Cave he had found "the earlier and more primitive
stratum of culture" (Nelson 1917b:70). The critical point here is that,
clearly, the savagery–barbarism–civilization model of cultural evolution
had not yet been replaced, at least in Nelson's mind. It is clear in his
writings twenty years later (e.g., Nelson 1937) that it still had not been
replaced.

Nelson (1918) clearly did not excavate "stratigraphically" in Florida.
There, in 1917, he spent three days inspecting the remnants of a large
shell mound that was being destroyed by road-building activities. He indicated that his own observations of the mound, "it must be admitted,
involved little more than a fairly thorough inspection of two [stratigraphic]
exposures [revealed by the road-building activities], amounting to some
three thousand square feet" (Nelson 1918:89). Did Nelson even excavate?
Yes, but apparently without paying attention to vertical provenience in
the sense that the study could be considered a case of stratigraphic excavation. "At a few points only, nearest the center of the mound, was any

actual digging done, and that in the practically sterile lowest horizon of the refuse" (Nelson 1918:89). The artifacts he discussed were collected by "picking the surface of the two [stratigraphic] exposures" revealed by the activities of steam shovels (Nelson 1918:89). He spent minimal time discussing temporal differences in the few artifacts he collected. Based on his observations of the stratigraphic profiles, Nelson made the critically important observation that "under certain conditions depth is an index of age [deeper being older]. The same rule is to be observed in shellmound investigation. But unless we take strict account of *the order of deposition,* the depth at which a given artifact occurs may signify little or nothing" (Nelson 1918:86; emphasis added). He then noted that some of the sherds he recovered from the exposed stratigraphic profile were deeper than other sherds but that all were of similar age, given their having been recovered from particular, sloping (nonhorizontal) strata. The importance of Nelson's observation on superposition was, as we indicate below, largely overlooked by the profession.

Nelson (1920) replicated his San Cristóbal excavation technique in 1916 when he spent two weeks at Pueblo Bonito in Chaco Canyon, New Mexico (Figure 3.3). There he excavated two stratigraphic columns in 6-inch arbitrary levels, one 16 feet deep and the other 11.5 feet deep. He then did percentage stratigraphy, noting the general form of the frequency distribution curves of several types of pottery. He did this for one simple reason. As he noted, "In spite of the comparatively uniform character of the broken pottery scattered about all but one of the ruins in the Chaco region, it seemed *a priori* impossible that stylistic changes should not have taken place during the long interval of occupation suggested by the size of the refuse heaps" (Nelson 1920:383). Stylistic change in pottery types was expected—the answer to a chronological question was presumed to be discoverable—so Nelson excavated accordingly. In Florida, he did not have the time to ask or answer that question, and at Mammoth Cave the appropriate artifacts—pottery—for answering the question were not in evidence, so he did not ask it.

At Gamio's suggestion, Kroeber (1925a) excavated at Teotihuacán in the Valley of Mexico (Figure 3.1) in 1924 in an attempt to sort out the "Archaic" cultural manifestations found there. He used percentage stratigraphy, but because it failed to produce a clear result, he seriated surface-collected Archaic materials. More importantly, in the 1920s he initiated his and his students' studies of Uhle's many pottery collections from Peru (e.g., Gayton 1927; Gayton and Kroeber 1927; Kroeber 1925c; Kroeber and Strong 1924a, 1924b; Strong 1925). The basic analytical procedure was spelled out in the first of several reports on those collections:

The plan is to examine separately and in detail the collections from each
district; to group together, according to the field inventory, specimens of
the same grave provenience; to group the graves according to type of artifacts represented in them; to assume that graves containing artifacts of
identical type belong to the same period, and that those containing artifacts of consistently different types belong to different periods; and then,
from the overlapping of types and whatever other evidence, direct or indirect, may be available, to attempt to establish a sequence of the periods.
In this work the authors have followed one principle as basic: to proceed objectively, giving consideration only to the specimens themselves
and the collector's unqualified statements of fact concerning them, and
disregarding for the time being all interpretations embodied by him in his
records. . . . Their aim . . . is to establish, so far as may be possible, findings incontrovertibly substantiable by evidence and free from opinion or
subjective interpretation. (Kroeber and Strong 1924a:5–6)

They used several other rules of thumb to interpret the collections.
When an abundance of a particular style of vessel believed to signify a
particular culture (e.g., "Inca") was found at a site, they suggested "it was
the style rather than the pottery itself that was imported" (Kroeber and
Strong 1924a:12). The presence of distinct types in one geographic place
was thought to represent temporal differences (Kroeber and Strong
1924a:22), though "a distinct style is not necessarily proof of a distinct period" (Kroeber 1925c:229). Typological similarity suggested cultural "influences" and proximity in time of similar types (Kroeber and Strong
1924a:22–23). Although stratigraphy helped confirm various portions of the
chronology (e.g., Strong 1925), the absence of stratified deposits did not
hinder the development of a chronology since "continuous [cultural] development" was revealed by typological similarity between cultural "phases"
(Kroeber and Strong 1924b:96–97); that is, such continuous development
was presumed to be responsible for a particular style sharing "certain traits
with those [styles] assumed to precede or succeed it" (Kroeber and Strong
1924b:103). This was phyletic seriation.

The probability of the presumed succession was strengthened by reference to multiple types. The proportions of various pottery types per
phase were "particularly impressive" (Kroeber and Strong 1924b:104) and
tended to describe normal curves; this was frequency seriation. Nonetheless, this apparent grounding in the materialist metaphysic was obscured
by reference to particular "culture types" (e.g., Kroeber and Strong
1924b:108) as manifest in particular combinations of pottery styles. Further, ethnographically observed acculturation and enculturation processes
were called on to account for what appeared to be "transitional" cultures
(Kroeber and Strong 1924a:49). Such "transitional or wavering phase[s]"

of cultural development (Kroeber and Strong 1924a:54) underscored the fact that types were extensionally defined. Particular trait lists (e.g., Kroeber and Strong 1924a:46) were correlated with and thus denoted real cultures in an ethnographic sense, reflecting the essentialist metaphysic. Such a notion would continue to plague culture history.

Spier (1918a, 1919) followed up his work near Zuñi by reporting on collections of pottery from various sites in the general area. He used some of the same interpretive principles used later by Kroeber to interpret Uhle's pottery collections, the most obvious one being that typological similarity denoted historical, or phyletic, connection. The lack of such similarity denoted no such connection, and thus typologically distinct pottery had to have come from elsewhere because it represented a different cultural affiliation. Such a notion was supposedly confirmed when a particular type or several related types of pottery were found to have a limited spatial distribution somewhat distinct from the spatial distribution of another particular type or set of types. Spier (1918a:345, 1919:386) spoke of "groups" moving across the landscape in such a manner as to refer simultaneously to sets of distinct pottery styles and to human populations. Thus, his archaeological manifestations represented distinct ethnic populations and/or cultures. Spier (1918a, 1919) used the materialism-based technique of examining relative frequencies of pottery types, but his conflation of this technique with essentialism-based interpretations came to exemplify the culture history paradox.

The influence of the innovative analytical techniques perfected by Nelson, Kidder, Kroeber, and Spier was not as widely felt in the discipline as it might have been. Several individuals working with the American Museum of Natural History, where the focus on shifting frequencies of artifact types originated, used these techniques. Erich F. Schmidt (1927, 1928), working in the Gila–Salt region of southern Arizona, was one. He trenched around a sediment block so that three or four sides were exposed, and then excavated each stratum separately. He used percentage stratigraphy to work out the history of pottery change, and he also inferred population movements based on the types of pottery included in the sequence. Another was George C. Vaillant (1930, 1931, 1932, 1935a, 1935b; Vaillant and Vaillant 1934), who did virtually the same thing working in the Valley of Mexico in the late 1920s and early 1930s. Neil M. Judd (1954) used percentage stratigraphy in the 1920s at Pueblo Bonito in Chaco Canyon (Figure 3.3), but because he was excavating in secondary deposits he had little luck working out the chronology. He eventually turned the problem over to Frank H. H. Roberts, Jr. (Stephenson 1967), who used it as a dissertation topic (Roberts 1927).

In a retrospective look at the discipline, Roberts (1935:3–4) himself commented on the matter:

> Recently [Kroeber's, Nelson's, Spier's, and Kidder's method of examining the percentage representation of pottery types] has fallen into discard. Just why this should be the case is not apparent. It is true that under certain conditions it is not an infallible source of evidence, particularly in chronological studies based solely on surface material. Nevertheless it is helpful in outlining the main characteristics of a district and in indicating where intensive work should be undertaken. In a study of the ceramics of a single site it has more than enough merit to warrant its retention in archaeological procedure. It graphically demonstrates the true nature of the pottery complex. One explanation for the failure to make use of the system is, perhaps, that the workers have become so absorbed in a detailed study of pottery *per se* that they have forgotten the important factor of giving percentages. It is only from such data that the real significance of each group [read *type*] in the series [of pottery types] can be judged.

Roberts was, in this statement, perhaps a bit too negative, as several individuals working in the Southwest were studying variation in the relative abundances of pottery types and were using percentage stratigraphy (e.g., Alexander and Reiter 1935; Dutton 1938; Hawley 1934; Martin 1936:98–114; Reiter 1938b) or seriation (e.g., Martin 1938:268–281, 1939:454–455) in their efforts to measure time. Only a few others working elsewhere examined the fluctuations of type frequencies (e.g., Kniffen 1938; Olson 1930; Rouse 1939). But overall, Roberts was correct. Why did the discipline largely abandon the materialist analytical techniques pioneered by Nelson, Kidder, Kroeber, and Spier? Roberts was at least partially correct in his answer to that question, but as we explore in Chapter 4, the complete answer involves much more than "a detailed study of pottery *per se*." Before turning to that topic, however, it is important here to make a final observation regarding the birth of culture history.

The Direct Historical Approach

What came to be known in the 1930s and 1940s as the *direct historical approach* had been used years earlier by Nelson, Kidder, Kroeber, and Spier (Spier 1931; Steward 1942). Given that they had no way to determine which way time was going in a sequence of pottery types that had been seriated by type frequencies or by a continuity of features, they began with types that were known to have been made in the historical period. Kidder (1916:120), for example, made it very clear that he chose Pecos for excavation not only because it seemed to have stratified deposits and also seemed to have "practically all the types of prehistoric wares known to occur in the upper Rio Grande district," but also because the occupation of Pecos extended into the historical period. Given such a chronological anchor, one could thus work backward through time either by excavating through a superposed series of strata or by arranging collections in a seriation—either of the frequency or phyletic sort—with the historical-period types at the top of the arrangement. Thus, with one end of the temporal continuum anchored in the historical period, one could "carry the story of Pueblo arts" from the present into the remote past and thus address questions of the relations of historically documented ethnic groups (Kidder 1916:120).

The direct historical approach was popularized by various individuals, in particular by William Duncan Strong (1935, 1940) and Waldo R. Wedel (1938, 1940), both of whom worked on the Plains, a region rich in ethnographic information. Julian H. Steward (1942), a student of Strong's at Columbia University, provided a simple but rather thorough programmatic statement on the approach. Aside from noting that it provided a chronological anchor, Steward (1942:337) indicated that it was "far more important" to note that the approach "provides a point of contact and a series of specific problems which will coordinate archaeology and ethnology in relation to the basic problems of cultural studies." In this respect, Steward (1942:339) lamented that ethnology was tending to ignore the results of archaeology, whereas the latter seemed preoccupied with method and establishing ceramic sequences. He thus called for an integrated historical anthropology that allowed generalized data on cultural change, process, and dynamics to be integrated into what he called "theories." In Steward's view, the direct historical approach was the integrative device of choice. "[I]f one takes cultural history as his problem, and peoples of the early historic period as his point of departure, the difference between strictly archaeological and strictly ethnographical interest disappears" (Steward 1942:341). We need now to turn to the 1920s and 1930s to examine the adolescent years of culture history, for it is at that time that other central tenets of the paradigm first were formalized.

Notes

1. Interestingly, Nelson also made use of what has become known as the "heirloom" hypothesis (Schiffer 1987:319).
2. We successfully replicated Spier's (1917a) regression formulas for the eight surface samples listed in his table VIII, but we could only approximate his regression formulas derived from the values in his table VI by using the median frequencies of white ware and of corrugated ware for all sites that had the same

relative abundance of red ware. Spier's use of an interval-scale statistic to correlate percentages was not statistically sound, but, given that his interest was largely in establishing the direction (increasing or decreasing) of frequency changes rather than the *rate* (slope) of change, the method was acceptable. However, his figure 6 and its associated discussion are unacceptable.

4

After the Revolution

The demonstration in the teens that culture change was analytically visible in the shifting frequencies of pottery types was truly innovative and revolutionary. Stratigraphy, or more correctly, superposition of pottery assemblages, *confirmed* that such shifts in frequencies were chronological indicators. But while stratigraphic excavation had initially served a confirmational role in chronology building and continued in that role, it quickly—by the mid-1920s—came to serve a largely creational role. As Judd (1929:408) observed late in that decade, "Chronology is the key that will unlock many secrets of American prehistory and stratigraphy is the stuff of which chronology is made." Nelson (1937) made virtually identical remarks a decade later. Neither mentioned that it was percentage stratigraphy and seriation that had made culture change visible or that superposition had long been known to document the passage of time. Such statements no doubt contributed to the perception of many historians of Americanist archaeology that there was a "stratigraphic revolution" in the teens. The substantive literature of the time also no doubt contributed to that perception.

In this chapter we explore changes in the discipline that occurred beginning about 1920, and we start with an evaluation of the impact of the so-called stratigraphic revolution. There are several aspects to this revolution that had far-reaching implications for how culture historians went about their business—implications that in some cases were useful (they allowed the measurement of time) and in others were ultimately quite deleterious. Next, we review the work of several individuals whose contributions epitomize how culture history operated in that period. Finally, we turn to classification, since the manner in which the formal dimension came to be dealt with in the 1920s and 1930s was intimately tied to attempts to monitor time and to measure culture change. This brings our discussion up to about 1970.

Measuring Time with Strata

Immediately on the heels of work by Gamio, Nelson, Kroeber, Kidder, and Spier, numerous individuals (e.g., de Laguna 1934; Ford 1935a, 1935b, 1936a, 1936b; Gladwin and Gladwin 1929, 1935; Harrington 1924b; Haury 1936a, 1936b, 1937a; Hawkes and Linton 1916, 1917; Loud and Harrington 1929; Martin 1936, 1940; Roberts 1929, 1931; Vaillant 1930; Webb and DeJarnette 1942; Willey 1939) excavated in such a manner as to use superposition to allow them to measure time. Attempts were even made to derive an absolute time scale from strata (Jochelson 1925:117–119), as Dall (1877) had earlier, but those efforts were viewed as faulty (e.g., Schenck 1926:208–212). It also was quickly suggested that the use of stratigraphy to provide a relative time scale was not without difficulty. For example, strata might be "dislocated" or "inverted," or the contents of strata might be "mixed" (e.g., Colton 1946:297–299; Crabtree 1939; Hawley 1934, 1937; Holmes 1919:67, 80).

The Trouble with Superposition

The difficulties were perceived because archaeologists strayed from the geological conception of superposition (Stein 1990; see also Praetzellis 1993). The law of superposition relates only to layers—units of deposition typically called *strata*—not to the age of the sediments or particles (including fossils and artifacts) making up the layer. This was Nelson's (1918:86) earlier point regarding "the order of deposition." Some mid-twentieth-century introductory geology texts refer to the law as a *principle* and note that the relative age of the depositional units runs from the oldest unit on the bottom to the youngest unit on top, but only if the column is undisturbed (e.g., Longwell et al. 1969:122, 660; Pearl 1966:184). Such wording no doubt contributed to confusion among archaeologists simply because (1) the age of the depositional event is *not* distinguished from the age of the constituent parts of the depositional unit representing the event and (2) the notion was referred to as a principle rather than as a law.

The order of deposition might or might not be related to the age of the sedimentary particles. The misconception that the two are always related was, and still is, perpetuated in textbooks, such as that by Meighan (1966:26), who stated that "the layers deposited first must be the oldest, and the levels above must come later in time. This explains why archaeologists are so careful to record the depth at which objects are found—the depth usually has a bearing on the age of the find, at least in relating it to other finds from the same site." The first sentence seems to concern the age of the depositional event, but the second sentence conflates the age of the event with the age of the sedimentary particles. More recent treatments perpetuate the confusion (e.g., Drucker 1972). There also has long been a misunderstanding of what superposition actually measures. John C. McGregor (1941:45–46), for example, wrote that

> to the most uninitiated it is obvious that the lowest layer must have been laid down first to support those resting upon it. Thus the lowest layer is oldest, the next above younger, and so on to the top, where the most recently laid down layer, or stratum, is found. A study of the contents of these layers will then give some idea of the relative ages of the strata. . . . The most recent or latest material will come from the top layers; the earliest or most ancient, from the bottom. The archaeologist then need only arrange these objects in the order in which they were uncovered from the bottom up and he has a sequential evolution of the culture of the people who made them.

Clearly, McGregor had the order-of-deposition part correct, but the part regarding the age of the particles making up the depositional units is potentially incorrect.

Florence M. Hawley's (1937) response to George C. Vaillant's (1936:325) comment that "objects at the base of an undisturbed midden must be older than those at the top, which were obviously the most recently deposited" further epitomizes the misunderstanding. Based on her work at Chetro Ketl in Chaco Canyon, New Mexico (Figure 3.3), Hawley (1934) concluded that the stratigraphy of the "east dump" had been "inverted" by the activities of ancient human inhabitants (Hawley 1937:298). Excavating in 8-inch levels, Hawley (1934:32–35) found that her pottery types, which had not been constructed "with a preconceived idea of a series of classes necessarily representing a chronological sequence," were, "in general, sequential." But, she discovered something else as well: "contradictions appeared in the fact that some of the apparently latest strata and latest pottery appeared low in the pile, but the variation in soil makeup of the various strata and the dating made possible by collected charcoal indicated that almost one half of this dump was of material much older than the rest and out of chronological order. Briefly put, part of the dump was upside down" (Hawley 1934:35).

Hawley's (1934:51–57) data consisted of dendrochronologically dated pieces of charcoal that were out of sequence within the stratigraphic column. Importantly, she presumed that the dendrochronological dates "closely dated the [stratigraphically] associated pottery, for the potsherds and the charcoal from the house fires had been thrown out together" (Hawley 1937:298). Thus, Hawley concluded—more by implication than by explicit statement—that superposition measured the *order of deposition* of the various strata making up the east dump but did not measure the respective ages of the charcoal nor of the pottery particles making up the strata. That her conclusion invalidated not the law of superposition but rather the presumed direct relation between the age of a depositional event and the age of the sedimentary particles making up a stratum was not made explicit by Hawley.

Index Fossils

Geologists have long used fossils included in units of deposition to cross-correlate those layers (Rudwick 1996), but they typically are careful to use only organisms likely to be contemporaneous with the depositional event represented by the layer (see Hancock 1977 and Mallory 1970 for historical reviews). Their choice of such *index fossils* is empirical; one has to examine many exposures to determine which kinds of organisms were unique to and diagnostic of a particular stratum and time period (Hancock 1977). Archaeologists typically have omitted such bridging arguments for two reasons. First, the rationale linking organisms to depositional units is implicit (Hancock 1977; Mallory 1970; and references therein) and thus cannot readily be converted to an application linking artifact manufacturers to depositional units. Further, the implication that an organism represented by a fossil was alive at the time the depositional unit containing the fossil was laid down is an interpretation; a similar interpretation is required when artifacts are involved (Stein 1990:516). Early biostratigraphers did not make this interpretive leap explicit (Hancock 1977). Second, because archaeologists focus on artifacts, it is not surprising that they would label some stratigraphic sequences "reversed," as this refers "to the temporal order of the age of manufacture for [artifacts] contained in the deposit. The stratigraphic order of the layers is not reversed with regard to superposition" (Stein 1990:519). In other words, the *depositional sequence* is not reversed. Paleontologists and geologists struggled mightily with the notion of biostratigraphic correlation throughout the nineteenth and into the mid-twentieth century (Hancock 1977). The notion came to approximate its modern form—at least in North America—only in the 1930s and 1940s (Mallory 1970).

Stratigraphy and Empirical Standards

Once it was clear that culture change was analytically visible in the American archaeological record, stratigraphic excavation became commonplace, and excavation techniques subsequently were described more explicitly in the literature than they had been previously (see Praetzellis [1993] for a history). Superposition and stratigraphic excavation provided empirically sufficient standards by which one could test a suspected sequence of artifact forms. The necessary standard that superposed artifacts represented the passage of time was dealt with by referring to selected strata—depositional units—as *mixed* or *reversed in chronological order* when two or more sequences of artifacts failed to align with one another. Such ad hoc rationalization attends the fact that "Superposition does not order the contents of layers unless there is a systematic relationship between the contents and layer deposition" (Dunnell 1981:75) and underscores the commonsensical approach to chronology typical of the culture history paradigm. Use of vertical units—whether depositional strata or of the arbitrary metric sort—ultimately led to big problems.

Strata as Units of Time and Units of Association

Wissler (1916b:190) stated that Nelson's (1916) work in New Mexico was an excellent example of how a scientific result "depends upon the method of handling data," citing "Mr. Nelson's *decisive chronological determinations* in the Galisteo Pueblo group" (emphasis added) as an example. Most importantly from the perspective of stratigraphic excavation, in the first edition of his classic, *The American Indian,* Wissler (1917a:275) remarked that the "uninterrupted occupation of an area would not result in good examples of stratification [of cultures], but would give us deposits in which culture changes could be detected only in the qualities and *frequencies of the most typical artifacts*; for example, Nelson's pottery series from New Mexico" (emphasis added). Here was a hint that strata, as units of time and as units of associated cultural materials, would come to have much more significance to the culture history paradigm than perhaps was originally intended, that the presence of strata—discrete and distinct depositional units—implied an occupation by multiple, distinct, successive cultures. As Fowke (1922:37) noted several years later, "The intermittent character of occupancy is . . . shown by the distinct segregation of numerous successive layers of kitchen refuse."

On the one hand, Wissler (1916a:487) spoke of "cultural strata," but he did not mean depositional units; rather, he meant cultural evolutionary stages that happened to occupy different stratigraphic units. On the other hand, most archaeologists in the 1920s spoke of the remains of different "cultures" being found in distinct strata (e.g., Gamio 1924; Harrington 1924b; Hawkes and Linton 1917). Judd (1929:416) spoke of "superimposed cultures." Each culture was represented by the artifacts associated within a vertical unit, whether that unit was arbitrarily defined by metric levels or by the boundaries of natural depositional units. This is not surprising given that each such unit—particularly natural depositional units—was thought to represent an "occupation," whatever that was. Wissler's and Fowke's suggestions were reinforced by the notion that a small site represented a brief occupation by one culture and thus was to be preferred when one sought to identify the constituents of a cultural phase (e.g., Colton 1939:11; Martin 1936:111). Haury (1937b:20–21) took this notion to the extreme with his suggestion that

> Rubbish in pits proved to be of the highest value in giving unmixed samples because of the short time represented by the accumulation of the deposits. More than two phases were seldom represented. . . . Being relatively small, the time required to fill them was usually too short for the material to change. . . . With much of the pottery found in pits it was easier to determine those traits which constituted one phase ceramically than would have been possible with pottery from other sources. Once these were determined, however, larger accumulations, such as rubbish mounds, gave invaluable data on succession.

Ultimately, the essentialist view that each culture was preceded and succeeded by other such units was reinforced by the use of vertically superposed depositional units as units from which artifacts were collected. Such a collection strategy would characterize archaeology beyond culture history's fall from favor, a point to which we return several times in later chapters, but which is well exemplified by work that took place in the late 1920s and early 1930s. To demonstrate this, and to characterize the status of culture history at the time, we turn now to the work of an individual whose contributions to the discipline epitomized the paradigm at the beginning of its heyday.

George C. Vaillant

Vaillant had worked with Kidder at Pecos Pueblo in 1922 (Kidder 1924:28). Under the direction of Clark Wissler and Clarence L. Hay of the American Museum, he worked in the Valley of Mexico from 1928 to 1936, spending the vast majority of his time at the sites of Zacatenco, Ticomán, and El Arbolillo (Figure 3.1). His initial goal was to build on earlier efforts by Gamio (1913) at Atzcapotzalco and by Kroeber (1925a) at Teotihuacán (Figure 3.1) and establish a sequence of cultures and cultural remains (Vaillant 1930:17–18). His work has not been the subject of any detailed scrutiny by historians of Americanist archaeology, though in it we find an excellent characterization of culture history as it was practiced in the late 1920s and early 1930s. For example, Vaillant (1937:307–309) indicated that the "aim" of archaeology was "the study of the Indian material culture, its history and development, and its interpretation in terms of human history. One of the chief aims of this branch of research was to try to establish the relative age of the different monuments and cultures."

Vaillant knew well the details of archaeological research that had preceded his own in the area where he worked (e.g., Gamio 1913, 1924; Kroeber 1925a), and he devoted space in many of his reports to reviewing available data. As did his predecessors and contemporaries, Vaillant believed that at least some of the variation in pottery was attributable to difference in age. Given his research goal, once in the field Vaillant first sought a site "possessing deep beds of débris"; that site was Zacatenco (Vaillant 1930:18) (Figure 3.1). Vaillant (1930:19) noted that although modern activities had disturbed some of the site, they also had exposed "the deepest bed of continuous early culture débris he had seen up to that time, [and he] immediately decided to trench it." Natural erosion and human activities had "confused the depositions of débris," but Vaillant (1930:19–21) focused on the overall thickness and depth of the deposit— more than 3 m—noting in particular that "Even if one had no sure geological demarcations of strata, at least with such depth one could arrange time periods from the different styles of artifacts found at various levels. If the rainy season washed the upper strata down over the lower in later times, it must have done the same each year in early times, so that although the original position of the débris might be altered, it would nevertheless preserve an equivalent deposition on its new bed" (Vaillant 1930:20).

Importantly, Vaillant elaborated on the potential obfuscating factor of what came to be known as reversed stratigraphy:

> It is theoretically possible . . . to have, through such agencies [as rainy-season erosion], a reverse stratification, i.e., when the successive removal of strata by erosion presents the original layers reversed in the new accumulation. A pit dug into normal strata may produce this phenomenon in the excavated dirt. . . . The possibility of a reverse stratification must be considered, but, for several reasons it can only superficially affect the interpretation of the site. [Erosion of strata from topographically high to topographically low areas might produce a reversed stratigraphy, but] At some point on the slope one could detect the interlaminations of the strata and derive therefrom a true picture of past conditions. (Vaillant 1930:20–21)

Given this cautious awareness of the potential trouble with stratified deposits, Vaillant (1930:22) indicated that

Reliance had to be placed on the objects themselves and constant care exerted to extract them from their relative positions. Working against a hillside absolute depth meant little. The variability of the strata made it impossible to work by peeling of layers; and the material occurred more often in lenses than in prolonged depositions. To keep some relative control of the position of the objects, we moved into the deposits on a series of floors. Later, when the trench was opened completely, we could trace the débris lenses and fix the position. By recording the daily progress of excavation in section and plan it was subsequently quite easy to compare a digging level and the objects which it yielded on any given day with the actual deposition of the lenses, which could not be understood until after complete excavation of the trench. Except to begin a trench, no digging was ever done straight down. We worked against a vertical face in front, so that three faces, the front and the sides of the trench, were always exposed; and control was thereby established on dips in the strata.

This, simply put, was what we earlier labeled as the Harrington-Peabody excavation technique, similar to that used by Kidder at Pecos in some of his excavations. Vaillant used it to excavate a number of trenches at Zacatenco, and (1) having "arrived early in the work at a recognition of three main types of material, Early, Middle, and Late," (2) failing to find continuous artifact-bearing strata segregated by "sterile layers," and (3) recognizing redeposited materials, Vaillant (1930:28) was left with "the only alternative of deductive stratification on the most common occurrence of types of figurines and pottery." That is, horizontally separate strata in his various excavations were correlated using their artifact contents—a form of biostratigraphy, or more correctly, artifact or ceramic stratigraphy.

Vaillant's (1930:66–77) chronology of pottery at Zacatenco aligned with those developed by earlier workers at nearby sites (e.g., Gamio 1913; Kroeber 1925a). Like many culture historians, he cautioned that "Further studies must follow to corroborate the data acquired and refinements, both in excavation and typology, are essential to a more complete understanding of the problem of the cultural and chronological position of the early cultures in the Valley of Mexico" (Vaillant 1930:66). His reports included rather exhaustive descriptions of the materials he recovered—with numerous photographs and drawings—typically arranged by material, type, and chronological position. Most of his types were largely commonsensical categories, many with functional names such as spindle whorls, gorgets, arrowheads, manos, and the like. Importantly, however, his pottery types were largely based on decoration, such as a "blue white" type and a "red-on-black" type. His typology of figurines, on the other hand, was unusual. Types were labeled with a capital letter, sometimes followed by a lowercase

Roman numeral. In his initial report Vaillant (1930) had little to say about the reasoning behind this classification system.

During the second field season, Vaillant excavated at Ticomán (Figure 3.1), and in his report he provided some initial, if incomplete, insight into the purpose and reasoning behind his classification:

> The method evolved for the classification of pottery types from Zacatenco and Ticoman is not an absolute technical arrangement but a more or less eclectic grouping that, while following basal similarities in composition, at the same time lays stress on the *stylistic vagaries which, resulting from the whims of fashion, reveal, in consequence, chronology.* Figurines are sorted on a similar basis. . . .
>
> The bewildering number of designations for pottery styles and of letters to indicate figurine types need not unduly intimidate the student as they are meant purely to facilitate brevity and accuracy in exposition and reference. Eventually, *when the groundwork for a chronology will have been completed, the student will be able to seize the main definitive types of each period and the elaborate preliminary nomenclature will be happily forgotten.* Yet, in these first steps one must follow a fairly refined system of grouping material, lest one slur over details that might hold subsequent importance.
>
> However, to simplify this detail as much as possible, we have labeled by the term, *time-bearer,* the more important chronological indications of the following digest of elements comprising culture sequence at Zacatenco. (Vaillant 1931:210; emphasis added)

The preceding citation reveals numerous features of the culture history paradigm in the 1920s and 1930s. Types were constructed extensionally by trial and error and thus could be modified in light of new material. Once types that allowed the measurement of time had been constructed, the fine details of the exploratory classification system could be dispensed with. Some types that allowed the measurement of time were ones that had rather limited temporal distributions and thus were more or less equivalent to index fossils—Vaillant's "time-bearer" types. Other types might have other analytical uses.

In his summary descriptions of the cultural materials associated with each of the periods in evidence at Zacatenco, Vaillant (1931:211–219) noted that some historical types tended to have unimodal frequency distributions through time. He used percentage stratigraphy to determine this, but he failed to note that those historical types tended to have larger temporal distributions than did his time-bearer index fossils. Vaillant (1931:218) also noted that "new" types that appeared in the middle of the sequence "very likely entered from some other source. Thus there is the strong probability of the fusion of two peoples." That is, types with no apparent evolutionary ancestral type must be intrusive (Vaillant 1936,

1937), a notion begun with Spier (1917a, 1918a, 1919) and perpetuated by Kroeber and Strong (1924a), Schmidt (1928), and others (e.g., Ford 1935b, 1952) throughout the tenure of the culture history paradigm.

Excavations at Ticomán were meant to refine the chronology evidenced at Zacatenco and to test this later notion of fusion. Vaillant collected fifty-two samples of sherds and figurines from stratigraphic proveniences at Ticomán and after studying them concluded that "we were dealing with an autochthonous evolution. In other words, the development of material culture was self-contained and was subject neither to the amalgamation of foreign with indigenous elements [as at Zacatenco]. While each class and style of object went through change in the course of its history at Ticomán, there was really no simultaneous shift [in styles of both figurines and ceramic vessels] such as one would expect were fusions or dispersals of peoples involved" (Vaillant 1931:251).

Vaillant's interpretive algorithm was becoming commonplace in culture history. On the one hand, abrupt shifts in the styles or types of pottery or figurines suggested immigration or at least a nonindigenous source and thus perhaps diffusion or trade (e.g., Ford 1935b; Haury 1937a). Vaillant had shifts in both ceramic vessels and figurines at Zacatenco, which reinforced the interpretation of the appearance of a new group of people rather than merely the diffusion of a few new ideas; that is, the scale or magnitude of the change was, implicitly at least, critical to inferring whether diffusion or migration was the cause of change. The interpretation of immigration was reinforced as well by the appearance of "a slightly different [human] physical type" (Vaillant 1936:325) coincident with the replacement of pottery and figurine styles. Referral to what was often termed changes in "somatotype," in those instances when human remains were available, came to be commonplace in the operations of culture history (e.g., Ford and Willey 1941).

On the other hand, at Ticomán the deposits were thin, apparently lacked "consecutive strata," and thus seemed to represent a single period. Recall Wissler's (1917a) earlier suggestion that the lack of strata denoted continuous occupation. Thus, "as is so commonly the case in the history of a single people, there were no simultaneous shifts of the various styles of artifacts, so that a chronology for one class of object was not necessarily the same as for another" (Vaillant 1931:329). That is, styles of figurines changed independently of styles of pottery through time. Just as Charles Darwin had recognized seventy years earlier, each species (type) had its own tempo of evolution (Mayr 1982:433). One could trace the *in situ* evolution of a culture by distinguishing stratigraphically superposed figurine styles that evolved "one from another" (Vaillant 1936:325); in short, a phyletic seriation such as Kidder's (e.g., 1917a) denoted a lack of outside, or nonindigenous, influence. Thus, the facts that (1) the two categories of ceramics evolved independently, (2) neither changed abruptly, and (3) there was no evidence of simultaneous abrupt change in both indicated *in situ* evolution of a single culture. Vaillant's (1931, 1936, 1937) equation of particular sets of artifact styles with particular "peoples," "civilizations," or "tribal entities" reflects the attempts of culture historians to keep their research anthropological and the fact that they could not escape the essentialist metaphysic. Vaillant (1936:325), as many of his contemporaries and subsequent culture historians did, noted that one could not speculate "as to the identity and tribal affiliation of the [early pottery and figurine] makers," but this did not dissuade him from believing that "from the styles and types of their artifacts we can readily distinguish whatever sites they occupied." Nor did his caution keep him from speculating on ethnic identities.

Later field seasons saw additional excavations at other sites in the Valley of Mexico (Vaillant 1932) and a continued search for "culture complex[es]" (Vaillant and Vaillant 1934:15). Some excavations were not clearly stratigraphic, and others used 50-cm-thick arbitrary levels (Vaillant and Vaillant 1934:16). One important innovation in reporting was the plotting of particularly diagnostic styles of figurines—time-bearers—on the drawings of stratigraphic profiles (e.g., Vaillant 1935b:149, 151, 154; Vaillant and Vaillant 1934:17, 19). As well, the figurine typology was described in slightly more detail, and an attempt was made to legitimize it:

> Letters are used to designate major types and supplementary numbers in Roman numeration indicate the sub-types formed by minor stylistic variation, sometimes ethnographically and sometimes chronologically significant. Considerable legitimate criticism may be brought to bear on this method of nomenclature as being too elaborate and too difficult to remember. But the use of regional or type site names would be even more confusing, for several types often occur at the same site. Thus the letter and numeral system of classification lends itself to exacter reference. The underlying idea is not to classify in an arbitrary manner, but to present to students the kinds of figurines found at different levels and at different places. At the same time, it is desirable to have a classification sufficiently elastic to include the expansions made necessary by fresh research. (Vaillant and Vaillant 1934:24)

At this time James A. Ford (1935b, 1936a; Ford and Griffin 1938) was grappling with precisely the same problems in his classifications in the Southeast (see Chapter 5). But it is clear that by the early 1930s Vaillant's figurine types were *classes*—ideational units—that could display distributions over space and through time. Thus, they could perform analytical work; they could serve as measurement scales or measuring devices. Vaillant's (1935b:159) chronological periods were "figurine periods"

or "figurine phases." Further, Vaillant (1935b:189), at the end of his research, was explicit about the fact that figurines and pottery vessels comprised two divisions of ceramic art, "each susceptible of close classification
and capable of use as a control for the historical analysis of the other."
That is, because each of the two divisions had a unique evolutionary and
developmental history, the chronological implications of one could serve
as a check on the chronological implications of the other when types of
the two categories were found associated, a fact made explicit again 35
years later (Dunnell 1970). This is the materialist metaphysic.

But Vaillant (1935b:189) still resided largely in the essentialist (anthropological) camp: "emphasis is laid on the differentiation between the
pottery styles of various peoples and various times." This point is very clear
in Vaillant's (1936, 1937) two semipopular summations of his excavations.
There, he spoke of figurine types, "usually female," having perhaps "been
used as votive objects or as household images of saints," of "ornamental
vessels [serving] in rituals," of "peoples" as equivalent to cultures or periods, of different "tribes" being represented by different ceramic styles, and
of the different sociopolitical organizations that characterized various cultural periods (Vaillant 1936:324–326). There was, of course, no way to test
such statements, but referral to his archaeological materials in such terms
rendered them anthropological and thus meaningful in a commonsense
manner. Interestingly, Vaillant also spoke of distinct "culture levels [that
differed] from each other in the form and decoration of their pottery, in
the artistic styles of their stone and clay sculptures, and in their architecture. Through the study of the strata in the rubbish heaps, minor time
stages can be distinguished within each culture group" (Vaillant 1937:313).
Thus, while his empirical evidence suggested that culture change was apparently gradual and continuous—a materialist conception—he leaned
more strongly toward the essentialist camp and spoke of fifty-two-year-long
cultural periods, based on the Aztec calendar, when cultures generally were
static (Vaillant 1937). Cultural transformations occurred more or less
abruptly at the end of each period; this, too, was essentialism.

In his final site report, Vaillant (1935b) again repeated his earlier
statements about the classification of figurines, but this time he added several critical details. In particular, he noted that specimens were grouped

> on the basis of the sum total of all their parts, plus their position in time
> and space.
>   Under this system a group of figurines, restricted to a single site and
> a single period, would therefore present a greater variation in its constitu-
> ent specimens, than would a group which could be subdivided into chrono-
> logical divisions or regional styles. In this latter circumstance differences
> in the minutiae of detail would receive greater emphasis than the gross

resemblance of the plastic technique as a whole. Thus [a] group of figurines which is widely distributed in time and space must be divided into a quantity of sub-types to distinguish these aspects, whereas [a] group which is confined to [one] culture phase exhibits no comparable range in local or chronological variations and does not require such subdivision. However, in some cases subdivisions were made when it seemed probable that future research would show this chronological and regional differentiation. . . .

In general the letters of the alphabet indicate the broad divisions of figurines according to technique and time. The numerals following indicate subdivisions on the basis of regional styles or a cross-cutting of a major group by time periods. Letters in small case following such numerals are the result of the discovery of time or regional variations in a type previously classified. (Vaillant 1935b:190)

Type definitions thus clearly were extensionally derived, but they also were constructed by trial and error to reflect small chunks of the time–space continuum or the continuum of cultural development. This was typical of culture history procedure (e.g., Haury 1937a; Sayles 1937). The basic structure of Vaillant's classification system seems to have been a logical predecessor of the type–variety system of the 1950s. The system was devised to "preserve data of potential historical worth, until sufficient information is amassed for secure recognition of the inter-play of culture in Mexico. Then a simpler system can be confidently adopted, with a nomenclature indicative of tribe and period" (Vaillant 1935b:190). Similar but less lengthy comments were made regarding the classification of ceramic vessels (Vaillant 1935b:190–191). Despite the regular and evermore elaborate repetition of such statements, Vaillant never once provided an explicit definition of any of his figurine or vessel types; that is, he never listed the *significata* of his classes. What he regularly did was provide elaborate descriptions of many of the *denotata*—the members—of each type. Thus, Alfred Tozzer (1937:340), not surprisingly, complained that he had tried to apply Vaillant's classification, but the latter "had to come to [the former's] rescue."

Vaillant (e.g., 1935a:294) was thinking about culture change in materialist terms: "[T]he minute differentiations in technique and style that are indicative of changes in fashion, and, therefore, time, were stressed to the exclusion of broader resemblances such as would be considered in a philosophic or artistic evaluation of the material culture of these people." Tozzer (1937) complained about this too, arguing that it was doubtful all of the variation reflected in Vaillant's classification reflected time; it was more likely, Tozzer reasoned, that it reflected "personal and chance variations." But Vaillant was clearly stuck in the essentialist metaphysic. Two of the principal results of his many excavations were "the definition of *three culture*

groups [and] the establishment of a *culture sequence,* if not a chronology"
(Vaillant 1935a:296). He called upon the popularity principle as well as
invention, diffusion, trade, migration, and other ethnographically documented historical processes to account for the culture history he perceived.
His constant referral to the correlation of a particular type or set of types
with a particular tribal, ethnic, or cultural group of people demonstrates
the paradigm's regular conflation of the materialist and essentialist metaphysics. Vaillant's efforts epitomize how culture history was operating by
the mid-1930s. Clearly, one of the major problems concerned how to deal
with the formal dimension, the subject to which we turn next.

The Formal Dimension—Early Thoughts

In the introduction to his final volume on the pottery from Pecos
Pueblo, Kidder (1936b:xx) provided a comment that epitomized much of
the thinking prevalent in Americanist archaeology during the first several
decades of the twentieth century—a comment that underscored the conflation of the materialist and essentialist metaphysics:

> The division of the Glaze ware of Pecos into six chronologically sequent
> types is a very convenient and, superficially, satisfactory arrangement. For
> some time I was very proud of it, so much so, in fact, that I came to think
> and write about the types as if they were definite and describable entities.
> They are, of course, nothing of the sort, being merely useful cross-sections
> of a constantly changing cultural trait. Most types, in reality, grew one
> from the other by stages well-nigh imperceptible. My groupings therefore
> amount to a selection of six recognizable nodes of individuality; and a
> forcing into association with the most strongly marked or "peak" material
> of many actually older and younger transitional specimens. . . . This pot-
> tery did not stand still; through some three centuries it underwent a slow,
> usually subtle, but never ceasing metamorphosis.

Kidder's comment reveals the fundamental paradox in the early foundations of the culture history paradigm. The conceived materialistic "slow,
usually subtle, but never ceasing metamorphosis" of artifact forms through
time was monitored using typological, essentialist, "recognizable nodes of
individuality."

One can plot the phyletic history of the metamorphosis of types, as
Kidder (1915, 1917a) and Haury (1937a) did for pottery (Figure 3.7) and
Sayles (1937) did for stone tools (Figure 4.1). Haury (1937a:169-170) noted
with respect to pottery from Snaketown, Arizona (Figure 3.3), that transitional specimens were useful: "Although the pottery of Snaketown was particularly susceptible to division into types [indicating types were extensional

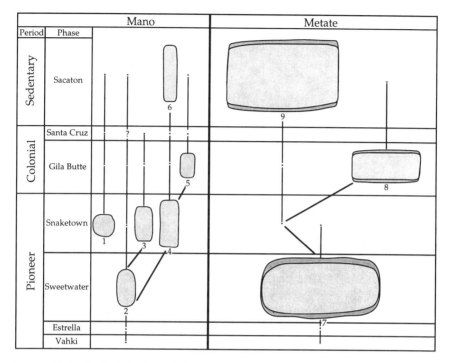

Figure 4.1. E. B. Sayles's chart of the development of manos and metates at Snaketown. Each numbered form is a type; each type is illustrated within the phase when it was found in greatest frequency. Connecting lines denote phyletic relations (after Sayles 1937).

derivatives], we found that some pieces could not be admitted into definite categories because they shared the elements of two types. Such transitional or borderline specimens are thrown into prominence as tangible evidence of continuity in the development of pottery." That is, transitional specimens provided evidence of the "genetic relationship" (Haury 1937b:212) of sequent types. Transitional specimens are, however, a direct result of how typologies were being built—extensionally—but this escaped notice at the time. The use of extensionally defined types to illustrate phyletic histories gives those types an appearance of being real, essentialist units, as Kidder noted. Further, types built by extensional trial and error that were meant to measure time were sure to eventually become index fossils as their definitive criteria were refined so that the type units reflected ever smaller chunks of the time–space continuum.

In his efforts to understand the cultural chronology of Georgia and Florida, Gordon Willey (1939:142) found percentage stratigraphy to be inconclusive in some cases, a result of what he termed stratigraphic "disturbance" and "mixing." Thus, he later turned to type fossils, where the use of such units to measure culture change conceived in materialist terms is revealed in comments echoing those of Kidder:

> Any pottery type is based on a number of stylistic features found in combination, but changes occur through time, and transitions are often so gradual as to prevent sharp distinctions. However, the periods into which the pottery types have been grouped are each based on one or more "key" or "marker" types, which have been found to be sufficiently restricted in range and distinctive in appearance to allow their occurrence to be quite positively determined. (Willey and Woodbury 1942:236)

Willey's problem was the same as Kidder's—cultural development conceived in materialist terms but perceived, or at least thought only to be measurable, in essentialist terms. Transitional specimens were the obvious results of the use of extensionally defined units as well as of the failure to distinguish between empirical and theoretical units. The latter reinforced the notion that type fossils were somehow real because of their narrow temporal–spatial distributions; they represented particular cultures in the sense of an ethnographic unit.

The seriations of Kroeber and Spier were different creatures because they provided detailed measurement of continuous change. Specifically, they employed percentages of *ideational* units as they were represented by samples of *empirical* units in order to mark the passage of time. Such seriations required historical types with long temporal durations so that their changing relative frequencies through time could be measured (Dunnell 1970, 1981). Thus, the method was founded in a materialist metaphysic. Kroeber suggested, and Kidder and Spier used, superposition as a means of testing the temporal significance of seriations. That the seriated units were *at least* ideational if not also theoretical was a requirement of the method (Dunnell 1970). This went unremarked in the literature of the time, however, probably because nearly everyone constructed types extensionally. The synergism and mutually reinforcing character of seriation and superposition, even though the latter was perceived to be the final arbiter of chronological questions, no doubt contributed to the discipline-wide shift by the early 1920s to asking chronological questions. A potential flaw was that the greater trust placed in superposition for addressing chronological issues probably contributed to the essentialist conception of types, particularly index fossils; historical types should, it was thought, have stratigraphically demonstrably short temporal durations. As well, this in turn no doubt reinforced the feeling that such types were somehow real.

It actually was several decades before it was argued that seriation could serve as a check on an ordering based on superposition (e.g., Brainerd 1951a:312; Rowe 1961). Since the time of Nelson, Kidder, Kroeber, and Spier, archaeologists have found out that artifact assemblages recovered from subsurface contexts can be just as biased as artifact collections gathered from the surface (e.g., Dunnell and Dancey 1983; Schiffer 1987). Seriation was not a theoretical triumph; it was very much ad hoc and empirical, as our discussion of its origins shows. Seriation worked. That was the important thing, not *why* it worked. Indeed, whenever questions arose, they were effectively derailed by citing a commonsense description of the seriation phenomena—waxing and waning of popularity was *why* frequency distributions appeared as they did. The lack of theory meant that there were no guidelines, no rules, no principles for constructing units that would describe archaeological assemblages so that the observed variation was temporal.

We return to seriation in Chapter 5. Here, it is sufficient to note that early on, methodologically, type formation was largely trial and error. Absent an explicit rationale, a certain schizophrenia entered Americanist archaeology that persists to this day. Although all investigators recognized that the units they discussed were constructions of archaeologists, justifications of the units almost always were reduced to claims that the units—types—were real; that is, they were inherent in the data. Such a justification no doubt was reinforced (at least subconsciously) by the fact that type definitions were extensionally derived. The essentialist metaphysic—often finding expression in the popularity principle—plagued, and continues to plague, attempts to construct units. There are, then, two questions that need to be addressed. First, where did the types used by Nelson, Kidder, Kroeber, and Spier come from? Second, what happened to classification efforts once it was shown that types could be constructed in such a manner as to allow the measurement of the passage of time? We address each of these in turn, only touching briefly here on the former before turning to the latter in the next section.

The Origins of Types

The origins of the types used by Nelson, Kidder, Kroeber, and Spier have gone largely unremarked in the literature. As noted in Chapter 3, Kroeber's types were largely accidental constructs that resulted from the particular sites he happened to encounter and from which he gathered surface materials. His type units seem to have been largely post hoc descriptions of average-looking specimens that were extensionally derived. Spier merely used types that were similar to those described by Kroeber and found by Nelson to measure time. Nelson (1914, 1916) is not at all clear about how he constructed his type units. He reasoned that there were surely at least two basic kinds of pottery, glazed and unglazed, that were no doubt extensionally derived but that also tended to be associated with, respectively, large and small ruins. Further, there were so many sites in the region where he focused his attention that he believed they must have been "occupied successively" because to presume they were occupied simultaneously would result in a population "out of all proportion to the known historical facts about the Tanos and about the Pueblos of the Southwest as a whole" (Nelson 1914:31–32). Superposed sherds and a vague concept of pottery development no doubt reinforced his notion of sequent occupations. Variations in decoration surely, he reasoned, reflected stylistic pulsations or changes in fashion. Thus his types were extensionally derived units the temporal significance of which was confirmed by stratigraphic excavation.

Kidder (1915) had a suspected chronology of types before he ever excavated at Pecos. His types were founded on implicit notions of the evolution of decorative motifs (e.g., Kidder 1915, 1917a) and technology. They were extensionally derived constructs based largely on (1) associations between various kinds of pottery and different sorts of architecture or (2) the apparently distinctive spatial distributions of pottery kinds. For example, he noted that "the pottery of the small houses is entirely unlike that of the larger groups" (Kidder 1915:412). Three "wares"—black-and-white, red-and-black, and corrugated—were associated with small ruins, and four "wares"—red-and-glaze, biscuit, incised, and black—associated with "great" ruins (Kidder 1915).

That the first chronological schemes were derived from pottery rather than from, say, stone tools, has gone largely unremarked (but see Dunnell 1986b for an important exception). In 1938, Nelson reviewed the several basic types of materials from which artifacts might be manufactured and remarked that

> Of these basic materials stone is one of the most ancient in service and, up to the introduction of metal, the one almost always present in archaeological sites. In spite of its apparent refractory nature, it is capable of being worked in a variety of ways, and its products therefore lend themselves readily to technological and typological studies that are as a rule capable of chronological interpretation. The same is true also of pottery, once it arrives on the scene. As a plastic medium clay lends itself to being modeled into any shape that circumstances require or fancy may suggest; and its additional possibilities for accessory ornamentation are similarly almost limitless. These attributes of plasticity or workability, inherent in clay and ordinary stone, therefore enable their resulting artificial products to serve as fairly authentic guides. They present *genetically related series*

constituting gradually modified or specialized form groups such as are required, in the absence of stratigraphy, for determining the time order of most of the other associated fragmentary traits. (Nelson 1938:152; emphasis added)

Thus, by the late 1930s it was apparent that both pottery and stone tools might be classified in such a way as to allow the measurement of time. A mere decade earlier the consensus seemed to be that stone tools would not allow the building of chronologies. As Vaillant (1930:12) observed,

> Pottery making received, as it were, a tribal stress, so that it became a universally practised art, psychologically strongly controlled by the group. At the same time, it was neither a specialized fine art nor the product of a guild of artisans. Thus socially conserved it would tend to change more from whim of fashion than individual vagary. The relatively standardized technique of house building and stone work throws pottery into strong relief as the one cultural element in which changes would produce a time sequence otherwise difficult of detection.

Kidder (1924:45) made a similar observation: To detect the passage of time in the archaeological record, "the investigator must select for study those phenomena which most accurately reflect changes in culture or, what amounts to the same thing, cultural periods. Pottery has so far provided the most useful material for such studies, as it is abundant at all sites except the very earliest, is readily classifiable, and is a highly sensitive register of cultural change." In a footnote appended to this statement, Kidder noted that "Valuable but much less easily acquired evidence is provided by architecture, physical type, skull deformation, mortuary customs, sandals, etc."

The reason that pottery received the lion's share of the culture historians' attention resided in how artifacts were classified—extensionally. Pottery was readily classified in this manner because sherds, particularly decorated ones, displayed so many kinds of attributes—temper, color, surface manipulation, etc.—in so many different ways. This was empirically obvious, and extensional definition was, at least initially, easy. This escaped notice (except for Kidder's comment cited above that pottery "is readily classifiable") at the time, despite the fact that it was a change in classification procedures—from cultural traits per se to variants of a trait—that had resulted in the birth of culture history. The classification of pottery played the seminal role in culture history largely because of the earlier classification efforts of Holmes (1886a, 1886b, 1886c). Ways to classify pottery such that it could be used as an analytical tool for measuring variation in time and space were developed by Holmes, and these were mimicked by Nelson, Kroeber, Kidder, and Spier in their work in the Southwest. Similar efforts followed slightly later in the Southeast (e.g., Collins 1927a). The explosion of pottery types and of suggested attributes and procedures one might use to classify pottery that followed the birth of culture history (e.g., Drier 1939; Ford 1935b, 1936a; Gillin 1938; Guthe 1927, 1934; Hargrave 1932; Hargrave and Smith 1936; March 1934) signaled a new purpose to classification that came to be a signature of culture history.

Classification of Artifacts—The Search for Historical Types

After 1916, artifact types came to be more than simply communication facilitators. From our above discussion, it should be clear that types that were temporally sensitive were the kind of units desired. Typically termed "styles" (e.g., Kidder 1916:122; Kroeber 1916b:36; Nelson 1916:162; Spier 1917a:277; Wissler 1916b:195), the ability of such types to measure time could be tested empirically using superposed collections from a column of sediment. As a result, chronological inquiry came to dominate archaeological research during the first half of the twentieth century (Dunnell 1986b:166). Classification efforts became very narrowly focused on one and only one kind of unit—the historical type. Functional variation in artifact form, still speculative in terms of methodological consideration, was effectively eliminated from discussion, despite calls for its examination (e.g., Steward and Setzler 1938). As Brew (1946:230) noted, such calls were merely ignored—not derogated—because of the singular focus on chronology. This focus created problems at the time as well as later in the history of the paradigm. The first problem, however, involved the construction of historical, or chronologically sensitive, types.

Kidder (1915:453, 1917a) discussed different kinds of pottery, or "styles," in terms of ancestral–descendent relationships. One pottery type might, for example, "father" another (Kidder 1915:453), and a pottery type might also become "extinct" (Kidder and Kidder 1917:348). Kidder's types, and perhaps to a lesser degree Kroeber's, Nelson's, and Spier's, were units that, it was hoped, reflected the passage of time *as well as* cultural evolutionary—that is, phyletic—relationships. Kidder (Kidder and Kidder 1917:349) stated that "One's general impression is that [the types] are all successive phases of [particular pottery traits], and that each one of them developed from its predecessor." Note that Kidder's word "phase" does not denote the units later termed cultural phases; it is a commonsense English word denoting a portion of a continuum. Hence, variation in pottery was temporally continuous, a notion that would be explicitly modeled in the 1950s. To measure time, Kidder erected types that were both "more or less arbitrarily delimited chronological subdivisions of material" (Kidder 1936b:xxix) and "chronologically seriable" (Kidder 1936a:625). Types had to undergo a test of "chronological significance [via] stratigraphic tests" (Kidder 1936b:xx). Kidder's types thus were theoretical units constructed to measure time: Conceptually, (1) variation is continuous—things are in the continuous process of becoming, and thus kinds, or types, are artifacts of observation (of the etic sort); and (2) change in the frequencies of variants reflects the passage of time. This is, simply, the materialist metaphysic.

This position is in stark contrast to the essentialist underpinnings of common sense and ethnology, both of which were (and still are) involved heavily in archaeological interpretation and explanation. This obviously created a fundamental contradiction (Dunnell 1980, 1982). As Julian Steward (1941:367) remarked, "the purpose [of archaeology] is to represent the development, interaction, and blending of diverse cultural streams." Evolutionary biologists use the same aquatic metaphor when they speak of the "evolutionary stream" (Mayr 1972:987). Thus, on the one hand, human history was a stream of attributes, ever changing, flowing from past to future; on the other hand, experience suggested that humanity was divisible into more or less discrete groups or cultures and it was these groups that required explanation. Recall, for example, that Kidder's types were "recognizable nodes of individuality." The implications for classification were enormous. In the materialist view, types, cultures, and units in general were artifacts of observation; they were tools used to measure variation that constituted the past and of which the present was just a terminal snapshot. From the essentialist view, however, types, cultures, and units in general were empirical and real; they were the things to *be* explained, not the means *of* explanation.

Kidder's (1936b:xx) "recognizable nodes of individuality" represented "ceramic periods" (Kidder 1936b:xxi) as well as distinct cultures (Kidder 1936a:623, 1936b:xxviii). This is essentialism; it decidedly is not materialism. Kidder's goal was the formulation of "ceramic periods" (Kidder 1936b:xxi) and the identification of "nuclear cultures" (Kidder 1936a:623) that would allow him to write culture history. He believed that one could trace "the descent of types and [establish] collateral relationships" between types and cultures (Kidder 1936b:xxviii). The influence of cultural anthropology's essentialist viewpoint is clear: Cultures, real cultures, were the subject of anthropological and archaeological study. Culture traits—shared ideas (after Tylor's [1871] definition)—expressed as archaeological types could be used to tell time, and they could also be used to discuss population movements and the cultural relations of sites from which artifact assemblages were collected. But by structuring change as discontinuous nodes—a position culture historians were forced into by failing to make explicit distinctions between ideational and empirical units—explanations had to be of the transformational sort, in which differences between the discretely variable nodes (essentialist artifact types) are noted rather than the materialist measurement of change as the differential persistence of variants (Dunnell 1995:34–35; see also Mayr 1959). Such conflation of the materialist and essentialist metaphysics was common in the first half of the twentieth century and is no less so today.

In the Southeast

As time went on, successively more and more kinds of pottery were found and described—some not very well, which led to further problems in communication among archaeologists. While standardization of stone tool classification was attempted at the same time (e.g., Black and Weer 1936; Finkelstein 1937), most efforts dealt with pottery. One result was that two major centers of discussion of classification appeared—one in the Southeast and one in the Southwest.

Much of the significant early work in the Southeast was done by James A. Ford, whose work we examine in detail in Chapter 5. Here we touch on only one of his more significant early contributions. By the mid-1930s, there were no formal Southeastern pottery types, though there was some standardization in pottery terminology. Lengthy descriptions of pottery assemblages were the rule, as were tabular summaries of data (e.g., Griffin 1938, 1939), both of which limited one's ability to compare materials from different sites. To remedy the situation, Ford and James B. Griffin (1937) proposed that a meeting of major figures in Southeastern archaeology should take place, at which time rules and procedures for building typologies would be established. The resulting "Report of the Conference on Southeastern Pottery Typology" (Ford and Griffin 1938[†]), provides detailed insight into how various individuals in the Southeast viewed typology. The recommended structure for the typology was, Griffin (personal communication 1996) indicates, a mix of the Southwestern format, Carl E. Guthe's (1927, 1934) recommended list of analytical features, and Griffin's (1943) Fort Ancient format. The original proposal for this important conference (Ford and Griffin 1937) and the report that resulted from the conference (Ford and Griffin 1938) were reprinted in 1970 in the *Newsletter of the Southeastern Archaeological Conference* (Vol. 7).

Pottery types in the Southeast were created explicitly to integrate form with both time and space: "Types should be classes of material which promise to be useful as tools in interpreting culture history. . . . A type is nothing more than a tool, and is set up for a definite purpose in the unfolding of culture history" (Ford and Griffin 1938:3). Types were ideational units in the sense that "A type must be defined as the combination of all the discoverable vessel features" and "A type should be so clearly definable that an example can be recognized entirely apart from its associated materials"; thus, "it is necessary to select a set of mutually exclusive features to serve as a primary framework for the classifications" (Ford and Griffin 1938:4). Because sherds rather than whole vessels were to be expected, surface finish and decoration were to serve "as the bases for the primary divisions of the material" (Ford and Griffin 1938:5).

Importantly, then, types were defined, ideational categories. That they were extensionally defined as opposed to simply described is suggested by the statement that "two sets of material which are similar in nearly all features, but which are divided by peculiar forms of one feature may be separated into two types *if there promises to be some historical justification for the procedure*" (Ford and Griffin 1938:4; emphasis added). The implication is that if one thinks a difference in a single character state is temporally and/or spatially significant—that is, that it will allow differences in time and/or space to be measured and thus allow analytical work to be done—then use that difference as part of the definition of a type.

On the one hand, the meeting participants indicated "there is no assurance that [the included attributes] can be considered as genetically related" (Ford and Griffin 1938:7), which was by that time a far cry from what their colleagues in the Southwest were saying. Similar to their Southwestern brethren, on the other hand, Southeastern archaeologists were to name types based on geographic location and description (Ford and Griffin 1938:10). Further, specimens representative of each type were to be held by each institution working in the area, and a review board was established "to control and unify the processes of type selection, naming, and description" (Ford and Griffin 1938:10–11). The procedure for proposing a new type involved inspecting sample specimens, producing a tentative description, and documenting "the range of variation allowed for the type" (Ford and Griffin 1938:16).

These aspects of the proposal indicate that types were extensionally defined, historical accidents dependent for their existence on the specimens at hand when a type was proposed. Types obviously were viewed as important for revealing culture history, but no tests were suggested for establishing the validity of the units for actually measuring temporal or spatial dimensions. This lack reveals the atheoretical nature of the proposed system. Common sense was to be the guide: The "usual range of [a] type [is indicated by] sites at which [a] type is found in sufficient abundance to be considered native" (Ford and Griffin 1938:16). Numerous papers describing various Southeastern ceramic types appeared shortly after the conference (e.g., Caldwell and Waring 1939; Ford and Willey 1939a, 1939b; Haag 1939; Jennings and Fairbanks 1939), just as they were also appearing in the Southwest.

In the Southwest

Things were not much better in the Southwest. A number of monographs produced in the 1920s and 1930s attempted to standardize descriptions of various pottery forms and surface treatments (e.g., Gladwin and Gladwin 1928, 1930b, 1931, 1933; Haury 1936a; Hawley 1936). Similar to efforts in the Southeast, Southwestern pottery types were to integrate the dimensions of time, space, and form, but they were also to do something else. In naming a type, temporal placement and comparative terms were to be omitted, and a binomial nomenclature was to be used. Color or surface treatment constituted the first ("genus") part of the type name, and geographic locale constituted the second ("species") part (Gladwin and Gladwin 1930a:4; see also Gladwin 1936:256). In this respect, the Southwestern naming system was similar to that of the Southeast, only the order of terminological categories used was reversed. Unlike biological nomenclature the procedure of the Gladwins and their colleagues resulted in listing the "species" name before the "genus" name of a pottery type, as with "Tularosa black-on-white" (Gladwin and Gladwin 1930a:5).

Having first been suggested at the original Pecos Conference in 1927 (Kidder 1927:490), the binomial pottery classification procedure grew out of a consensus reached at the first Gila Pueblo Conference in 1930 (Gladwin and Gladwin 1930a; see also Brew 1946:58; Gladwin 1936:256). This nomenclature system was used throughout the Southwest and resulted in the naming of numerous types. Procedures and rules for naming new types were produced (e.g., Colton and Hargrave 1937) and were repeated in following decades (e.g., Colton 1965). Brew (1946:58) later suggested it was precisely this pottery nomenclature system that resulted in the " 'family tree' concept of culture classification designed to describe all Southwestern prehistory," probably in large part as a result of the work of Lyndon L. Hargrave (1932) and Harold S. Colton (e.g., 1932). That the resulting units were at least sometimes not intensionally defined classes is evident from Colton's (1932:12) early statement that "Since the Pecos Classification was published the pottery types associated with the culture periods . . . have become more distinct." This suggests that at a minimum the types were extensionally derived units the definitions of which could be modified as more specimens were examined.

Colton and Hargrave's study of the pottery of northern Arizona, published as *Handbook of Northern Arizona Pottery Wares* (Colton and Hargrave 1937[†]), was ostensibly an attempt to integrate form, space, and time. In all senses, it represented a complete break with the tradition of Kroeber, Kidder, Spier, Nelson, and others. Colton and Hargrave (1937:2–3) defined a pottery *type* as "a group of pottery vessels which are alike in every important characteristic except (possibly) form"; a pottery *ware* as "a group of pottery types which has a majority of [the important] characteristics in common but that differ in others"; and a pottery *series* as "a group of pottery types within a single ware in which each type bears a genetic relation to each other." The problems are immediately apparent in this scheme. Colton and Hargrave conflated the necessary and sufficient conditions of membership in a class (type, ware, series)—the definition or significata of a class—with interpretations of *specific* classes. Thus the difference between type and ware seems to reside in the number of attributes held in common (though which attributes is not specified), but the difference between series and type or series and ware resides in the interpretations given them. Types and wares were units for measurement; series comprised phyletically related types.

Curiously, Colton and Hargrave's scheme had elements of modern dimensional, or paradigmatic, classification (*sensu* Dunnell 1971b)—note, for example, the vessel rim dimensions and attributes listed in Figure 4.2—though this part of the system was devised simply as a means of facilitating communication. In constructing the rim classification, Colton and Hargrave employed three dimensions—side-wall shape, lip direction, and rim form. One class, then, might be II-B-4 and another II-B-5, the two differing only in terms of rim form. They recognized that the attributes they listed (Figure 4.2) did not form a closed system: "This method is flexible and can be used on any forms of pottery vessels by adding to the chart any forms not previously recorded" (Colton and Hargrave 1937:11).

One thus could make the claim that the classification was intensional—that is, it did not depend solely on the actual specimens being analyzed for its structure—but it falls short on several counts, not the least of which is that the creators never told us why these particular dimensions or their particular character states or attributes were selected as opposed to others. This caused them to resort to common sense—hence their use of terms such as "proper" and "obvious"—as their warrant for selecting dimensions and attributes. In commenting on Colton and Hargrave's classification, Paul Reiter (1938a:490) saw it as "stimulat[ing] suspicion that the potters of northern Arizona must have been parsimoniously impeccable in their adherence to ceramic creeds." Neither he nor Colton and Hargrave saw the originality in the system—it was clearly an etic construct—as a direct result of their viewing such constructs as empirical or emic units.

They might have been unclear on several counts, but Colton and Hargrave certainly were clear about the historical relatedness of the types. Their emphasis was on the relatedness between and among the *types* that were created and not on the relatedness between and among attributes (in terms of what replaced what). In addition, there was, of course, no warrant

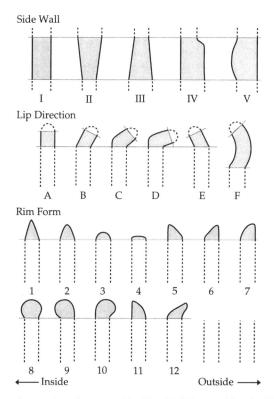

Figure 4.2. Dimensions and attributes used by Harold Colton and Lyndon Hargrave to class-ify Southwestern rim sherds. Although they did not use the terms "dimension" and "attribute," their system is a paradigmatic classification (Dunnell 1971b), in which classes are created by the intersection of attributes of analytical dimensions (after Colton and Hargrave 1937).

for the phyletic interpretation of a series, though this did not stop Colton and Hargrave from distinguishing among derived, collateral, and ancestral types nor from graphing the relations among the types, similar to what biologists do in cladistic analysis. Their graph showing these relations is reproduced in Figure 4.3. Their unabashedly biological model of pottery classification was, however, flawed because common sense underpinned the key notion. That notion was that related forms were related because they were similar. In fact, it should be the other way around—similar forms are similar because they are related (e.g., Simpson 1961:68–69). The problem was that Colton and Hargrave offered no argument—nor did anyone else at the time—that the similarities described were of the homologous sort, hence Kroeber's (1931a, 1943) lament (see also Neff 1992, 1993).

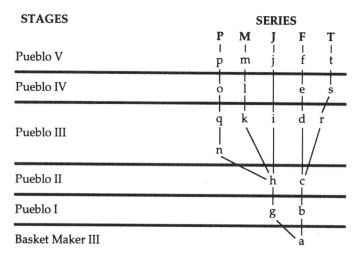

Figure 4.3. Harold Colton and Lyndon Hargrave's hypothetical representation of the relation between a series and its types. In the example, series F comprises types *a, b, c, d, e,* and *f*. Type *a* is ancestral to all other types; type *c* is ancestral to types *d, e, f, r, s,* and *t*; type *c* is collateral to types *d* and *r*, derivative from type *b*, and ancestral to types *f* and *t*; all types are related to each other through type *a*; types *i, j, k, l,* and *m*, are related to each other through type *h*; types *q* and *n* are both ancestral to type *o* but collateral to each other, and are derivative from types *h, g,* and *a*. Note one peculiarity of the system: Colton and Hargrave state that type *c* is collateral to types *d* and *r*, and they also state that types *q* and *n* are collateral to each other. This is sheer nonsense and is strictly a function of where one draws lines between stages (after Colton and Hargrave 1937).

Kidder's (1915, 1917a) less elaborate classification scheme denoted some of the same sorts of relations between types, but his contemporaries did not level the kind of criticism against him that they did against Colton and Hargrave. Given the degree of criticism, it was not accidental that their model was short lived. In his review of their handbook, Ford (1940:264) commented that Colton and Hargrave did not consider "the utility of the types for discovering cultural history." Ford was more optimistic than some regarding the determination of the genetic relations among types and wares within a series. He noted, however, that Colton and Hargrave ignored the problem of selecting "a class of features [attributes] which will best reflect cultural influences [e.g., transmission via contact], and which in their various forms will be mutually exclusive, to serve as guides in the process" of determining ancestral–descendant relationships (Ford 1940:265). Ford was, we think, without using the term, speaking of homologous similarity, but he failed to make this clear and in fact would fall prey to exactly this pitfall in his later work.

In another review of Colton and Hargrave's handbook, Reiter (1938a:490) noted that he "was unable to find a single instance of proof of [the genetic relationships of pottery types]." Reiter (1938a:490) also noted that the typology tended to ignore variation, and he insisted that "variation tendencies cannot be overlooked if genetic or chronologic emphasis is strong." Reiter's comments were on the mark because Colton and Hargrave's units were empirical groups, not intensionally defined classes. For example, they stated that "types vary in time [and] from place to place at a given time" (Colton and Hargrave 1937:1). Their units were data, not tools that could be used to measure variation, since the units varied by location in time and space. Types did not measure time; rather, their locations in time were to be determined by stratigraphy or dendrochronology (Colton and Hargrave 1937:23). Colton and Hargrave had confused empirical and theoretical units, as evidenced by their suggestions that "there are sherds that are intermediate between types" (Colton and Hargrave 1937:31) and that the members of a type "will not [always] fit the [type] description perfectly" (Colton and Hargrave 1937:30). Their types could *never* be theoretical units, the empirical representations of which should display certain distributional properties if properly structured (like Kidder's). Rather, they were simply shorthand notations of what a "typical" (Colton and Hargrave 1937:31), or average, specimen looked like.

Colton and Hargrave (1937) provided no examples of the genetic relations of their types. This is hardly surprising because, as indicated earlier, those types were empirical units rather than theoretical ones. They did not develop Kidder's (e.g., 1915, 1917a) evolutionary speculations into a theoretical account of the behavior of historical types. While the structure of their types–series–wares scheme was clearly hierarchical, that structure was essentially void of explanatory content. Colton and Hargrave (1937:2–3, 5) indicated that genetic relations among types were "obvious" and "clearly revealed" and that "definite evolutionary characters were recognized," but they provided no list of them nor did they provide guidance as to how such characters were to be identified, as Kidder (e.g., 1915, 1917a) had done two decades earlier. In simplistic form, they, as well as others (e.g., Beals et al. 1945; Haury 1937a; Sayles 1937), merely mimicked Kidder's procedure, which, as we have seen, was derived from Petrie's (1899, 1904) method.

The problem is this: To hypothesize that two sets of things are related in an ancestral–descendent fashion demands specification of how that relationship is generated. Lacking theory, Colton and Hargrave provided no such specification. Although they added structure to Kidder's (1915, 1917a) method, they (Colton and Hargrave 1937:xii) were forced to warrant those additions by reference to ethnographic data such as (1) indigenous pottery will be made of local materials, (2) changes in technology represent changes in "people," and (3) styles of design diffuse. These suggestions were derived from Colton's (e.g., 1936:339) limited observations of the behaviors of living Puebloan peoples. The use of such warrants underscores the atheoretical nature of culture history and its dependence on empirical generalizations derived from ethnology and anthropology.

J. O. Brew and the Death of Phylogenies

As indicated in J. O. Brew's *Archaeology of Alkali Ridge, Southeastern Utah* (Brew 1946[†]), many individuals—including Brew—were not happy with what might be called the Gladwin–Colton scheme of establishing phyletic relations (e.g., Reiter 1938a; Steward 1941). Perhaps most problematic in the scheme were its evolutionary implications, which Brew (1946:53) found unacceptable: "[P]hylogenetic relationships do not exist between inanimate objects." As Brew (1946:54–56) pointed out, biologists were aware that the Linnaean taxonomic system did not *necessarily* denote phylogeny, although it might. In the 1930s and 1940s that particular taxonomy did not explain the categories of phenomena it sought to arrange for at least two reasons. First, the Linnaean taxonomy was in use well before any notion of evolutionary descent with modification was generally accepted and had not yet been modified in light of that notion (Mayr 1982). Second, the categories—biological taxa—were typological (essentialist) entities (Mayr 1959, 1982) with temporal and spatial locations. How could such essentialist categories possibly be modified via descent?[1] Brew (1946:49) noted that Kidder (1936b:xx) was well aware of this characteristic of his pottery types when the latter stated that "Most types, in reality, grew one from the other by stages well-nigh imperceptible." But neither Kidder nor virtually anyone else perceived that the difficulty lay in having a materialist conception of cultural evolution but operating within an essentialist metaphysic when analyzing and interpreting the archaeological record. Brew alone appears to have come close to recognizing this paradox; at least he alone was explicit about the problems that resulted from it.

Brew (1946:46) argued that (1) classifications are arbitrary constructs of the analyst—"no typological system is actually inherent in the material"; (2) there is no ideal classification allowing the solution of a set of heterogeneous problems; and (3) the classification should fit the purpose of the investigation. For the last point, Brew (1946) was explicitly following Kluckhohn's (1939b:338) comment that archaeological typologies were being "proliferated without apparent concern as to what the concepts involved are likely to mean when reduced to concrete human behaviors." Others recognized these problems as well. For example, Bennett (1946:200) wrote that "a classification is a relative affair, determined entirely by the problem at hand," and "Archaeological classifications and typologies are abstractions which are really bundles of testable hypotheses about the nature of correspondence of culture objects to the dynamic culture-historical pattern which bore them."

Brew (1946:64) clearly recognized the interplay of theory and unit construction, for he argued that we should change our classifications "as our needs change and as our knowledge develops." He held the typical conception of cultural change: "We are dealing with a constant stream of cultural development, not evolutionary in the genetic sense, but still a continuum of human activity" (Brew 1946:63). But Brew was more perceptive than many of his contemporaries: "We must ever be on guard against that peculiar paradox of anthropology which permits men to 'trace' a 'complex' of, let us say, physical type, pottery type, and religion over 10,000 miles of terrain and down through 10,000 years of history while in the same breath, or in the next lecture, the same men vigorously defend the theory of continuous change" (Brew 1946:65). The paradox emanates "from the belief that the manufactured groups [types] are realistic entities and the lack of realization that they are completely artificial. . . . Implicit in [the belief] is a faith . . . in the existence of a 'true' or 'correct' classification for all object, cultures, etc., which completely ignores the fact that they are all part of a continuous stream of cultural events" (Brew 1946:48). The paradox identified by Brew is the essentialist belief in real types and the materialist conception of change as a continuous stream. Thus Brew (1946:63) correctly recognized that "The 'intermediate' types are *not* unimportant, to be eliminated, as is often done, by disregarding them"; such types were the stuff of the materialist metaphysic.

Brew's (1946:65) solution to the paradox—more new classifications— reveals the pervasive lack of archaeological theory. The kinds of classifications and the kinds of units necessary to resolve the paradox were unspecified. For example, Brew did not tell us how to deal with intermediate types because he did not recognize that such units were the result of extensional definitions. Further, while recognizing that his functional types were perhaps incorrectly labeled as knives, scrapers, and such, because a "knife" can be used as a "scraper" (Brew 1946:235), he did not explore any possible ways to correct the problem. He could only warrant his own use of the classifications of others such as Kidder, Gladwin, and Colton as a desire for comparability (Brew 1946:87–88, 92–96, 252–254). This is probably why Brew's discussion had only one apparent impact on Americanist archaeology—to drive the final nail into the coffin containing the Gladwin–Colton scheme (recall Reiter's and Steward's criticisms; Gladwin had abandoned the scheme a decade earlier).

Earlier, some (e.g., Kroeber 1931a; Steward 1941) had suggested that biological phylogeny was not an accurate model of cultural evolution—the former was monophyletic, the latter often polyphyletic. Others (e.g., Beals et al. 1945; Reiter 1938a) suggested that genetic relationships could not be demonstrated with the scheme; still others were more optimistic (e.g., Ford 1940) but could offer no map for finding a way out of the paradox. Brew's (1946:53) explicit statement that inanimate objects do not interbreed was the final blow, and it was repeated by others (e.g., Beals et al. [1945:87], who saw Brew's Alkali Ridge manuscript before it was published). Interestingly, Brew (1946:55) suggested that "The only defense there can be for a classification of [artifacts] based upon phylogenetic theory is that the individual objects were made and used by man." He failed to make the conceptual leap to "replicative success" (Leonard and Jones 1987)—one cornerstone of evolutionary archaeology—for two reasons.

First, evolution for him seems to have involved only the processes of genetic transmission and genetic change. Thus, he perceived only a weak correlation between an organism and the "artifacts" that that organism might produce, such as birds and eggshells or mollusks and mollusk shells, and no connection at all between people and their artifacts (Brew 1946:55–56). Since artifacts were not genotypic phenomena, they were not subject to evolutionary forces. That it is the phenotype—of which artifacts are an expression—that undergoes selection escaped Brew's and contemporary biologists' attention for a number of years (Leonard and Jones 1987; Mayr 1982). Second, he quoted a single biologist, geneticist Thomas H. Morgan, who argued that a phylogenetic (or phyletic) history did not explain organisms; hence, to Brew, it could hardly explain artifacts: "This is a most important point, and I wish to emphasize it here," Brew (1946:56) noted. Perhaps the deficiencies of biological evolutionary theory of the 1930s and 1940s led archaeologists to abandon the inclusion of that theory into their field. In any event, Brew certainly made no attempt to eliminate any such deficiencies, nor did he attempt to build an explicitly archaeological theory of culture change.

It is likely that conceptions such as Kidder's (1936b) regarding types and Colton and Hargrave's (1937) intuitive, commonsensical rephrasing of them set Southwestern pottery classification on a course from which it has yet to recover and which sets it apart from the developments in most other areas of the New World. In particular, in the Southwest, where superposition was first used so effectively and where dendrochronology also provided absolute chronological information, definitions of historical types were extensional and thus could be continuously refined in light of new information. This led to the creation of historical types with extremely narrow temporal distributions—in essence, index fossils (e.g., Breternitz 1966). Their utility for analytical exercises such as seriation, which requires historical types with long temporal durations, was thus compromised.

The Formal Dimension—Post Hoc Synopses

Given the plethora of handbooks and procedures that appeared in the 1930s, it is perhaps not surprising that some, such as Roberts (1935:4), would observe that archaeologists had become "so absorbed in a detailed study of pottery *per se* that they have forgotten the [purpose of their discipline]." Willey and Sabloff (1993:118) later observed that during the 1920s and 1930s, "The potsherd grew steadily farther away from the whole pot, from the larger cultural context, and from the people who made the pottery. . . . such potsherd archaeology represented the vanguard in American studies." Of course, what these commentators failed to realize is that since about the middle of the 1920s, the major purpose of classification had been to construct units that allowed the measurement of time. That such was indeed the purpose of "potsherd archaeology" did not escape detection at the time.

Beals et al. (1945:13) explicitly stated that "There is no magic and no inherent virtue in potsherds taken simply by themselves. To the archaeologist they are primarily time fossils, and are valuable so far as their objective characteristics can be utilized to indicate temporal or regional differences or similarities between the sites from which they come." A few years later Haag (1961:19) made a similar observation: "If one examines the history of the development of any science or individual discipline, early in its story there is a necessary preoccupation with classification. This is often deplored because many students forget that classification is only a means to an end, that it is only sorting the cards in order to play the game properly." This was precisely the case in the history of biology where the purpose of systematics was forgotten at various times (Mayr 1982). The game in the case of archaeology was to measure time. That typological units might also be used for something else was, at least in the early stages of unit construction, of little concern. Irving B. Rouse (1939) and Alex D. Krieger (1944) were explicit about the chronological purposes of the typological constructions then being erected, and offered programmatic, post hoc statements on how such measurement tools were to be constructed.

Irving B. Rouse

In his classic *Prehistory in Haiti,* Rouse (1939[†]) distinguished between (1) the set of necessary and sufficient conditions for placing a specimen within a type and (2) the specimen or specimens placed within or identified as examples of a type. The ideational units that could be used as significata of a type he termed *modes* to distinguish them from *attributes,* which under our framework would be referred to as empirical units. This distinction between ideational units (modes and combinations of distinctive modes making up types) and empirical units (specimens displaying certain modes) allowed one to measure change through time and difference across space because the units of measurement—modes and types—were immutable, atemporal, and aspatial, just as is a unit of measurement such as an inch or a gram. Modes and types are not and *cannot* be actual attributes or artifacts, since attributes and artifacts have specific positions in time and space and because they differ from all other specimens in at least some formal properties (Rouse 1939:19–21). Rouse (1939:20, 147–159) was specifically interested in modes that allowed the construction of historical or chronological types, though other modes, for example, functional or technological modes, could be studied, perhaps for purposes other than chronology (Rouse 1944).

Rouse stressed that modes and types were units created by the archaeologist; in our terms, they were intensional units. He allowed the possibility that these units might reflect a mental template or idea in the mind of the artifact maker, but he did not mix the measurement purpose of the units with such interpretations of them (Rouse 1939:20). When he interpreted the units, Rouse (1939:18), like his predecessors and contemporaries, called on common sense to explain the distribution of modes and types through time and space: "Each type is a pattern of artifact characteristics [that supposedly] is the result of conformity . . . to a cultural standard. . . . Each mode . . . is a cultural pattern, or standard of behavior which influences the artisan's procedure . . . a community-wide technique, design, or other specification to which artisans conformed." Thus, modes and types could come into existence by "origination," disappear via "extinction," or undergo "replacement" by another mode or type (Rouse 1939:14), much as a cultural trait might (e.g., Wissler 1916b).

Rouse's procedure for choosing modes was inductive: "attributes which seemed to be most significant for a culture historical study" were selected (Rouse 1939:26). The procedure Rouse (1939:13) used produced an empirically testable result; empirical manifestations of modes and types should, for example, have a basically unimodal frequency distribution through time when measured across specimens of different age (Rouse 1939:141, 151). The result was a set of artificial units—modes or types—that measured temporal differences. The unimodal frequency distributions of modes and types might reflect the waxing and waning popularity of cultural norms or customs. Thus Rouse (1939) fell squarely within the

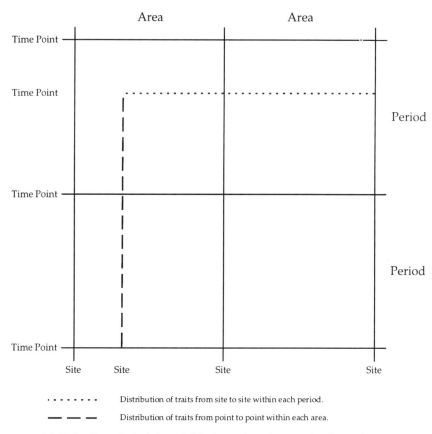

Figure 4.4. Irving Rouse's depiction of diffusion and persistence of traits. Each area on the diagram denotes a homogeneous unit of culture, considered geographically, and each period likewise marks off a homogeneous unit of culture, considered chronologically. The distribution of modes from time point to time point is the basis for the concept of persistence—a temporal concept. The distribution of modes from site to site indicates diffusion—a spatial concept. Rouse's point was that both the temporal and spatial aspects of types or modes must be considered (after Rouse 1939).

materialist camp (variation reflected the passage of time) but acknowledged the essentialist camp (the meaning of types was inherent in the data).

Although his units were first and foremost of the theoretical sort, there was no theory but only common sense to account for them. Rouse (1939:14) called on *diffusion* to explain the spatial distributions of modes and types, *persistence* to explain their temporal distribution (Figure 4.4), *origination* to refer to the "means by which a type or mode comes into existence," *extinction* to refer to when a "type or mode dies out," *replacement* to refer to one type or mode taking the place of another, and the *popularity principle* to explain frequency distributions of types and modes. Other commonsense principles—some related to the age–area notion—were also borrowed from ethnology (Rouse 1939:34). Although in large part he followed his predecessors by merely describing his procedures, based as they were in ethnology, Rouse (1939:139) was not only explicit about the borrowing, but also cautious: "the technique employed . . . represents an attempt to apply the ethnological methods of reconstructing culture history to archeology. Providing that the procedures followed . . . are technically sound, the conceptual technique should have as much utility as American techniques for reconstructing ethnological history." He was, in short, stuck like his contemporaries in the commonsense understanding of culture-historical processes being discussed by the ethnologists of the day (Rouse 1939:144–159), a result of the lack of a theory of culture history applicable in archaeological settings to which he could turn for guidance.

Rouse (1941:14–15) later made a distinction between *ordinary, alternative, optional,* and *deviant* modes. The first were the "standard" and accurately reflected "a rule to which the artisans conformed" (Rouse 1941:14), whereas alternative modes reflected replacement, optional modes reflected a lack of replacement, and deviant modes reflected deviations from normal behavior. Rouse later (e.g., 1952, 1960) abandoned the last three kinds of modes. While recognizing that the study of historically significant modes and types was "the *sine qua non* of archaeological research," Rouse (1944:203) saw other uses for other kinds of modes and types. One might, Rouse (1944:203) suggested, study variation in the form of stone tools from a technological or functional perspective rather than only the temporal position of artifacts. Study of the temporal distribution of technological modes, for example, would allow the writing of their histories (Rouse 1939:140).

In a similar vein, Steward (1954) distinguished among morphological or descriptive types, historical-index types, and functional types, noting a distinct analytical purpose for each. Brew (1946:46) advocated "*more* classifications [each one] personal to the student and his problem and . . . conditioned by the nature of the information he seeks to extract from his [specimens]." These suggestions were not seriously pursued with any intensity for several decades. Why? Probably because only the concept of historical type was sufficiently well developed to allow empirical testing. And it was empirical testing that was the standard for evaluating the correctness of a chronological interpretation.

Alex D. Krieger

Another archaeologist who considered types and how they could be used was Alex D. Krieger. As Rouse (1939, 1941) had earlier indicated, the formation of types by an archaeologist is an inductive procedure, a point with which Krieger agreed: The initial sorting of specimens "into trial patterns is largely experimental" (Krieger 1944:280). Hence, types are "discovered" (Krieger 1944:273, 1960:142). Clearly, there was no theory to inform the construction of the units called types; thus the units were built by trial and error and were of the extensional sort. Krieger's contributions to the issue of typology, which are seen most clearly in "The Typological Concept" (Krieger 1944[†]), resided in his explicit statements that the usefulness of types was testable: "In simplest terms, [for Krieger] the test of historical significance requires that all types must display temporal–spatial contiguity" (Dunnell 1986b:170). That is, archaeologically useful types are those "that have been demonstrated empirically to have chronological and geographical meaning"; types—termed "styles"—that "had limited and coherent temporal and spatial distributions" were Krieger's goal (Dunnell 1986b:171, 175). Types, then, were viewed as organizational tools that allow the grouping of specimens into sets that "have *demonstrable historical meaning*" (Krieger 1944:272); each type should "occupy a definable historical position . . . its distribution is delimited in space, time, and association with other cultural material" (Krieger 1944:277–278). Hence, types are tentative—inductive, trial-and-error—constructs until their "geographical (i.e., site-to-site), temporal, and associational occurrence" have been ascertained and found to be limited, and the co-occurrence of their attributes has been found to be consistent (Krieger 1944:280–281). Krieger's blueprint for type construction is shown in Figure 4.5.

Krieger perceived types to be "arbitrary" constructs of the archaeologist (Krieger 1960:145). But in the absence of theory, he rationalized and provided a warrant for them using common sense, and thus his types were of the essentialist kind. Types became real categories interpretable in terms of "the mental patterns which lay behind" them (Krieger 1944:272) and the "concrete human behaviors" they represented (Krieger 1944:271). Variation among specimens placed within a type was noise that distorted the archaeological image of a mental template held in common by the makers of the artifacts; such variants were attributable to a lack of social recognition and were of little historical significance (Krieger 1944:272). This stance was not unusual for the time, as archaeologists searched for types that variously had "temporal, areal, and/or cultural significance" (Whiteford 1947:228). Only the first—temporal significance—and the second—spatial significance—were, however, empirically

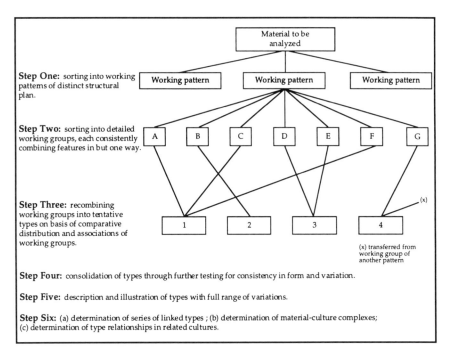

Figure 4.5. Alex Krieger's six-step method for constructing archaeological types (after Krieger 1944).

testable in a nontautological manner. Everything else was unwarranted assertion founded in common sense.

The ability to test the historical significance of types and the potential to use them for chronological purposes resulted in a very narrow problem orientation in Americanist archaeology of the early mid-twentieth century. By the middle of the 1920s, the purpose of classification had become largely one of measuring temporal differences among assemblages based on their included styles: Attributes and types "may be eliminated from later recordings if it has been satisfactorily demonstrated that they have no [chronological] significance" (Whiteford 1947:236). This had not always been the case, particularly in the Southwest where, as we have seen, not only was establishing chronological relations important—and Kidder (1936b) had already mentioned the "chronological significance" test of types—but establishing phyletic relations between types was also an important goal that was perceived as being, but in fact is not, separate from the chronological goal.

The Type–Variety System

The synthesis of chronology and artifact form, the roots of which can easily be traced to Kidder, is attributable to the work of Ford, Rouse, and Krieger. To them, types were theoretical units—combinations of modes— that possessed historical significance; that is, they displayed temporal and spatial contiguity (Dunnell 1986b:174). The size of the temporal or spatial distributions of types could, however, be markedly different, and the term *type* was found to be inconsistently applied in terms of its scale of inclusiveness. Ironically, the final iteration of the culture-historical-type concept was developed after Spaulding's (1953b) assault on the concept.

The problem of scale of inclusiveness was straightforward. Given a culture-historical type that "is recognizably distinct in terms of certain visual or tactile characteristics, and [that] has explicit temporal and areal associations," if each slightly variant form that differed from a type "only in very minor ways" was given a separate type name, then "the practice of giving them all equal status as types [results] in attaching too much significance to the variant" (Wheat et al. 1958:34–35). There was thus a need for a unit that allowed the placement of each specimen "in a category according to its degree of distinctiveness, some method . . . to designate entities which do not differ markedly from a described type and yet are useful if given separate recognition" (Wheat et al. 1958:35). Joe Ben Wheat, James C. Gifford, and William W. Wasley, in "Ceramic Variety, Type Cluster, and Ceramic System in Southwestern Pottery Analysis" (Wheat et al. 1958[†]), formalized a method known as the type–variety system for dealing with just this problem.

The type–variety system suggested that historical types of the Ford–Rouse–Krieger school, which "vary considerably in their areal and temporal distributions, and thereby utility, [be] systematically sorted on the basis of their distributions and differentiated into varieties and types" (Dunnell 1986b:174). Thus, a variety "generally is more restricted in one or both of [the time and space dimensions]" (Wheat et al. 1958:35). In this respect, the type–variety scheme was an improvement over earlier formulations. Wheat et al. (1958) explicitly noted, for example, that their concept of variety subsumed the poorly defined concept of subtype and also provided a new conception of variants. Varieties were "useful if given separate recognition" for denoting "minor regional or temporal departure from the [type] standard" and thus were not noise that was explicable only as individual variation (such, as they noted, Colton had earlier suggested) or as deviation from a cultural norm (Wheat et al. 1958:35–36). Wheat et al. clearly were concerned with the significance of variation in artifact form across space and through time. A variety thus could manifest itself in "any of 3 possible ways and we may speak of 3 aspects of variety: (1) technological or stylistic, (2) areal, (3) temporal" (Wheat et al. 1958:36). The first was definitional, the last two were inferential and subject to empirical testing.

The Gladwin–Colton conceptualization—particularly Colton's version—of pottery evolution had an influence on Wheat et al.'s (1958) type–variety system. They (Wheat et al. 1958:35) discussed pottery "sequences," which were intended to connote "evolutionary development" among the styles included within them, and contrasted those with a ceramic "series," which were "essentially geographical [units]." They were unclear how evolutionary relations were to be determined among pottery types, other than to more or less echo Colton's earlier formulation: "A ceramic sequence is composed of pottery types similar to each other in decorative style and other manifestations which have evolved, one from another, from early to late times" (Wheat et al. 1958:35). Their lack of theory is apparent because they did not specify the relevant kind of (homologous) similarity, nor did they specify a mechanism (transmission) for such evolution.

For Wheat et al. (1958:38, 39) a "type cluster consists of one type together with its varieties. . . . A type cluster is as restricted in time and area as the temporal and areal value of the type *plus* any additional time and area encompassed by the varieties within its sphere. . . . A ceramic type cluster takes its name from the established type." Thus one could have an established type, ABC, that included not only ABC but also an ABC–X variety and an ABC–Y variety (Figure 4.6).

Philip Phillips (1958:118) did not agree with the implied "sense of importance [and] ranking" that appeared to differentiate an established type from its related varieties (as indicated by the type cluster), because the two units—established types, related varieties—seemed to him to represent "precisely the same kind of entities," that is, theoretical units that allowed the measurement of time. The concept of varieties "had not received much attention" in the Southeast, and Phillips (1958:118) saw his chance to clean up the type–variety system before it caught on there. He proposed replacing the term "established type" with "established variety" and Wheat et al.'s "type cluster" with "type." This scheme would result in a type that "always includes its varieties . . . varieties are always varieties of the type; there is no occasion to speak of the type *and* its varieties at all" (Phillips 1958:119; see also Gifford 1960).

Ford (1935b:8) had earlier suggested that "Typologically related decorations [on pottery] found together in the same collection [could be taken as] indicating the probability that they represented variations of one major idea [read *type*] of decoration." He later modified this somewhat for the Southeast when he, along with James B. Griffin, stated that "two sets of

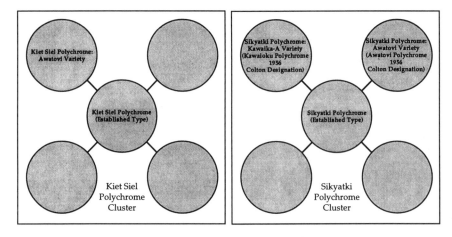

Figure 4.6. Two pottery clusters illustrating the Wheat–Gifford–Wasley type–variety system. In the Kiet Siel Polychrome cluster there is an established pottery type, Kiet Siel Polychrome, and one variety. The empty circles represent not-yet-discovered varieties. Similarly, Sikyatki Polychrome has two recognized varieties, though future analysis might allow more to be recognized (after Wheat et al. 1958).

material which are similar in nearly all features, but which are divided by peculiar forms of one feature may be separated into two types if there promises to be some historical [read *archaeological*] justification for the procedure. Otherwise they should be described as variants of one type" (Ford and Griffin 1938:4).

The type–variety concept played a major role in Americanist archaeology both in Mesoamerica (e.g., Sabloff and Smith 1969; Smith et al. 1960) and in the Mississippi Alluvial Valley. Working in the latter area, Phillips, Ford, and Griffin (1951:63), in their *Archaeological Survey in the Lower Mississippi Alluvial Valley, 1940–1947,* noted that "the most carefully defined types always overlap" and as such are *"created units of the ceramic continuum."* The frequently implied goal of their typological framework was to identify variation that allowed distinct time–space contexts to be distinguished. Phillips et al. (1951:69) described twenty ceramic types for the Mississippian period (post–ca. A.D. 900) in the Mississippi Valley.

Despite much debate in the 1950s and 1960s over the relative merits of type–variety classification schemes versus simple type classification (e.g., Ford 1954c, 1961, 1962; Phillips 1958; Smith et al. 1960; Wheat et al. 1958), the Phillips et al. (1951) types were standards until Phillips published his two-volume monograph *Archaeological Survey in the Lower Yazoo Basin,*

Mississippi, 1949-1955. In that study, Phillips (1970) expanded the original twenty types into a system of over forty types and eighty-eight varieties in an attempt to refine the existing ceramic categorization system. Types, according to Phillips, should be established primarily on the basis of paste (e.g., clay-tempered, coarse-shell-tempered, fine-shell-tempered), surface treatment (e.g., plain-surface, cordmarked), and design (e.g., incised, stamped). A secondary set of dimensions—modes of form and modes of decoration—should then be used to establish varieties within types. Phillips's view was that types reflect temporally and/or spatially widespread cultural and historical relations. Varieties of ceramic types, in contrast, "reflect specific areal and temporal variations in the norms of the type" (Phillips 1970:25). Thus, for Phillips, the type–variety system was a nested series of units. All included varieties were implied by a type; varieties merely have to be recognized and named when encountered; varieties are not "as readily sortable as types" because they "intergrade" or are transitional forms (Phillips 1970:25).

Phillips rationalized the utility of varieties precisely because to him they were intergrading units that "represent narrow intervals on the sliding scale of time and area" (Phillips 1970:26). Both the Phillips et al. (1951) typology and the Phillips (1970) type–variety system contained built-in overlap between and among types. As Phillips (1970:26) stated, "Intergrading [of types] is inevitable; it is in fact their very nature. As data accumulate and the sorting criteria become more explicit, two varieties juxtaposed in time or space naturally become more sortable." There are clear-cut cases in the archaeological record where the type–variety system has been used to create and refine those "narrow intervals" that Phillips spoke of, but the record is replete with cases that are not so clear-cut (Fox 1992; O'Brien and Fox 1994)—a fact not lost on Phillips (1970:26), who, having made the claim that new data allow troublesome types to become sortable, continued, "just about that time we begin to discern an intermediate category and the problem of sortability is with us once again."

The problem is, in part, technical. Phillips's descriptions of types and varieties do not distinguish between the necessary and sufficient conditions for membership in an ideational unit—significata—from the characteristics of extensionally defined empirical units. Recognizing this, it is understandable that Phillips was faced with "the problem of sortability" every time new specimens were collected. Phillips's efforts were further hampered by his essentialist view, a view reinforced by his notion that once sufficient data were available, all specimens would be sortable into types. This could only be true if his types were inherent in the specimens themselves.

Some Final Efforts to Control the Formal Dimension

As noted earlier, Rouse (1939) was the first to note the distinction between theoretical and empirical units (he did not refer to them as such)—a distinction he made throughout his career (e.g., Rouse 1944, 1952, 1960, 1972). For example, he defined a *class* as the "series of objects which are grouped together" (the empirical, existing items) and a *type* as the "series of attributes [modes] which are shared by [a class] and which distinguish them as a class" (Rouse 1953:62). Types and modes were theoretical units that one would use if "primarily interested in defining units of culture for use in distribution studies or for some other interpretative purpose" (Rouse 1953:62). By distinguishing between the groups of specimens (Rouse's classes) and the theoretical units used to record them (Rouse's types), Rouse (1952:327) was able to note that some types or combinations of modes constituted *styles,* whereas others did not (see also Rouse 1953:62). By "style" he meant a type with a distinctive time–space distribution (following Kroeber and Strong 1924a).

Rouse (1939) originally suggested that modes might reflect customs, but subsequent to Walter W. Taylor's (1948) arguments and the regular suggestions of others (e.g., Krieger 1944), he later changed his wording somewhat but not his conception. In 1939, a mode "supposedly [was a] cultural standard [or] pattern" (Rouse 1939:18). Early in the 1950s, Rouse (1952:325–326) indicated that modes were "culturally distinctive" and reflected "ceramic customs." Otherwise, a "mode is a kind of part of artifacts. It consists of *the character, form, or structure common to [a part] of a number of artifacts and distinguishing them as a class*" (Rouse 1952:326–327). In other words, in 1952 a mode was an ideational unit, just as it was in 1939. The part of a ceramic artifact under consideration might be handles, the possible forms or modes of which could consist of, for example, a "loop handle" and a "D-shaped handle" (Rouse 1952:325).

Rouse (1960[†]) maintained the distinction between ideational and empirical units in a still later paper entitled "The Classification of Artifacts in Archaeology," in which he reiterated many of his earlier points but also introduced several new items. His definition of a mode was the same as it was two decades earlier, with the explicit addition of cultural transmission as the explanation for the distribution of modes. A mode was "any standard, concept, or custom which governs the behavior of the artisans of a community, which they hand down from generation to generation, and which may spread from community to community over considerable distances" (Rouse 1960:313). Modes, as they were in 1939, were artificial—the result of human activity—"diagnostic" attributes; they were ideational

(Rouse 1960:314) though "modes are inherent in one's collection" (Rouse 1960:318). By "inherent" Rouse meant conceptually or definitionally inherent rather than inherent in the sense of an essence. Demonstrating that modes in fact reflect "customs" was, of course, impossible, and Rouse really never pursued such demonstrations (e.g., Rouse 1965a, 1965b). Rather, he merely maintained such a notion—as did some others (e.g., James Ford)— as a commonsense warrant for his type units.

Rouse (1960) pointed out that taxonomic classification uses multiple kinds of modes simultaneously and is hierarchical in structure. In taxonomies, modes are weighted or "require selection of only a few [distinctive/diagnostic] modes from among many" if the artifacts are complex (Rouse 1960:316). The strong point of Rouse's discussion was his distinction between historical and descriptive types. Clearly, each is defined by a set of modes, but if one wishes to construct historical types, then the "modes [must] have been selected, consciously or unconsciously, for their time-space significance" (Rouse 1960:317). Selection of such modes by the archaeologist makes historical types theoretical units—ones that measure differences in time and space—regardless of their possible emic content. "Descriptive types" for Rouse seem to have been ad hoc selections of modes that were essentially meaningless because they lacked an archaeological or analytical purpose.

Confusion over empirical and theoretical units permeated much of the literature on classification and typology during the 1960s. Continued attempts by others to standardize terminology (e.g., Krieger 1964) did little to clarify matters. This confusion did not, however, permeate one of the few other papers on typology and classification published at the time, "The Use of Typology in Anthropological Theory" by cultural anthropologist Clyde Kluckhohn (1960[†]). In that paper, Kluckhohn (1960:135) noted that (1) "Most classifications are still either crudely empirical or grossly impressionistic" and (2) "we are relatively rich in content [empirical] categories but poor in conceptual or relational [theoretical] categories." It appears that by "empirical classifications" Kluckhohn meant descriptive types in the sense that they provide general characterizations of specimens in each of several piles but otherwise have little analytical or interpretive utility.

Despite a rather haphazard use of key terms such as class, type, and group, Kluckhohn (1960) made a number of important points. Kluckhohn, like Rouse, appreciated the fact that there are two kinds of types. On one hand, a culture historian's historical types are used to build chronologies and time–space frameworks and are conceptual or relational, that is, they are "theoretical" because they "shed light on the relation between one set of facts and another" (Kluckhohn 1960:134), and "One makes certain that the criteria [attributes] chosen are actually relevant to the purpose or purposes at hand" (Kluckhohn 1960:136). On the other hand, empirical categories—a culture historian's "descriptive types"—are ad hoc selections of modes that allow grouping of objects and simplify description; they are not, however, analytically useful.

Another important point Kluckhohn made, following Rouse (1939), was that "there must be a discontinuity between a class and its members" (Kluckhohn 1960:135); that is, a class is an ideational (theoretical) unit that specifies the necessary and sufficient conditions for membership, whereas the members of the class are empirical specimens. There is a two-step process involved. First, analysts are "faced with discovering what measurements are crucial or most economical to obtain [correct assignments of specimens to classes]" (Kluckhohn 1960:135). This is where a major problem resides. Theory plays a critical role as it informs us as to which attributes are relevant and thus "crucial." The absence of theory reduces the choice of attributes to the status of a guessing game. Constructed classes make one's fundamental divisions "completely explicit [and one must follow] them consistently" when "assigning" a specimen to a class (Kluckhohn 1960:136). The latter is the second of the two-step process, and it introduces a second potential problem. Kluckhohn (1960:135) indicated that one must "carefully distinguish those phenomena [attributes] which tend to be associated with a particular category [class] from those which are essential criteria for membership in that class." In other words, one must keep the definitive, or diagnostic, attributes—the significata—separate from attributes that just happen to be associated with them on various specimens.

As we have discussed, the first problem—lack of theory resulting in ad hoc attribute selection—plagued culture history virtually from its start and resulted in trial-and-error formulations of units. The second problem too was a chronic failing of culture historians at both the artifact and assemblage scales, manifest as the type description and the trait list, respectively, to follow a procedure such as Kluckhohn's (1960). Such failures resulted in the accuracy of assignments of artifacts to types and determinations of such things as "cultural affiliation" being assessed on the basis of the expertise of the individual doing the assignments and determinations.

One's expertise depended on the number of years and kinds of apprenticeships one had experienced. Thompson (1956b:332, 1958b:8) stated, "The final judgment of any archaeologist's cultural reconstructions must . . . be based on an appraisal of his professional competence." Spaulding (1985:307) spoke of the pre-1950s "ineffable expertise communicable only by apprenticeship." Adams (1968:1188) wrote, "Long experience in an area is almost a necessity in fashioning a valid ecological approach" such as was demanded by processual archaeology. Taylor (1969:383) was even more explicit when he indicated that given the inferential character of the conclusions being produced, "Our only tribunal is professional acceptability or our personal values." Apprenticeships constituted the bulk of archaeological training within the culture history paradigm, and this was ultimately part of the reason for the development of the new archaeology of the 1960s (e.g., Binford 1968a:14). There had to be a better way to judge the correctness of a conclusion than through reference to someone's expertise.

A final example of the failure to distinguish between theoretical and empirical units is an article by Jeremy A. Sabloff and Robert E. Smith entitled "The Importance of Both Analytic and Taxonomic Classification in the Type–Variety System" (Sabloff and Smith 1969[†]). Sabloff and Smith (1969:278) suggested an advantage of the system was that it "is dependent on the recognition and use of *all* attributes of the ceramic collection" (emphasis added), which indicated that they did not have clearly in mind a problem in need of a solution. They rationalized their position on the type–variety system's advantages by noting that different kinds of attributes distinguish between (1) *wares* (paste composition, surface finish), which were viewed as having larger temporal–spatial distributions than types and varieties; (2) *types* (decorative technique, vessel form), which were viewed as being indicative of a specific time interval in a specific region; (3) *varieties*—"minor, but significant, variations within a type [that may include attributes of] decorative technique and vessel form, or . . . change in design style or the use of a different temper"; and (4) *groups*—sets of "closely related [and] (roughly) contemporaneous types" (Sabloff and Smith 1969:278–279). Most of these units were supposed to have particular time–space positions, but why they *should* have such positions was not specified, indicating the atheoretical nature of the system.

Sabloff and Smith (1969:280) suggested that "one of the major aims of [the type–variety system] should be to provide the readers with sufficient data, without undue repetition, for any approaches, be they ones of intersite comparisons or total reanalysis of the ceramic data, that they may care to take in future studies." Thus, "emphasis on the identification of types and the criteria used in establishing them and differentiating them from other types and varieties" was recommended (Sabloff and Smith 1969:280). These statements, too, suggest there was a strong atheoretical aspect underlying the system as conceived by Sabloff and Smith because the results of applying the system could be used for solving any problem and answering any question. Not surprisingly, then, the procedure and rules for selection of criteria for creating types and varieties were unspecified. The notion of an ideal, all-purpose classification had died decades earlier in biology (e.g., Hull 1970; Mayr 1981, 1982, 1987, 1995), but it was alive and well in the article by Sabloff and Smith.

A *mode* was defined by Sabloff and Smith (1969:279, 281) as a "selected attribute or cluster of attributes which display significance in their own right." Thus, they did not follow Rouse's (1939) seminal definition of a mode as a single character state, and it is also unclear if their modes were ideational or empirical units. A mode, they noted, could be used "to delimit an area of occurrence, to mark a specific period in time, or to emphasize a design style" (Sabloff and Smith 1969:281). Here, modes seem to have been empirical. Types were to be delineated by a set of "principal identifying modes [that] immediately give the reader an idea of the criteria which the archaeologist has used to identify a type" (Sabloff and Smith 1969:282). This statement implied that modes were ideational, but it failed to clearly distinguish the necessary and sufficient conditions for unit membership from characters that happen to be displayed by unit members. Whether types were construed as being ideational or empirical thus was unclear, particularly when Sabloff and Smith (1969:283) indicated that it "remains to be seen" if new specimens disrupt the structure and content of the—by implication, extensionally defined—units (see also Dunnell (1971a[†], 1971b).

Summary

Empirical units can be a rather mixed bag. If a set of specimens is associated as a unit, it is a *group,* but only if the set represents the denotata of a theoretical unit will it be clearly explicable in theoretical terms and unambiguously capable of doing analytical work such as marking a point in time. The absence of theory, and thus of theoretical units, typically results in awkward trial-and-error efforts to sort specimens into meaningful groups capable of getting some analytical job done, such as measuring time (e.g., Thomas 1981). Such efforts are ripe for all sorts of counterclaims and arguments over the meaning of groups (e.g., Flenniken and Raymond [1986] vs. Thomas [1986]; Flenniken and Wilke [1989] and Wilke and Flenniken [1991] vs. Bettinger et al. [1991] and O'Connell and Inoway [1994]). In the absence of theory, there is no way to resolve the resulting debates. As we have seen, efforts to classify artifacts became narrowly focused on one problem—measuring time—in the second and third decades of the twentieth century. The ability of types to do the desired analytical work, to measure time, could be tested independently of the classification by using the principle of superposition.

Theoretical units circumvent the difficulties of empirical units. Theoretical units are units that *explicitly* specify the necessary and sufficient conditions for group membership; they are definitions that are atemporal and aspatial, though their *empirical manifestations* have distributions in time and space. The advantage of theoretical units is that the choice of criteria for sorting specimens is explicit and *theoretically linked to the problem to be solved.* Further, insofar as two analysts agree that the position of notches on projectile points, for example, is analytically important and agree on the distinction between basal notches and side notches (e.g., Beck and Jones 1989), they will *identify*—Kluckhohn's (1960) "assign"—the same specimen in a collection of artifacts as a member of the same particular theoretical unit. All specimens will be inspected for the presence or absence of notches and their placement on individual specimens. Because the definitions can be written before the collection is sorted into internally homogeneous piles of like-looking specimens, the *intensional* choice of the kinds of variables to use in constructing the theoretical units—that is, in writing the definitions—must be made explicit.

Here is where the research goals of the analyst come into play: Which of the infinite number of attributes are to be included? *Theory justifies the choices.* If one wishes to compare assemblages of stone tools in terms of function, then one would need to use a set of functional artifact types, with types—theoretical units—defined by functional attributes to describe (measure) the assemblages in a relevant fashion. Functional attributes such as use-wear, edge angle, and similar kinds of variables that attend object–environment interaction—Rouse's (1939) modes—would be theoretical units. Stylistic modes (Dunnell 1978) would be inappropriate for constructing functional types. Culture historians regularly failed to make such distinctions and instead simply offered functional "interpretations" of types (groups of like-looking specimens) that were largely stylistic (*sensu* Dunnell 1978) and had passed the historical significance test. Another advantage to building theoretical units is that their definitions can be expanded by adding a new kind or dimension of variation (e.g., kind of material) if it is determined that that particular variable (dimension) is important to the analysis. Similarly, if it is found that a dimension is irrelevant or has been inconsistently applied (e.g., Beck and Jones 1989), it can be omitted.

After about 1916, culture historians' interests quickly became focused on one aspect of types—their ability to measure time. That ability was founded in superposition, itself a misinterpreted concept that, with its focus on strata, was to introduce another significant problem—the recognition of assemblages—that we briefly introduced early in this chapter and will take up in more detail in Chapter 6. Lacking theory, superposed artifacts, believed to reflect the passage of time—an empirical generalization—had to be sorted by trial and error until each pile occupied a more or less distinctive position on the temporal continuum. The appearance that culture history was scientific was maintained by the testability of proposed chronologies of artifact types.

Thus, whether types were empirical or theoretical units was of little immediate concern, despite Rouse's (1939, 1952, 1960) regular efforts to point out the importance of the distinction. The fact that types, once properly constructed, could be used to measure time was sufficient. Such units were warranted on the basis of common sense, particularly on the basis of the popularity principle. That this principle had never been consciously and empirically tested was not pointed out until fifty years after its adoption (Adams 1968:1188). Kroeber's (1919) study was construed by him as a test of the popularity principle, but it was not truly a test. He proclaimed that the variation he measured was "purely stylistic" because it did "not vary in purpose" (Kroeber 1919:239), but he provided only minimal theoretical warrant for this proclamation. More significantly, although he suggested that the curves he derived denoted change and underlying "drifts and tendencies," the curves fluctuated more than the popularity principle allowed. This, Kroeber (1919:242) thought, resulted from his use of small samples; larger samples would have resulted in "smoothing and increased regularity of the plotted curves . . . and some segregation of the present irregularities into historically true ones." This is known today as evolutionary "drift" (e.g., Dunnell 1980; O'Brien and Holland 1990).

The essentialist metaphysic was reinforced by such commonsense, ethnologically based understanding and simultaneously (1) usurped the necessity of a materialist metaphysic for studying change (reinforced by the failure to distinguish between empirical and theoretical units) and (2) demanded discontinuous units that permitted (and themselves demanded) differences to be detected. Change might have been conceived in materialist terms as slow and continuous modifications of variants, but perceptions of change were measured as differences between discontinuous units. This paradox also permeated the one truly archaeological method that was developed by culture historians—seriation—one of the topics to which we next turn our attention.

Note

1. Debate over the species concept and its utility for determining phyletic relation is still going on (see references in Cracraft 1989 and Mayr 1996).

5

Artifact Classification and Seriation

The mid-1930s through the early 1950s were, in several respects, the heyday of the culture history paradigm. Superposed artifact collections and the development and perfection of typologies allowed culture historians to identify various prehistoric cultures and to place them in their proper time–space positions. Various federally sponsored relief projects poured a huge amount of money and labor into archaeology during this period, especially in the Southeast (e.g., Haag 1985, 1986; Jennings 1985; Lyon 1996), and as a result the data base for many areas grew geometrically. By 1935, the discipline had become sufficiently formalized that the Society for American Archaeology was founded in an attempt to solidify and align the efforts of avocational and professional archaeologists (Griffin 1985; Guthe 1967).

On the methodological front, things were moving at a rapid clip. Seriation had become one of the backbones of archaeology, especially in the Southwest, though it tended to play a lesser role than percentage stratigraphy during the 1920s and early 1930s, as evidenced by the work of Ford (1935b), Hawley (1934), Roberts (1927), Schmidt (1928), and Vaillant (1930, 1931, 1935b). As we discuss below, seriation reemerged and underwent some major development and refinement in the 1940s and early 1950s, in large part as a result of the efforts of Ford. Various problems with classification that had been built into culture history from the start reached a boiling point as several of the leading figures in the paradigm, including Ford, argued over the basic procedure for, as well as the meaning of, the various units that resulted from building typologies. Though it was unclear at the time, those debates signified the beginning of the end of culture history as the leading paradigm in Americanist archaeology.

We begin this chapter with a review of Ford's work and his epistemological position and then turn attention to various developments that occurred in seriation. Then we review one of the major substantive contributions to the paradigm that appeared early in the 1950s—a contribution that serves as an excellent vehicle for examining the basic tenets of, as well as the contradictions built into, culture history. In the final section, we discuss the important debates over artifact classification that appeared in the 1950s. Discussion of the classification of larger units variously known as cultures, foci, or phases is reserved for Chapter 6.

James A. Ford

When Ford began working in the Southeast in the late 1920s and early 1930s, his formal training had been minimal. What he learned of archaeology in his early years was the result of working with Smithsonian archaeologists Henry B. Collins (1926, 1927a, 1927b) in Mississippi and Frank M. Setzler (1933a, 1933b, 1934) in Louisiana. Collins, along with several colleagues, spoke at the seminal *Conference on Southern Pre-History* sponsored by the National Research Council and held in Birmingham, Alabama, in December 1932—a meeting Ford attended. Collins (1932:40) described how the geographic distribution of historical-period pottery types in Mississippi aligned with the distribution of various ethnographically documented tribes, just as he had five years earlier (Collins 1927a), and he emphasized the importance of the direct historical approach to solving chronological problems. Winslow Walker, who a year earlier had begun excavating beneath the large mound at Troyville, in Catahoula Parish, Louisiana (Walker 1936), noted at the conference that "It is not permissible to assume that all [artifacts] are the products of the same makers, merely because they happen to be found in the same mound or village site. Unless the method of excavation employed is such that the exact vertical as well as horizontal position of all the artifacts can be determined, it is useless to attempt further classification based on typology alone" (Walker 1932:45). Matthew Stirling (1932) underscored the arbitrary nature of culture areas and the fact that one culture would "influence" another's development. Ford would, a few short years later, use many of the same words and notions to discuss his findings in Louisiana.

Armed with what he heard at the conference and with the training he had received from working with Collins both in the Southeast and in Alaska, Ford (1935a, 1936b) developed what we term his four tenets: (1) geographically adjacent sites in Louisiana and Mississippi contained rather different kinds of pottery (Ford 1936a:4), just as Kroeber had observed in the Southwest; (2) gradual change and development in culture was an undeniable fact (Ford 1935a:8–9, 1936a:5); (3) the archaeological measurement of time—the determination of chronological relations—was of utmost importance (Ford 1936a:7, 1936b:102); and (4) stratigraphy could help solve the chronology problem, though few stratified sites were known in the region (Ford 1935a:9, 1936b:103). Early on, Ford was explicit about his view of culture, culture change, and how to document culture change: "Culture is in reality a set of ideas as to how things should be done and made. It is in a continuous state of evolutionary change since it is constantly influenced both by inventions from within and the introduction of new ideas from without the group. . . . All [artifacts] were subject to the principle of constant change, hence those on any one site are *more or less* peculiar to the time that produced them" (Ford 1935a:9). Because revealing the culture history of an area was a primary goal of archaeology, and because a chronology was required to reveal that history, Ford (1935a:9, 1936a:6) concluded that he had to "develop a measure of time in terms of cultural change" that could, once stratified sites were found, be tested via excavation. Like many of his predecessors in the Southwest and his contemporaries in the Southeast, Ford chose pottery as the medium for his measurement scale.

From the perspective of the late twentieth century, it appears that Ford independently invented various techniques (he did not reference some of the relevant literature in his early works), but later, after receiving his Ph.D., he integrated the work of others into his own. Beginning in the late 1940s, his references were more thorough, and his terminology was more in line with that of his contemporaries. It is quite likely that Fred B. Kniffen introduced Ford to some of the techniques that had been worked out in the Southwest. Kniffen, a geographer, had been trained in large part by Kroeber at the University of California. He had witnessed Kroeber, along with his fellow students William Duncan Strong and Anna Gayton, ordering Max Uhle's pottery collection from Peru, using phyletic seriation, frequency seriation, and the little evidence of superposition available to them in Uhle's notes (Gayton 1927; Gayton and Kroeber 1927; Kroeber 1925a, 1925b; Kroeber and Strong 1924a, 1924b; Strong 1925). Thus Kniffen (1938) was familiar with such methods as seriation and percentage stratigraphy. He arrived at Louisiana State University in 1929 to begin a distinguished career in the department of geology and geography (anthropology was later included in the title). Ford was accepted as a research assistant and student at LSU in 1934, more or less under Kniffen's sponsorship. In the foreword to his "Analysis of Indian Village Site Collections from Louisiana and Mississippi," Ford (1936a:3) stated that Kniffen's "constant encouragement, advice, and frank and penetrating criticism have been invaluable." The evidence is circumstantial, but if Kniffen truly gave Ford advice and criticism, it is inconceivable that he wouldn't have taught him the basics of seriation and percentage stratigraphy.

Recall that (1) Kidder had been a student of Reisner, who in turn was a student of Petrie, one of the originators of developmental seriation (Petrie 1899, 1901, 1904), and (2) Kidder's arrangements either were of the developmental, or phyletic, sort (e.g., Kidder 1915, 1917a) or were—like Nelson's—based on the superposition of his samples (e.g., Kidder and Kidder 1917) and thus comprised percentage stratigraphy. Ford eventually did something rather different. Initially, however, Ford (1935b:1–2) mimicked—without citing them—the efforts of Kidder and Nelson and distinguished seven "decoration complexes," or groups "of pottery decorations characteristic of an area at a definite period of time," in northeastern Louisiana and southwestern Mississippi. Each complex consisted of several categories—generally termed "types" by Ford—of pottery. He established the temporal relations among three of the complexes by excavating the Peck Village site in Catahoula Parish, Louisiana. He used pottery decoration as the basis for his categories because it "is the most prominent feature of design which is readily determined from potsherds" (Ford 1935b:7; see also Ford 1936a:15). He assumed that changes in the styles of pottery denoted temporal difference and that "Questions of the degree of variation from the mean allowable within a type must in large degree depend upon the judgment and experience of the classifier" (Ford 1935b:8; see also Ford 1936a:18). This suggests that while his units were classes, at the very least the definitions of his units often were of the extensional sort.

In his excavation of Peck Village, Ford used arbitrary levels, the thicknesses of which were determined by the amount of material collected; each level—termed a "section" by Ford—contained "an appreciable amount of material" (Ford 1935b:6). Given his belief that culture change was continuous and gradual, it is not surprising that he used such an excavation technique. As he observed years later, "It is as absurd to dig automatically in ten-centimeter levels as it is to separate collections only by visible stratification" (Ford 1962:45). This is so, in short, because such vertical units are depositional accidents or accidents of where one locates a datum plane to which arbitrary levels are tied, given that culture change is continuous through the vertical sedimentary record. Ford no doubt later discounted Emil Haury's (1937b:20–21) suggestion that pottery sherds recovered from refuse pits provided the best and clearest evidence of the "traits which constituted one phase ceramically" because such pits took such a short time to fill that material change was unlikely.

Thus, Ford's excavation method was implicitly founded on the notions that more deeply buried artifacts were older than those that were buried in more shallow positions and, uniquely, that the thickness of his arbitrary levels was unimportant. One needed sufficiently large samples to monitor culture change without fear of sample-size effects, but they did not have to come from strata of equal thickness. After excavating his samples from Peck Village, Ford plotted the proportional frequency of each pottery type in each level/section of each excavation unit. He then used percentage stratigraphy and plotted the proportion of "marker type" pottery for each of his three decoration complexes per level/section. A *marker type* was a kind of pottery that "typified," was "peculiar to," or "statistically dominated" the pottery of a particular decoration complex. Ford noted that the proportions of marker types changed monotonically from the bottom to the top of each unit and concluded that the complexes (and by implication the marker types) must therefore be chronologically sensitive. Thus, he explicitly tested the chronological significance of the decoration complexes and their included marker types and simultaneously produced an empirical— but not a theoretical—warrant for the popularity principle.

Ford (1935b:23) noted that the "most important implication of the Peck Village situation is that with the passage of time, while deposition of the [unstratified] midden was in progress, the ceramic art of the inhabitants was slowly changing." There was "no typological connection" between the two most frequently represented of the three decoration complexes, so Ford (1935b:24) concluded that "the change in ceramic art is probably not the result of local evolution of [one complex] out of [the other], but rather [it was a] gradual replacement of complexes, [as] indicated by the smooth changes in proportion" of the marker types. "Replacement" was a commonsensical word with no attached theory and thus had no real explanatory power. Shortly thereafter, Ford's (1936a, 1938) observations led him to focus his attention on developing methods for using surface-collected materials to measure time. In brief, he wanted a means of distinguishing "the relative ages of the different schools of ceramic art" (Ford 1936a:10). Excavation was destructive and nonreplicable; establishing chronological control without excavating allowed "more intelligent observation" of excavated material if its temporal significance was known before it was excavated (Ford 1936a:7).

For his study of surface-collected sherds from Louisiana and Mississippi, published as *Analysis of Village Site Collections from Louisiana and Mississippi,* Ford (1936a[†]) modified his original classification scheme and designated three dimensions for study—motif (plan of decoration), elements (means to express motif), and manner of application (arrangement of elements)—each of which had a series of possible expressions designated by numbers. The numbers designating the particular expression of each dimension were placed in the order listed and separated by semicolons. Specimens with multiple features to be listed could be designated by listing one over the other—separated by a horizontal line—in the number sequence. This system, like that of Colton and Hargrave (1937) for northern-Arizona rim sherds (Chapter 4), was paradigmatic, or dimensional, in structure (Dunnell 1971b). Ford's units were classes, meaning the significata were explicit. They were particular combinations of attributes and were immutable, atemporal, and aspatial; that is, the symbols 41;21;5 denoted a class and specified the necessary and sufficient conditions for the membership of a specimen within that class, regardless of the temporal–spatial location of the specimen. Ford's (1936a:23) system allowed him to tally the frequency of any attribute—be it a particular motif, an element, or an application—as well as the frequency of representation of any class. That is, the number of specimens displaying a particular attribute or the number of specimens displaying a particular combination of attributes—the denotata—could be tallied.

Ford (1936a:250) believed that pottery complexes differed from each other as a result of either temporal difference or geographical isolation. He knew the basic chronological sequence of his surface samples based on superposition of the marker types at Peck Village and a few other sites in Louisiana and southern Arkansas that had been excavated recently. This allowed him to integrate and relate his site-specific assemblages into a time–space distributional chart (Ford 1936a:271). He mentioned the possibility that trade and diffusion could be detected from such charts (Ford 1936a:252; recall Spier's [1917a, 1918a, 1919] similar suggestions) and concluded that the chronology should be checked by excavation (Ford 1936a:270). The net result was that Ford proposed an innovative way to classify pottery; his units at the scale of discrete objects—pottery sherds— were classes, the distributions of which could be plotted in time and space. But they were ad hoc units because they were built extensively by trial and error rather than being theoretically informed constructs.

In "A Chronological Method Applicable to the Southeast," Ford (1938:262[†]) stated that the "repeated occurrence of a certain decoration [complex] at separate sites [indicates] the decoration [complex] represents a real and significant type." Thus, one might think that at the scale of multiple types (something similar to Colton and Hargrave's [1937] *ware*), Ford's units were "real" because they were inherent in the data. This is incorrect. It is true that Ford, like virtually all of his contemporaries, wanted to discuss the history of "ancient cultures" and "different groups of people" (Ford, 1935a), both of which are ethnographic units of the essentialist sort. But Ford (1938:263) was clear that "it cannot be accepted that these ceramic complexes will represent different cultures or culture phases. . . . What the method attempts to do is to use ceramic decoration, probably the most flexible of the remaining cultural features, as 'type fossils' to distinguish the passage of time." That his archaeological units might represent ethnographic units of a particular sort was an interpretation—a commonsense warrant—and represented his first encounter with the essentialist–materialist dichotomy. He ignored it here because he recognized neither it nor its significance.

For Ford (1938:262), regularly associated decoration types represented a decoration complex that, if found over a restricted area, in turn represented "a distinct time horizon. [Once decoration complexes are determined, such] stylistic time horizons that have existed in [an] area may now be logically separated." Ford (1938) did not make it clear that his decoration complexes comprised marker types that had passed the historical significance test. While a horizon style represented by a decoration complex might be construed as a synchronic slice of time, clearly this is not true in practice. Ford's (1938:261) decoration complexes are shown as boxes in Figure 5.1 and were meant to represent spans of time such as the "length of tenure of a village site" or "the time when one complex of styles was in vogue"; simply put, they represented "periods"—not points—along the continuous dimension of time. Ford's illustration implies that the appearance or disappearance of a style—a marker type—or decoration complex denotes the position on the continuous time scale where boundaries should be drawn between periods. Such criteria for defining period boundaries differ from those apparently used by Kroeber (e.g., 1916a, 1916b; see Chapter 3) for constructing internally homogeneous–externally heterogeneous periods and appear to align better with Kidder's (e.g., 1936b) nodes or peaks of occurrence. Elements of both can, however, be perceived in Ford's earlier (Ford 1935b) and his later (Ford 1949; Ford and Quimby 1945; Ford and Willey 1940) work.

Ford emphasized several important points in his 1938 article. First, samples must be representative "of the full range of the people's ceramic styles" and thus perhaps should be collected from "village refuse" rather than from burials, as grave goods were not likely to be representative (Ford 1938:260). Second, like Kidder and others working in the Southwest, Ford indicated that decorative complexes evolved from one into another. His graphic model (Figure 5.1) did not make this clear for several reasons. It did not indicate that pottery type "*1*" was different in each complex, although this was implied in the text (Ford 1938:262). While pottery type "*2*" might link complex A and B, it might be more abundant in one than the other and thereby *mark* the former. Third, to determine which way time was going one had to study historical- and protohistoric-period collections (just as Nelson, Kroeber, Spier, and Kidder had done) to establish which decoration complex was the most recent. This was the direct historical approach. Fourth, Ford indicated that stratigraphic data could be used

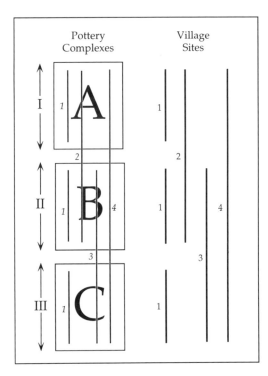

Pottery   Village
Complexes   Sites

Figure 5.1. James Ford's model of pottery-decoration complexes (A–C), pottery types (*1–4*), and village sites (1–4). Some "style types," as Ford referred to them, such as those represented by *1,* might occur in only one complex, though there is nothing to keep them from extending through two (*2* and *3*) or three decoration complexes (*4*). Village occupations (1–4) can act in similar fashion (after Ford 1938).

to test the results of applying his method. Ford (1936b:103) had earlier remarked that stratigraphically superposed collections constitute "the best basis for relating time changes," a position he would retain throughout his career. He did not use the term "seriation" in the 1930s.

A few years later, as a result of his continuing attempts to place pottery collections recovered from different sites within their proper temporal positions relative to one another, Ford perfected his graphic technique of percentage stratigraphy, eventually producing bar graphs that showed the waxing and waning of a style's popularity at a glance (e.g., Ford and Quimby 1945; Ford and Willey 1940). The analytical technique of using bar graphs to manually sort collections into what was hoped to be a chronological sequence was used by one of Ford's collaborators in the Southeast (Willey 1949). It was also adopted in the Southwest, where Paul S. Martin and colleagues were seeking "trends within pottery types and any other significant observations that might accrue from a comprehensive visual presentation of data [and thus they] decided to employ a graphic method similar to that used by James A. Ford" (Martin et al. 1949:196). Their continued use of that technique (Martin et al. 1949:192–193; Martin and Rinaldo 1950a:531, 1950b:372–373; Rinaldo 1950:95) was founded in part on their belief that the method "gives a more precise picture of the changes through time than the less complex curve that represents the differences between phases only" (Rinaldo 1950:94) and because it provided "a more complete conception of the changes in popularity of each of the various pottery types" during the span of individual cultural phases (Martin and Rinaldo 1950b:370).

Importantly, Martin and his colleagues examined the variation in proportions of pottery types recovered from different contexts within individual sites. On the one hand, when they found that "the frequencies of wares were either erratic or fairly constant, and, when plotted, either by actual number of sherds or by percentages, did not approach a normal frequency curve," they concluded that a site "was occupied but once and for only a short time" (Martin 1938:271). On the other hand, when they seriated collections from individual houses within a pueblo site on the basis of their conjecture that all of the houses "were not occupied at the same time" (Martin et al. 1949:191), they sometimes found that they were able to confirm that proposition (Martin et al. 1949:198) and to demonstrate "that the position of each house or room in the series represents the approximate order in time in which each house was last occupied" (Martin and Rinaldo 1950b:530). They often checked the results of their seriation of pottery assemblages from individual houses with dendrochronological and stratigraphic data.

Ford conducted research for his dissertation as a member of Gordon R. Willey's Virú Valley (Peru) Project, famous for its seminal study of settlement patterns (Willey 1953c). Lesser known—or at least less often cited—is Ford's (1949) contribution to the project. A decade after his initial work in the Southeast, Ford was still concerned with establishing control over time. In his dissertation, later published as *Cultural Dating of Prehistoric Sites in Virú Valley, Peru* (Ford 1949[†]), Ford, for the first time in his career, performed a frequency seriation, using the bar-graph technique he had developed when using percentage-stratigraphy data. But like Willey (1949), Ford used superposed collections and percentage stratigraphy data as the basis for his chronology and then seriated his surface collections by "interdigitating" (Willey 1949:82, figure 101) them with the master chronology. We use the term *interdigitation* to distinguish this technique from that of sorting or ordering collections purely on the basis of their artifact content—termed seriation—without reference to superpositional data.

Ford (1949) presented arguments regarding, and methods testing, the reliability and validity of the chronological implications of his surface samples. Some of the arguments echoed statements he had made a decade earlier (Ford 1935a, 1935b, 1936a, 1936b, 1938), but some were new, such as his clever assertion that the problem that large pots produce more sherds than do small pots can be circumvented by shifting the scale of analysis from pottery types to attributes of pottery (Ford 1949:37). He followed Brew (1946) in noting that the utility of an artifact classification scheme resides in its ability to measure "culture history in time and space. . . . to measure culture and trace its change through time and over area" (Ford 1949:38; see also Ford 1940); more explicitly, a proper type "is primarily a time–space measuring tool" (Ford 1949:40). Thus, Ford (1949:38) noted that the utility of a classification "must be tested by the question of how well it serves [its] end purpose." Ford (1949, 1952:328–331) grappled with the assumptions underlying the commonsense conception of culture change and contact as a braided stream, but he lacked the tools—the theory—to help explain the model, though his discussion helped illuminate its structure.

Ford made a number of important points, some of which echoed his statements of the 1930s: (1) "culture [is] a stream of ideas" (Ford 1949:38); (2) within a restricted geographic area, cultural change normally is gradual—there is a "slow shifting of norms"; (3) abrupt or rapid change suggests "external pressure" (Ford 1949:39); (4) culture history has the appearance of biological history or evolution, but because (i) genes only flow down through generations whereas (ii) ideas flow up as well as down between generations and also flow between individuals within a generation, evidence of evolutionary or phyletic relations must await the establishment of chronological relations (Ford 1949:39); (5) types are "artificial units" created by the archaeologist "for one purpose: to serve as a measure of time and space" (Ford 1949:40); (6) types reflect to some unknown and probably unknowable degree the ideas or cultural norms of the people who made the artifacts; and (7) because of all of the above, properly distinguished types should display approximately normal frequency distributions through time. Thus a "type will appear to have been made first in very small quantities. As time passes it reaches its period of maximum popularity, more or less great. Then it declines in popularity and finally vanishes" (Ford 1949:41).

The crucial point here is that the last statement is simply the popularity principle. Ford, like his predecessors, lacked a theoretical rationale for the normal frequency distributions displayed by his types, and thus he was forced to fall back on common sense. To Ford (1949:40), a "type is nothing more than material that exhibits a high degree of similarity in the features that reflect the influence of ideas prevailing in the ancient cultures. Each type established will . . . grade insensibly into other materials." Types were extensionally derived from the continuously changing culture trait known as pottery. As a result, different analysts may place the same specimen in different types "without being in essential disagreement at all" (Ford

1949:41). While Ford's discussion hinted at an explanation in the sense of a theoretical model—transmission of ideas influences the frequency of their empirical manifestations—he neither elaborated on it nor developed a theoretical model of it in evolutionary terms such as those that had been used by Kidder.

Despite his lack of grounding in theory, Ford displayed tremendous insight into various critical issues. He noted that the particular frequency pattern displayed by a type is created in part by how that type is constructed by the archaeologist. Thus, how the units termed types are constructed might produce less than perfect normal curves (a point later emphasized in a review of Ford's results [Bennyhoff 1952]). Ford (1949) recognized that every archaeological phenomenon is a palimpsest at some scale (e.g., Brooks 1982). As a result, some of the predicted fluctuations in frequency curves (Kroeber 1919; Neiman 1995) will be muted by the diachronic nature of the samples (Teltser 1995).[1] Further, sampling error could create inexplicable features in the curve, as could disturbance to the deposits producing the samples. Ford (1949:49) thus smoothed his frequency-seriation curves by simple inspection of the distributions as opposed to using any statistical procedure. Again, his lack of knowledge of particular analytical tools—here, statistics—is revealing. This deficiency in methodological sophistication ultimately led to some accurate criticisms, but simultaneously Ford's work was misconstrued.

Clifford Evans (1951:271) was impressed with Ford's (1949) "fundamental contribution to theoretical and applied archaeological methodology." So was J. A. Bennyhoff (1952:231, 233), who found Ford's bar graphs to be "ingenious" and his graphic procedure of interdigitation to be "one of the foremost advances in American archaeology." This was an accurate evaluation because such a graphic technique had been very rarely used prior to Ford's (1949) work. Ford had approximated such graphs a few years earlier (Ford and Quimby 1945), but that was to illustrate the percentage-stratigraphy data at a single site. Similarly, most previous graphs, while of a form different than Ford's, also were to illustrate percentage-stratigraphy data. Seriating percentage-stratigraphy data from multiple sites via interdigitation originated (so far as we can determine) with Ronald L. Olson's (1930) work on materials from the Channel Islands off the coast of southern California. Olson earned his master's degree from the University of Washington under the tutelage of Leslie Spier and his Ph.D. from Berkeley under the direction of A. L. Kroeber. It is thus clear where Olson's ideas originated. Rouse (1939) used the same analytic and graphic technique and explicitly acknowledged that he was mimicking Olson. Only Ford's version of the technique was the subject of detailed comment.

Ford's (1949) statements on culture change and how it could be measured were later misconstrued as "normative theory" and characterized, along with those of other culture historians, as an "aquatic view of culture" that could offer no more of an explanation of culture change than to suggest that the flowing stream of ideas "periodically 'crystallized' . . . resulting in distinctive and sometimes striking cultural climaxes which allow us to break up the continuum of culture into cultural phases" (Binford 1965:204). Ford's aquatic view is apparent in his writings, but the normative aspect—expressed as periodic crystallization producing discrete cultural phases—clearly is not. Kidder's (1936b:xx) "recognizable nodes of individuality" denoting ceramic periods could be appropriately criticized in this fashion. Ford recognized the continuous flow of culture streams and created his decoration complexes and marker types as merely arbitrary constructs—ideational units—meant to measure the current; his percentage stratigraphy and frequency-seriation curves showed the current. In his summary of Virú Valley prehistory (Ford 1949:fig. 8), he followed the lead of his predecessors and sliced the culture stream into *arbitrary* periods and then described the ceramic complex of each. Recall that Kroeber (1916a, 1916b) apparently sliced up the continuum somewhat on the basis of maximizing within-group homogeneity and between-group heterogeneity, but his slicing was not explicitly intentional in this respect. Hence his periods had the appearance of being arbitrarily sliced out of a continuum.

Ford (1949:45) assumed "each pottery type selected by the classifiers from the ceramics made in Virú had undergone a popularity cycle through time that resembled a normal distribution." Then, each site-specific set of percentage stratigraphy data was aligned on a common graph and interdigitated with every other set of such data, each being expanded or compressed "in order to make it fit the others" (Ford 1949:45) in a manner that resulted in the frequency distribution of each type approximating a normal frequency distribution. The final master graph was "presented as the story of the popularity of the pottery types described in Virú Valley" (Ford 1949:47). Ford (1949) divided the story into time periods, the dividing lines being placed where one or more types decreased in abundance or disappeared, and one or more types increased in abundance or first appeared.

In a slightly later publication (Phillips et al. 1951), the procedure involved moving the seriation graph for each spatial unit up and down "until the same [artifact] types showed comparable relative quantities" at the same vertical position across all graphs (Phillips et al. 1951:228). At those positions, a horizontal line was drawn—a slice was made—to break the graphed continuum into segments. The plethora of compromises that had to be made to ensure that all of the several graphs had the horizontal lines drawn in similar positions relative to type frequencies (see Phillips et al. 1951:228) underscored the arbitrary positional character of the dividing lines or slices. Precisely the same technique was being used in paleobiology at the time. The boundary between ancestral and descendent species was drawn by "select[ing] some feature or features of essential importance characterizing a genus or species and [drawing] the line where this character becomes dominant or universal in the evolving population," but this procedure was there, too, not an easily applied one (Simpson 1943:172–173).

Why slice the temporal continuum of culture into discrete periods, such as Ford, his predecessors (e.g., Kroeber, Kidder), and his contemporaries (e.g., Willey) did? Willey, who collaborated with Ford (Ford and Willey 1940, 1941) offered an explanation. He stated that "the appearance or disappearance of a pottery type [can be] capitalized upon as markers on the time scale" and cautioned that "the simple presence of a pottery type is not always enough to denote a specific period; its association with other types and its percentage relationships with these types in context [are] more often significant factors" (Willey 1949:4–5). Of the ceramic periods designated using such criteria, Willey (1949:4) suggested that while "the basic assumption [is] that culture changes through time[, t]he culture period is the means of measuring and describing cultural forms . . . as these have existed in a time continuity." It seems, therefore, that the notion was to create units of a larger scale than merely a type of artifact—a unit that was somehow equivalent to an ethnographically documented culture. The result was the conflation of the materialist and essentialist metaphysics.

Americanist archaeology of the 1920s through today has followed Willey's program, comparing the contents of periods. This forces one away from monitoring the differential persistence of variant forms through time, explicable in Darwinian evolutionary terms, to comparing the contents of temporal units and explaining their differences in transformational—historical and ethnological—terms (Dunnell 1980; O'Brien and Holland 1990; Teltser 1995). The ultimate reason for the slicing resides in the explanatory system implicitly held by culture historians, common sense as informed by anthropology and ethnology. Such a sense-making system uses essentialist categories for analysis, and it is a sense-making system from which Americanist archaeology has not yet divorced itself.

Seriation Matrices

At the same time that Ford (1949, 1952) was perfecting his techniques of chronological ordering—percentage stratigraphy, interdigitation, frequency seriation—and thinking about the cultural implications of such orderings, attempts were being made to render the technique of ordering more "objective" (Brainerd 1951a:303). Early attempts to use statistical techniques focused on a select few of the numerous historical types or known index fossils (e.g., Beals et al. 1945:166–167). How could all the data be considered simultaneously? With the help of statistician W. S. Robinson (1951), George W. Brainerd (1951a) developed a mathematical technique for measuring the *similarity* of pairs of assemblages. Using the new mathematical technique, "collections with closest similarity in qualitative or quantitative listing of types lie next to each other in the time sequence" because of the "concept that each type originates at a given time at a given place, [each type] is made in gradually increasing numbers as time goes on, then decreases in popularity until it becomes forgotten, never to recur in identical form" (Brainerd 1951a:304). Thus, the rationalization for arranging collections based on their similarity was the typical, commonsensical one—popularity. What was new was the explicit statement that similarity was conceived and thus measurable in quantitative terms. As Robinson (1951:293–294) put it, "similarity of percentages of different types of pottery in use is evidence that the deposits are close together in time, and dissimilarity of percentages is evidence that the deposits are far separated in time."

The mathematical "indexes of agreement" (Robinson 1951:294) that result from the quantitative measurement of similarity, which became known as "Brainerd–Robinson coefficients," are arranged in a matrix such that the largest values are closest to the diagonal and the lowest values are farthest from the diagonal and in the corner of the matrix. The technique has served as the foundation for numerous technical developments within (Marquardt 1978) and beyond seriation that we do not explore here. More important is Brainerd's discussion of the seriation method in general, which appeared as "The Place of Chronological Ordering in Archaeological Analysis" (Brainerd 1951a[†]).

Brainerd (1951a:302) began by echoing Ford's statement regarding the importance of sound chronologies both to writing culture history and to reconstructing culture (the latter having recently been called for rather loudly as a goal of archaeology by Walter Taylor [1948]): Artifact forms (types) must be placed in their correct time–space frameworks for either of these goals to be reliably and validly attained. Brainerd (1951a:302–303) underscored the importance of typology to such an endeavor; typologies need not be functionally oriented if one seeks to measure the temporal dimension with artifact form, and he implied that such "cultural interpretation" of artifacts as provided by functional typologies may weaken the validity of any chronological implications derived from such typologies. Brainerd's discussion reveals his atheoretical, commonsense rationalization of types; he elaborated on this rationalization a few months later (Brainerd 1951b). "Each [type] must be of such complexity in number and organization of attributes that the presence of an artifact belonging to it suggests that its makers lived in the same cultural milieu as that of makers of all other artifacts classified into the same sorting group; thus all artifacts classified from one group must have been made at approximately the same time and place" (Brainerd 1951a:304).

Types, to Brainerd, reflect "cultural standards" if they are marked by the presence of a "constant combination of [complex] attributes" (Brainerd 1951a:305). The constant recurrence of attribute combinations was to become the cornerstone of Spaulding's (1953b) "emic type" two years later. The notion came from Brainerd (1951b). For Brainerd (1951a:303), the archaeological utility of types construed as recurring combinations of attributes was to be evaluated on the basis of their "sensitivity and reliability" for distinguishing temporal–spatial differences, with "sensitivity" depending on "the judgment of the typologist." Clearly, Brainerd was using the same commonsense rationale as his contemporaries and predecessors. There was no theoretical basis for such an argument.

Brainerd did make some important points, not the least of which was spelling out the basic requirements that collections to be seriated must meet. Types must be historical, and while this cannot be known with certainty, if they can be seriated, then, he reasoned, they must be historical. Artifacts must represent the same "cultural milieu" (Brainerd 1951a:304), which ensures against a frequency seriation measuring ethnic (and perhaps spatial) variation rather than time. Seriated collections must be relatively synchronic; a fundamental assumption is "that each collection consists of artifacts made during a shorter time span than that covered by the whole group of [seriated] collections" (Brainerd 1951a:308–309). The effects on the solution of mixed collections and collections representing varied durations were to be explored via bootstrapping (Brainerd 1951a:309–310; see also Dunnell 1981), though Brainerd's suggestion that one may eventually be able to determine the relative time spans of different collections incorrectly presumed a constant rate of change. Assumptions underlying the method were explicit: (1) historical types will display unimodal frequency distributions through time (Robinson 1951:293); (2) similarity in form (measured as relative frequencies of types) denotes similarity in age (Brainerd 1951a:304); and (3) an order derived via frequency seriation does not indicate the direction of time's flow (Brainerd 1951a:312)—points all made earlier, if less eloquently, by Ford (1935b, 1936a, 1938, 1949).

A correct solution was represented by a unimodal frequency distribution—what Brainerd (1951a:305) termed "lenticular"—for each type and could represent a chronology but "does not conclusively rule out the possibility of factors other than chronology causing the sequence" (Brainerd 1951a:305). As Robinson (1951:294) noted, the assumption that similar percentages of types represented similar position in time was "an argument from consequence to cause, and it is therefore properly suspect." He therefore regularly referred to orders of assemblages resulting from application of the technique as "presumptively chronological" and cautioned "The existence of order among the data . . . is not enough to guarantee that the order is a temporal one. [It may be the result of] some other factor such as geographic proximity" (Robinson 1951:295). Robinson's warrant for the accuracy of the temporal inference was superposed collections. As we have seen, Brainerd's warrant was the popularity principle.

By the early 1950s, then, similarity in form—whether measured as similar kinds of specimens (Ford 1938; Kidder 1917a) or as similar frequencies of particular kinds within different assemblages (Brainerd 1951a; Ford 1949; Spier 1917a)—represented similarity in time. Formal difference was measured by creating typologies, the types of which were demonstrably, via stratigraphic context, temporally distinct portions of the temporal continuum of a cultural stream of ideas. Types were recurring combinations of attributes; the recurrence property was definitional and took care of the "shared" aspect of the conception of culture as shared ideas. The view that culture caused behavior took care of the "ideas" part of that conception. But types as purely ideational units used as tools for measuring time were thought to be insufficiently warranted. Thus, types as constructs of the archaeologist were rationalized by suggesting that they reflected the "ideas" in the mind of the makers of the artifacts, which in turn warranted subscription to the popularity principle. Again, this commonsense approach to explanation and rationalization reveals the atheoretical nature of the culture history paradigm.

The successes of culture history in constructing time–space frameworks set the stage for its own undoing. By midcentury, led by Taylor's (1948) unsympathetic critique, more and more archaeologists wanted to go beyond chronology and do what came to be known as cultural reconstruction and to get at the people responsible for the artifacts (recall that Taylor's was not the first such plea; Bennett [1943], Steward and Setzler [1938], and Strong [1936] had made similar pleas). As Frederick Barth (1950:339), for one, noted, "It can no longer be the archaeologist's ultimate ambition to make chronological charts of cultures; that can be done through cooperation between a chemist and a bulldozer." Barth's brief comment is typically overlooked by historians of archaeology, but it reflected the tone of the time. He argued, for example, that the study of culture change should focus on the adaptational history of cultures.

If culture was shared ideas, then for archaeology to be anthropological, techniques to get at the ideas of the prehistoric artisans had to be devised. Types that passed the historical significance test had an obvious purpose; they allowed the measurement of the passage of time and the building of chronologies. But the fact that those types might also reflect the ideas in the minds of the makers of the artifacts had served for years as a commonsense rationale for them above and beyond their obvious ability to perform chronological work. This was the metaphysical paradox identified by Brew (1946), though he did not recognize it in those terms. To illustrate the status of culture history in the mid-twentieth century and to help clarify the metaphysical paradox that had become built into it, we now turn to one of its most classic products.

The Lower Mississippi Alluvial Valley Survey

Many archaeological projects that had been initiated prior to World War II were completed shortly after its end.[2] One of the most revealing of these for gaining insight into the culture history paradigm was the collaborative study by Philip Phillips, James A. Ford, and James B. Griffin (1951) of the ceramic-period record of the Mississippi Valley from roughly the Missouri–Arkansas border on the north to the Arkansas–Louisiana border on the south (Figure 5.2). This study was a landmark both substantively and methodologically (Dunnell 1985), but in many respects it captured a major weakness of the culture history paradigm—the conflict between the commonsense, essentialist metaphysic and the materialist metaphysic. The historical significance of the work of Phillips et al. in the development of Americanist archaeology is documented in detail elsewhere (Dunnell 1985; O'Brien 1996b). Our critical examination here should in no way be construed as denigrating the pioneering efforts they made in furthering our understanding of a very complex archaeological record.

The greatest value of the monograph *Archaeological Survey in the Lower Mississippi Alluvial Valley, 1940–1947* (Phillips et al. 1951[†]), is found in the dialogue among its three authors, whose differences of opinion—founded in conflicting metaphysics—are highlighted in various sections of the report. The dialogue-like text provides much more interesting reading than do contemporary programmatic accounts (e.g., Phillips and Willey 1953) of how the culture history approach was to be operationalized.

All three authors worked on the classification of the pottery, but the final decisions on what to include and how to phrase the discussion resided with Griffin (Dunnell 1985). The authors conceived of a pottery type as demanding "hair-splitting," arbitrary decisions, because types have more or

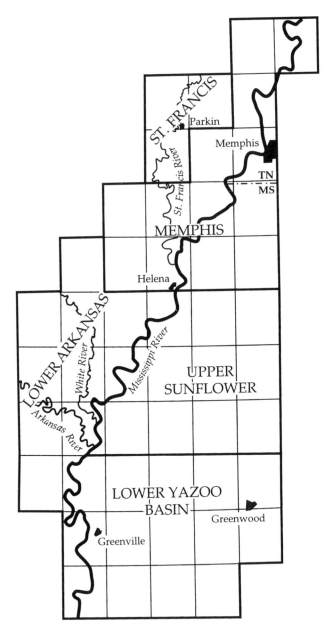

Figure 5.2. Map of the central Mississippi River valley showing the analytical quadrats employed during the Lower Mississippi Alluvial Valley Survey (after Phillips et al. 1951).

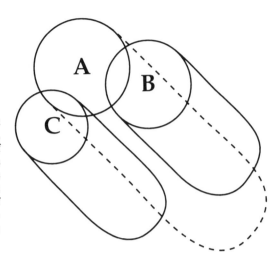

Figure 5.3. Model of the way in which Philip Phillips, James Ford, and James Griffin conceived of pottery types. Each letter denotes a type, the circle around it denotes the range of formal variation within the type, and the length of the cylinder represents the temporal range of a type (after Phillips et al. 1951).

less continuous distributions in time and space, as shown in Figure 5.3. A type to Phillips et al. was a stylistic norm that shifted so gradually across space and through time that the shifts were undetectable, making the distinctions of types arbitrary (Phillips et al. 1951:64). In that manner, their types were ideational units, the time–space boundaries of which were supposed to be limited in order to allow them to write culture history, specifically, to measure time–space differences. But the theoretical content of their types was compromised by their commonsense rationale; their types would "finally achieve cultural meaning" when they—through trial-and-error extensional redefinition—showed approximate "correspondence to ethnographic distributions in time and space" (Phillips et al. 1951:64).

Types were supposed to measure time; to determine whether they actually did so, one checked them with superposition. The ethnographic implications of the Phillips et al. types, however, were not testable because there were no clear constructional features that gave types those kinds of properties, nor were there any theoretically informed tests to ensure that the constructed types had them. Like Krieger (1944) and others with similar views, Phillips et al. reverted to commonsense rationalization. For example, change in "ceramic features" was conceived as gradual because types were supposed to reflect prehistoric norms, or what they termed "the consensus of community opinion" (Phillips et al. 1951:62) of what a proper-looking pot was. And "the characters we select as criteria for type definition . . . are bound to correspond to characters that might have served to distinguish one sort of pottery from another in the minds of the people who made and used it" (Phillips et al. 1951:63), but Phillips et al. never presented a warrant for determining what went on in the heads of the vessel manufacturers. Such information is impossible to generate from sherds.

They subjectively chose geographic "popularity" centers, out from which they expected types to gradually drift or "creep" into other types, a reflection not only of the extensional character of their type definitions but also of the notion that culture is transmitted and shared:

> Each community that had reached a certain level of sophistication in pottery-making will be found to have been maintaining side by side several different vessel styles [read *types*]. . . . Between these centers, styles vary and trend toward those of other centers in rough proportion to the distances involved, subject of course to ethnic distributions and geographic factors.
>
> Thus we have in mind the concept of a continuously evolving regional pottery tradition, showing a more or less parallel development in and around a number of centers, each of which employs a number of distinct but related styles, each style in turn being in process of change both areally and temporally. With this remarkably unstable material, we set out to fashion a key to the prehistory of the region. Faced with this three-dimensional flow, which seldom if ever exhibits "natural" segregation, and being obliged to reduce it to some sort of manageable form, we arbitrarily cut it into units. Such *created units of the ceramic continuum* are called *pottery types*. (Phillips et al. 1951:62–63)

Thus their types were arbitrary constructs founded on their notions of cultural change; types—rationalized as stylistic norms—were sections of the braided stream of cultures' shared ideas.

Phillips et al. constantly warned archaeologists of the dangers of blindly accepting and using their ceramic typology without revision. This warning indicates that their types were not classes but rather extensionally defined groups; the definitions thus should and would be modified as more specimens were examined, and eventually the groups might become classlike once their historical significance was confirmed. They also provided one of the most insightful comments on ceramic typologies ever written because it identified the same paradox identified by Brew (1946) a few years earlier—the difficulty of conceiving of change in materialist terms but structuring observations in essentialist terms:

> Exigencies of language require us to think and talk about pottery types as though they had some sort of independent existence. "This sherd *is* Baytown Plain." Upon sufficient repetition of this statement, the concept Baytown Plain takes on a massive solidity. The time comes when we are ready to fight for dear old Baytown. What we have to try to remember is that the statement really means something like this: "This sherd sufficiently resembles material which *for the time being* we have elected to call

Baytown Plain." Frequent repetition of this and similar exorcisms we have found to be extremely salutary during the classificatory activities. (Phillips et al. 1951:66)[3]

The breadth and extent of this paradox was so far-reaching that one of the collaborators was made to publish some of his work elsewhere (Ford 1952). It is important, then, to examine this paradox internal to Phillips et al.'s conception of types and the purposes for which they were suited.

The section of Phillips et al. (1951:219–236) on seriation and inter-digitation—the latter serving as the major basis for the chronologies—re-iterated much of what is found in Ford's (1949) Virú Valley report, which is not surprising since it was authored largely by Ford. But it included considerations of the spatial dimension not found in such detail in his earlier works. The authors "went to great pains to set up and adapt each type [as a measurement unit] for a continuous stream of changing cultural ideas" (Phillips et al. 1951:22) across space and through time. They believed that pottery types would display unimodal or normal frequency distributions through time—the popularity principle—and that "all the pottery-type frequency curves [will] be different in each part of the area on each time horizon, and a distinct pattern will appear when each part of the area is viewed through time" (Phillips et al. 1951:223). The metaphor of a braided stream makes this clear: Each individual trickle contains different proportions of the main stream at different positions as one moves down the braid and the trickles variously join, mingle, and separate into new trickles. Thus, while Phillips et al. (1951:224) refrained from drawing "iso-ceramic lines," they divided the valley into five arbitrary subareas on the basis of the distribution of pottery types dating to the latest time horizon; to return to the metaphor, they arbitrarily defined five trickles of the braided stream at one point along its continuous flow. They produced frequency seriations of pottery in each of the five areas and then correlated them by aligning relative frequencies of each of the five graphs "until the same types showed comparable relative quantities" (Phillips et al. 1951:228). Thus, they not only explicitly recognized the role of diffusion and community interaction in the flowing braided stream of culture, but they also recognized the fact that the spatial dimension must be controlled; otherwise, variation in ethnic origin or in cultural tradition could obscure the temporal meaning of a seriation. Lipo et al. (1995) have recently shown the wiseness of Phillips et al.'s (1951) intent, as well as where they erred.

In his slightly later monograph entitled *Measurements of Some Prehistoric Design Developments in the Southeastern States,* Ford (1952[†]) was explicit about the influence of the spatial dimension and diffusion on the frequency distribution of types through time. There will be a time lag, he

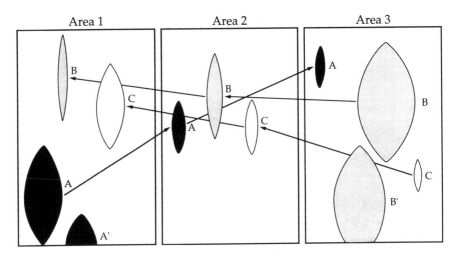

Figure 5.4. James Ford's model of the diffusion of types across space, illustrating change in frequency and time lag—phenomena Ford believed must be considered in making temporal alignments of relative chronologies. Each letter and kind of shading denotes a distinct type (after Ford 1952).

noted (Figure 5.4), between the age of a type in its area of origination and its age in the area(s) to which it diffuses—later formally termed the "Doppler effect" by Deetz and Dethlefsen (1965[†]; see also Dethlefsen and Deetz [1966]). Ford suggested that the direction of diffusion could be ascertained (1) by the decreasing relative frequency of a trait as one moved away from its area of origin or (2) more "reliably" by the detection of ancestral forms of the trait in the area of origin. In more modern terms, primitive attributes or forms should be found in the area of origin, whereas attributes or forms derived from the trait will perhaps display wider distributions. The validity of the spatial distribution of a trait or form as a measure of its age had been seriously questioned before (Dixon 1928:69–72). But overall, Ford's (1952) discussion reflected his lack of theory, for which he attempted to compensate by calling on commonsense notions of popularity and a sort of distance–decay function to rationalize how he identified ancestral forms of a trait.

Whereas Ford (1935a, 1949) viewed culture change as gradual and steady—a "placid stream of pottery continuity" (Phillips et al. 1951:427; see also Ford 1951:91–100)—Phillips and Griffin conceived of the flow as jerky or punctuated. This latter view emanated in part from the inherent discontinuity of stratigraphic units (Phillips et al. 1951:428); thus the breaks in the flow that Phillips and Griffin perceived tended to correspond to stratigraphic boundaries. But this is exactly as Griffin and Phillips had expected the archaeological record to be arranged—nice, orderly units that had highly visible discontinuities between them. For Ford, pottery

> was developing in a continuum throughout its entire history in the Mississippi Valley, that whether new types evolve by modification of older ones or come in as new ideas from the outside, they take their place in an uninterrupted cultural flow. The logical consequence of such a view is that, in most cases a "mixed" pottery complex represents a single brief span of time on the continuum, an "instant" for all practical purposes, when both elements of the mixture were being made and used side by side. The importance of this postulation for the seriation method can hardly be exaggerated. Ford does not deny that mixed complexes sometimes do result from reoccupation of sites. Such collections he frankly banishes from his graphs and says so. . . .
>
> Griffin and Phillips, on the other hand, while not rejecting the general theory of continuity, are inclined to feel . . . that there are more instances of mixture through reoccupation of sites than Ford has recognized. In particular . . . they have tended to see indications of at least one significant break in the otherwise placid stream of pottery continuity at the point where the tempering material shifts from clay to shell, in other words between the Baytown and Mississippi periods. They feel that, by including mixed collections on the graphs, Ford has effected a spurious transition that seems to prove his continuity hypothesis, but in reality leaves the question open. (Phillips et al. 1951:427)

Several decades of excavation in the meander-belt portion of the Mississippi Valley would demonstrate that although there *was* a change from clay-tempered pottery to shell-tempered pottery, in many localities that change was not as abrupt as Griffin and Phillips had forecast.

Phillips and Griffin were willing to admit that seriation (including interdigitation) and stratigraphy (site-specific percentage stratigraphy and, particularly, ceramic stratigraphy) were "independent methods of analysis" (Phillips et al. 1951:239), and they correctly noted that the stratigraphic exposure of a 2-m^2 excavation unit was accurate for that exposure only and should not be extrapolated over an entire site or over the surrounding region (Phillips et al. 1951:291). But Phillips and Griffin's essentialist notions of "abrupt cultural change" demanded, in the end, that they view many sites as stratigraphically "mixed" when they showed no such abrupt change (Phillips et al. 1951:291–292). Similarly, Ford's surface collections were viewed by Phillips and Griffin as mixed, and thus when seriated they consisted of false "transitional" collections "that are actually the result of reoccupation" (Phillips et al. 1951:292). This was one reason Phillips and Griffin made Ford (1952) publish his study of design elements across the

Southeast elsewhere. How Ford's colleagues knew the surface collections and the collections from their stratigraphic tests were mixed highlighted their essentialist stance. They could not empirically test such an inference except to cite those cases of clear stratigraphic separation of types as accurate reflections of reality and to discount cases where the types were stratigraphically associated.

An excellent example of Phillips and Griffin's perspective is given in the discussion of the pottery from the Rose Mound site in Cross County, Arkansas. There, they excavated a single 2-m^2 unit in arbitrary 10-cm levels; a total of twenty-two levels was excavated, and the authors noted that "The stratification of this [unit] has a particularly important bearing on the interpretation of the pottery stratigraphy" with regard to the shift from sand-tempered to shell-tempered pottery, or what was then termed Baytown to Mississippian pottery (Phillips et al. 1951:286–287). A graph of the type percentages constructed as a bar chart (for which Ford was famous) was superimposed on a composite stratigraphic profile that showed the location of the boundary between the two lowest stratigraphic units (Figure 5.5). Phillips et al. (1951:288–289) concluded (at least Phillips and Griffin did) that

> the effect of this slope [of strata boundaries] on the pottery stratigraphy is to introduce a spurious transition of a new and insidious kind. . . . The resulting pottery graph could not fail, therefore, to show a smooth transition in [pottery types]. To judge correctly the stratigraphic relationship between [the two stratigraphic zones, the five arbitrary levels containing the boundary between the strata] would have to be eliminated from consideration. *The resulting conclusion is that there was an abrupt shift from a pure Baytown to an equally pure Mississippi pottery complex* [emphasis added].

Although Ford might have agreed the five levels were mixed, he certainly did not, in light of his seriations, agree with the "resulting conclusion."

Beyond Seriation—The Debate Begins

We noted above that as a result of these differences with his collaborators, Ford was forced to publish some of his results elsewhere. There were other differences as well, one of which involved how Ford wanted to interpret the chronologies constructed as a result of the Lower Mississippi Alluvial Valley project when those chronologies were compared with others in the greater Southeast. Ford (1952) believed that the similarities of those various chronologies in terms of both sequence and included types denoted the various braids of the braided stream of the cultural continuum. He

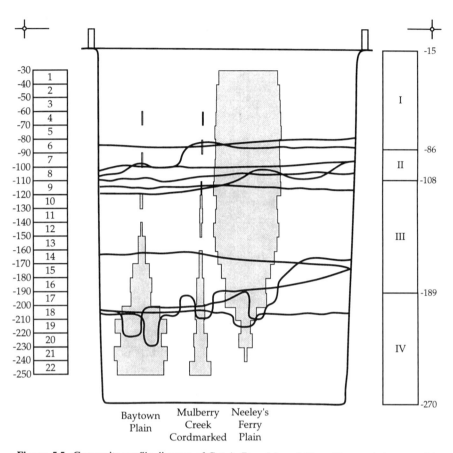

Baytown   Mulberry   Neeley's
Plain   Creek   Ferry
              Cordmarked Plain

Figure 5.5. Composite profile diagram of Cut A, Rose Mound, Cross County, Arkansas, with relative percentages of three pottery types by excavation level superimposed. The negative numbers on the left correspond to depth (in cm) below the top of the excavation stakes (upright rectangles at the edges of the graph). The numbers in boxes refer to 10-cm excavation levels. Roman numerals I-IV represent idealized strata obtained by averaging the four walls of the 2-m^2 excavation unit. Heavy undulating lines in the center are boundaries between strata from all four walls of the excavation unit. The width of a horizontal bar denotes the relative abundance of a pottery type in a particular excavation level. Sherds of the types Baytown Plain and Mulberry Creek Cordmarked are predominantly clay tempered; those in the type Neeley's Ferry Plain are shell tempered. Notice the gradual replacement of clay-tempered by shell-tempered pottery (after Phillips et al. 1951).

therefore sought not only to "align ceramic chronologies in adjacent geo-graphical areas somewhat more accurately than has been done previously" (Ford 1952:318), but also to "trace evolving strains [read *idea streams*] through time and across space and measure them qualitatively and quan-titatively" (Ford 1952:319). Ford (1952:322) explicitly noted that he sought to "follow some of the more prominent streams of ideas." He then cited Kroeber's (1948:260, fig. 18) illustration of biological evolution as involving only branching and cultural evolution as "a tree in which the branches grew back together as readily and frequently as they separated" and indicated that his graphic technique for illustrating the latter sort of evolution was at best imperfect.

Ford (1952) constructed chronologies for several different areas of the Southeast using percentage stratigraphy, seriation, and interdigitation. He correlated the various areal chronologies by "focusing attention on the pat-terning formed by type maximums and by placing less weight on the ap-parent starting and stopping points of type occurrences" (Ford 1952:331). He had long recognized that (1) the end points in the temporal range of a given type might be obscured by various processes such a mechanical mixing of types in a vertical column of sediments and (2) seriating mixed surface collections might produce a too-long temporal range for a type (Ford 1952:344). Ford (1935b, 1936a, 1949) was also very aware of the fact that small samples could provide incorrect information on the initiation and termination of a type. Given these problems, the actual end points of a type's distribution in time and space were obscure. Thus, Ford (1952:344) noted that "For these reasons, it seems best to place more weight on the temporal position of the type maximum than on the apparent vertical po-sition of its initial [or final] appearance." The type maximum was likely to provide the best approximation of the "mean," or average (Ford 1949), age of a type.

Similar factors caused the type frequency distributions to fluctuate and thus diverge from the perfect " 'battleship' frequency curves" (Ford 1952:344) that a historical type was expected to display. He therefore visu-ally smoothed the frequency curves and then correlated the various areal chronologies, explicitly acknowledging (Ford 1952:343) that the final ar-rangement was probably not exactly correct but that there were probably no "major errors" and begged the reader's acceptance of the arrangement for purposes of discussion.

In aligning the various areal chronologies he compared, he was seeking to track the movement of what he termed "cultural influences" (Ford 1952:329). This merely followed what Willey (1953a:363) would later refer to as an "axiom" of culture history—"typological similarity is [an] indicator of cultural relatedness." Once the areal chronologies were correlated, Ford

(1952:343) examined the history of what he termed "eight ceramic decorative traditions," each representing a "selected stream of ideas across space [that had developed] through time." He spoke of one design type leaving "no direct descendants" (p. 347), of one design type evolving from another (p. 350), and of particular design types and elements displaying "close kinship" to one another (p. 355). In other words, formally similar types were phyletically related; their similarity was of the homologous sort. There was no theoretical warrant for such interpretations, only Ford's commonsense notions of the braided stream of cultural evolution.

While Ford's (1952) analysis was not unique in technique—others (e.g., Willey 1949) had done more or less the same thing—it was unique in breadth of data coverage along the time, space, and form dimensions, and it was also rather unique for the combination of methods used. Albert C. Spaulding (1953a) made it clear that he was not particularly impressed with Ford's (1952) methodological procedures. Spaulding (1953a:589) viewed Ford's measurements as nothing more than "counting and ranking" of pottery types—a procedure that was, in his opinion, neither measurement nor scientific. Although he apparently agreed with the assumption underpinning Ford's seriations—"that two assemblages which resemble each other closely are not far removed in time" (Spaulding 1953a:589)—Spaulding found Ford's sole use of "graphical methods" to seriate collections as lacking methodological rigor and sophistication and thus to be highly questionable (see also Spaulding 1978). Ford could "only assert that his final ordering is the best possible under the circumstances and reproduce the graphs to substantiate the assertion. The absence of any mathematical expression of degree of fit leaves the skeptical reader with no recourse other than reproducing the component histograms and trying new arrangements himself, a task which is made difficult by the absence of the original counts on which the percentages were calculated" (Spaulding 1953a:590–591). In one of the great quotes from the debate, Spaulding (1953a:591) compared Ford's smoothing of curves to a "bloody amputation."

In his response to Spaulding's (1953a) review, Ford (1954b:110) could only weakly protest that "measurements" was not his wording but rather that of the editors. And the mathematical technique recently proposed by Brainerd (1951a) and Robinson (1951) (1) was unnecessary "to demonstrate what appears to be obvious by inspection" (Ford 1954b:110); (2) "cannot take into account areal variation in type frequencies" (Ford 1954b:110); and (3) produced coefficients that do "not distinguish between frequency agreements that are to be found at either end of the time span of a type" (Ford 1954b:111). The first point underscored Ford's lack of methodological sophistication; for him, such sophistication was unnecessary because the solution was obvious. The second point identified Ford's misunderstanding of the Brainerd–Robinson technique because the analyst selects—perhaps on the basis of their spatial distribution—the assemblages to be seriated, regardless of whether those assemblages are seriated visually or with coefficients of similarity. The third point reinforces points derived from the first two. Ford apparently did not understand that a Brainerd–Robinson coefficient measures the total similarity of two assemblages based on the complement of the sum of the differences between relative frequencies of *multiple* types. His dreaded "frequency agreements" at either end of the duration of a type simply will not be found *if* the types are historical.

In his reply to Ford's response, Spaulding (1954a:113) reiterated that "Ford simply does not know what the word 'measurement' denotes." He continued, "in scientific usage it . . . definitely does not include ranking" (Spaulding 1954a:113). This simply means that Spaulding was using "ranking" as a synonym for sorting, interdigitating, or seriating. Any arrangement resulting from using such an ordering technique will be an order of collections, but in Spaulding's view it would not necessarily "measure" anything. The last is so for Spaulding (1954a:113) because, to him, "In ordinary usage [measurement] refers to comparison with a scale subdivided into equal units of specified size, and in scientific usage it has a considerably more technical meaning which definitely does not include ranking." Thus, what would today be termed ordinal scales of measurement (Stevens 1946) were not, in Spaulding's view, *scientific* scales of measurement. But the problem was actually deeper than that.

Spaulding (1954a:113) also argued that "time relationships were in large part inferred by means of relative frequencies of ceramic types [but type] counts and locus, not time, were the empirical data of the study. [Thus] A general murkiness of exposition, of which the infelicitous use of measurement is an example, is a persistent stumbling block in understanding the arguments advanced" by Ford (1952). This very complex statement is the key to the Ford–Spaulding debate. Spaulding was suggesting that one cannot measure geographic distance with units such as years, that one cannot measure time with units such as kilometers, that one cannot measure temporal change in cultural ideas with arbitrary units called types (see also Spaulding 1957, 1960b). Spaulding was questioning the warrant for the inference that Ford's arrangements of type frequencies in time and space measure the temporal flow of streams of cultural ideas. Ford (1954b:110) had no theoretical warrant for such an inference and could only suggest that Spaulding's criticism was founded on "a lack of familiarity with certain characteristics of the *mechanics of cultural development and diffusion* which were used as basic assumptions" (emphasis added). It was such commonsensical warrants—the popularity principle in this case—that characterized the weaknesses of the culture history paradigm in general and Ford's graphical ordering techniques—seriation, interdigitation, percentage stratigraphy—in particular.

It was debate over the nature of culture change and the meaning of types that resulted in a serious challenge to the culture-historical type of Kidder, Ford, Rouse, and others. Previous rationalizations had, as we have shown, been founded on commonsense notions such as the popularity principle. The paradox presented by adopting a materialist conception of culture change as continuous and gradual yet using a method that structured observations in essentialist terms had reached a breaking point, as epitomized by Phillips et al.'s (1951) disagreement. Was there a way out of the morass? Could one, for example, show that types were not arbitrary analytical constructs and simultaneously provide more than a commonsense warrant for them? Without recognizing them as such, one might have predicted that determining which view—materialist or essentialist—was correct might be difficult. The result was, then, merely a replacement of the commonsense rationale with a methodological one founded in empiricism.

The Empiricist Challenge to Artifact Classification— The Debate Continues

Until the early 1950s, most archaeologists were content to worry about the chronological placement of the types they constructed. These units *might* reflect cultural norms or customs, but such suspicions were merely commonsense rationalizations for the units; they were not empirically testable save in a tautological manner, such as in Brainerd's (1951a) rendition that the popularity of norms produced normal frequency distributions of types through time, and thus empirical manifestations of such frequency distributions denoted norms or customs. Nonetheless, lacking theory, the commonsense understanding grew, and as we have seen in Phillips et al. (1951) and elsewhere, the possibility that types were somehow "real"—read "emic"—units grew stronger, probably being helped along with statements such as Taylor's (1948) admonition that archaeology should be anthropological. In 1953, Spaulding published a paper describing a technique for discovering "real" types (Spaulding 1953b). Ford (1954a) responded, Spaulding (1954b) replied in kind, and Ford (1954c) finally produced a more programmatic statement concerning his views of classification.[4] This often heated exchange came to be referred to as the Ford–Spaulding debate (e.g., Thompson 1972:36). It is, we think, important to begin with a bit of background to the debate in order to set the proper tone for its evaluation.

Fordian types—that is, ones constructed for purposes of culture history such as advocated by Kidder, Rouse, and Krieger—were theoretical units initially formed by trial and error and then tested to ensure that they measured time. With no theoretical foundation, such types had a somewhat arbitrary appearance—admitted by the culture historians—and certainly had no clear sociobehavioral meaning. Spaulding (1953b) usually is credited with revolutionizing these aspects of archaeological typology (Dunnell 1986a:37; 1986b:178), but we suspect he merely formalized a growing dissatisfaction by providing an explicit alternative that was, it seems, originally suggested by someone else. In his seldom-referenced writings on typological nomenclature, Spaulding (1948a, 1948b) never mentioned how type units might be constructed. He did, however, indicate what he desired a year later in commenting on the Midwestern Taxonomic Method (discussed in Chapter 6). Spaulding (1949:5) wanted to develop a classification technique that omitted the problem of transitional assemblages and "expressed at one stroke the classifier's opinion of the cultural relationship and the chronological position of an assemblage," as such a technique would allow "a combined presentation of [the] independent units of chronological position and cultural affinity in either narrative or chart form."

The avenue to explore in attempting to erect such a classification technique was apparently unclear to Spaulding in 1949–1950. But in 1951, the avenue was identified for him. Spaulding (1951) presented a paper at a conference on archaeological method sponsored by the Viking Fund and held at the University of Michigan. George W. Brainerd (1951b) presented a paper, entitled "The Use of Mathematical Formulations in Archaeological Analysis." He had just published his landmark paper on objectifying the sorting procedures of the seriation technique (Brainerd 1951a), a paper with which Spaulding (1953a, 1954a) clearly became very familiar and which he used to criticize Ford's "bloody amputations." In his seldom cited "Mathematical Formulations" paper, Brainerd made two observations that undoubtedly influenced Spaulding. First, Brainerd (1951b:117) indicated that "Archaeological taxonomy [read *typology*] is in itself a generalizing procedure which ultimately depends for its validity upon the archaeologist's success in *isolating the effects of culturally conditioned behavior* from the examination of human products" (emphasis added). His second point is extremely important, and we thus quote it in full:

> The first step of procedure in artifact analysis is usually the formulation of types, groups of artifacts, each of which shows a combination of similar or identical attributes or traits. . . . If [the observation quoted above] is acceptable, the systematics used must have cultural validity in that they must mirror the culturally established requirements met by the artisans. In his search for these tenets of the unknown group it behooves the

archaeologist as a scientist to work objectively, free of a priori conceptions. The attributes used in sorting artifacts into types should thus be *objectively chosen as those which occur most often in combination in single artifacts.* Criteria based upon subdivisions of an attribute which occurs in a continuous range through the material are preferably used only when the distribution curve of the attribute in the archaeological samples shows binodality, and *the dividing line for sorting should be drawn between the nodes.* By use of the above requirements for type attributes, the archaeologist can *objectively describe the cultural specifications followed by the artisans. Statistical procedures for the formulation of, and sorting of specimens into, types satisfying these requirements are feasible,* and may in some cases be useful. It seems conceivable also that mathematical studies of attribute combinations may demonstrate more finely cut cultural differentiation without the use of the intermediate concept of types, for types are, after all, simplifications to allow qualitative division of the material into few enough categories to permit inspectional techniques of analysis. (Brainerd 1951b:118–119; emphasis added)

Brainerd (1951b:122) argued that his suggested use of mathematical or statistical techniques would eliminate one of the problems with the Midwestern Taxonomic Method noted by Spaulding (1949)—that of transitional collections. Further, Brainerd (1951b:123) indicated his suggested techniques would eliminate the problem of existing typologies falling "far short of full utilization of archaeological materials for the recovery of information on culture." He continued, "In such analyses, it is conceivable that a bridge may be found uniting the objectivity of the taxonomist to the cultural sensitivity of the humanist. Cultural intangibles can, if they exist, be made tangible. *Better technique is the solution"* (Brainerd 1951b:124; emphasis added). Thus, the other problem earlier identified by Spaulding (1949)—that of getting at culture and cultural relations by studying artifacts—could be eliminated by better technique or method. Statistics was that better technique. Here, in one package—statistics—was the solution to the two problems Spaulding had identified in 1949.

Spaulding's (1953b[†]) article "Statistical Techniques for the Discovery of Artifact Types" addressed both issues that concerned culture historians. His statistical approach appeared to eliminate trial and error and the arbitrariness of the Fordian approach, and it provided a warrant for sociobehavioral meaning. The warrant was, however, entirely illusory. His statistical method received little comment. His definition of a type as "a group of artifacts exhibiting a consistent assemblage of attributes whose combined properties give a characteristic pattern" (Spaulding 1953b:305) was compatible with earlier definitions because of the recurrence of attribute combinations (recall Brainerd's [1951a] earlier "constant combination of attributes") The difference was that for Spaulding, recurrence was *empirically determined;* for Ford and some others (Rouse 1939), recurrence was *definitional.*

Fordian types were extensionally defined combinations of attributes with limited temporal and spatial distributions and thus were theoretical units that, upon (deductive) testing and refinement, measured time. Those types might or might not have cultural or anthropological or human behavioral significance. Spaulding's types were different. For Spaulding, following Brainerd (1951b), types were real and inherent in the specimens; in other words, they were essentialist, empirical units. Thus to Spaulding (1953b:305), "Classification into types is a process of discovery of combinations of attributes *favored by the makers* of the artifacts, not an arbitrary procedure of the classifier" (emphasis added). Because types are inherent in the data, they must be discovered, inductively, and statistical techniques, as suggested by Brainerd (1951b), provided the objective means of determining which attributes regularly, and more often than random chance would allow, co-occur on specimen after specimen.

To Spaulding, who, like his contemporaries, viewed artifacts as products of human behaviors, discovery of recurring attribute combinations denoted *the discovery of human behavior concerning which attributes should be combined to produce a normal, or favored, specimen.* Spaulding's types were of the emic sort. While Spaulding's technique was designed to receive input only from the specimens themselves, it originally (1953–1954) left unresolved the issue of choosing particular attributes—just as Brainerd's (1951b) seminal comments had—the combinations of which were to be the subjects of statistical testing. His later reductionist discussion of this problem in "Statistical Description and Comparison of Artifact Assemblages" (Spaulding 1960a) merely pushed the problem to one of similarly unspecified choices of attributes of attributes.

Because Spaulding's units were empirical, they had time–space locations; that is, they occurred in single components. Application of his method was restricted to one assemblage—a time and space-bound unit—at a time. Fordian types, by contrast, were theoretical and thus had measurable distributions in time and space and could be found in more than one component at a time. Ford's orientation was narrow; types were analytical tools that the archaeologist constructed in such a manner as to permit chronological ordering of assemblages. But Ford's attempts to explain the culture-historical paradigm to which he subscribed were "badly muddled by a conflation [of] the definitional and interpretive meanings attached to [the] type [concept] and by frequent recourse to intuitive rationales necessitated by the lack of any truly theoretical justification for the culture-historical position" (Dunnell 1986b:172). That is, Ford never clearly distinguished between theoretical units and empirical units. His theoretical types were definitional and thus immutable; their empirical frequency distributions characterized culture change. Their meaning to Ford in terms of the braided, flowing stream of cultural ideas involved commonsense interpretation that made those types seem like real, essentialist units.

In his "Comment on A. C. Spaulding's 'Statistical Techniques for the Discovery of Artifact Types,'" Ford (1954a[†]) protested that Spaulding's approach was "amazingly naive" because it only suggested cultural norms; it did not help write culture history. In his response, "Reply to Ford," Spaulding (1954b[†]) noted that Ford had not "challenged the validity of the techniques [Spaulding] used to discover [attribute] clusters" (Spaulding 1954b:393) and underscored the procedural murkiness in Ford's constructions of "attribute combinations." Spaulding proclaimed that his "attribute clusters" were "functional types" (Spaulding 1954b:392), not in the post-1960 general sense of the term (e.g., Wilmsen 1968a, 1968b) but in the sense that because they "include inferences as to the behavior of the makers of the artifacts," they were "culturally meaningful" in an emic sense.

Faced with the question of the utility of his units and the lack of a nontautological test of their interpretive meaning, Spaulding was forced to turn to his method as justification, much as had been implied by Brainerd's (1951b) suggested use of the division of types by identifying "nodes" or, more correctly, statistical modes, and drawing a line between them. The legitimacy of the claim that discovered attribute combinations reflected human behavior and were culturally meaningful had to come from method—the statistically significant patterning of the attribute combinations—as there was no other place from which it could come. Such combinations were clusters of attributes that reflected "the cultural specifications followed by the artisans" for Brainerd (1951b:118) and a "social behavior pattern" for Spaulding, and thus they must have a restricted distribution in time and space (Spaulding 1954b:392)—the typical commonsense explanation of Brainerd's and Spaulding's contemporaries. Justification for the presumed human behavioral meaning of Spaulding's types was the same as that for Brainerd's and involved the facts that (1) the artifacts existed as human creations and (2) they were sortable into recognizable (discoverable, empirical, essentialist) sets; thus, they *must be* real. They could, however, do no analytical work for archaeology such as Ford's seriable types could.

Ford's (1954c[†]) paper "On the Concept of Types: The Type Concept Revisited" was published as a direct result of the debate between him and Spaulding and was written not only to refute Spaulding's claims but to clarify Ford's conception of types. On the very first page, Ford expressed doubt that Spaulding's (1953b) statistical method would allow the discovery of a "cultural type" because types were, in Ford's view, simply shorthand devices for both anthropologists and the makers of artifacts. Ford's discussion focused on the fictitious Gamma-gamma people who occupied the Island of Gamma. His discussion of Gamma-gamma architecture clearly reflected (1) the ceramic continuum model (Figure 5.3) and (2) Ford's model of culture as a braided stream. With regard to the former, Ford's (1954c:46) figure 1 was merely the end of one of the cylinders of the continuum model and showed the variation contained within that circle as variation in the architecture of Gamma across the island. His figure 2 (Ford 1954:48) was a slice through the continuum showing the ends of several cylinders as variation in the houses on the Island of Gamma and several adjacent islands. With regard to the latter, Ford referred to the "fluid process" of cultural change, to "streams of thought," and to "one stream of cultural development [being] replaced by another" (Ford 1954c:51). His summary illustration (here reproduced as Figure 5.6) showed both the temporal and spatial continuum of Gamma Island architecture. Ideational units would be required to measure that variation, but Ford failed to make this point clear.

Cultural, or emic, types certainly exist, Ford thought, as the houses of the Island of Gamma and nearby islands indicated. But what Ford (1954c:52) wanted were "type groupings consciously selected [by an archaeologist to produce] a workable typology . . . designed for the reconstruction of culture history in time and space." Ford never specified how such groupings were to be extracted from the constantly changing braided cultural stream. He never spelled out what a type "designed for the reconstruction of culture history in time and space" should consist of or how one knew one had such a type. Instead, in this paper Ford chose to illustrate the continuous and braided-stream character of culture development and to show that a great deal of formal variation existed at any time–space position in the continuum. That variation might "tend to cluster about a mean, which [the ethnologist could] visualize as the central theme of the type [read *the type definition*]. [But] the ethnologist cannot rely upon the culture bearers to define this central theme. They may or may not be aware of it. . . . The [type], then, is an abstraction made by the ethnologist and derived from the cultural activity" (Ford 1954c:45). An artifact might "illustrate the aborigine's ideas as to the proper ways to construct dwellings" or ceramic vessels (Ford 1954c:47), but it comprised a constellation of *alternate* ideas about how things might be done; a type perceived by an anthropologist or archaeologist was "not a natural cultural unit" (Ford 1954c:48) but rather a sort of short-hand or abbreviated description. The ethnologist or archaeologist might choose the wrong scale of idea combinations to examine—house form *versus* how a roof was thatched—or the wrong combination of attributes. Even the Gamma-gamma people didn't know what a

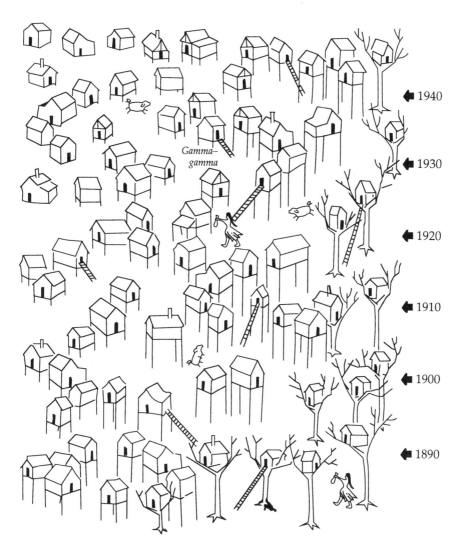

Figure 5.6. Variation in housing through time on James Ford's fictitious island of Gamma. Basically, what Ford was trying to show in this confusing diagram was the considerable spatial and temporal variation in housing. The "typical" structure is shown just above the woman in the upper half of the diagram. A line drawn vertically through that house would represent the mean house for each decade; geographic variation is shown to the right and left of that line. Notice that, in general, there is a decrease in house elevation through time. There is a concomitant decline in the number of houses built in trees, but this is a separate issue from house elevation. Conflation of such issues, as with confusion over stylistic and functional traits (linking, for example, the dimension "kind of construction material" with the dimension "color of trim"), is still fairly common in archaeology (after Ford 1954c)

typical house looked like, didn't know what their own emic types consisted of, in part because they had only a vague notion of what was acceptable at a given time–place position.

In Ford's view, discontinuities along the time or space dimensions of the archaeological record gave the archaeologist a sort of natural (in no way to be confused with cultural or essentialist) seam by which the time–space continuum could be broken into chunks. Types were therefore accidents of the samples available: "[T]he particular locality where an archeological collection chances to be made will be one of the factors that determines the mean and the range of variation that are demonstrated in any particular tradition in the culture that is being studied" (Ford 1954c:49). Chance samples of the continuum would provide discontinuous snapshots of that continuum, and as such "Types are easily separable and they look natural [read *emic* or *real*]" (Ford 1954c:52). The fact that types were extensionally defined didn't help matters, but Ford failed to make this point. To Ford, Spaulding's argument was flawed because his type definitions were founded on the discontinuous nature of the samples generally available to archaeologists. "Permitting sampling chance to determine typology operates very well so long as the archeologist has only a spotty sampling of the culture history" (Ford 1954c:52). Not surprisingly, then, too much data in the hands of an archaeologist would result in an "overlapping of types [and] a meaningless conglomeration" of such units if the typologist were naive (Ford 1954c:52); typological creep and a smearing and blending of type boundaries would occur if the typologist didn't pay close enough attention.

In the end, Ford's strategy for refuting Spaulding's position backfired because his allusions to cultural customs and standards gave Spaulding's types something of a claim to such meaning. Cowgill (1963:697) went so far as to remark that "the Spaulding and Ford views about the discoverability of artifact types are not contradictory." Spaulding's types were, on the one hand, "founded in the essentialist view of variation. They presume that significant variation occurs as more or less discrete packages and that variation not assignable to such packages lacks explanatory significance" (Dunnell 1986b:181). Comparison of Spaulding's "real" types had to be qualitative and to focus on differences between them. Fordian types, on the other hand, stemmed from a materialistic conception of reality; variation in form was continuous across space and through time. The division of that continuity into units we call types was a trial-and-error process, the successes of which Ford, and others, chose to evaluate with the historical-significance criterion. As Dunnell (1986b:173) later noted, this criterion did not ensure that Ford's and others' types were all stylistic in the sense that the historical types so identified were selectively neutral variants (Dunnell

1978), though they *were* dominantly stylistic (Dunnell 1986a:31). The problem was that functional and technological types and attributes might also measure time, but the former potentially conflated homologous similarity with analogous similarity and thus made the writing of developmental histories of cultures difficult.

Given the general belief that types probably have some cultural meaning (Brainerd 1951a, 1951b; Krieger 1944), it is not surprising that some Americanist archaeologists believed that the type–variety system, which resulted in the classification of the same scale of phenomena (sherds) at different levels of inclusiveness (varieties, types, wares) would also reveal aspects of culture at different scales. Gifford (1960) suggested, on the one hand, that a variety represents individual or small-group social variation within a society. On the other hand, a type is "the material outcome of a set of fundamental attributes that coalesced, consciously or unconsciously, as a ceramic idea or 'esthetic ideal'—the boundaries of which were imposed through the value system operative in the society by virtue of individual interaction on a societal level. These ceramic ideas occurred in the brains of the potters who made the ceramic fabric that constitutes a type, and they are not by any means creations of an analyst" (Gifford 1960:343). His rationalization of his units was the typical one: Potters "tend to conform to the demands of a majority of the norms that are a part of their culture at a particular time in history" (Gifford 1960:343), and cultural phenomena are not randomly distributed in time and space (Gifford 1960:342). Thus, despite the lack of citation, Gifford (1960:342), like Spaulding (1953b) before him, believed that an inherent—essentialist—order of the data was discoverable and that "Classificatory schemes . . . are in part useful as a means toward this end." Others (Smith et al. 1960) suggested that such cultural significance may reside in the units designated by the type–variety system, but they were much less strongly committed to such a viewpoint.

Summary

In the end, the Ford–Spaulding debate was something of a catalyst for the new archaeology of the 1960s. Spaulding's (1953b) view, clearly having a precedent in Brainerd's (1951b) work, represented an entirely new approach to the archaeological record: Appropriate methods would allow the detection of emically significant properties of that record—properties that revealed human behaviors (Binford 1968a:23). That (1) the new archaeology lacked a theoretical basis for such claims and (2) its results were not testable in a nontautological manner escaped serious notice for nearly two decades (Dunnell 1978), though some weaknesses were detected earlier

(Taylor 1969, 1972). Spaulding's clear and concise statement of the importance and objectivity of method swayed many archaeologists, however, and thus much effort was subsequently focused on developing an appropriate method for grouping specimens (reviewed in Dunnell 1986b:176–190). But without theory from which one could derive performance standards—What analytical work are the groups of things called types and built by these methods supposed to do?—the programmatic literature was reduced to meaningless squabbling over which method was better. If a purpose was proposed for a set of types, it often was written in Ford's culture-historical terms, with all the attendant commonsense justifications attached.

Even as we approach the twenty-first century, the lack of theory still plagues the classification of those discrete objects we call artifacts. To be sure, significant advances have been made in specifying attribute combinations that tend to measure time, or technology, or function, rather than some combination of these or other properties, a consideration earlier noted as important by Brew (1946), Brainerd (1951b), Steward (1954), and others. But by and large, these are ad hoc formulations founded on experience gained over the past eighty years or so of trial and error. Significantly, the lack of theory within the culture history paradigm resided not just with the classification of artifacts but elsewhere within the paradigm as well. In Chapter 6 we turn attention to other fundamental issues of classification, but we shift the scale from discrete objects or artifacts to aggregates of artifacts variously termed assemblages, components, collections, and the like. It was in dealing with such sets of discrete objects that (1) dependence on the geologically—and thus by implication temporal—vertical boundaries of the sets and (2) continuing efforts to be anthropological exerted additional influences on the ontogeny of the culture history paradigm.

Notes

1. Similar fluctuations characterize drift in biological evolution (Gould et al. 1977).
2. One of the seminal manuals in archaeological field techniques was published about this time (Heizer 1949, 1950).
3. The phrase "for the time being" also suggests their types were extensionally defined.
4. A few other individuals put in their two cents worth at the time (e.g., Evans 1954; Steward 1954).

6

Classification of Artifact Aggregates

Early twentieth-century Americanist archaeologists worried not only about how to measure time and how to classify artifacts in such a manner as to *allow* them to measure time, but also about how to build units larger than types of discrete objects—units that would allow some synthesis and comparison of the cultural manifestations they studied. That is, they worried about classifying cultures as those were represented by the sets, or aggregates, of artifacts that were regularly found associated with each other. Ultimately, archaeologists wanted to determine how such aggregates of forms were related in time and space and how they were related to each other developmentally (e.g., did one somehow influence another). In the Southwest, dendrochronology had begun to help sort things out according to calendrical time (Douglass 1919, 1921; Gladwin 1936; Hawley 1934; Wissler 1921), and though the same technique was attempted in the Southeast (Willey 1938), in the latter area stratigraphic excavation received the lion's share of attention in chronological matters (Willey 1939).

As we have shown in preceding chapters, the materialist–essentialist paradox permeated most interpretive efforts. Artifact types that allowed measurement of the time–space continuum were actively sought but were also typically warranted as reflecting ideas in the heads of the artisans. Culture might have been thought of as a constantly flowing braided stream of idea sets, but the individual histories of what were thought of as cultures were monitored as a series of isolated frames within a motion picture. Those isolated frames, as we will see, came to be viewed not so much as a random selection of snapshots along the continuum but as real *periods of cultural stasis* that were separated by nearly instantaneous alterations in idea sets. The shallow time depth of one's own lifespan, in conjunction with the culture-area concept, probably subconsciously reinforced such essentialist notions of time- and space-bound cultural stability and discontinuity. The root of the problem seems to have resided in the ongoing attempts of culture historians to legitimize what they were doing by making it anthropological. In this chapter we limit our discussion mainly to the manner in which culture historians addressed one question: How were archaeologically manifested cultures, which to most archaeologists were the time- and space-bound units actually being studied, supposed to be identified? In the end, what we really are examining is how archaeologists turned those units *into* cultures.

The Midwestern Taxonomic Method

By the 1930s, Americanist archaeologists had come to something of an impasse over the means and terms used to describe and discuss assemblages or collections of artifacts. The term "culture" was ubiquitous in the role of a grouping unit, but it varied tremendously in scope and meaning from one application to the next. "This vague and varying use of the word 'culture' to describe manifestations which were so unlike in scope and character, of which some were culturally correlative—but in different degree, while others lay wholly outside the specific field of relationship, led logically and necessarily to taxonomy" (McKern 1943:313).

The Midwestern Taxonomic Method (MTM) was created in the 1930s to rectify those problems by providing a broadly useful means of categorizing assemblages. To wit, "the archaeological classification necessarily must be based upon criteria available to the archaeologist" rather than on temporal, spatial, or ethnographic criteria (McKern 1937:71, 1939:303). The method is intimately associated with William C. McKern and has been called the "Midwestern Taxonomic System" (Binford 1968a; Brew 1946; Cole 1943; Dunnell 1971b; Lewis and Kneberg 1946; Rouse 1953; Taylor 1948; Willey 1953b), the "McKern Taxonomic System" (Cole 1943), the "Midwestern Classification," the "Midwestern System," and the "Midwestern System of Classification" (Taylor 1948).

As McKern (1939) pointed out, it was the product of a consensus reached about a proposal originally made by him but which had been subjected to broad discussion, including a polling of the profession with a questionnaire, over a period of years (McKern 1934, 1937; see Griffin [1943, 1976], Haag [1961], Kehoe [1990], and McKern [1939] for histories of the development of the method). Thus, while McKern was the guiding light, many other leading archaeologists of the day (e.g., Fay-Cooper Cole, Thorne Deuel, James B. Griffin, Carl E. Guthe, Arthur R. Kelly) had a role in the ultimate formulation that was largely completed in 1933 and

1935 (McKern 1934, 1937) and published by McKern as "The Midwestern Taxonomic Method as an Aid to Archaeological Culture Study" in 1939 (McKern 1939[†]).

In outline, the method is quite simple. The entities arranged—the building blocks of the method—are called *components*, which are assemblages of associated artifacts that represent the occupation of a place by a people. Thus a component is not equivalent to a site unless a place has experienced *only* a single occupation (McKern 1939:308, 1944:445). In practice, components are defined on the basis of trait similarity. Similarity in trait lists, in turn, is used to assign components to groups. Five levels of groups are recognized in the method. From least to most inclusive, these are *focus, aspect, phase, pattern,* and *base.* Components belonging to a single focus share most traits, and the traits (e.g., particular designs) are specific. Foci that share many, usually more general, traits (e.g., technique of decoration) than those used for establishing foci are grouped as an aspect and so on until one reaches the base where only a few, often inferential, traits (e.g., agriculture) are held in common. Three kinds of traits are distinguished: *linked traits* are common to more than one unit; *diagnostic traits* are limited to a single unit; and *determinants* are traits that occur in all members of a unit but in no other unit (Figure 6.1).

McKern's (1939) description of the method was typical of the time. He described a procedure, and while he made some astute points, they were made in ad hoc fashion (e.g., representative samples are necessary [McKern 1939:304]). Further, he avoided some of the most critical issues, such as how traits were to be defined and what "similarity" meant and how it was to be measured. For example, McKern (1939:306) noted that traits may be of varied scales, such as an attribute of an object or a type of object; cases of the former tended to involve complex artifacts such as pottery. McKern (1939:306, 311, 1940) did worry about some of these issues, but subsequent users of the method did not. Reliance on common sense to justify such crucial decisions gives the MTM an intuitive aura to the modern reader, as it did to some of McKern's contemporaries (e.g., Cole and Deuel 1937; Deuel 1935; Griffin 1943, 1976; Guthe 1936; McGregor 1941; Ritchie 1937; Steward 1944), some of whom, according to McKern (1938, 1940, 1942, 1943, 1944), misunderstood and misused the method.

Analysis of the MTM makes it clear that it was a grouping system. Its units were not classes to which assemblages were assigned but rather were aggregates of assemblages per se. McKern was explicitly clear that the units did not necessarily have any temporal or spatial meaning; such meaning had to be acquired independently of the method. It was founded purely on the formal similarity of units (Spaulding 1949, 1957). In modern terms,

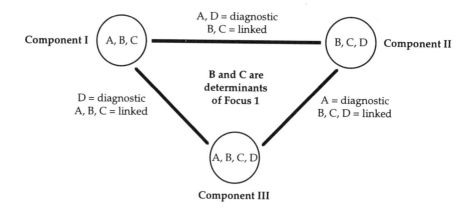

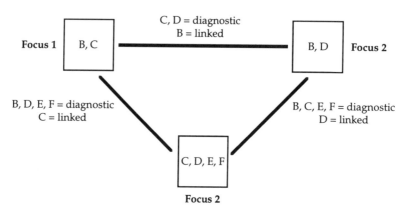

Figure 6.1. The analytical relations among traits (capital letters), components (circles), and foci (squares) in the Midwestern Taxonomic Method. Because components I, II, and III share traits B and C, they are linked traits in this comparison; other traits are diagnostic. Traits B and C are determinants of focus 1; components not containing traits B and C are not members of focus 1.

the method is an application of numerical phenetics, or numerical taxonomy, without recourse to the actual measurement of similarity (see Sokal and Sneath [1963] for discussion of phenetics and Mayr [1969:203–211] for contemporary criticism). McKern's contemporaries were quick to point out that the failure to measure similarity quantitatively was a major flaw of the method (Kroeber 1940[†], 1942). The difficulties in such measurement were, however, underestimated by the critics. For example, numerical phenetics would not come into its own until the 1960s, when inexpensive computing became available, and even then it was applied for only about twenty years and almost exclusively in biology (Hull 1988:519; Mayr 1981).

Despite its shortcomings, the MTM was widely applied in North America over the 1940s and 1950s (e.g., Lewis and Kneberg 1946; McGregor 1941). Why? Because McKern's determinants cleverly circumvented the grouping problem by using extensionally defined units. Within the MTM, inspection of components assigned to a focus or higher-level unit resulted in the identification of traits common to all *and* limited to members of the unit. Such identifications provided criteria for the addition of future members: "Classification is nothing more than the process of *recognizing* classes, each class identified by a complex of characteristics" (McKern 1939:304). "Once [the set of determinants] has been determined . . . any manifestation found to show this complex of [determinant] traits may be classified by definition" (McKern 1940:19). This meant that the particular traits that met the conditions—they were present in all inspected units but in no others (determinants)—depended on the components polled. Thus the list changed as knowledge of the archaeological record grew and more components were examined. The price paid was that all foci, aspects, and so forth were historical accidents comprising assemblages known at the time the determinants were derived.

The critical issue here concerns the unit termed *component*, defined as "the manifestation of any given focus at a specific site" (McKern 1939:308). Units of this sort were often referred to by McKern as "manifestations" of one of his larger units. A component, then, is an empirical unit made up of a set of associated artifacts. Artifact types or their distinctive attributes are the cultural traits that serve as determinants: "A simple type of artifact may serve as one element in a trait complex for one cultural division, and therefore may serve in some comparison as a determinant for that division. . . . However, when a comparatively complex type of pottery is characteristic for one of the more specific cultural divisions [aspect, focus], the question arises as to whether it should be considered as a trait or as comprising a number of trait elements" (McKern 1939:306). If a culture's trait list, manifest as a set of associated artifact (and/or attribute) types, "is found to recur in characteristic purity and practical completeness at [multiple] sites, to an extent suggestive of cultural identity, this recurring complex [of traits] established . . . [a] focus" (McKern 1939:308). The extensional nature of the significata of a focus is apparent in McKern's wording.

The critical issue remains, however. One must build trait lists from a set of associated artifacts. How does one determine if two or more artifacts are associated? McKern was hardly explicit, but, simply put, a component represents a single occupation of a site—"a single specified manifestation at a site"—and thus is distinguished from a site, which "may bear evidence of several cultural occupations" (McKern 1939:308). McKern (1940:18) offered an ethnological rationale for the trait lists derived from components: "A complex of traits determined at a site [read *a component*] may represent the customs and ways of living (culture) of a local group representing a single variety, or band, of Indians, sharing an identical lot of cultural habits." This commonsense warrant is also an inference, but it is one that is impossible to test in a nontautological manner without the help of theory. Further, what remains unspecified is the answer to the question posed at the beginning of this paragraph: How does one determine if two or more artifacts are associated? The answer is, of course, by using some sort of depositional (empirical) unit, such as a stratum, that has visible boundaries in order to conclude that a set of artifacts contains items that not only are associated archaeologically but were associated systemically (*sensu* Schiffer 1972) as well.

The emergence of the culture history paradigm in the 1920s and 1930s was heavily predicated on stylistic descriptions because they allowed the measurement of time as a result of their homologous character. As McKern (1937:78–80, 1939:307–309) himself implied, stylistic traits dominated the lower-level units in the taxonomic hierarchy—focus and aspect—whereas functional traits tended to dominate the higher-level units. Thus it is not surprising that the focus, and to a lesser extent the aspect, were the principal units of the MTM to find application (e.g., Griffin 1943; McGregor 1941), since they allowed the identification of unique time–space positions. As a result, with few exceptions, the higher-level units were eventually largely abandoned. The highest-level unit, base, was included in the original scheme, later eliminated, then reinstated, and finally omitted: "It has served little or no purpose as yet and is generally omitted from classifications" (McKern 1943:313).

The temporal dimension was explicitly omitted from the MTM, and the method was criticized on this point. Steward (1942:339) noted that the method was flawed because it produced a "set of timeless and spaceless categories." In response, McKern (1942) protested that he had merely set those dimensions aside for the moment in favor of the formal dimension; he had explicitly not discarded the time–space dimensions. Steward's (1944:99) rebuttal entailed two elements. He simply could not conceive how a taxonomic or hierarchical classification, which for him denoted branching evolution, could be forced onto cultural phenomena that not only branched or diverged through time but also converged to create a reticulate form of evolutionary descent. Second, Steward could not find any utility in the MTM because it seemed to lack any reference to theory. The later was one reason numerical phenetics fell from favor in biology several decades later, but Steward's observation had minimal impact on archaeological thought.

Some thought such criticisms were largely misplaced (McKern 1942; Spaulding 1949, 1957). Others saw a flaw in the fact that the ethnological implications of the units—foci, aspects, and so forth—were left undeveloped. Such perceived deficiencies no doubt prompted some Americanists to worry about how the method could be modified in such a manner as to rectify the problems (Colton 1939; Gladwin 1936). Other perceived problems included Lehmer's (1952:336) observation—seemingly founded in the materialist metaphysic—that the culture continuum was obscured by the method. He proposed therefore that the Southwestern term "branch" used by Gladwin and Gladwin (1934) be employed to imply or denote "a cultural development through time within a specific area, a cultural development characterized by the appearance of new traits, the modification of existing traits, and the loss of old traits, but a development which is basically a cultural continuum."

Similarly, in reviewing an application of the MTM (Lewis and Kneberg 1946), Jennings (1947:192–193) complained that "When a continuous flow of cultural traits can be seen to persist from period to period, the new periods being different in the possession of new traits, but retaining many old ones, the injection of a phase, focus, or pattern, before admitting a chronological and/or genetic relationship seems to serve no purpose beyond adding to the suspense" and "forcing a clear, sharp stratigraphic sequence of cultures whose distant cultural equivalents are known, and whose chronological position is amply demonstrated in the [Midwestern Taxonomic Method's] classificatory pigeon-holes is wasted effort." Comparing trait lists, demonstrating similarities and differences between such lists, showing their relative chronological positions, and thereby establishing the relationships of the lists "paid the historical debt [and is] what archaeology is expected to do," according to Jennings (1947:193). Spaulding (1957) thought this was nonsense, as the MTM was explicitly concerned solely with the formal dimension; the temporal and spatial dimensions were to be added later, and then the phyletic relations of essentialist units would be determined.

Although its terminology passed from the scene in the 1960s, units such as "Archaic," "Woodland," and "Mississippian"—units still very much alive—either originated as higher-level units in the MTM or were passed on to us through it. More importantly, the phase unit proposed by Phillips and Willey (1953) that came to dominate Americanist archaeology in the 1960s is, in many respects, simply the result of reworking the MTM, jettisoning the higher-level units, and modifying the focus to include explicit temporal and spatial parameters (as suggested by Gladwin 1936 and Colton

1939). Many phases are the very same constructs first proposed as foci in the MTM (O'Brien 1996b). This, of course, means that many of the basic units of prehistory are historical accidents that exist solely because particular assemblages were known when the MTM was applied in a given area (e.g., Stephenson 1954). The impact of the MTM on contemporary ideas of prehistory remains enormous, if largely unremarked (Chang 1967; Mason 1970; Trigger 1968). One of its greatest impacts at the time it was being formulated was on the archaeology of the American Southwest.

In the Southwest

Brew (1946:32) suggested that it was in the first decade of the twentieth century that "the concept arose of the development of cultures as the proper field for archaeological research in the Southwest." Prehistoric "cultures" were identified on the basis of such things as aggregates of artifacts, associated architectural features, and anatomical features of associated human skeletons (e.g., Kidder 1917b). Stratigraphic excavation provided the means by which the goal of the "proper field for archaeological research" could be obtained. All artifacts in a stratum were associated and constituted an assemblage or aggregate of artifact types worthy of study. By 1927, sufficient observations had been made that it became obvious that if progress was to be made in reaching the desired goal, some consensus had to be reached regarding nomenclature and method.

That year, Kidder hosted the first Pecos Conference, held at Pecos Pueblo, New Mexico, the purpose of which included identifying fundamental problems of Southwestern prehistory, formulating research plans, and producing a unified nomenclature (Kidder 1927). One product was the Basketmaker I-III–Pueblo I-V sequence for northern Arizona. Opinion was unanimous at the conference that "the development of [Southwestern] culture was essentially autochthonous" (Kidder 1927:489). In an attempt to establish "a basis for more precise definition of culture-stages [and] to arrive at agreement as to diagnostic culture-traits . . . [p]ottery, it was agreed, is at the present time the most abundant, convenient and reliable criterion, and the cooking wares the simplest type for preliminary chronological determinations" (Kidder 1927:490). In outlining the sequence of Basketmaker and Pueblo culture periods, it was noted that the earliest unit was only "postulated," and other periods were dichotomized as exhibiting such things as agriculture or not, pottery-making or not, groups living in either small or large communities, and craft specialization or not. This mixed use of inferences and artifact types, and the noting of the presence or absence of cultural traits to characterize cultural periods was typical of later culture history formulations both in the Southwest (see Brew 1946:35) and elsewhere (e.g., the Midwestern Taxonomic Method).

At the seminal Pecos Conference, the potential for confusion was built into the sequence by occasional indications of architectural types associated with various periods, but it was unclear if those were definitive criteria of one or more periods or if they were merely associated with some typically unspecified (at least in Kidder 1927) pottery type meant to be diagnostic of a particular period. This ambiguity became a part of typical culture history procedure, despite at least some recognition of the problem (e.g., Brew 1946:37–43, 76–78). In the Southwest, as in those areas where the Midwestern Taxonomic Method was used, a set of associated artifacts was rendered as a trait list said to represent a "culture." Theoretical warrants for designating the boundaries of the sets were nonexistent and unnecessary because, as we will show, such sets of things seemed, from the implicitly held essentialist view, to be self-evident when encountered in the field.

The Globe Conference of 1931, convened by Harold S. Gladwin and held at Gila Pueblo, Arizona, was organized to deal with Hohokam materials from southern Arizona in a manner not unlike that in which the Pecos Conference was handling much of the rest of the Southwest. As discussed earlier, a system of pottery nomenclature and classification loosely based on a biological model had been adopted a year earlier (Gladwin and Gladwin 1930a, 1934). From this emerged the Gladwins' "comprehensive scheme by which relationships and relative chronology could be expressed" (Gladwin and Gladwin 1934:8–9). They believed that all prehistoric groups in the Southwest had passed through the same cultural stages but at different times in different places—classic unilinear cultural evolution. Consequently, they differentiated among the terms *peoples, cultures,* and *periods.* Their system of nomenclature was taxonomic in structure, and from top (most inclusive level) to bottom consisted of four basic units. *Roots* represented groups of people; *stems* represented distinct geographic areas occupied by specific groups of people (root); *branches* corresponded to "culture areas" (at a much lower and finer level than Kroeber's [1939] culture areas) and represented "the various [cultural] developmental series [of phases] which have sprung from roots" (McGregor 1941:6); and *phases* were time- and space-bound cultural variants within branches that contained characteristic features (associated modes and types of artifacts and architecture) (Gladwin and Gladwin 1934:9–10).

Although Gladwin (1936[†]) perceived major similarities between his scheme and the Midwestern Taxonomic Method then being outlined by McKern (1934), such similarities were superficial. To illustrate the similarities, Gladwin aligned the units of the two schemes as shown in Table 6.1. Gladwin and Gladwin (1934:10) originally merely indicated that phases had

Table 6.1. Harold Gladwin's Alignment of
Archaeological Units Used in the Southwest with
Those of the Midwestern Taxonomic Method

Gladwin[a]	MTM[b]
Root	Basic culture (later, "pattern")
Stem	Phase
Branch	Aspect
Phase	Focus
[Unspecified unit]	Component

[a] Gladwin (1936).
[b] From McKern (1939).

"characteristic features." Gladwin (1936:258) later indicated that in the Southwest, "Components have been listed in our Phases, but not named as such. This designation will be added in our next revised edition." In a later publication (Gladwin 1937:249), he indicated that phases were distinguished by various kinds of things such as types of architecture, types of pottery, and, less frequently, types of stone tools. It is, of course, here and only here where the similarity resides. On the one hand, McKern's units were merely groups that increased in generality as one read up the list. Temporal, spatial, and phyletic relationships were not only not to be implicated, they were explicitly denied. Gladwin's units, on the other hand, explicitly implied (at least initially) temporal, spatial, and phyletic relations.

Shortly after his original formulation appeared in print, Gladwin (1936:258) noted that he felt that because the use of "a generic and a specific name for pottery types implied a biological analogy [it] was a mistake. The idea is being carried too far along biological or zoological lines, and men do not realize the profound differences which exist between zoological species and the things which have been made by men and women. Zoological species do not cross and intergrade [and biological evolution] is so slow as to be hardly distinguishable." He believed cultural evolution was much more rapid and involved "merging and cross-influences. . . . We are really dealing with [cultural] varieties rather than species, and, in consequence, there are bound to be a great many intermediate and transitional types" (Gladwin 1936:258). His skepticism was to be echoed for the next decade as the biological analogy was made ever more rigid by some of his contemporaries.

For the purpose of understanding not only chronological issues but cultural developmental issues as well, Gladwin's scheme was modified by Colton and Hargrave (1937; Colton 1939, 1942) by "fusing it with

McKern's" method (Kluckhohn 1939a:160). Colton (1939:6–8) eventually borrowed the concepts of *determinants, components,* and *foci* from the Midwestern Taxonomic Method (see also Reed 1940). This was "a step in the right direction," according to Kluckhohn (1939a:160), who had been worried about determining which traits were diagnostic of (essentialist) cultural units; he even used the term "type fossils" (in quotes).

Given Kidder's (e.g., 1915:453; Kidder and Kidder 1917:348) earlier discussions of pottery types as having not only ancestral–descendent relationships but also the capacity to become extinct, it is perhaps not surprising that Gladwin at least initially took the biology-like approach that he did. Colton was a biologist by training (Brew 1946:58; Gallagher 1978), and Hargrave had been trained as an archaeologist but had a deep avocational interest in biology, particularly ornithology, and had spent most of his career working for and with Colton (Carothers 1978). Both Kidder's and Gladwin's writings, and Colton and Hargrave's intellectual expertise and interests, probably contributed greatly to the latter two adopting Gladwin's ideas even as Gladwin was abandoning them.

Colton (1939, 1942) in particular followed Gladwin's lead, and his goal was "to outline the cultural units of Northern Arizona and show . . . their relationships" (Colton 1939:3). Noting that the habits, customs, languages, social patterns, and material cultures of extant tribes all differed to similar degrees, he believed that use of the archaeologically accessible material culture traits should permit one to establish how "closely related" prehistoric cultural units were (Colton 1939:5). Marked differences in material culture denoted distantly related (if at all) entities that "might loosely [be called] tribes" (Colton 1939:5). Conversely, similar material cultures denoted closely related tribes. Following McKern (1934, 1937, 1939), the "characteristics that distinguish these 'tribes' are called determinants" (Colton 1939:5). Following Gladwin and Gladwin (1934), a phase was "a fundamental unit in the culture of a human population of an area" made up of "contemporaneous prehistoric sites [the] determinants [of which show] great resemblances to one another"; "genetically related [phases] are grouped together into a branch"; and "We can think of a branch as representing an Indian tribe" (Colton 1939:6).

For Colton, following Gladwin, related branches made up a stem, and related stems constituted a root. Thus, unlike the Midwestern Taxonomic Method, which expressly disavowed such phyletic implications, Gladwin—at least initially—generally, and Colton particularly, offered a warrant of sorts for their groups. This warrant was, however, not well developed and merely used evolutionary terms, the meanings of which were intuitively known to everyone. But simply because the scheme was cast in evolutionary terms did not make it a theoretical system for determining ancestral–descendent relationships. It did not, for example, address the fundamental problem of distinguishing between analogous and homologous similarity. Nor did it specify how phyletic relations between artifact or culture types were to be determined. As it turns out, Colton seems to have merely borrowed the units and grouping procedure of the Midwestern Taxonomic Method; to have applied some of Gladwin's terms to some of the units; and ultimately to have applied to the units a set of evolutionary terms that were generally understandable.

Following McKern's (1934, 1937, 1939) terminology, a component was "merely the expression of a focus at a given site" and was used "to indicate the presence of a focus in a large site where several foci are indicated" (Colton 1939:7, 9). A phase's "description" was based on pottery traits, architectural traits, and "traits in stone, bone, wood, and textiles" (Colton 1939:10–11). "In selecting a type site to illustrate a focus, a small site should be chosen, one in which the time of occupancy was so short that the focus will not be blurred by the mingling of traits from components older or younger than the focus to be described" (Colton 1939:11). A single component representing a brief occupation could serve to provide the significata for a phase, and other components would be grouped with that phase on the basis of those significata. Phases were, therefore, extensionally defined classificatory accidents founded on available samples.

Reviewers focused on Colton's phyletic interpretations rather than on his methods. On the one hand, Reed (1940:190) thought Colton's scheme was a reasonable one: "The genetic and temporal approach seems more desirable in a region such as this where chronology is relatively well-known." On the other hand, Steward (1941:367) remarked

> It is apparent from the cultural relationships shown in this scheme that strict adherence to a method drawn from biology inevitably fails to take into account the distinctively cultural and unbiological fact of blends and crosses between essentially unlike types. . . . It is true that cultural streams often tend to be distinct, but they are never entirely unmixed and often approach a complete blend. A taxonomic scheme cannot indicate this fact without becoming mainly a list of exceptions. It must pigeon-hole. . . . the method employed inevitably distorts true cultural relationships.

In a later statement, Colton (1942:34) explained that the scheme he had borrowed from Gladwin and used for his 1939 monograph was "a classification of prehistoric human groups" and was not a classification of cultures. Colton (1943:264) indicated that "In the reconstruction of history two essential factors are required, the recognition of human social units by objective characters [determinants], and the construction of a time scale." He hinted at a theory of transmission but did not clarify the fact that ideas, rather than genes, were transmitted and inherited. At the time, no one was talking about the transmission or inheritance of traits other than those that were genetically controlled (Brew 1946). Although Colton may have implicitly recognized the significance of what he was proposing, and certainly he possessed the requisite background in biology to have perhaps done so, his lack of exposition of transmission and inheritance mechanisms incorporated within a theory of cultural development failed to convince his contemporaries that what he was doing was somehow warranted. It is unlikely that his (Colton 1939, 1942) mixture of inferences of social organization, religion, and the like with archaeologically visible determinants (material culture traits) contributed to this failure because such was typical practice at the time.

As with the Midwestern Taxonomic Method, Colton's (1942:34, 36) low-level units—phases and branches—were distinguished largely on the basis of stylistic traits such as "pottery designs," whereas his higher-level units—stems and branches—were based on technological and functional traits. While again this was typical of the time, it would ultimately limit the utility of the system. Confusion was compounded by Colton's (e.g., 1939:13–14) lack of specification of the necessary and sufficient conditions for membership in his various phase and branch units; thus Gladwin (1943:22) lamented that he could not determine which sites represented which phases in Colton's (1939) analysis. Colton's system seems to have been largely a grouping method not unlike the Midwestern Taxonomic Method; his definitive criteria for phases were extensional derivatives of all cultural manifestations occupying the same position in time (Colton 1939:15). Thus, quite often, the significata—the necessary and sufficient conditions for unit membership—of a phase were not distinguished from the denotata—the unit members.

Phases, Components, and Stratigraphy

In the Southwest, the earliest use of the term *phase* is found in Gladwin and Gladwin (1929:51), where the term was used as a synonym for *stage* (Olson 1962:458).[1] The term *phase* took on a different meaning when Gladwin and Gladwin (1934:10) used it to denote cultural variations in time and space and suggested that phases be assigned geographic names. A few years later, Gladwin (1937:247–248), following McKern (see also Gladwin 1936), indicated that a phase was a unit of time of relatively brief duration, whereas a cultural stage was of longer duration than a phase (although implying a stage would have a particular place in time), and implied that stages tended to display more significant changes than phases did. Importantly, Gladwin

(1937:248, 249) twice indicated that it was unwise and "not safe to create a phase on [the basis of] only one component."

For Gladwin (1937) and others, a "phase was assumed to have a certain temporal uniformity [and] the search went on to discover what the period of regularity was," and such units were "given inflexible limits and it was assumed that phases could be correlated on a one-to-one basis" (Olson 1962:459). In the 1930s, "A dominant pottery type was the prime indicator for phases" (Olson 1962:460; see Gladwin [1943] and Haury [1937a] for examples); such types were, following Kidder, often ideational units that were extensionally defined and subsequently refined in the light of new evidence until they became *type*, or *index, fossils* that occupied very limited time–space positions. Olson (1962:460), without using the terms, was unsure if Gladwin's cultural units were theoretical or empirical: "It is unclear whether Gladwin was segmenting cultural streams by means of a taxonomic structure [read *classification*] or whether he was implying that the Mogollon *made* the phases, which could be later recognized by the archaeologist." Gladwin's (1943:28) statement that "There is nothing so convincing as repetition [of descriptions of multiple specimens] in establishing a type" leads one to suspect his units for discrete objects were extensionally defined classes. Phases and larger units were identified on the basis of "the presence or absence of various types of pottery" (Gladwin 1943:53), suggesting that these units were also extensionally defined classes.

Stratigraphic excavation allowed a phase's significata to be extracted from the vertical—and thus time-sensitive—spatial units of archaeological sites. Either natural stratigraphic units or arbitrary levels provided sets of artifacts that were by definition temporally associated; from those assemblages could be extracted a list of traits—manifest as artifact types—that had demonstrably (after some trial-and-error refinement) limited temporal distributions. In turn, comparing these temporally diagnostic traits across the geographic space occupied by multiple sites allowed one to select those traits that were linked—held in common by multiple components—and those that could serve as determinants—distinguished by vertically superposed components. Those index fossils came to designate cultures.

The paleobiological approach to identifying species was similar in the 1940s and 1950s and took one of two forms. Either one used stratigraphic discontinuities to define a set of fossils that, through extensional definition, provided the necessary and sufficient conditions for unit membership, or one included within a fossil species only a range of variation in form similar to that evidenced by extant species (Simpson 1943, 1961). The latter progressively became less available as an option to archaeologists as the borders between spatial units, such as cultural areas or Holmes's (1903) ceramic groups, became progressively more blurry throughout the twentieth century.

In the Southwest, Haury (1936b:80) used stratigraphy to help designate phases: "The sequence of phases was first determined by stratigraphy of pottery types, and the association of these types with houses." Haury (1937b:19–20) clearly specified the procedure for defining phases: First, establish pottery types; second, determine the stratigraphic positions and relations of types "to provide the primary diagnostic of phases"; and third, examine other categories of artifacts—architecture, figurines, stone tools— "to round out and complete the list of phase components." That last word, *components,* is a term that designates parts, elements, or constituents and was an unfortunate choice, since the term "component" was coming to mean something else entirely as a result of the Midwestern Taxonomic Method (Gladwin 1936, 1937; McKern 1934, 1937, 1939). But the significant point here is that Southwestern cultural phases were constructed on the basis of types that had limited time–space distributions; that is, they were stratigraphically *confirmed* (the historical-significance test). Thus the types became index fossils that designated phases (Gladwin 1943; Haury 1937a).

In retrospect, it seems to us that in light of the general conception that culture was akin to a continuously flowing braided stream of ideas, the so-called stratigraphic revolution was, in the long run, more damaging than helpful. True, it allowed the measurement of time, but it measured time in discontinuous chunks we call strata or arbitrary levels and reinforced the essentialist metaphysic typically used—if implicitly—to structure and explain the archaeological record. An excellent example of this is found in Haury's (1937a, 1937b) discussion of the excavations at Snaketown. Haury (1937b:20) noted that

> Rubbish pits proved to be of the highest value in giving unmixed samples [of pottery] because of the short time represented by the accumulation of the deposits. More than two phases were seldom represented [because] [b]eing relatively small, the time required to fill them was usually too short for the material to change. . . . With much of the pottery found in [such] pits it was easier to determine those traits which constituted one phase ceramically than would have been possible with pottery from other sources.

Stratigraphic excavations confirmed the sequence of types in some cases; in other cases strata "had relatively little value as far as phase changes were concerned, i.e., the changes took place too slowly to have been registered between any two contiguous strata" (Haury 1937b:25). The use of strata as collection units, then, and the use of essentialist type fossils disallowed the detection of continuous change at the level of culture units.

As well, the use of type fossils resulted in the detection of strata containing what were interpreted as "mixtures" of pottery representing two or more phases (Haury 1937b:27). At the level of a cultural unit, there was, then, no change but only transformations from one phase to the next. Detection of "early, full, and late" manifestations of a phase was the result of finding pottery with poorly developed attributes of a particular phase, well-developed attributes of that particular phase, and a mixture of the well-developed attributes with attributes of the succeeding phase (Haury 1937b:21). Haury (1937a:169–170) wrote that "such transitional or borderline specimens are thrown into prominence as tangible evidence of continuity in the development of pottery" and demonstrated a "genetic" relation between different pottery types (Haury 1937a:212). The confusion of ideational and empirical units is clear in this wording, just as it is elsewhere. A demonstrably gradual, continuous evolution of pottery was cut up into stratigraphically documented chunks termed *phases*, which in turn were treated as real culture units.

Colton (1939:9) used McKern's (1939) term *component* in the same sense that McKern did—"to indicate the presence of a focus in a large site where several foci are indicated." But he also equated the term *phase* with McKern's *focus:* A phase–focus was "a fundamental unit in the culture of the human population of an area" (Colton 1939:6). A phase–focus unit was distinguished from antecedent or later units "by the differences in material culture traits, sometimes very slight" (Colton 1942:34). Kidder et al. (1946:9) defined a phase as "A cultural complex possessing traits sufficiently characteristic to distinguish it for purposes of preliminary archaeological classification, from earlier and later manifestations of the cultural development of which it formed a part, and from other contemporaneous complexes." For Martin et al. (1949:17), a phase referred to "an interval of time and to specific pottery types, bone and stone tool types, and house forms, all of which we have deliberately and arbitrarily set up as classifications." A few years later, Martin et al. (1952:30, 31) stated that "a phase is an artificial and chronological system superposed on man-made materials. . . . [W]e know that there is no break between phases and that phases are merely *arbitrary culture groups* set off in arbitrary units of time. . . . [A] phase may mean a moment, a span of centuries, a cluster of traits, or none of these; but rather an endless moving belt of progress—a continuum."

Sets of artifacts contained within the discontinuous chunks of the stratigraphic record that Martin et al. (1952) dealt with "were assigned to specific phases on the basis of their ceramic assemblages" (Olson 1962:467). Once temporal and spatial boundaries were set for ceramic types, other traits were imported to describe the phase, and sherds and pots were relegated to a position where they had "no more emphasis in synthesis than any other item of material culture" (Olson 1962:469). That is, artifacts of various kinds—not necessarily (and often not at all) structured as Fordian types (time-sensitive ideational units)—that were geologically associated *with* Fordian types were appended to the descriptions of individual phase-focus units. The result was a mixing of various kinds of things, some that were clearly what we would term Fordian types that were dominantly stylistic (Dunnell 1978) and others that were variously descriptive, technological, or functional in nature. The end product of such exercises, whether one worked in the Southwest, the East, or the Midwest, was the construction of " 'periods' [that] will prove to represent distinct cultures when the bare skeleton of a ceramic chronology has been given flesh and body in the form of a full and 'functional' culture description" (Willey and Woodbury 1942:236).

Just as he pointed out some of the weaknesses inherent in the classification of artifacts, Brew (1946) identified weaknesses inherent in the building of cultural sequences in the Southwest. Because most of the schemes being generated began with what were termed "basic cultures," Brew focused his remarks on that concept:

> In arranging the archaeological finds of the Southwest into groups the practice has been similar to the custom now commonly used in biology in the classification of species. Groups of trait [read *artifact type*] assemblages having a large number of common characteristics have been banded together in "cultures." Under this system the assemblages (sites) in any one of the cultures have more traits in common with each other than with any assemblage in one of the other cultures. . . .
>
> All this has been done informally. There has not been a definite, agreed-upon, set of rules for such classification. Specifically, there has been no definition of the number of traits in common or of the degree of divergence from other cultures necessary in order to permit the creation of a new basic culture.
>
> Consequently it seems legitimate, first of all, to ask the question: what is a basic culture, in terms of traits common internally and traits divergent externally. Since "basic cultures," like genera and species, are arbitrary concepts of the students working in the field, it seems that we should have some sort of definition so that when a new basic culture is announced, we may have some way of determining its status in comparison with the basic cultures already established. (Brew 1946:76–77; see also Brew 1942:192–193)

Do not confuse Brew's "basic culture" with that of McKern (1939). Brew's comments were directed at least in part toward McGregor's (1941:120) seminal definition of a basic culture as "the base or foundation upon which later cultures might have been built. Thus a basic culture might be defined as the earliest definite culture from which others might be traced. To do this with accuracy it is necessary to be able to show that the later people are definitely, even genetically, related to the first or earliest known group. This requires a detailed knowledge of the archaeological history of the cultures considered." As with cladistics (Forey 1990), one might wonder how far back was far enough (Daifuku 1952:194).

Brew believed that there was an even more important problem. He implied that the problem reduced in part to improper assignment of cultural traits (manifest as artifact types) to particular cultures: "This is one of the most glaring faults of our classificatory systems. They force such assumptions and the result is a peculiar warping of comparative trait lists. If we could devise some method of determining invariant indices of differences and likenesses of cultural traits, we might perhaps avoid this difficulty by eliminating the cultural labels" (Brew 1946:76). On the one hand, the method Brew suggested for "determining invariant indices of differences and likenesses of cultural traits" was analysis of variance, in which one could, Brew (1946:76) reasoned, separate what we would today term functional and stylistic variants (Dunnell 1978). Brew lacked the theory requisite to such a method. On the other hand, proper assignment of a trait was likely to result, Brew thought, from accurate dating of a trait (see also Ford 1952). This, of course, presumed that one not only knew when a particular culture existed but also knew the significata (read *assemblage of associated types*) of a culture. Brew failed to notice that if we know these last two things, then the problem of trait assignment disappears *if* the types and assemblages are "arbitrary," or ideational, classes. The problem exists because the units are extensionally defined and the significata and denotata are not kept separate conceptually.

Brew's (1946:77) final plea for "no more [newly proposed] basic cultures in the Southwest until we have a workable definition of 'basic culture'" not only failed to address the real issue but also revealed his failure to recognize the problem. In Brew's terms, basic cultures were denoted by banding together trait assemblages with a large number of common characteristics. And it is this statement of procedure that revealed the real issue: Trait assemblages were constructed from a list of associated artifact types. Then, the spatial boundaries of a set of artifacts were taken to represent the boundaries of a prehistoric culture. In lieu of a theoretical warrant for boundary specifications, stratigraphic boundaries were often used as a surrogate. Thus problems of comparability emerged because, as we all know now, different strata can represent time spans of rather different magnitude. Colton's (1939) suggestion noted earlier that a small site should be used to illustrate a cultural phase acknowledged this fact and was an attempt to place the compared assemblages on more equal footing. Of course, it assumed that site size is systematically and directly related to duration of occupation—an assumption that might be true in some general sense but which is, in reality, often untrue. More importantly, it would fail to fulfill its purpose even if the assumption were met all of the time because it conflates the materialist cultural continuum with essentialist culture units.

Brew's failure was not his alone. His contemporaries fell prey to the same problem. It seems they all held what appears today to have been an essentialist notion of culture development; that is, cultures were real and discontinuous units that could be discovered. Kidder's (1936b:xx) "recognizable nodes of individuality" as representing ceramic periods come to mind. Such a notion circumvents the necessity of a theoretically informed designation of temporal–spatial boundaries for aggregates of artifacts. The aggregates are already bounded by unique time–space stratigraphic boundaries, and so theory is unnecessary; commonsense ascription of stratigraphically bounded aggregates of artifacts to cultural units is possible once the significata for the units are discerned. The latter are in turn derived extensionally from selected components and thus are historical accidents.

Southwestern archaeologists were not very successful in grappling with the paramount issues of classifying aggregates of artifacts, and they continued to muddle along into the mid-twentieth century using procedures developed in the second and third decades. Most archaeologists, however, abjured what they saw as the genetic implications of the Gladwin–Colton system, either because they disapproved of the evolutionary constructions in principle (e.g., Brew 1946; Reiter 1938a; Steward 1941) or because they thought the data required to make such connections were lacking (e.g., Ford 1940). There was, as we have seen, no theoretical basis for any such conclusion, and thus there were no methods for detecting phyletic relations.

Formalization of the Classification of Aggregates

Philip Phillips and Gordon R. Willey published a programmatic statement entitled "Method and Theory in American Archaeology: An Operational Basis for Culture-Historical Integration (Phillips and Willey 1953[†])" as an attempt to formalize the classification of aggregates. That paper, along with a later one (Willey and Phillips 1955), were combined to form the basis of a book, *Method and Theory in American Archaeology* (Willey and Phillips 1958), that summarized much of the conceptualization of Americanist archaeology and prehistory in the 1950s. Their earlier paper (Phillips and Willey 1953) was largely a post hoc description of the manner in which many archaeologists of the time more or less operated, though they offered a few suggestions of their own as to how to classify aggregates.

Their 1953 article seems to have grown out of, particularly, Willey's (1953b) perception of a growing disparity between practice and the central tenets of the Midwestern Taxonomic Method. The MTM, although disavowing any phyletic implications of its taxonomic structure, was founded on typological—that is, formal—similarity. Within archaeology, it was "axiomatic" that typological similarity was an "indicator of cultural relatedness," and thus "a common or similar history" for units judged to be similar was automatically implied, despite protestations of McKern to the contrary (Willey 1953b:363–364). Further, Willey (1953b:369) noted that equating similar appearance with similar history was methodologically flawed: "The processes by which, or through which, cultural continuity and change are maintained or accomplished have not received study and reflective thought commensurate with the way these concepts have been invoked by American archaeologists." Finally, the equation was theoretically flawed: "it appears that evolutionary theory has been very naïvely applied. Monogenesis of southwestern cultures is a postulate to be tested, not an axiomatic explanation" (Willey 1953b:369; see also Phillips and Willey 1953:630–631). The Gladwin–Colton scheme was in need of testing prior to its being used as an explanatory device. No theory of cultural development was available, and using biological evolutionary terms with commonsense connotations was not a good substitute for theory. The alternative proposed by Phillips and Willey was, however, not much better than the scheme they sought to replace.

Phillips and Willey (1953:617) suggested that "an archaeological culture is an arbitrary division of the space–time–cultural continuum" and thus followed some of their predecessors in conceiving culture history as a braided stream—a materialist conception. They began their discussion by noting that any archaeological unit is "the resultant combination of three unlike basic properties: space, time, and form" (Phillips and Willey 1953:617). Spaulding (1957) found this line of reasoning to be fundamentally in error due to the fact that space, time, and form were rather different properties of phenomena and thus each required quite distinct scales of measurement. Phillips and Willey (1953) gave explicit definitions of three spatial units of different scales—*locality* (often a site), *region,* and *area*—the first two of which they aligned, admittedly tentatively, with a community (or local group) and a tribe (or society), respectively. This reflected their essentialist viewpoint: Their units had some reality in a social or anthropological sense that could perhaps be discovered. Their formal units began, not surprisingly, with *components* and *phases.* The latter was chosen over McKern's *focus* because Phillips and Willey preferred the "stronger temporal implication" of *phase,* precisely the point Gladwin (1936) had made earlier (a point not acknowledged by Phillips and Willey).

A component was approximately equivalent to the sociological units of band, neighborhood, and village (Phillips and Willey 1953:621), and a phase was approximately equivalent to a society (Phillips and Willey 1953:622). This attempt to align archaeological units with sociocultural ones revealed that Phillips and Willey (1953) were thinking in essentialist terms; their component and phase units were justified because they had some objective and empirical reality. There was, of course, no theoretical basis for such interpretations of components and phases, though the interpretations rendered in ethnographic terms provided a commonsense warrant for the archaeological units in lieu of a theoretical one. It was, after all, Phillips (1955:246–247) who two short years later coined that oft-repeated phrase "New World archaeology is anthropology or it is nothing" (repeated in Binford [1962:217], Deetz [1970:115], Flannery [1967:119], and Willey and Phillips [1958:2]; Flannery incorrectly attributed the phrase to Willey). Such a commonsense position had already cast a cloud over culture history—a then-unappreciated sign that a storm was brewing.

Following McKern (1939:308), Phillips and Willey (1953:619) defined a component as "the manifestation of a given [phase] at a specific site." A phase was conceived of as being temporally, spatially, and formally "sufficiently characteristic to distinguish it from all other units similarly conceived"; "components are combined into phases because analysis reveals cultural uniformity amounting to practical identity" (Phillips and Willey 1953:620, 630). The latter echoed McKern's (1939) discussion and reveals the influence of the MTM on Phillips and Willey. But while the MTM was a grouping technique, Phillips and Willey formalized this aspect of culture history procedure into one involving *classes*. McKern (1939) and his contemporaries (e.g., Gladwin 1937) were explicit in stating that a phase–focus unit could not be represented by a single component, indicating that theirs was a grouping procedure for extensionally defined units. Phillips and Willey (1953:620) stated that "In practice . . . it often happens that a phase is initially defined on the strength of one component . . . but the expectation is implicit that other components will be found and the original definition modified accordingly." Thus, a phase was a class that could be named and its definition specified on the basis of a single component. The necessary and sufficient conditions for membership were extensionally determined from that single component; the extensional aspect was underscored by the potential for definition modification in light of newly discovered components. For example, when several local sequences—where "a local sequence is a series of components found in vertical stratigraphic relationship in a single site" (Phillips and Willey 1953:623)—are correlated, the correlation is generally "accompanied by a progressive generalization of the definitions [of phases] until their original usefulness is impaired. . . . [I]n the process the original formulations [of local sequences] are retailored to fit the wider spatial and (perhaps) deeper temporal requirements" (Phillips and Willey 1953:623). Phases were viewed as accidental constructs largely dependent on the first component or set of components specified.

The usual problem remained: How were sets of things to be identified so that their similarities could be measured? Phillips and Willey's first requirement was to identify the boundaries of the sets. What helped here was the suggestion that "a site or a level within a site" could be a single component and thus represent a phase (Phillips and Willey 1953:620). Thus, spatial boundaries, whether naturally or arbitrarily defined, dictated what went into a component and thus what went into a phase; all artifacts within the boundaries were included within the sets of things to be compared. Otherwise, Phillips and Willey were as obtuse as their predecessors: Phases are classes of components, and components are empirical manifestations of phases. Thus, one must have the phases (classes) in order to recognize or identify components, but one needs components to write the phase (class) definitions. The result is that a phase is extensionally defined on the basis of one component. This is acceptable given Phillips and Willey's commonsense warrants for their units: Phases are somehow real, being approximately equivalent to real societies, as required by their notion "that you cannot hope to shed light on processes by means of abstractions [read *phases as classes*] that have no theoretically possible counterparts in cultural and social 'reality'" (Phillips and Willey 1953:629). Their "theory," unfortunately, is not theory in the usual sense but rather a theoretically vacuous hypothesis concerning a possible relation between an archaeological unit and an ethnological unit, a fundamental problem that had been identified earlier (Guthe 1952; Jennings 1947).

This leaves the critical question unanswered: What, precisely, is a component? That a component is supposed to be equivalent to a band, neighborhood, or village provides a clue. It is, as in the MTM, the manifestation of a single occupation; thus it is a set of temporally, spatially, and behaviorally associated artifacts. As Willey (1953b:363–364) noted,

> the concept of the assemblage is implicitly grounded in the historical validity of the artifact–feature complex as a *unit*. Such a unity, by the very nature of its internal associations, bespeaks spatial–temporal correlates. . . . [T]here is [therefore] covert historical theory in the assemblage concept. . . . The unity of the assemblage, if historical unity can be assumed, must lead to the conclusion that we are dealing with the remains of an integrated cultural complex in the case of the *component*.

That an assemblage represents a temporally associated set of artifacts is a hypothesis that warrants investigation (e.g., Schiffer 1987). Unfortunately, Americanist archaeology still lacks a theory for specifying what aggregates of artifacts should consist of and how to specify temporal–spatial boundaries of the aggregates such that they are relevant to the analytical problems at hand (Dunnell 1971b:149–152, 1995).

The locations of the temporal–spatial boundaries of an assemblage are vague because that is all they can be in the absence of theory. Stratigraphic boundaries are thus typically called on in lieu of a theoretically informed specification of boundaries. Implicitly, the reasoning is that stratigraphic boundaries are empirical and do not require theoretical specification. As Rouse (1953:59) noted, stratigraphic excavation provides collections of artifacts that "are segregated by layers of refuse and subdivisions thereof, in order that the succession of *occupations* may be determined" (emphasis added). This echoed Clark Wissler's (1917a) and Gerard Fowke's (1922) earlier remarks that a single continuous occupation will occur in an unstratified deposit, whereas multiple occupations will each occur in a separate stratum. The degree to which the artifacts included in an assemblage from a single depositional unit represent a palimpsest (e.g., Brooks 1982) is not considered because it *cannot* be from such an empirical perspective. Rather, one (implicitly) assumes the stratigraphic boundaries somehow correspond to the problem at hand—identifying "cultures" as represented by single occupations. Thus, the creation of artificial boundaries, such as when one excavates in arbitrary levels, is to be avoided in order to "prevent contamination of one classified culture type by another" (Phillips 1942:200).

It is interesting that Phillips (1942)—a staunch essentialist—should have derogated others for using arbitrary levels to bound aggregates in order to maintain the identity of essentialist cultural units. His abhorrence resided in the fact that in the absence of natural stratigraphic boundaries, rather than create artificial ones, "Your archaeologist unhampered by a classificatory bias, would find no trouble at all in breaking [a chronological series of artifact types] down in sequent periods, each marked by the appearance of a new type of material" (Phillips 1942:198). In other words, the lack of stratigraphically bounded aggregates is not a problem; the boundaries are inherent in the artifact data themselves.

To Phillips and Willey, the apparent stability of phases was not totally an artifact of the geological boundaries of their member components. The "material traits [of a phase] can, under certain circumstances, be remarkably stable" (Phillips and Willey 1953:622). Recall that Kidder's (1936b:xx) ceramic periods were rendered as "recognizable nodes of individuality." One could construct local sequences, regional sequences, and period and area chronologies that, while increasing the spatial scale, "still maintain contact with the primary stratigraphic data" (Phillips and Willey 1953:624) but simultaneously reflect Kidder-like nodes or peaks of occurrence. This is the essentialist metaphysic. To extend the metaphor, the materialist's braided stream of culture no longer flows gradually and continuously; its rate of flow is jerky, generally slow but punctuated by temporally brief, fast stretches (see also Spaulding 1957). This notion that there are periods of stasis in the flowing braided stream of cultural history is one significant legacy of the culture history paradigm. Unfortunately, the resulting units— typically called phases—are perceived to be analytical tools rather than mere descriptions or classes, an issue to which we return below.

In their later formulation, Willey and Phillips (1958:24) noted that as "typological and stratigraphic analyses become more refined, it often becomes desirable to subdivide phases into smaller (primarily temporal) units, and it seems best to regard these as *subphases*." Subphases can be distinguished by "differences [in] a few specific items of [phase] content or where such differences are expressible only in variations in frequency" (Willey and Phillips 1958:24). The latter was no doubt a nod to James Ford, to whom Willey and Phillips dedicated their book and for whom cultural periods were marked by shifting frequencies of artifact types. For Willey and Phillips, phases and subphases are classes constructed to measure temporal–spatial differences in the distributions of artifact forms. Being extensionally defined, those definitions are modified as new components are found, until some are so refined that they denote smaller segments of the time–space continuum than other, less refined classes. The former are subphases, and the latter are phases.

Rouse responded to Phillips and Willey's (1953) original reasoning in an article entitled "On the Correlation of Phases of Culture" (Rouse 1955[†]). Rouse expressed concern over Phillips and Willey's handling of the distinction between empirical and theoretical units (our terms, not Rouse's), and he sought to clarify it (see MacWhite [1956] for other thoughts on Phillips and Willey's discussion). He noted that, on the one hand, a component is an "analysis unit" that has "objective and physical reality" (Rouse 1955:713). The objectivity derives from its boundedness, and the boundaries are often, if not always, stratigraphic. That a component represented "one occupation" (Rouse 1955:713) was the typical inference well prior to Rouse's statement (e.g., Brew 1946; McKern 1939). On the other hand, "a phase is an abstraction [read *ideational unit*] from the reality of components" (Rouse 1955:713). This unit is rendered as "a complex of traits which recurs from component to component and which serves to distinguish its particular components from others" (Rouse 1955:713); a phase is a class consisting of an extensionally derived list of significata. To clarify his point, Rouse (1955:714) drew an analogy between a pottery type (significata) and the sherds (denotata) of that type.

One might well ask at this stage what Spaulding, who had earlier offered an empirical challenge to culture historians regarding their artifact classifications, thought of Phillips and Willey's formulation, particularly of their notion that "an archaeological culture is an arbitrary division of the space–time–cultural continuum. . . . an arbitrarily defined unit or segment of the total continuum" (Phillips and Willey 1953:617). In an article entitled "Prehistoric Cultural Development in the Eastern United States," Spaulding (1955) used the term *assemblage* as a synonym for component. Once components, or assemblages, are arranged in time, "chronological periods [are defined] in terms of important cultural innovations" (Spaulding 1955:13)—the presence or absence of traits. Spaulding made this point again in a letter to Willey and Phillips that they published in their 1958 book:

> It is true that any assemblage represents a segment of a continuous stream of cultural tradition extending back into time, but once you grant the purpose of a scientific exposition of culture history, the process of classifying the time stream with respect to its cultural characteristics is anything but arbitrary. It should be classified in terms of events so as to yield a succession of distinct culture types. . . . [W]idely accepted cultural theory indicates that the normal pattern is one of relative stability, then rapid growth through the introduction of a critical new element followed very quickly by a number of other new elements, then a period of relative stability, and so on. . . . [T]he recognition of the sharp [changes] is a scientific obligation of the archaeologist. The segments so recognized are certainly not the result of arbitrary classification. . . . So time itself is continuous and proceeds at an unvarying rate, but culture change in relation to time probably never proceeds at an unvarying rate, and useful archaeological classifications of chronology are those which have sharp rate changes as their limiting points. A good chronological classification yields a number of periods, each of which is characterized by a distinctive "culture" ("culture type" in my terminology). (Spaulding, in Willey and Phillips 1958:15–16)

To Spaulding then, there was a set of natural joints, or inherent discontinuities, in the continuum (see also Spaulding 1957, 1982:11). Thus in his dealings with aggregates, as in his dealings with artifacts, Spaulding held an essentialist view. Similarities among components through time and across space "can be related to the proposition that culture change is systematic rather than capricious and to the auxiliary proposition that an important basis for the systematic behavior of culture is its continuous transmission through the agency of person to person contact" (Spaulding 1955:14; see also Rouse 1939). Formal similarity between components implied similarity in their time–space distributions, and vice versa. Major differences in culture types suggested invasion, and minor shifts suggested diffusion as the process responsible for culture change. Thus, in many ways, Spaulding echoed the words of those whose artifact classifications he questioned. But he also reinforced Phillips and Willey's and others' essentialist notions of the discontinuous flow of the cultural braided stream.

In response to Spaulding's onslaught, Willey and Phillips (1958:16–17) modified their original wording and indicated that they now preferred "the concept of an archaeological unit [read *culture*] as a provisionally defined segment of the total continuum, whose ultimate validation will depend on the degree to which its internal spatial and temporal dimensions can be shown to coincide with significant variations in the nature and rate of cultural change in that continuum." Archaeologists were to make every effort to "understand precisely what quantities of space and time are involved in the formulation" of such culture units (Willey and Phillips 1958:17). This concern attended the notion of the *tempo* of culture change; is it slow or fast, is it gradual and continuous or punctuated and discontinuous, is it some combination of both, and if so, when is it one and when the other? Having only recently been provided with a nearly universally applicable absolute chronological scale in the form of radiocarbon dating (Johnson 1951; see Marlowe [1980] and Taylor [1985, 1987:147–170] for histories of the development of radiocarbon dating), it is not surprising that questions concerning the tempo of culture change could only now be seriously asked and answered. Dendrochronology had provided some earlier insight to such matters, but it was limited temporally and geographically. Radiocarbon dating had no such limitations, and answers to questions of duration and tempo forced considerable rethinking (e.g., Johnson 1961:5).

In the volume stemming from their survey-and-excavation work in the Mississippi Valley, Phillips et al. (1951:455) made the following statement: "We stand before the threat of the atom in the form of radiocarbon dating. This may be the last chance for old-fashioned, uncontrolled guessing." Sixteen years later, Frederick Johnson (1967; see also Johnson 1961) summarized the benefits that had come to archaeology from this "threat": Suspected sequences could be checked, different local sequences could be correlated, and the absolute ages of important events such as the first peopling of the Americas and the appearance of domestication could be determined. But Phillips et al.'s caution was not entirely misplaced. Luther Cressman (1951:311) immediately pointed out that "The C14 method is no miraculous tool for the archaeologist." One had to be sure, Cressman cautioned, of the association between the dated samples and the items one wished to date. He made it clear that radiocarbon dating, just like dendrochronology, was an indirect dating technique and demanded good archaeological technique in the field. Where, for example, had dated charcoal samples come from in a site? As Johnson (1967:165) noted later, there was a "return to the trenches for a more careful look at the provenience of samples."

Interestingly, Johnson (1961:4–5) also noted that dendrochronological dating had been "responsible for now forgotten pangs and heartbreaks among archaeologists because the estimates of ages in relative chronologies based on assumptions of the rate of culture change frequently differed significantly from dates derived from counting tree-rings. This situation is rather amusingly similar to the uncertainties, misconceptions, and face-savings which, in the early 1950's, accompanied the introduction of radiocarbon dates." But the net result of the development of radiocarbon dating was that stratified deposits or thick deposits that could be excavated in arbitrary levels were no longer mandatory to work out a sequence, nor were percentage stratigraphy and seriation. All one needed were radiocarbon dates associated with artifacts. Archaeologists began to forget basic culture-historical methods in their attempts to establish chronological sequences. Those methods had been focused on making the temporal dimension visible; they now were viewed in large part as unnecessary, given that radiocarbon dating made that dimension readily visible.

Building local sequences of cultures or phases was not, however, the ultimate step in culture history procedure. A later step was to "historically integrate" (Phillips and Willey 1953:628) components and phases into some sort of meaningful structure in the sense of cultural development and cultural processes. To perform the integration, Phillips and Willey (1953:629) advocated the use of "concepts that make no pretense to sociological [read *ethnological*] or any other kind of reality. Tools like traditions and horizon style have come into existence precisely in response to an awareness that the main currents of culture flow through space and time without regard for social and political boundaries." The Midwestern Taxonomic Method could not serve such an integrative function because with its successively larger and more general units, "phases [foci] tend to drop out of sight. We propose to keep them in sight" because they are to some degree ethnographically real (Phillips and Willey 1953:629). Phillips and Willey (1953:629), and their predecessors and contemporaries, were "concerned with process as well as history." To address the concern with process, different kinds of integrative units were necessary. It is to these kinds of units that we now turn.

Horizons, Horizon Styles, and Traditions

Emil Haury (1937b) spoke of "horizons," but he used the term more or less as a synonym for cultural phases in the sense of Gladwin (1936). As we have seen, Ford (1938:262) discussed "distinct time horizons" represented by decoration complexes, and he suggested that while these would be found over "a restricted area," they could serve as "stylistic time horizons" over larger areas. A few years later, Ford and Willey (1941) presented a synopsis of the prehistory of the eastern United States in which they (1) identified a number of transects across portions of the eastern United States as horizontal lines across geographic space, and for each of those transects they (2) presented "chronological profiles," or sequences of cultures, that were variously crosscut by sloping lines that represented "cultural horizons" (Figure 6.2). Herbert Spinden (1928) had earlier spoken of various "horizons" of culture and had illustrated them as sloping through time as they passed through space (see Willey 1981 for discussion); Ford and Willey's figures seem to have been heavily modeled after Spinden's, though the horizons of the latter appear to have encompassed inferred forms of adaptation such as "arid lands agriculture," whereas the horizons of the former included burial-mound forms only. William G. Haag (1942) and John W. Bennett (1944) appear to have mimicked Ford and Willey's (1941) connotation in their use of the term *horizon*.

A. L. Kroeber (1944:104), credited by Willey and Sabloff (1993:204) with formalizing the concept, indicated it had become common practice in South American archaeology to think of a *horizon style* as a unit "showing definably distinct features, some of which extend over a large area, so that its relations with other, more local styles serve to place these in relative time, according as the relations are of priority, consociation, or subsequence." Shortly after Kroeber's (1944) discussion, Willey (1945) offered his own definition of the concept of horizon style and simultaneously introduced a new conceptual unit. Willey (1945:49–50) suggested two criteria were fundamental to the horizon style: "first, that there shall be resemblance among the style groups so classed; second, that there be uniformity in relative position in the sequence on the part of the style as it occurs from region to region. Resemblances among component regional styles of a horizon style are established on the basis of very definite sets of features." Willey (1945:49, 53) implied that the "artistic similarity" representing a horizon style was "an integration of artistic elements which has been widely diffused at a given time period," indicating a horizon style could exist at the scale of an attribute or mode (*sensu* Rouse 1939). A horizon style could also exist at the scale of discrete object (artifact type) or at the scale of complexes or sets of discrete objects (multiple associated types) (Willey 1945:50). Horizon styles could be used as "style markers for specific time horizons"; in other words, "horizon styles are the horizontal stringers by which the upright columns of specialized regional development are tied together in the time chart" (Willey 1945:53, 55).

Willey (1945:50) cautioned that "Horizon-style resemblance, although specific, does not indicate cultural identity of the groups who participated

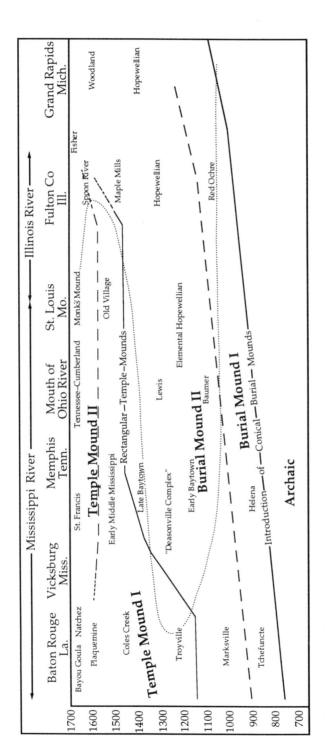

Figure 6.2. James Ford and Gordon Willey's alignment of archaeological phenomena along a south-to-north transect from Baton Rouge, Louisiana, to Grand Rapids, Michigan (after Ford and Willey 1941).

in the style." In a later paper (Willey 1948:8), he indicated that a horizon or horizon style

> is an abstraction based upon the recurrence of specific features of style or manufacture in prehistoric artifacts, mainly pottery, from one region to another so that the phenomena [allow us to] coordinate our knowledge of the past in a broad temporal and spatial scheme. This integration is made possible when the same stylistic or technical complex of traits is found in the respective cultural sequences of geographically widely separated regions, and by this means the two or more sequences are brought together and equated in time.

Still later, Willey (1951:111) was even more explicit: "The historical uniqueness of stylistic pattern is the fundamental assumption underlying the concept of 'horizon style.' As the result of this uniqueness, the presence of any style in two or more places has a high synchronic value." Overall, then, horizon styles were formed as theoretical units meant to measure the similarity in time of similar forms of artifacts or their attributes, and thus to allow different cultures to be correlated temporally. That the similarity was of the homologous (common ancestry) sort is indicated by the requisite assumption of historical uniqueness and by the implication that a horizon style diffuses—the cause of the similarity (the transmission of an idea from one population to another). Such similarity does not indicate cultural identity because the latter is conceived at the much larger scale of "culture complex" (Table 6.2).

The new concept, *tradition*, had been around for some time in vague form as the persistence of one or more culture traits through time (e.g., Rouse 1939:14), but Willey formalized it. He defined a tradition as comprising "a line, or a number of lines, of pottery development through time

Table 6.2. Scale Relations of Some Culture History Units

Scale of unit		Historically equidistant	Extensive space, brief time	Extensive time, small space
Empirical	Conceptual			
Attribute of discrete object	Mode	Mode	Horizon style	(Pottery) tradition
Discrete object	Class	Type	Horizon (style)	Tradition
Aggregate of discrete objects	Assemblage	Phase	Horizon	Whole culture tradition

within the confines of a certain technique or decorative constant" (Willey 1945:53). Thus, a tradition could be denoted at the scale of attribute or mode. "A pottery tradition includes broad descriptive categories of ceramic decoration which undoubtedly have value in expressing historical relationships when the relationships are confined to the geographic boundaries of" what Willey (1945:53) described as "a unified culture area [wherein] important cultural developments were essentially local and basically interrelated for at least a thousand years [thereby demonstrating a] fundamental cultural unity." A tradition could also be denoted at the scale of discrete object. A pottery tradition "lacks the specific quality of the localized pottery style. . . . In successive time periods through which the history of ceramic development can be traced, certain styles arose within the tradition" (Willey 1945:53). It is at the scale of large complexes of types that traditions became what were later termed "whole culture traditions" (Table 6.2).

A tradition contrasted with a horizon style in that the former underscored "the point that generic similarities in decoration and form of ceramics do not necessarily indicate stylistic complexes diffused rapidly through space in a relatively short period of time" (Willey 1945:55). To Willey, traditions demonstrated "the staying power [read *persistence*] of certain regional-cultural ideas; but, for the present at least, it tells us little else" (Willey 1945:56). That is, one might perceive the persistence of a class (ideational unit) in terms of its empirical representatives being found throughout a stratigraphic sequence. In lieu of a theoretical justification, however, such continuous representation demonstrated by a class is warranted simply in commonsense terms—it represents the "persistence" of an idea through time. No theoretical consideration of the perceived continuity demanding the mechanisms of transmission and heritability accompanied these musings.

Early on, then, a tradition told us little because there was no means of explaining why a class persisted. Willey (1945:56) did, however, cite Ralph Linton's (1944) study of the persistence of certain attributes of Woodland pottery. Linton (1944:369) proposed that the attributes that persisted concerned the functional properties of the vessels: "Simple tools and utensils which serve their purpose adequately are among the best guides to culture origins and continuities. They become integrated into the largely unconscious business of daily living and tend to persist untouched by contact with neighboring cultures or by changing fashions." What we would today term *stylistic* attributes and types are more prone to change, Linton reasoned, than functional ones: "The main stress was laid upon painted wares and shapes having an aesthetic appeal. This is quite in agreement with the frequently observed fact that culture elements [or *traits*] which do not involve change in long-established habits or basic economic techniques are accepted much more readily than those which do" (Linton 1944:380). This followed earlier thinking such as Haury's (1937a:223) that "utilitarian" ceramic types were "less subject to rapid changes than painted pottery."

Here, then, was an early hint that perhaps horizons and traditions were concerned with different kinds of theoretical units; the first might consist of stylistic attributes or types, the latter of functional attributes or types (Dunnell 1978), though in the absence of theory such a difference was probably mostly an accidental result of analysis. Failure to pursue and develop theoretical accounts of this potential difference between the two concepts, together with the persistent confusion of theoretical and empirical units, would continue to plague the use of, as well as the explanatory potential of, horizon styles, traditions, and what came to be known later as horizons.

Phillips and Willey (1953) used the terms *horizon* and *horizon style* interchangeably (a fact they later acknowledged [Willey and Phillips 1958:31]) to characterize similarity in form across a large expanse of space and through a *brief* period of time. To characterize formal stability over a *long* period of time across an expanse of space (usually small), they used the concept of *tradition*. Similar to Willey's (1945) earlier discussion, these "units" (Willey and Phillips 1958:29) were viewed as "integrative devices" that were "fluid historical concepts" and that made "no pretense to sociological or any other kind of reality" (Phillips and Willey 1953:625, 629). The units are of the theoretical sort, as their definitive criteria—classes of whatever scale (Table 6.2)—have *distributions* in time and space. Components and phases "are located in space and time but are not dependent on these properties for their meaning" (Phillips and Willey 1953:630). In other words, these particular units merely exist in formal terms: "The phase [in particular] is a formal abstraction that can be manipulated independently of space and time" (Phillips and Willey 1953:630). A Willey-and-Phillips phase is a class, an ideational unit. But because a component is a manifestation of a phase at a site, it must be—contrary to Phillips and Willey—an empirical unit and thus have a *position* in time and space. Phillips and Willey's consistent confusion of empirical and ideational units is thus apparent here.

Horizons and traditions clearly are both ideational units that, like phases, have distributions in time and space. The difference between them and phases is that a phase supposedly is equivalent to an ethnological unit, whereas horizons and traditions have no such ethnological equivalent. Rather, "the temporal and spatial ingredients are dominant" in horizons and traditions (Phillips and Willey 1953:631) because those units are meant to reveal relations among parts of different phases. "Components and phases enter into traditions and horizon styles, [and] their external relationships may be revealed and expressed by them, but they are not in any manner combined to form them" (Phillips and Willey 1953:631). A horizon style is "roughly defined as a specialized cultural continuum represented by the wide distribution of a recognizable art style" (Willey and Phillips 1958:32). A horizon is *"a primarily spatial continuity represented by cultural traits and assemblages whose nature and mode of occurrence permit the assumption of a broad and rapid spread.* The archaeological units linked by a horizon are thus assumed to be *approximately* contemporaneous" (Willey and Phillips 1958:33). Thus, a horizon style is conceived at the scale of type, a horizon at the scale of an aggregate of multiple types.

As explained by Rouse (1953:70), horizons allow "synchronizing periods over a large region," whereas traditions imply the survival of culture traits "from period to period within a single geographic area." These are units for integrating and relating phases or similar units in time and space. But as we saw in the discussion above concerning Willey's (1945) earlier conception of horizon styles and traditions, there is no theoretical basis for these units. Instead, they are justified in commonsense terms as exemplifying the diffusion or persistence of traits, respectively. Why culture traits do or do not diffuse or persist was thus not addressed and remained opaque in Phillips and Willey's (1953) early formulation. Willey and Phillips (1958:31) did not provide a theoretical explanation in their later formulation either, other than to suggest that such integrative units were "culturally determined," as they must be if one seeks ultimately to achieve some sort of understanding of culture history when that history is conceived as a braided stream.

Rouse (1955) sought ultimately to determine the evolutionary, or phyletic, relations among phases—manifest as sets of aggregates of all artifacts found in association—rather than merely to trace the distributions of a few classes, as the horizon and tradition units dictated. Thus he described three ways to correlate phases. First, one might use an MTM-like procedure to group phases that shared traits. Why the traits were shared was a separate issue that involved determining if they were the result of similar adaptations (analogous similarity), similar developmental stages (echoing the model of cultural development proposed by Willey and Phillips 1955, 1958), or phyletic connection (homologous similarity). Second, one could note similarities in the time–space distributions of phases precisely because they were *classes* (in Rouse's usage) and thus had distributions rather than pointlike locations in time and space. Identical or adjacent positions of two or more phases in either or both the time and space dimensions did not necessarily signify that phyletic relations existed between them (Rouse 1955:716). Such propinquity "establishes contemporaneity and contiguity, or lack thereof, and nothing else" (Rouse 1955:717). To argue that contemporaneous phases were phyletically related "because they share a given horizon style . . . is on the genetic rather than the distributional level of interpretation, for it requires an assumption that the style has diffused from one phase to the others with little or no time lag" (Rouse 1955:718). Here Rouse underscored the assumption of temporal synchroneity of different manifestations of a horizon or horizon style.

Third, one might trace the evolutionary—"genetic"—relations among phases. To accomplish this, one first had to establish the time–space distributions of phases and their formal similarities (Rouse 1955:719) in order to demonstrate that they had been in "contact." Second, one needed to distinguish between what we have called analogous and homologous similarity, the linchpin to the third kind of comparison. The modeled result of such analyses is shown in Figure 6.3. Efforts to accomplish this last step, however, would be thwarted not because of any weakness in Rouse's formulation but because culture-historical interests had three decades earlier become narrowly focused on stylistic phenomena that allowed one to measure and read time. Thus there had been no effort to build a theoretical model of phyletic-like culture history—a model begun by Kidder, Gladwin, and Colton but discounted by many, with the final blow being delivered by Brew in 1946—and no effort to develop analytical methods for distinguishing between analogous and homologous similarity. Because styles performed so well in working out chronological relations, culture historians wrongly assumed they could be used for other analytical purposes as well. And while culture-historical artifact types tended to be somewhat stylistic

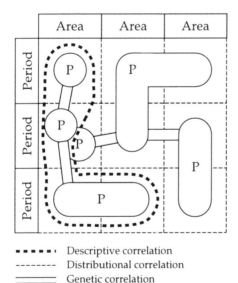

Figure 6.3. Irving Rouse's model of the results of comparing phases (P) to show their relative positions in form, space, and time. He saw three approaches to the correlation of phases—descriptive, distributional, and genetic—each requiring different concepts and methods. Descriptive and distributional correlations could, in Rouse's view, be used to derive "genetic" connectedness between phases—in other words, to show that one phase was derived from another—but he viewed it as more unreliable than making descriptive or distributional correlations (after Rouse 1955).

■ ■ ■ ■ ■ ■ Descriptive correlation
------- Distributional correlation
======= Genetic correlation

(*sensu* Dunnell 1978), given their subjection to the historical-significance test (they displayed temporal and spatial continuity in their distributions), such testing did not guarantee that they were completely or even mostly stylistic. Thus the extent to which they measured homologous similarity and phyletic relations was unclear. In lieu of theory, Willey's (1953b) axiom that typological similarity indicated cultural relatedness and thus a common or similar history was the best culture history could offer.

This is exemplified in Willey and Phillips's (1958) response to Rouse's (1955) suggestions. They argued that his "genetic" relations could only "be revealed and expressed by means of integrative concepts that are culturally determined" (Willey and Phillips 1958:31). The phrase "culturally determined" underscored their essentialist warrant for phases as having some ethnographic reality: Clearly, ethnographic units such as communities and bands interacted and shared ideas and occasionally genes. It was here that Willey and Phillips differentiated between *horizon* and *horizon style*. A horizon style consisted of a kind of artifact, technology, or other culture trait "that indicates a rapid spread of new ideas over a wide geographic space" (Willey and Phillips 1958:32). A horizon was "a primarily spatial continuity represented by *cultural traits and assemblages* whose nature and mode of occurrence permit the assumption of a broad and rapid spread" (Willey and Phillips 1958:33; emphasis added). In short, horizons and horizon styles were seen to reflect transmission or diffusion over space. A tradition was "a (primarily) temporal continuity represented by persistent configurations in single technologies or other systems of related forms" that operated at Rouse's (1955) "genetic level of interpretation" (Willey and Phillips 1958:38). Traditions were seen to reflect transmission or diffusion across time. In other words, Willey and Phillips's styles could detect transmission across space as well as through time. Thus, in a way, Willey and Phillips's conception of cultural development was well captured by the flowing braided-stream metaphor. Each trickle is a tradition that to varying degrees meets and mixes with other trickles as denoted by horizons and horizon styles. How they chose to discuss that metaphorical model is particularly interesting.

As noted earlier, Willey (1953b) in particular disliked the Gladwin–Colton scheme of deriving phyletic relations, and thus Phillips and Willey (1953:631), following various of their predecessors, stated that the "use of the organic evolutionary model is, we believe, specious." It is not surprising that nowhere did Willey and Phillips (1955, 1958; Phillips and Willey 1953) explicitly specify how to establish phyletic relations. The single exception—Willey's (1953b:363) earlier-mentioned dictum that "typological similarity [denotes] cultural relatedness"—is precisely the point with which Rouse (1955) attempted to contend. His point was that proximity in time and space, in conjunction with similarity in form, does not necessarily denote a phyletic relation. Couching the discussion within a progressive evolutionary scheme of cultural stages, as Willey and Phillips (1955, 1958) did, was no solution to this dilemma.

Willey and Phillips perceived no dilemma, however, because their horizons and traditions provided the empirical warrants for discussing the historical development of cultures. They were "integrative" units that denoted "some form of historical contact" *rather than* "implications of phylogeny" (Willey and Phillips 1958:30). Culture history, in their view, demanded "culturally determined" integrative concepts, not genetic or phyletic ones (Willey and Phillips 1958:30–31). Willey's (1953b:368) suggestion that "principles of continuity and change are expressed in the degrees of trait likeness and unlikeness which are the mechanisms of establishing the genetic lines binding the assemblages together" thus was metaphorical and underscored the commonsense approach to explanation. One has to wonder, however, how cultural or historical "relatedness," when couched within a temporal framework aimed at studying the development of cultures, could fail to be phyletic in the sense of Darwinian evolution.

Culture historians had learned via trial and error to address one problem—time. Time could be measured with artifact types that passed the historical-significance test. But culture historians also attempted to do more than simple chronology; they wanted history—specifically cultural developmental history—to be read from their chronological orderings. In the end, temporal difference was interpreted as historical difference expressed as difference in evolutionary, or developmental, stages (a framework we return to in Chapter 7), all woven together with horizons and traditions. That the system was not very sturdy is clear. It was hardly a theoretically founded structure; units might indisputably measure time, but no technique existed for testing their measurement of ancestral–descendent relations. The focus on stylistic—homologous—similarity, even had it not been somewhat accidental, was only half of the necessary equation. That limited focus, along with the commonsense approach to explanation, permeated the paradigm throughout the 1950s. These two aspects of the paradigm found major expression in the middle of that decade as archaeologists grappled with various notions of the braided-stream model.

The 1955 Seminars

In 1954 the Carnegie Corporation of New York made funds available to the Society for American Archaeology (SAA) to sponsor a series of seminars on archaeological method and theory. Four seminars were held in different cities in the summer of 1955, during which various Americanist archaeologists discussed important issues of the day. Both the participants and the seminar themes were chosen by the executive committee of the SAA (Wauchope 1956). Each seminar produced a report under the general editorship of one of the participants, none of whom "asked or expected individual credit for the ideas or the writing" (Wauchope 1956:vii). The four reports were published the following year as the eleventh memoir of the SAA, under the general editorship of Richard B. Woodbury (1956). Two papers from that volume are of particular concern here because they capture much of the thinking at the time on the integration of the three dimensions of archaeology—time, space, and form—and how one might deal with phenomena such as diffusion and persistence.

Culture Contact

An issue that one set of seminar participants considered was the identification and interpretation of culture-contact situations (Lathrap 1956). The participants indicated that theirs was only the second paper to deal with such events, citing Willey (1953a) as the first. Willey had described archaeological evidence for three prehistoric cases of what he considered to be culture-contact episodes. Invasion, to Willey (1953a:370, 374), was indicated by "stark" and "striking" differences between archaeological cultures superposed in the stratigraphic record. Diffusion or acculturation was represented by "a blend of the intrusive elements and the old local forms" (Willey 1953a:379). Such ideas can be traced as far back as Kidder's (1924) work. Gladwin (1943:53) had suggested that the relative abundance of a pottery type within an assemblage could be taken as evidence of the indigenous or intrusive (read *traded in*) status of the type. A similar suggestion is found in Ford and Griffin (1938).

Seminar participants suggested (Lathrap 1956:7) that their recognition of eight "types" of culture-contact situations rested on "the nature of the contact and its results," two dimensions of variation. The "nature-of-contact" dimension could involve intrusions at the "site-unit" level or at the "trait-unit" level; the former denoted immigration of a unique ethnic group to an area, and the latter denoted the movement of a single culture trait such as "a stylistic or technological feature or complex" (Lathrap 1956:8). The "results" dimension consisted of several possibilities, depending on the level or magnitude of the contact. For example, the trait list and traits of the receiving, or indigenous, culture could dominate the intrusive culture's trait list or traits, or those of the latter could dominate those of the former.

The intent of the seminar was to provide examples and definitions of the eight types of contact situations in strict archaeological terms without recourse to "ethnographic reconstruction" (Lathrap 1956:7). Ethnographic terms and concepts were, however, used heavily. Lathrap (1956:10), for example, spoke of Ciboney sites, a Ciboney chronology, a set of Ciboney sherds, a Ciboney culture, a Ciboney people, and Ciboney influences. All of these were used in an essentialist fashion—that is, in terms that suggested they had some objective and empirical (emic) reality. As a result, seminar participants provided rather nebulous *interpretations* of contact events, such as the following: "The fact that Ciboney influences did enter Arawak culture and vice versa suggests that it was not entirely hostile [contact], while the rarity of indications of weapons and the complete lack of fortifications among both groups suggest that the meeting may have been entirely pacific" (Lathrap 1956:10). Trait similarity might denote some contact, but as Rouse (1955) had noted, this was an assumption, the proof of which required various analyses and the distinction between homologous and analogous similarity. This distinction was not discussed during the seminar.

Seminar participants went to great lengths to present archaeological examples of each of the eight types of contact situations, but each example was represented by an *interpretation* of archaeological material and thus exemplified the type of contact situation it was meant to represent. Why a particular example characterized a particular type of contact was not clear for want of theory. The closest the seminar participants came to discussing theoretical units for measuring contact is found in the statement that "Situations of culture contact are identified archaeologically by the observation of the intrusion of elements of one culture into the area of another. . . . [A]n element is intrusive in one area when we find it occurring at an earlier date in another. The probability of intrusion is strengthened if the element has immediate antecedents in the area where it occurs earlier and none in the area where it occurs later" (Lathrap 1956:7).

Such a statement was little more than a verbalization of Ford's (1952:330) earlier discussion (see the discussion associated with Figure 5.3), and, like that discussion, begged the question of how evolutionary antecedents—*primitive forms*, in paleontological terms—were to be identified. Later discussions of such culture-contact episodes came under serious attack from the processualists (e.g., see the exchange between Sabloff and Willey [1967] and Binford [1968b], and Erasmus's [1968] discussion). Criticisms were couched in terms of the search for laws, however, and thus (1) missed the important point of explicating how culture contact was to be detected archaeologically and how different kinds of contact were to be analytically distinguished and (2) failed to consider why a contact episode occurred the way it did in the first place and why it might have had the result that it did. In short, the later criticisms were not informed by any theory of cultural development and contact.

Participants in a symposium (Thompson 1958a) held three years after the 1955 seminars used basically the same archaeological criteria to identify contact events as had the seminar participants and Willey (1953a). Those criteria included such things as the degree of trait similarity, demonstrable historically antecedent forms of traits, and the like. Symposium participants, as had those at the seminars, failed to explain how analogous and homologous similarities were to be distinguished.

Culture Stability

The second contribution to the 1955 seminar volume that is relevant here, edited by Raymond H. Thompson and entitled "An Archaeological Approach to the Study of Cultural Stability" (Thompson 1956a[†]), concerned stability and persistence in cultures or traits—that is, in culture traditions. Recall that Phillips and Willey (1953) had suggested a commonsense, essentialist model of culture change with their statement that material traits can, "under certain circumstances, be remarkably stable." This followed the notion of Kidder (1936b:xx) and others that "recognizable nodes of individuality" in pottery types represented ceramic or cultural periods.

This notion was axiomatized by seminar participants (Thompson 1956a:37), who suggested that (1) "shifts from one culture type to another are comparatively rapid" and (2) a graph of cultural complexity against time would produce a curve "characterized by a series of sharply rising escarpments connected by slightly sloping plateaus." Thus, culture change no longer was conceived as a flowing stream that might vary its rate of flow somewhat along the continuum—a materialist conception—that was perforce merely perceived in essentialist terms. The continuum was now conceived as a series of long, quiet pools separated by short but violent rapids. As we discussed earlier in this chapter, a similar conclusion was reached by Willey and Phillips (1958:16–17) under the rather forceful suggestions of Spaulding.

The implications of this change in the conception of culture development on the classification of aggregates of artifacts were enormous. Types of artifacts had been analytical tools that were rationalized by common sense as reflecting customs or shared ideas. This notion shifted in 1953 with Spaulding's (1953b) argument, following Brainerd (1951b), that types were real; they no longer were solely analytical tools. Phases had been more or less arbitrary sections of the continuum of culture change for Phillips and Willey (1953) and some (e.g., Ford 1949; Rouse 1939), but not all (e.g., Haury 1937a, 1937b), others. Constant repetition of the common-sense, ethnological rationale for these units made them *seem* real. The use of stratigraphic boundaries for identifying sets of artifacts thought to represent a single occupation within which there was no cultural change reinforced the *appearance* that real units were being discovered. Together, these two facts strengthened the essentialist notion that real cultural units were being studied. The near discipline-wide change in conception from thinking of units as arbitrary (conceptual or ideational) to units as real—Ford (1962) was a notable exception—was a predictable outcome.

The source of the new model of culture change was said to have been "the general body of anthropological theory," though it was also reported that it could have been derived solely from archaeological data (Thompson 1956a:37). In point of fact, the new model lacked an empirical basis altogether but was simply the current expression of very old interpretive ideas. The Spencer–Morgan–Tylor unilinear, progressive evolutionism reborn at the hands of Leslie White (e.g., 1938, 1945, 1949) and Julian Steward (e.g., 1955), despite the criticisms of Kroeber (1946) and others, seems implicated (but see the discussion in Chapter 7). The archaeological data referred to in the seminar paper resulted from associations between artifacts in stratigraphically bounded units; *occupations* were manifest as *assemblages* (recall Wissler's [1917a] earlier statement). This is evidenced by Thompson's (1956a:36) noting the tendency of archaeologists to "treat the site as [providing] a unit of artifact association for analysis and synthesis. . . . [F]orm classes of artifacts and [such] a unit of artifact association provide the necessary data for quantitative description and comparison."

The seminar participants' analytical units—assemblages of associated artifacts representing occupations and interpreted as "cultures"—were naturally structured in a manner that matched their model of culture development—periods of cultural stasis punctuated by relatively brief and abrupt change. Thus, the so-called stratigraphic revolution resulted in the notion that one might monitor continuous change rendered as shifts in the frequencies of variant forms, but why bother when the differences between analytical units termed *cultures* or *phases* were real (e.g., Spaulding 1955, and in Willey and Phillips 1958:15–16). One seminar participant recognized the most pressing problem: "How do we reduce any kind of cultural change to quantitative manipulative terms?" (Wauchope 1966:19). The answer—the use of ideational units such as modes (*sensu* Rouse 1939) and classes as analytical tools for measuring continuous change—escaped recognition. So, too, did the fact that by using stratigraphically bounded assemblages, culture historians were being opportunistic rather than theoretically rigorous. Ford (1962:45) recognized this fact and insisted "the vertical separation of potsherds and other cultural materials only by the observable breaks

in the deposit would be an archaeological variety of cataclysmic geology. . . .
By this procedure, we have allowed the history [of a site] to be separated
into periods by chance historical [depositional] events. . . . The chance that
a neighboring site, occupied for the same span of time, was subjected to
the same sequence of events seems remote."

Seminar participants characterized a tradition as "a socially transmitted form unit (or a series of systematically related form units) which persist
in time. . . . [P]otentially . . . a tradition may exist for any cultural trait or
combination of traits. . . . A tradition is a socially transmitted cultural form
which persists in time" (Thompson 1956a:38, 39). Joseph R. Caldwell
(1958:3) echoed this notion when he suggested that a tradition consisted
of "any culturally transmitted pattern of action seen through time." Thus,
a tradition (1) could be identified at any scale, such as an attribute of an
object, a kind of object, or a kind of aggregate of objects (part of
Wauchope's [1966] objection); (2) persisted through time; and (3) represented socially transmitted ideas. The last two points required that traditions at all scales be the result of transmission. If archaeologists wanted to
identify traditions, they had to select something that persisted through time
as a result of inheritance—Caldwell's cultural transmission. In lieu of a
theoretically informed selection of units, selection had to be based on trial
and error, such as is exemplified by attempts to find specimens of an ideational unit in a temporal—say, superposed—sequence. The resulting units
of such efforts—historical types—may or may not be stylistic in the sense
that they denote homologous similarity and are selectively neutral (Dunnell
1978; O'Brien and Holland 1990).

To seminar participants, a tradition could remain stable or persist, or
it could converge or diverge, elaborate or reduce (Figure 6.4); in short, "a
tradition may change form" (Thompson 1956a:42). Each "tradition segment" consisted of a combination of attributes of whatever scale, signified
in Figure 6.4 as capital letters and termed "traits" in the discussion. The
traits were theoretical units because they allowed one to measure (1) their
presence in, or absence from, a segment and (2) their addition to and sub-
traction from consecutive segments: Trait "A" is always the same regardless
of which segment(s) it falls within, and the same is true for Trait "B," Trait
"C," and so on.

Traditions were viewed as units to be identified on the basis of ideational units termed traits. They represented, in their consecutive tradition
segments, the social transmission of ideas manifest as traits and thus were
conceptually grounded in homology. They were supposed to be stylistic
units (*sensu* Dunnell 1978). Whether they in fact were or not, and, if so,
the degree to which they were, is unclear. In lieu of theory, the history of
a tradition—that is, the form it takes—was said to result from sociocultural

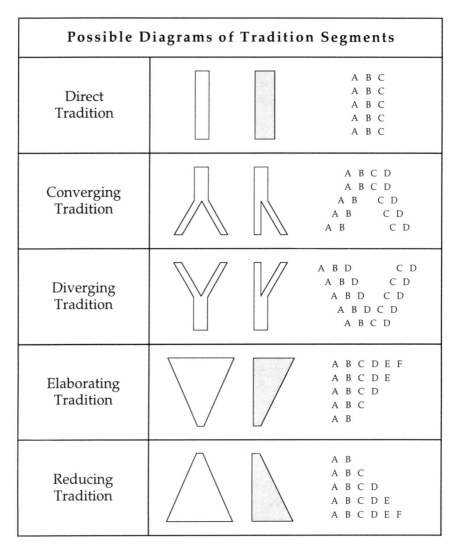

Figure 6.4. Five types of tradition histories recognized by participants in the 1955 Society for American Archaeology-sponsored seminar on cultural stability showing how traditions can change through time. Each capital letter represents a cultural trait at whatever scale; each row of capital letters represents a "tradition segment" (after Thompson 1956a).

factors such as "the interests of the culture" or a culture's "value system," which determines if a culture is conservative or innovative (Thompson 1956a:52). Such a teleological, intent-ridden, explanation for persistence or change in form of a tradition merely represented a commonsense, ethnologically derived basis for the possible histories of traditions.

In short, then, all culture-historical types are units that display time–space contiguity once they have successfully passed the historical-significance test of Kidder and Krieger. Those that display extensive distributions in time and limited distributions in space are termed traditions. A tradition can be designated at the scale of an attribute (Rouse's *mode*), at the scale of a type (discrete object), or at the scale of assemblage (sets of objects or associated types). Those historical types with extensive distributions in space but restricted distributions in time are termed horizons or horizon styles, and they also can be designated at any scale. The degree to which these units monitor homologous similarity—the degree to which they are styles (*sensu* Dunnell 1978)—is unclear.

Later formulations did little to clarify or resolve critical issues. Donald J. Lehmer and Warren W. Caldwell (1966:515) redefined a horizon as "a cultural stratum which includes two or more phases, or putative phases, which were approximately coeval and which are characterized by enough common traits, or variants of the same trait, to appear as manifestations of the same basic culture complex." Horizon styles were viewed as "widely distributed and distinctive traits or trait complexes which serve as hallmarks of the horizon" (Lehmer and Caldwell 1966:512). In other words, Lehmer and Caldwell extended the scale of inclusiveness of horizons from that originally proposed by Willey (1945, 1948)—mostly at the scale of attribute or type of discrete object—to one that included the designation of horizons at the scale of similar assemblages. Of course, this begs the question of how similar is similar enough.

Joe Ben Wheat et al. (1958:42) indicated that a "ceramic system may be defined as representing a certain class of pottery, made or used by the people of a certain archaeological culture, in a certain area during a certain period of time" and that a ceramic system "should be thought of in terms of a time *period* rather than a phase." Continuing, the "ceramic system is usually and most usefully short in time duration, showing little or no evolution among member type clusters, but is wide in geographical range by comparison with a ceramic sequence which shows a demonstrable evolution among member type clusters but is limited in [geographic] range and long in duration" (Wheat et al. 1958:42). As Figure 6.5 shows, the member type clusters in a ceramic sequence are plotted as discontinuous units vertically

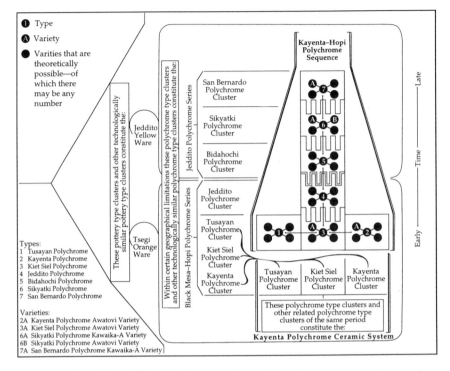

Figure 6.5. The Wheat–Gifford–Wasley conception of the relations among pottery variety, type, type cluster, series, ceramic system, ceramic sequence, and ware. All of those units were used as taxonomic devices to show technological, temporal, cultural, and areal interrelationships and similarities among certain ceramic manifestations. Note the implied "genetic relatedness" among types (after Wheat et al. 1958).

(against time), and the member type clusters are plotted as discontinuous units horizontally (across space). One suspects the interdigitation of the jagged horizontal lines separating the member type clusters of the ceramic sequence are meant to model a gradual replacement of one type cluster with another, but the passage of time is nonetheless modeled as discontinuous chunks and is marked by differences between essentialist type clusters rather than by changes in the frequencies of variant forms. Change is thus of the transformational sort and is explicable in commonsense terms. One type cluster "evolves" into another, but this key term is neither theoretically defined nor is any justification for it provided, giving the whole model an intuitive, commonsensical feel. Thus, types are species, varieties are subspecies or races, and subspecies are incipient species.

Area Co-traditions and Whole-Culture Traditions

Various statements on the utility of the concept of tradition appeared between Willey's (1945) original formulation and the mid-1950s (see references in Phillips and Willey 1953). One expansion of the concept was the *area co-tradition*. Wendell C. Bennett (1948:1) first used this term—originally proposed by Ralph Linton—to signify the addition of time depth to Kroeber's (1939) notion of a culture area. The purpose in doing so was to form "a meaningful unit for archaeological–historical interpretation. . . . [A]n area co-tradition is the over-all unit of cultural history of an area within which the [constituent] cultures have been interrelated over a period of time" (Bennett 1948:1). For Bennett (1948:1), each culture included in an area co-tradition "has its own history, its own persistent traditions. The coined . . . co-tradition, refers, then, to the linkage, the interrelationships of these cultural traditions in time and space." Linkages are noted as horizons and horizon styles that connect local cultural sequences. "The principal elements or characteristics [of an area co-tradition] should be found in each [constituent culture] and in each major time period" (Martin and Rinaldo 1951:216).

Rouse (1954) provided a clarification of the area co-tradition concept, likening it to a rectangular piece of cloth, the side edges representing the geographic limits of both the culture area and the co-tradition and the top and bottom edges representing the temporal limits of the two:

> The warp threads of the cloth consist of a series of regional traditions running from the bottom towards the top of the cloth, while the weft is composed of a number of horizon styles which extend from one side of the cloth towards the other. The cloth is decorated with a series of irregularly arranged rectangles, each representing a single culture, and these are so colored that they appear to form a series of horizontal bands, representing the various stages in the development of the co-tradition. (Rouse 1954:222)

That one could misinterpret Bennett's original formulation as characterized by Rouse's cloth was pointed out by Rouse. A unit proposed as an area co-tradition could have irregular side edges and be "composed of gauze, in which a regular series of warp and weft threads . . . are replaced by loosely twisted threads in an irregular arrangement" (Rouse 1954:223). Nonetheless, the area co-tradition was a "useful tool for [detecting culture change], rigid and specific though it may be" (Rouse 1954:225).

Another significant extension of the tradition concept was that, while originally conceived of as involving a certain technology (such as that for manufacturing a kind of pottery—hence Willey's [1945] pottery tradition), the concept came to mean much more. Willey and Phillips (1958:37–38), for example, wrote that

> traditions may be based on more complex systems of forms than that represented by a single technology. We have in mind something like the functionally interrelated trait complexes of the ethnographer. About the same amount of expansion is involved in substituting the concept of horizon for the horizon style. The working relationship between horizon and tradition, therefore, remains the same as between horizon style and pottery tradition.

The expansion of a tradition to include "trait complexes" exemplified, according to Willey and Phillips (1958:38), the 1955 seminar. While seminar participants acknowledged scale differences in the inclusiveness of traditions, they were more concerned with what Willey and Phillips termed "whole culture traditions" (Table 6.2). Willey (1966:4) later organized his grand synthesis of North American archaeology around the latter concept when he wrote

> By major cultural traditions I mean the principal native cultures or major cultural groupings as these can be discerned in geographical space. In every instance [in the book] these dimensions of space and time are appreciable. Each major cultural tradition is characterized by a definite patterning of subsistence practices, technology, and ecological adaptations. Each major cultural tradition also probably had a definite ideological pattern or world view.

Thus the notion of tradition came to signify not only the persistence of archaeologically visible phenomena such as a particular technology but also a set of ethnologically based inferences (e.g., Ascher 1961a; Thompson 1958a, 1958b).

Summary

Attempts to build chronological sequences of aggregates of artifacts had begun with Kidder (e.g., 1924) and others (e.g., Ford and Willey 1941). These efforts were accompanied by the adoption of several implicit operational principles, the most critical of which was Wissler's (1917a) implied belief that each depositional unit—whether a stratum or an arbitrary level—containing artifacts could be conceived of as a separate and distinct occupation. Artifacts were depositionally and thus temporally associated and therefore composed snapshots of the cultural continuum. But the focus on such aggregates of artifacts, combined with (1) attempts to document the history, development, and evolution of a culture and (2) an ethnologically dictated view of culture, resulted in the units becoming ever more real in an emic sense rather than staying the arbitrary chunks that they surely are, given the capricious nature of geological deposition and excavation by arbitrary level.

The focus on artifact styles allowed the measurement of time, and anthropological understanding of how cultures worked indicated the mechanisms of transmission across space (diffusion, trade, migration) and through time (persistence). But these were hardly robust notions, as evidenced by the general failure of culture historians to develop a theory of culture change—a theory that would have demanded, as noted by Kroeber (1931a) early on and later by Rouse (1955), the distinction between analogous and homologous similarities. Instead, understanding and explanation were derived from commonsense notions of culture change, such as the feeling that complex forms were less likely to be independently invented and more likely to be diffused or traded than were simple forms. The result was Willey's (1953b) dictum that typological similarity denoted similar histories, or more correctly, similar ancestry. Rejection of any phyletic, or evolutionary, implication of such similarity was, under this view, incongruous. It emanated from equating artifact types and cultures with species and noting that species do not interbreed, whereas cultures *do* "breed" via diffusion, trade, and the like. Innovation or minor change internal to cultures was left largely unaccounted for or was viewed as the result of nebulous outside influences, whereas major changes—the discontinuities in the continuum— were real and often represented instances of migration and acculturation. Of course, *why* change of either sort should have occurred in the first place was a major concern, and it is this topic to which we turn in Chapter 7.

Note

1. As John H. Rowe (1962b:40) made clear, "stages are units of cultural similarity, while periods are units of time, or, more specifically, units of contemporaneity." The concept of stages was abandoned by Americanist archaeologists prior to the middle of the twentieth century because stages had no chronological significance (Rouse 1953:71), but by mid-century they had been resurrected (Willey and Phillips 1955, 1958; see also Mason 1970).

7

Culture History, Cultural Anthropology, and Cultural Evolution

By the late 1940s and early 1950s, culture history was fully operational. Methods for controlling the formal dimension—sorting artifacts into types that permitted the measurement of time—had been perfected to such a degree that some types attained the status of index fossils and marked rather small chunks of the time–space continuum. Others had somewhat greater distributions and were useful in frequency seriation and percentage stratigraphy. The spatial dimension could be monitored with such units because they were founded largely on homologous similarity and were, therefore, the result of transmission. The time dimension, too, had become not only analytically visible using percentage stratigraphy and frequency seriation but was also brought into sharp focus, first by dendrochronology and later by radiocarbon dating. The goals of culture historians to document the development of cultures in particular places had been met by the late 1920s and early 1930s, and methods to do so had been formalized and axiomatized. Similarly, while previous efforts had been made to account for particular cultural sequences, by the late 1940s and early 1950s attempts were regularly being made to interpret the revealed documentation of culture development, and various axioms were formalized to help with this task.

In an examination of newly emerging conclusions on the developmental histories of cultures in several areas, Betty J. Meggers (1955:116) posed the question, "are the new ideas and interpretations 'scientific'?" She noted that various archaeologists working in different areas on different problems were using "the same basic cultural principles and have drawn similar general conclusions from them" (Meggers 1955:116). In brief, those principles were the following:

- "[T]he existence of a complex trait or group of traits in two geographically separated regions cannot be the result of independent development, but must be attributed to cultural contact" (Meggers 1955:116).
- The simultaneous appearance of a set of traits with noncontemporaneous origins in widely separated areas "represents a rapid movement of traits that have no apparent practical value to explain their swift spread" (Meggers 1955:117).
- "Rapid movements of whole complexes [of traits] seem to require the assumption of migration of peoples" (Meggers 1955:117).
- "[D]etailed resemblances [of traits] preclude the possibility of independent invention" Meggers 1955:117).
- "[D]etailed cultural resemblances are evidence of cultural diffusion whatever the obstacles to its occurrence appear to have been" (Meggers 1955:118).
- Unilinear progressive cultural evolutionism was assumed (a point to which we return below) (Meggers 1955:118; see also Binford 1968a:10).

In remarkable anticipation of the rhetoric of the 1960s, Meggers (1955:118) turned to physics as exemplary of "science" in order to answer her original question. She answered it in the affirmative because archaeologists "are proceeding in a scientific manner by applying to their problems basic explanations of cultural phenomena" (Meggers 1955:127). Noting that mid-twentieth-century American ethnologists tended to hold a point of view in which "archaeological results were stigmatized as being hopelessly deficient and relegated to secondary importance," she argued that contemporary archaeology was now following "the research paths opened by Tylor, Kroeber, Lowie, Wissler, and Boas" (Meggers 1955:128–129). It should be clear from previous chapters that in one sense Meggers was wrong; cultural anthropology in general and ethnological theory in particular *had* played a major if somewhat implicit role in culture history since its inception in the midteens. The popularity principle is a prime example. Another is the interpretation of the discontinuity of pottery styles as signifying diffusion or migration. Both of these uses concern discrete objects or artifacts—variation within the formal dimension. But in another sense Meggers was correct. Once methods were available to control the form, space, and time dimensions in some sort of rigorous fashion (this had occurred by about 1935 when the process of creating artifact typologies solidified around temporally sensitive styles), followed by formalization of procedures for classifying cultural units such as foci and phases, culture historians began to turn more explicitly and directly to culture theory to help them interpret the sequences of cultures their excavations revealed. We have noted both of these phases of the paradigm's use of cultural anthropology throughout this volume and have implied that such usage eventually contributed to the paradigm's fall from favor. In this chapter we explore that usage in more detail.

Cultural Anthropology

Interpreting cultural development and change was, of course, the central theme of Americanist archaeology virtually since the inception of the culture history paradigm. The ability to chronicle culture change prompted Wissler (1917b) to refer to early-twentieth-century archaeology as the "new archaeology," elsewhere referred to as the "first" new archaeology (Browman and Givens 1996). Clark Wissler (1917b:100) described this new archaeology as involving such questions as

> how long has man been in America, whence did he come, and what has been his history since his arrival? . . . [T]he archaeologist finds in the ground the story of man and his achievements. The new, or the real archaeology is the study of these traces and the formulation of the story they tell. . . . [The archaeologist] must actually dissect section after section of our old Mother Earth for the empirical data upon which to base his answers. It is not merely the findings of things that counts; it is the conditions and interassociations that really tell the story.

Wissler (1917b:100) went on to note that Nels Nelson's (1920) stratigraphic excavation at Pueblo Bonito in Chaco Canyon, New Mexico, in 1916 revealed "the story of the ruin" and that "Such are the results of the real, or new archaeology, as a part of the science of anthropology."

While seeing the value of stratigraphic excavation for the construction of cultural sequences, Wissler (1917a:274–275) also noted that stratified archaeological sites providing evidence of such sequences seemed to be largely limited to areas where evidence of "higher culture"—what would later be termed "formative" and "classic" culture—was found. Thus, at least initially, the perceived shallow time depth of the American archaeological record seemed to preclude the detailed study of culture change except where primitive cultures—that is, cultures that were not civilizations—had evolved into advanced cultures. But within a decade, on the basis of his work at Pecos, New Mexico, and the work of others, A. V. Kidder (1924:135) noted that "If a single outstanding fact has become apparent in our survey, it is the great value of stratigraphy, first for determining the sequence of local types and for solving local problems, secondly, for the possibilities that it holds out for providing crossfinds of contemporaneous non-local types and so for solving the broader and more important problems of inter-area chronology." It is, no doubt, statements such as this that have led to the perception that a "stratigraphic revolution" (Browman and Givens 1996; Willey 1968; Willey and Sabloff 1993) took place early in the twentieth century.

Concerning the goals of early-twentieth-century Americanist archaeology, Kidder (1932:8) observed that

> Archaeologists, noting that modern biology has mounted above the plane of pure taxonomy, have attempted to follow that science into the more alluring fields of philosophic interpretation, forgetting that the conclusions of the biologist are based on the sound foundation of scientifically marshalled facts gathered during the past century by an army of painstaking observers. This groundwork we utterly fail to possess. Nor will it be easy for us to lay, because the products of human hands, being unregulated by the more rigid genetic laws which control the development of animals and plants, are infinitely variable. But that is no reason for evading the attempt. It has got eventually to be done, and the sooner we roll up our sleeves and begin comparative studies of axes and arrowheads and bone tools, make classifications, prepare accurate descriptions, draw distribution maps and, in general, persuade ourselves to do a vast deal of painstaking, unspectacular work, the sooner shall we be in position to approach the problems of cultural evolution, the solving of which is, I take it, our ultimate goal.

Early explanatory efforts attempted to account for the temporal and spatial record of artifact styles. Thus, Kidder's phyletic seriations played a major role, particularly in the Southwest where his notions were taken to extremes by Gladwin and Colton. In the Southeast, Ford's marker types and decoration complexes played a similar role. Minor changes in style over time in one area denoted phyletic evolution; changes of larger magnitude and a lack of perceived continuity suggested outside influences. Culture historians also began to equate artifact styles with units at the scale of cultures, calling them phases, foci, and the like. Thus, explaining the documented instances of cultural stability and change in such units was merely a half step behind explanations of styles, and both efforts called upon ethnologically documented processes such as diffusion, migration, and the like to account for perceived changes. As Fred Eggan (1952:38) observed in the early 1950s, "recent developments in social anthropology hold out the possibility of reconstructing the social institutions of many prehistoric communities, without recourse to evolutionary or other formulas." In part this was so because of a shift in the late 1930s away from the concept of "culture area" and toward the concept of "culture type," which, according to Eggan (1952:37), "emphasizes similarities in culture content rather than geographical grouping, and offers a basis for the determination of genetic relationships." Willey's (1953b) axiom that typological similarity denoted a historical relation, while clearly present in archaeology (Kidder 1915, 1917a) and anthropology (Wissler 1916c) much earlier, thus received a significant degree of legitimacy from cultural anthropology.

By the 1950s, Americanist archaeologists had become quite adept at interpreting their chronological and spatial arrangements of "cultures," prompting at least one participant observer to christen this version of culture history the "new American archaeology" (Caldwell 1959). As Meggers's (1955) comments make clear, the second new archaeology was denoted by the fact that what had originally been commonsense warrants for units of whatever scale—a mode or type was a cultural custom or norm, a phase was a culture—ultimately became the ethnologically founded basis for interpretations of those units. Kidder's, Ford's, Nelson's, and others' original materialist conception of cultural evolution as a more or less gradually flowing braided stream had been replaced by essentialist periods of cultural stasis punctuated by brief but more or less violent episodes of change. Ethnology (e.g., Murdock 1956) provided the mechanisms of change (Table 7.1), and common sense provided the system of interpretation. *Archaeological* theory was unnecessary because ethnological or cultural theory—such as it was—fulfilled the requirements.

Willey (1953b) made two astute observations at the time that serve to illustrate the commonsense, anthropologically informed status of the culture history paradigm in the 1950s. Regarding the measurement of time using artifact form and recalling Wissler's (1917a) suggestion that stratified deposits represent multiple occupations, Willey (1953b:365) observed not only that "Sharp distinctions in physical strata were correlated with changes in cultural types," but also that merely observing the relative vertical positions of artifacts suggested change:

> One type was seen to "replace" another in this time story. If the stylistic division between an earlier and a later type was sharp, it was hypothesized that new or foreign elements were introduced into the life of the site at a particular point in its history. On the other hand, if the intrinsic qualities of two types showed strong similarity and if their frequency histories allowed it, gradual evolutionary change from one type into another was postulated. These *theories* [were] born in the techniques of stratigraphic chronological measurement. (Willey 1953b:365; emphasis added)

Table 7.1. List of Historical Culture Processes Called Upon by Culture Historians to Help Explain the Archaeological Record

Process	Definition/Description
Adaptation	*In situ* (generally) change directed toward better solutions to problems, often with teleological and progressive elements (people faced a problem and intentionally came up with a solution to it).
Diffusion	Movement of an idea from one culture to another (see migration, trade); may result in change in traits.
Invention	Innovation of a new trait/idea; change in trait list of a culture results from internal stimulus of the innovation, which may replace an older trait.
Independent invention	Innovation of a new trait/idea by two cultures independent of one another (syn. convergence; see parallel development).
Migration	Movement of a population from one area to another (see diffusion, trade); may result in change in traits.
Parallel development	Two cultures evolve along similar paths, more or less independent of one another.
Persistence	Maintenance of a culture trait/idea through long spans of time.
Popularity	A trait, if not present as a result of trade or nonconformist behavior, should display a unimodal frequency distribution through time.
Trade	Movement of an object from one ethnic group to another (see diffusion, migration); may result in change in traits.

Willey's use of the term "theory" denotes a basic misconception rampant within culture history. Simply put, there was no theory of culture change and development, save for what has been referred to as "cultural evolution" (e.g., Dunnell 1980), and that "theory" was not a theory in the usual sense of the word but rather a hypothesis (see below), a fact recognized by very few individuals during the 1950s (Swanson [1959] was an exception).

Surprisingly, Willey (1953b:369) himself recognized the lack of archaeological theory when he lamented, in remarkable anticipation of the rhetoric of the 1960s (e.g., Binford 1962, 1965), that

> The processes by which, or through which, cultural continuity and change are maintained or accomplished have not received study and reflective thought commensurate with the way these concepts have been invoked by American archeologists. "Evolution" and "diffusion" have been tag names employed, but these are broad categories rather than specific explanations, and there have been few clear theoretical formulations along these lines.

Willey was correct; there was no theory of cultural change couched in archaeological terms that provided explanations for why a culture might "evolve" or why a trait might "diffuse." In lieu of theory, all Willey (1953b:369) could do at the time was to state that "Adequate support for either class of theory [evolution or diffusion] will . . . be more effectively marshaled when greater functional understanding of the data in question is achieved." What Willey (1953b:364) meant by "functional" was the "ancient patterns of behavior that had been welded, with greater or lesser firmness, into a functioning whole"—that is, into a *culture*—denoted by a phase. Given such a conception, change had to be of the transformational sort—an abrupt transition from one steady state (one cultural form) to another. Constant referral to and use of Americanist anthropological theory in all its various forms placed culture history squarely in the essentialist camp; as we have seen, that metaphysic is not conducive to the stated goals of culture history—to document and study the historical development of cultures. But archaeologists wanted to be more than the bastard stepchildren of anthropology (e.g., Phillips 1955), more than the tail on the anthropological kite. Such a status for archaeology was reiterated by anthropologist Elman Service as culture history fell from favor: "The day-to-day work of an archaeologist (as an *archaeologist,* not as an archaeologist turned general anthropologist or philosopher) is to dig up the remains of peoples and their cultures, to map, measure, describe, count, and so on, and in his report to make an interpretation of what life was like 'then' " (Service 1964:364).

One of the individuals criticized by Taylor (1948) for not being anthropological looked back at the history of the discipline from the vantage point of 1952 and suggested that Americanist archaeology had been becoming more anthropological for "the last few decades." Strong (1952:319) indicated that, in his view, the integration of Americanist archaeology with "physical anthropology, linguistics, ethnology, theoretical anthropology, documentary history, and all the other social and cultural sciences" produced a significant enrichment of archaeology that he termed the "Synthetic-Anthropological" phase of Americanist archaeological research. The aim of this phase of research "is an attempt to join with our European and other colleagues in establishing the regularities, or *laws,* involved in world-wide economic and other cultural change or evolution" (Strong 1952:320; emphasis added). Phillips and Willey (1953) produced their programmatic statement with the same goal in mind (see also Phillips 1955). The desire of Americanist archaeologists in the 1950s to be anthropological had been clear for years; two decades earlier, Strong (1936:363), for example, had noted that anthropology in general was concerned with "two definitely historical processes, biological evolution and cultural development. . . . [T]he interrelationship in time and space of biological and cultural development, forms the background of all anthropological research." The problem perceived by culture historians was how to make the contemporary and static archaeological record look more like something in which an ethnologist might show some interest.

The methods used by culture historians to assign anthropological meaning to the phenomena they observed were hardly explicit and certainly not rigorous; they were founded in common sense. For example, in the first half of the twentieth century it was regularly suggested that types probably reflected customs and traditions (e.g., Rouse 1939); the artifacts were, after all, by definition products of human hands. When types displayed a unimodal frequency distribution across time, one could call upon the commonsense notion of the popularity principle to account for that distribution (e.g., Kroeber 1909, 1919; Nelson 1916; Wissler 1916b). Horizons and traditions suggested ways to measure historical relations among cultural units such as foci and phases but were founded on commonsense notions of diffusion across space and through time, respectively (Phillips and Willey 1953). Components or assemblages were thought to represent single occupations and so, by definition, must represent a homogeneous cultural group such as a band, clearly an ethnological unit (e.g., Colton 1939; Gladwin 1936; McKern 1937, 1939; Rouse 1955). A set of sites represented a community or tribe if the sites contained components belonging to the same phase—yet another commonsense warrant founded in cultural anthropology. Methods for drawing such correlations were rather informal, implicit, and agreed upon, and they rested on the notion that the archaeological record reflected human behavior in some sense, whether it was customs, norms, or culture contact. Such commonsense interpretations were, of course, not testable, but that was apparently of minimal consequence.

Willey and Phillips (1958) made clear the intellectual framework of *explanation* during the 1950s:

> "culture-historical integration," as it is used here, covers almost everything the archaeologist does in the way of organizing his primary data: typology, taxonomy, formulation of archaeological "units," investigation of their relationships in the contexts of function and natural environment, and determination of their internal dimensions and external relationships in space and time. However high-sounding these terms, it appears that the activities represented by them remain essentially on the descriptive level. Explanatory concepts, such as acculturation, diffusion, and stimulus diffusion, are utilized, but the aim is primarily to describe what happened to specific cultural units at specific times and places. . . . Culture-historical integration is thus comparable to ethnography with the time dimension added. . . .
>
> So little work has been done in American archaeology on the explanatory level that it is difficult to find a name for it. . . . We have [used]

"processual interpretation," which might conceivably cover any explanatory principle that might be invoked. In the context of archaeology, processual interpretation is the study of the nature of what is vaguely referred to as the culture-historical process. Practically speaking, it implies an attempt to discover regularities in the relationships given by the methods of culture-historical integration. . . . Perhaps it is fair to say that there has been a lack of progress in processual interpretation in American archaeology to date precisely because unit formulations have been put together with so little reference to their social aspect. (Willey and Phillips 1958:5-6)

What Willey and Phillips (1958:3-4) meant by the "social aspect" is not exactly clear, but they implied that they meant such things as symbolic behavior and political organization. Importantly, their integrative units of horizons and traditions were "culturally determined," and their components and phases were "theoretically capable of intelligibility in the social aspect" (Willey and Phillips 1958:31, 56). This allowed them and other culture historians working in the 1950s to produce "processual interpretations and explanations" in anthropological terms such as those listed in Table 7.1. Conflation of interpretation and explanation was not unique to Willey and Phillips but rather was a permanent fixture in culture history. However, failure to recognize that explanation is produced strictly from the application of theory and the empirical standards that stem from that theory was not the sole property of culture historians; that legacy carried over into processual archaeology as well (Dunnell 1978, 1982; O'Brien 1996a, 1996b, 1996c; O'Brien and Holland 1995a, 1995b).

Caldwell (1959:304) indicated that "The new archeology in America is tending to be more concerned with culture process and less concerned with the descriptive content of prehistoric cultures." He reiterated many of the interpretive principles stated earlier by Meggers (1955):

- "Whether or not changes were diffused from another region can be inferred from knowledge of whether or not they occurred earlier elsewhere."
- "That changes are of local development can be inferred when their prototypes occur locally at an earlier time."
- "A sudden change in a whole series of artifact forms may herald a prehistoric invasion."
- "[G]radual changes in forms occurring at different times suggests a period of comparative tranquility during which cultural development was not greatly influenced by outside areas" (Caldwell 1959:304).

Caldwell also rephrased what Willey and Phillips (1958) had said earlier: "The archeologist is inclined to see cultural patterns in developmental terms. A pattern represents some kind of regularity or organization. If a pattern can be recognized, the features we use to account for its presence may perhaps be stated in terms of the [cultural] processes which brought it into being or perhaps in terms of the factors which operate to maintain it" (Caldwell 1959:305).

In short, one had to somehow rend culturally meaningful units from the archaeological record so that ethnologically documented processes could be used to explain differences in those units (e.g., Sears 1961). That such a perspective had an early beginning within the culture history paradigm is exemplified by Jesse Jennings's (1947:192) statement that an "important problem is one of equating archaeologically built up foci with historic tribes." Carl Guthe (1952:3) noted that during the first quarter of the twentieth century there had been "continued use of ethnological terms which implied a direct link between historic tribes and archaeological cultures," and he argued that this was "a relationship which in most cases could not be proved," a point somehow missed by most culture historians as they sought commonsense warrants for their archaeological units.

The important question is, how did one really know, for example, that artifact types represented sociobehavioral norms, components represented communities, phases represented tribes, and the like? Brainerd (1951b) and Spaulding (1953b) suggested that rigorous method provided the way to know that artifact types represented norms and so on, and that position, simply put, created an opening for the new, or processual, archaeology of the 1960s to walk through unmolested. The concepts and procedures for this supposedly new kind of archaeology were spelled out in a series of papers by Lewis R. Binford. The requisite assumptions and the program or procedure for operationalizing the new archaeology were relatively simple and straightforward:

> The formal structure of artifact assemblages together with the between element contextual relationship should and do present a systematic and understandable picture of *the total extinct* cultural system. (Binford 1962:219)

> The loss, breakage, and abandonment of implements and facilities at different locations, where groups of variable structure performed various tasks, leaves a "fossil" record of the actual operation of an extinct society. (Binford 1964:425)

> The practical limitations of our knowledge of the past are not inherent in the nature of the archeological record: the limitations lie in our methodological naiveté, in our lack of development for principles determining the relevance of archeological remains to propositions regarding processes and events of the past. (Binford 1968a:23)

The first two quotations are warrants for an "archaeology as anthropology," and the last tells us how to do anthropological research with the archaeological record: Develop appropriate methods. This procedure sounds a lot like Brainerd's (1951b) and Spaulding's (1953b) method-dependent approaches.

The new archaeology of the 1960s hinged on rebuilding, reconstituting, and reconstructing the dynamics of a prehistoric culture at a particular position in the time–space continuum. Following Leslie White's (1949) definition of culture as humankind's extrasomatic means of adaptation, the focus shifted in the 1960s from the use of style (homologous similarity) of artifacts to measure time to function (analogous similarity) of artifacts in order to monitor adaptations. Binford (1962:220) characterized *style* as denoting group identity or ethnicity. Artifact function was characterized variously as technomic, sociotechnic, and ideotechnic (Binford 1962), or as primary and secondary functional variation (Binford 1965:206). The critical step in reconstruction had seen minimal development early in the 1960s, though Robert Ascher's (1961a, 1961b) and Raymond Thompson's (1958a, 1958b) efforts are noteworthy. Binford (1962:219) indicated that he considered "the study and establishment of correlations between types of social structure classified on the basis of behavioral attributes and structural types of material elements as one of the major areas of anthropological research yet to be developed." In short, material correlates of human behaviors had not yet been identified by culture historians, but attention turned to it rather quickly on the heels of Binford's polemic (e.g., Binford 1967).

Once such correlations were established, one seemingly had rather direct access to reading the dynamics of a working cultural system from the statics of the archaeological record. This made the third new Americanist archeology, that of the 1960s, attractive to some culture historians (e.g., Martin 1971), as it was precisely what they had been searching for all along. Thus, Robert Ehrich's (1965:6) illustrative suggestion (and it was only illustrative, as he thought such assumptions were unwarranted [Ehrich 1963:20]) made in the early 1960s that "We need only have postulated that either the potters were women living in a patrilocal society, or men living in a matrilocal one, to have a situation in which diffusion took place through the spread of pottery-makers rather than of the pots" was shortly thereafter to become a viable axiom of the third new archaeology (e.g., Deetz 1965; Hill 1966; Longacre 1964, 1966).

Echoing the new archaeology of the 1950s as characterized by Caldwell (1959), Meggers (1955), Phillips (1955), and Willey and Phillips (1958), the new archeology of the 1960s was interested in culture processes—"the dynamic relationships (causes and effects) operative among sociocultural systems, [the] processes responsible for changes observed in the organization and/or content of the systems, or . . . the integration of new formal components into the system. [In short, the] dynamic relationships operative among cultural systems" (Binford 1968a:14). To processualists, "Explanation . . . within a scientific frame of reference is simply the *demonstration* of constant articulation of [functional] variables within a system and the measurement of concomitant variability among the variables within the [cultural] system. Processual change in one variable can then be shown to relate to changes in other variables, the latter changing in turn relative to changes in the structure of the system as a whole" (Binford 1962:217). The possible catalysts for such change were to be sought "in systemic terms for classes of historical events such as migrations, establishment of 'contact' between areas previously isolated, etc." (Binford 1962:218). Interestingly, the historical *processes* of cultural change were exactly those of the culture historians (Table 7.1). This is not surprising, as discussions of the processes of culture change written by cultural anthropologists before 1960 (e.g., Spindler and Spindler 1959) sounded remarkably like those written after that time (e.g., Woods 1975).

As Clyde Woods (1975:ix) noted a decade after culture history had fallen from favor, "comprehensive treatments of [culture] change as a subdiscipline are practically nonexistent and good, predictive theory is seriously lacking." Woods (1975:12) suggested "the term evolution is appropriate to refer to [culture] change" and correctly underscored the significance of what he termed "the important difference between form and function" (Woods 1975:3), but he failed to make clear that this distinction involves, simply, the difference between homologous and analogous similarity as understood by paleobiologists. Rouse (1955) was well aware of this important distinction, remarking in the 1960s that "artifacts do not change in the same manner as organic objects. One task of anthropology in general and of archeology in particular is to formulate a theory of [artifact] change that will express differences between variation in artifacts and the evolution of plants and animals" (Rouse 1965a:94). He also noted that "A demonstration that two plants or animals are taxonomically related does not reveal how one changed into the other. To do this, it is necessary to study the genes which governed the change" (Rouse 1965a:95). And Rouse, in not so many words, argued that the basis of a theory of artifact change must reside in understanding how culture changes.

But rather than developing a theory of change using theoretical units for measuring and thereby explaining historical events, processual archaeology came to mean *deductive* archaeology; in short, it came to represent a particular method rather than a particular theory (e.g., Binford 1968a:16–23; Fritz and Plog 1970; Watson et al. 1971). Early on, Kidder (1917a:369) had suggested that "The only safe method for working out the developments in decorative art is to build up one's sequences from chronologically sequent material, and so let one's theories form themselves from the sequences." Such an inductive method was characterized as unscientific by processual archaeologists, who, following the wrong model of science (Dunnell 1980, 1982, 1989, 1992; O'Brien 1996b; O'Brien and Holland 1995a), pledged their allegiance to the deductive method (e.g., Binford 1968b; Fritz and Plog 1970; Watson et al. 1971). Given the preferred definition of culture as an extrasomatic means of adaptation, explanation for perceived change was forced to take the form of "cultures change because adaptations change" and so forth (O'Brien and Holland 1992). Binford's (1968a:15) dreaded "transformational sequence of [adaptational stages or] forms" was the direct result. Such things as evolutionary drift and nonadaptational change were precluded from discussion.

Cultural Evolution Did Not Die in 1896

Some commentators on the new archeology of the 1960s wondered "if archaeology really requires a set of specifically archaeological theory, other than the accepted principles of inference and interpretation and a hopefully augmented emphasis on method of field work and data collection, plus the *general framework of anthropological theory*" (Bayard 1969:382; emphasis added). By the 1950s, anthropological theory clearly had as one of its components what has been termed *cultural evolution* (Dunnell 1980). Received wisdom typically holds that "cultural evolution was generally anathema as late as the 1950s," only to be revived by the end of the decade (Willey and Sabloff 1993:220; see also Ehrich 1963:21). Not everyone agrees with this view (e.g., Trigger 1989:295). Willey and Sabloff's (1993:306) contention that cultural evolution was dead during the first half of the twentieth century is founded in part on the fact that "Haag's (1959) review article . . . indicates only a limited number of evolutionary efforts in the field." In our view, Haag's article is not an extensive review and thus cannot be considered to reference a representative sample of the Literature.

While not seeking to resolve the disagreement here, we underscore that the general notion of evolution, cultural or otherwise, played a major if implicit role in the growth and development of the culture history paradigm. How could it not have? Archaeology, after all, had one thing that cultural anthropology did not—access to an extensive temporal record. And, everyone knew that evolution takes place over time. Once it was clear that temporal difference existed in the archaeological record of the Americas, evolution of some form was an obvious if not always explicit or well-developed explanatory option.

Received wisdom also holds that Franz Boas killed any notion of cultural evolution at the end of the nineteenth century. However, leading figures in anthropology at the turn of the century did not reject outright the notion of cultural evolution. Although often attributed with just such a stance, Boas (1896:904) was merely concerned with the fact that the theory of cultural evolution resulted in a comparative anthropology founded on the "assumption that the same [cultural] features must always have developed from the same causes, [leading] to the conclusion that there is one grand system according to which mankind has developed everywhere; that all the occurring variations are no more than minor details in this grand uniform evolution." Given that the assumption was demonstrably wrong, Boas (1896:907) preferred the "historical method" and its ability to discover the processes that resulted in the *particular* development of different cultures. The historical method would ultimately reveal the laws of cultural evolution—inductively—rather than assume them as did the comparative method. The important point here is that Boas did not reject cultural evolution per se; rather, he rejected its interpretive assumptions. That at least some of his students (e.g., Kroeber 1909, 1916a, 1916b, 1919) followed suit is clear.

In the first edition of his classic *Anthropology,* Kroeber (1923a:3) used the term "tradition" to label the processes of cultural transmission and heredity to distinguish them from the biological "force" of (genetic) heredity. Both biological evolution and cultural development involved transmission, but because transmission within the latter could be between individuals that were not "blood descendants," the concept of evolution was "ambiguous" in a cultural setting (Kroeber 1923a:7). In Kroeber's (1923a:8) view "the designation of anthropology as 'the child of Darwin' is most misleading. Darwin's essential achievement was that he imagined . . . a mechanism [natural selection] through which organic evolution appeared to be taking place. . . . [A] pure Darwinian anthropology would be largely misapplied biology." What had "greatly influenced anthropology," according to Kroeber (1923a:8), "has not been Darwinism, but the vague idea of evolution. . . . It has been common practice in social anthropology to 'explain' any part of human civilization by arranging its several forms in an evolutionary sequence from lowest to highest and allowing each successive stage to flow spontaneously from the preceding—in other words, without specific cause." Kroeber saw this as nonsense. The development of a cultural lineage was historical, and historians "deal with the concrete, with the unique; for in a degree every historical event has something unparalleled about it. . . . [Historians] do not lay down exact laws" (Kroeber 1923a:5). This didn't mean that cultures did not evolve; it only meant that the Morgan–Spencer–Tylor model of such evolution was incorrect for its generality.

Kidder (e.g., 1915, 1917a) used evolutionary terminology in a meta-phorical sense precisely when the culture history paradigm was being born. Colton, Gladwin, Hargrave, Haury, Sayles, and others followed that lead, developing the notion perhaps beyond its practical limits. Importantly, when discussing then-available dating techniques, Kidder (1924:45) noted that

> Crude and primitive-looking remains, when compared with relics of an obviously more advanced type are usually, and doubtless often correctly, assumed to belong to an earlier period. This method of chronological evaluation must, however, be very cautiously applied and should always have the support of corroborative evidence, since in the history of the Southwest many cases of degeneration in culture and irregularity in cul-ture-growth have occurred. Care must also be taken not to mistake the survival of archaic traits in peripheral regions for evidence of antiquity.

In other words, the *progressive* aspect of cultural evolution as conceived by Morgan, Spencer, and Tylor (see Dunnell 1980) was alive and well, though it was also occasionally known to be an inaccurate portrayal of particular culture histories. Nonetheless, regular reference was made to "high" and "low" cultures, "advances in handiwork" (Vaillant 1937:313–314), cultural evolution shown by "chronological sequence, from exceedingly simple to very complex remains" (McGregor 1941:5), and "progressively increasing cultural complexity" through time (McKern 1946:35). Such interpretations no doubt fed the model eventually proposed by Willey and Phillips (1955, 1958).

Nelson provided one of the more elaborate and thorough discussions of the thinking on the evolution of culture—if not cultural evolution in the sense of Spencer, Tylor, and Morgan—during the 1930s. Nelson (1932:103) wrote of "implements or mechanical inventions, i.e., material culture phe-nomena, as parts of a unique unfolding *process* which has much in common with that other process observed in the world of nature and generally called organic evolution." But the progressive aspect of Morgan-like cultural evo-lution was paramount: Through the Pleistocene of Europe, Nelson (1932:115) reasoned, there was evidence for a "gradual *improvement* of nu-merous tools, weapons and ornaments made from stone, bone and shell" (emphasis added). Thus, possessing "a complete series of chronologically arranged specimens, [the archaeologist] will be perceiving how by slow stages of *improvement* the simple early inventions of stone, bone, wood and shell gave rise to our present metallic contrivances. This visible demonstra-tion of origin by gradual modification of most of our own material equip-ment for life is perhaps the greatest lesson in evolution that archeology has to teach" (Nelson 1936:257; emphasis added).

Although cultural evolution might be continuous, it also was apparently gradual in Nelson's view:

> [A] study of the history of mechanization reveals few if any absolutely original contrivances that were not essentially the results of gradual transformation or combination of older inventions; that in reality spurts, mutants or leaps are as rare among artificial (intellectual) phenomena as among natural phenomena. Progress in the former case is regarded as unthinkable except in terms of orderly sequence, process, or continuity, though the added increments that proclaim advance may not thereby be fully explained. Final explanations of this, as well as of the driving force and the ultimate goal of culture, may be left to the philosophers. (Nelson 1932:122)

This conception of culture change as continuous and gradual was reiterated by Ford (1935a) a few years later. Nelson actually had a form of explanation that would become all too familiar within the culture history paradigm of the 1950s. He wrote that "an invention is something that has been thought out, and by means of the hands tried out, until it was adapted to do the particular work for which it was intended"; in other words, "necessity is the mother of invention" (Nelson 1932:109, 111). Further, and importantly, "man, through the origination and development of his material culture, has created for himself a more or less completely artificial environment and thereby has placed himself in a corresponding measure out of direct reach of nature's molding influences—out of reach, that is, of the normal forces that make for natural selection and the survival of the fittest"; as a result, man is "no longer a true animal" (Nelson 1932:119, 120). Cultural evolution was a fact, but human biological history and human cultural history were hardly the result of such Darwinian evolutionary mechanisms as natural selection. That left a Morgan-like model of cultural evolution as the only viable alternative. Thus, *progressive cultural evolution*— improvement—was an *intentional* result of the human animal.

The seminal Pecos Classification of cultural units was progressive, unilinear, and evolutionary in structure, as was the original classification of cultures produced at Gila Pueblo (Daifuku 1952; Roberts 1935). In 1936, Byron Cummings presented a revised version of the Pecos Classification (cited in McGregor 1941:59–60) that had three major periods or developmental stages. During the 1940s, many individuals spoke of cultural "stages" of development (e.g., Ford and Willey 1941; Griffin 1946, 1952; McGregor 1941)—a patently cultural evolutionary concept. As Steward's (1948:103) discussion of his suggested classification of "American high cultures" indicates, "it appears that there may have been certain regularities in the development of [agricultural proficiency, population density, settlement patterns, sociological complexity, and craft technologies] in the different areas of native American high cultures. The present need . . . is a sequential scheme and corresponding terminology that takes into account basic technologies and associated socio-religious patterns rather than stylistic peculiarities" of artifacts.

The 1940s witnessed the rebirth of cultural evolution within cultural anthropology, largely at the hands of White (e.g., 1945, 1949) and Steward (e.g., 1955). But that notion had never really died in Americanist archaeology, as Kidder's and Nelson's remarks in particular make clear. Thus, culture historians were already tuned in to the appropriate wavelength when White and Steward began making their pronouncements. Various formulations of such a model appeared rather frequently in the 1950s (e.g., Daifuku 1952; Meggers 1956), with perhaps the most influential one being that of Willey and Phillips (1955, 1958). This and related schemes allowed one to place archaeological units such as phases in a unilinear, progressive evolutionary sequence. Explanation of a particular culture's lineage, change, and development would then, apparently, be self evident, reflecting the common sense approach of culture history in general (see Haag [1959:97] for an example). Evolutionary thinking was apparently so rampant that Eggan (1952:38), late in the 1940s, hoped for some explanatory and interpretive "formulas" that were *not* evolutionary.

Some individuals, however, were not fooled by evolutionary schemes. In commenting on Willey and Phillips model, Earl Swanson (1959:121) observed that "No theory has been developed. What is *assumed* is an evolutionary theory about the nature of culture, though Willey and Phillips are shy about admitting this. Moreover, no history has been written." This is precisely the problem Boas (1896) had had with Morgan-like schemes sixty years earlier. Writing at the same time as Swanson, Haag (1959:101) observed that Willey and Phillips "carefully avoid any contaminating *explanations* of culture change" and noted that what they are clearly suggesting "is an admirable statement of one of the tenets of evolutionism." That tenet was *progress*. Interestingly, McKern (1956) was not fooled either. He argued that "Any all-encompassing classificatory procedure which ignores the part played by ecology [read *adaptation*] in cultural determination and cultural history will find many of its approaches ending in 'taxonomic strain,' or, in the extreme, hopeless confusion" (McKern 1956:360). He then proceeded to argue that Willey and Phillips's placement of recent prehistoric Northwest Coast culture within their Archaic stage was surely incorrect and that such assignment indicated a too-heavy reliance on the presence or absence of agriculture as a definitive trait for various of their cultural stages.

But many *were* fooled. Thus, coincident with the centennial anniversary of the publication of Charles Darwin's *On the Origin of Species,* several edited volumes concerning the history and influence of evolutionary theory were published (e.g., Meggers 1959; Tax 1960). Willey (1960:111–112) contributed to one of those volumes, and therein reiterated his views: "There is abundant evidence from archaeology and history to see how man's technical culture, as directed toward the problems of subsistence, has evolved, more or less steadily, *toward greater effectiveness*. . . . [I]t is possible to trace a general evolution in [the history of social and political organization toward] increasing size and complexity." Thus, Willey (1961) found favor with various formulations of White's and Steward's models. Haag (1959:97), too, noted that "evolution is progressive if successful. The concept of 'stages' in the cultural history of mankind is a logical concomitant." Haag (1959:103) and Willey (1960:111) agreed that the "focal point of research efforts is adaptation" and that "the history of [cultural] adaptation is the story of cultural evolution," respectively. What a marvelous opening, in conjunction with the second new archaeology's attempts to invoke ethnologically documented mechanisms of culture change as explanations, for the new archaeology of the 1960s to walk through. And that, as we indicated earlier, was the opening it exploited.

The Fall from Favor

The opening was exploited by focusing on method. One needed some sort of warrant for the interpretive correlations of types with norms, sites with communities, and phases with tribes. Reasoning should be deductive, and laws of how cultures work should be derived from experiments and from tested analogies. This research process later became known as middle-range theory and was the vehicle by which the static archaeological record could be reconstituted into a set of dynamic cultural systems with a stronger methodological warrant than the commonsense one of culture historians. By explicitly revealing this avenue, describing how to traverse it, and arguing forcefully that it would provide the kinds of insights to the past desired by the culture historians of the 1950s, the processualists won the day. The culture history paradigm thus fell from favor, not without a bit of a fight, not completely in any event, and not for want of a salable product or lack of some rigorous method. It surely had both; for example, it had produced chronological results that were testable empirically. Suspected chronologies could be shown to be wrong. Where the paradigm got into trouble was in attempting to use archaeological units, which were etic and largely stylistic, as anthropologically meaningful and relevant ones, which were emic and functional. Perfecting the methods that underlay those attempts became the focus of the new archaeologists of the 1960s.

That focus, however, was incomplete for the development of a true processual, or scientific, archaeology. As Dunnell (1990:19) indicated,

> the culture historical paradigm represented a narrowing of inquiry from the eclecticism of the nineteenth and early twentieth century to focus on homologous similarities, similarities that arise in consequence of transmission. It was brought about by the invention of methods to detect homologous similarity and create chronologies. The product, time–space schemata, of course, mirrored the concentration of effort on macrotime and space relations. . . . The new archaeology [of the 1960s] focuses attention upon analogous similarities, similarities that arise in consequence of external constraints. This in turn led the new archaeology to pursue laws, rather than history, and to decry [culture-historical] pattern descriptions in favor of systemic, interactive descriptions.

In Chapter 1 we noted that Kroeber (1931a), early in the ontogeny of the culture history paradigm, had pointed out the necessity of not only distinguishing but utilizing both homologous and analogous similarity in writing evolutionary histories. The culture history paradigm had, with its intense interest in time and by making that dimension analytically visible, focused on variants of culture traits variously known as types and styles of artifacts. That they allowed the measurement of the time and space dimensions suggests they were largely founded on homologous similarities. Analogous, or functional, similarity, while occasionally pointed out as a potentially obfuscating factor (e.g., Rouse 1955), received little attention until about 1960 when culture historians began to be more explicitly interested in explanation (e.g., Ascher 1961a, 1961b). In conjunction with the continued desire to make Americanist archaeology anthropologically relevant (e.g., Phillips 1955), the shift in focus to functional and adaptational explanations in the 1960s resulted in a change from study of homologous similarity to analogous similarity. The study of both are necessary. It is little wonder that the desires of both culture historians and processual archaeologists to *explain* the development, the *evolution,* of cultures in theoretical and testable terms have not yet been fulfilled.

8

An Ending Note

In this book we have attempted to provide something of a critical history of the conceptual context of Americanist archaeology since the end of the nineteenth century and prior to the florescence of the new, or processual, archaeology of the 1960s and 1970s. That period, especially beginning in the midteens, was dominated by a particular view of archaeology that came to be known as culture history. Some of the benchmark papers from that period have been collected and reprinted elsewhere (Lyman et al. 1997), and they document the development of the first real paradigm in Americanist archaeology. Culture-historical research began inauspiciously but grew into something that occupied nearly the whole of the field until the 1960s, when it "officially" fell from favor. Yet culture history and various of the methods and concepts it spawned persisted in various guises and forms in later paradigms (e.g., Aberle 1970:216–217; Stanislawski 1973:118, 120), and parts of it—albeit in modified form—are seeing some resurrection as we near the end of the century (e.g., Teltser 1995; Tschauner 1994).

It was generally accepted prior to the end of the nineteenth century that superposed strata documented the passage of time. Attempts to use this fact during the first fifteen years of the twentieth century to document and study culture change met with minimal success and virtually no disciplinary approval because change was cast in essentialist terms, and thus only differences in lists of culture traits—generally construed as things rather than as *kinds* of things—were considered significant. Simultaneously, attempts to standardize the description of artifacts grew in number until, by the middle of the second decade of the twentieth century, so much variation was recognized that it was suspected that some of it denoted temporal difference. Within the short span of about three years, Nels C. Nelson and A. V. Kidder confirmed, using geologically superposed artifact collections, that some variation in artifact types—variants of culture traits—did in fact measure the passage of time. At virtually the same time, using percentage stratigraphy and frequency seriation, A. L. Kroeber, Leslie Spier, and Kidder demonstrated that those types also displayed a certain kind of distribution through time. Thus was born one of the central tenets of culture history—the popularity principle. It was not theoretically informed, being instead a commonsense warrant for a perception. That such could also be found in historically documented cultures (e.g., Kroeber 1919) set the tone for all future interpretations of the archaeological record. In short, anthropological theory, such as it was, served as the source of interpretive statements; an explicitly *archaeological* theory of culture development and change was unnecessary.

The effect of Nelson's, Kroeber's, Kidder's, and Spier's efforts on Americanist archaeology was immediate. No longer was the apparent absence of an extensive time depth to American prehistory a fatal problem in attempts to write the history of ethnographically documented cultures; no longer did one have to search for differences in superposed trait lists; and no longer did one have to search for elusive stratified deposits. Artifacts from any archaeological deposit of sufficient thickness could be chronologically ordered, as Spier showed, if those artifacts were categorized in particular ways. James A. Ford demonstrated the general applicability of percentage stratigraphy two decades later and the utility of frequency seriation in the absence of stratified or thick deposits a decade after that. A chronological ordering based on seriation—either of Kroeber's, Spier's, or Ford's frequency sort, or of Kidder's phyletic sort—was testable when stratified deposits were available or if one used other dating methods (e.g., dendrochronology early, radiocarbon later). Thus, *only* the kinds of types that allowed the measurement of time were desired because they allowed one to produce a testable product—a chronological sequence. The focus of classification efforts on this singular goal was due to the fact that "for the first time it was possible to do archaeology and be wrong! This jerked archaeology out of the business of speculative natural history and placed it firmly in the realm of science" (Dunnell 1986b:29).

Alex D. Krieger formalized the chronological-significance test for types in the 1940s, though there had been precedence in the work of Kidder, Ford, and others. The spatial dimension, largely as a result of the work of William Henry Holmes, Otis T. Mason, Clark Wissler, and finally Kroeber, was considered, but ethnic groups were not historically stationary (e.g., McKern 1946). Spatial variation in artifact form—or demonstrable temporal variation, for that matter—might signify prehistoric ethnic variation, and while this was not testable in the same sense as temporal variation, it was used as an explanatory algorithm for the archaeological record virtually from the birth of the culture history paradigm by Spier, Erich Schmidt, George Vaillant, and others. Thus, one spoke not only of types that might reflect cultural norms, but also of prehistoric cultural units as ethnically distinct phenomena that *might* reflect a band or community. It was, after all, learning and understanding the historical development of such units that was the explicit goal.

On the one hand, solving chronological questions initially resulted in Americanist archaeologists taking a materialistic view of the record: Variation in artifact form was a record of temporal change within the braided stream of the culture continuum. Styles in the sense of Kroeber were the basis of appropriate kinds of types because they denoted homologous similarity. Their frequency distributions reflected their popularity within a cultural lineage. On the other hand, the complexes, phases, and foci of W. C. McKern, Kidder, Harold S. Gladwin, and others represented the essentialist underpinnings of common sense, reasserted to interpret chronological sequences and to warrant such units. The traditions and horizons of Kroeber, Ford, and Gordon R. Willey were tools used to link such units in space and time, and they represented the intermingled channels of culture history's braided stream. By the 1940s, ethnologically documented historical processes such as diffusion, trade, migration, invention, and persistence were regularly being called on as "explanations" of temporal continuity and change and were measured by the degrees of similarities and differences between various artifact types and artifact assemblages. Progressive evolution underpinned much of the thinking about the history of the development of particular cultural lineages. That the artifact units were said to be styles and thus to represent homologous similarity did not, however, ensure that the units were adaptively neutral (in a Darwinian evolutionary sense) or even largely so. The notion that similarity in form denoted homologous similarity, while recognized as potentially false by Julian Steward and others and thus qualified to concern the complexity of the similar items and the magnitude of difference, became an axiom of culture history.

By the early 1950s, culture history was in its heyday. Ford had pretty much worked out most of the bugs in his frequency-seriation method, radiocarbon dating was now available (dendrochronology having been around for the previous thirty years in the Southwest [Douglass 1919, 1921; Wissler 1921]), and something approaching a consensus on the definitions of components, phases, and the like had been attained as exemplified by the work of Willey and Philip Phillips. Contributions such as the one by Phillips, Ford, and James B. Griffin (1951) represented the height of the paradigm, but that singular contribution also makes it clear that there were serious disagreements within the paradigm—essentially the paradox noted several years earlier by J. O. Brew that one might conceive of change in materialist terms but measure and interpret it in essentialist terms. Or, as evidenced by the 1955 seminars and by Spaulding's methods, one might conceive of change strictly in essentialist terms.

Walter W. Taylor's unsympathetic post–World War II review of Americanist archaeology heralded this trend toward essentialism. The pattern-oriented reconstructions of static cultures produced by culture history were to eventually give way to functional studies of dynamic, living cultural systems as proxies for the past. This had always been the ultimate goal of culture history; it had merely been put on hold while the temporal dimension was made analytically visible. Once the temporal dimension was sufficiently under control in particular areas, efforts there turned to attempts to interpret chronological sequences. Such efforts were doomed because the artifact units in use were inadequate and because attempts were made to interpret sequences of cultures rather than to explain why the archaeological record looked the way it did. Failure to deal rigorously with the construction of allegedly cultural units, in conjunction with a strong conviction to a Whitean view of cultural evolution, presented an opportunity ripe for exploitation.

The processual archaeology of the 1960s represented a shift away from explaining homologous similarities in the archaeological record to focusing on and explaining analogous similarities between living cultures and those of the past (Binford 1962, 1965). Thus there was a shift from ideographic history as explanation to a search for nomothetic laws as the *source* of explanation. The focus was still on cultural units rather than on the archaeological record. As a result, some of the commonsense, ethnologically based speculations about units and processes that were used by culture historians to rationalize why their largely empirical, trial-and-error procedure worked assumed a dominant role in the paradigm that succeeded culture history. Ideas that had been summarily recycled for decades by culture historians now made sense. A prime example of this is found in the empiricist challenge.

Spaulding's innovative way to create artifact types was rationalized as producing an accurate reflection of prehistoric human social behavior. His position became that of the new archaeology of the 1960s—those cultural norms archaeologists had only been talking about up to that point could be discovered. Rigorous method produced types that were "real," emic units in a human behavioral sense, or so it seemed. Some culture historians, such as Ford, simply couldn't buy such nonsense but, given the imperfect theoretical foundation of their own views, they could only protest weakly. Some post-Taylor, post-Spaulding culture historians made serious attempts to incorporate notions such as Spaulding's, as well as ethnological terminology, into the culture history paradigm. This is exemplified in Irving Rouse's more axiomatic discussion of modes in the 1950s and 1960s and in Phillips and Willey's modest attempts at alignment of components with communities and phases with societies. The culmination of such attempts was, of course, the birth of the new movement (Binford 1968a), which, in the end, disposed of some strengths while incorporating some of the same flaws that plagued culture history (Tschauner 1994:82–83).

In previous chapters we have sought to evaluate in rather rigorous fashion the central tenets of the culture history paradigm. Our evaluation has been couched within an evaluative framework structured in modern terms to reflect the explicit goals of the paradigm—the study of cultural history in a Darwinian sense. Throughout our evaluation, we have found a few glimmers of significant insight, but mainly we have found that culture history failed largely for want of an archaeological theory of cultural evolution. The paradigm fairly stumbled into a way to measure time using artifact form; the resulting units were largely stylistic in the sense of monitoring homologous relations, as they should be from a more modern theoretical perspective (Dunnell 1978). Frequency seriation and percentage stratigraphy were originally conceived in materialist terms to reflect the braided stream of culture history, not an unreasonable model (e.g., Dunnell 1980, 1982; O'Brien and Holland 1990).

But in lieu of theoretically informed unit construction, and given a large dose of anthropological reasoning, culture historians turned to commonsense ethnological warrants for unit formation and for interpretation of those units. Combined with the regular failure to maintain a clear distinction between empirical and ideational units, along with the commonsense use of stratigraphic units to define assemblages, the net result was an essentialist account of the history of successive cultural units. Change was of the transformational sort, and the gradually flowing braided stream became a series of intertwined placid pools punctuated by rapids. Cultures—the placid pools—as well as types, were recognizable to the trained eye because they were real. Transitional cultures or types were insignificant mixtures and constituted noise of little explanatory import.

In identifying the strengths and weaknesses of culture history, it is our hope that a better product will be constructed (e.g., Dunnell 1992, 1995; O'Brien 1996a, 1996c; O'Brien and Holland 1990, 1992, 1995a, 1995b; O'Brien et al. 1994). All three of us are strongly committed to making archaeology a science and to producing a scientific understanding of the past. And we are strongly committed to studying culture change and processes of change and stability. We thus have strong leanings toward understanding the past in terms of Darwinian, or scientific, evolution. Such leanings demand a materialist epistemology, well-conceived theoretical units for measuring change and stability, and well-developed theory for explaining the empirical phenomena we study. Much of the groundwork necessary to such an understanding—and many of the pitfalls to be avoided—can be found in the culture history paradigm. We need to understand that groundwork.

References

ABBOTT, CHARLES
    1877   On the Discovery of Supposed Paleolithic Implements from the Glacial Drift in the Valley of the Delaware River, near Trenton, New Jersey. *Peabody Museum of American Archaeology and Ethnology, Annual Report of the Trustees* 2:30–43.
    1888   On the Antiquity of Man in the Valley of the Delaware. *Boston Society of Natural History, Proceedings* 23:424–426.
ABERLE, DAVID F.
    1970   Comments. In *Reconstructing Prehistoric Pueblo Societies*, edited by William A. Longacre, pp. 214–223. University of New Mexico Press, Albuquerque.
ADAMS, RICHARD E.
    1960   Manual Gamio and Stratigraphic Excavation. *American Antiquity* 26:99.
ADAMS, ROBERT McC.
    1968   Archeological Research Strategies: Past and Present. *Science* 160:1187–1192.
AITKEN, ROBERT T.
    1917   Porto Rican Burial Caves. *Nineteenth International Congress of Americanists, Proceedings*, pp. 224–228.
    1918   A Porto Rican Burial Cave. *American Anthropologist* 20:296–309.
ALEXANDER, HUBERT G., AND PAUL REITER
    1935   Report on the Excavation of Jemez Cave, New Mexico. *University of New Mexico Bulletin, Monograph Series* 1(3).
AMSDEN, CHARLES AVERY
    1931   Black-on-White Ware. In The Pottery of Pecos, Vol. 1, by Alfred V. Kidder, pp. 17–72. *Papers of the Southwestern Expedition, Phillips Academy* No. 5. Yale University Press, New Haven, Connecticut.
ANONYMOUS
    1915   Museum Notes. *American Museum Journal* 15:30.
ASCHER, ROBERT
    1961a   Analogy in Archaeological Interpretation. *Southwestern Journal of Anthropology* 17:317–325.
    1961b   Experimental Archeology. *American Anthropologist* 63:793–816.
ASCHER, ROBERT, AND MARCIA ASCHER
    1965   Recognizing the Emergence of Man. *Science* 147:243–250.
BANDELIER, ADOLPH F.
    1892   Final Report of Investigations among the Indians of the Southwestern United States. *Archaeological Institute of America, Paper* 4:1–591.

BARTH, FREDRIK
1950   Ecologic Adaptation and Cultural Change in Archaeology. *American Antiquity* 15:338–339.

BAYARD, DONN T.
1969   Science, Theory, and Reality in the "New Archaeology." *American Antiquity* 34:376–384.

BEALS, RALPH L., GEORGE W. BRAINERD, AND WATSON SMITH
1945   Archaeological Studies in Northeast Arizona. *University of California, Publications in American Archaeology and Ethnology* 44(1):1–236.

BECK, CHARLOTTE, AND GEORGE T. JONES
1989   Bias and Archaeological Classification. *American Antiquity* 54:244–262.

BENNETT, JOHN W.
1943   Recent Developments in the Functional Interpretation of Archaeological Data. *American Antiquity* 9:208–219.

1944   Archaeological Horizons in the Southern Illinois Region. *American Antiquity* 10:12–22.

1946   Empiricist and Experimental Trends in Eastern Archaeology. *American Antiquity* 11:198–200.

BENNETT, WENDELL C.
1948   The Peruvian Co-Tradition. In A Reappraisal of Peruvian Archaeology, assembled by Wendell C. Bennett, pp. 1–7. *Society for American Archaeology, Memoirs* No. 4.

BENNYHOFF, J. A.
1952   The Viru Valley Sequence: A Critical Review. *American Antiquity* 17:231–249.

BETTINGER, ROBERT L., JAMES F. O'CONNELL, AND DAVID HURST THOMAS
1991   Projectile Points as Time Markers in the Great Basin. *American Anthropologist* 93:166–172.

BINFORD, LEWIS R.
1962   Archaeology as Anthropology. *American Antiquity* 28:217–225.

1964   A Consideration of Archaeological Research Design. *American Antiquity* 29:425–441.

1965   Archaeological Systematics and the Study of Culture Process. *American Antiquity* 31:203–210.

1967   Smudge Pits and Hide Smoking: The Use of Analogy in Archaeological Reasoning. *American Antiquity* 32:1–12.

1968a   Archeological Perspectives. In *New Perspectives in Archeology*, edited by Sally R. Binford and Lewis R. Binford, pp. 5–32. Aldine, New York.

1968b   Some Comments on Historical versus Processual Archaeology. *Southwestern Journal of Anthropology* 24:267–275.

BLACK, GLENN A., AND PAUL WEER
1936   A Proposed Terminology for Shape Classification of Artifacts. *American Antiquity* 1:280–294.

BOAS, FRANZ
1896   The Limitations of the Comparative Method of Anthropology. *Science* 4:901–908.

1900   Conclusion. In The Jesup North Pacific Expedition, edited by Franz Boas, pp. 387–390. *American Museum of Natural History, Memoirs* 2(4).

1902   Some Problems in North American Archaeology. *American Journal of Archaeology* 6:1–6.

1905   The Jesup North Pacific Expedition. *Thirteenth International Congress of Americanists, Proceedings,* pp. 91–100.

1912   International School of American Archaeology and Ethnology in Mexico. *American Anthropologist* 14:192–194.

1913   Archaeological Investigations in the Valley of Mexico by the International School, 1911–12. *Eighteenth International Congress of Americanists, Proceedings,* pp. 176–179.

1936   History and Science in Anthropology: A Reply. *American Anthropologist* 38:137–141.

BOCK, WALTER J.

1977   Foundations and Methods of Evolutionary Classification. In *Major Patterns in Vertebrate Evolution,* edited by Max K. Hecht, Peter C. Goody, and Bessie M. Hecht, pp. 851–895. Plenum Press, New York.

BOHANNAN, PAUL, AND MARK GLAZER (editors)

1988   *High Points in Anthropology,* 2nd ed. McGraw-Hill, New York.

BRAINERD, GEORGE W.

1951a   The Place of Chronological Ordering in Archaeological Analysis. *American Antiquity* 16:301–313.

1951b   The Use of Mathematical Formulations in Archaeological Analysis. In *Essays on Archaeological Methods,* edited by James B. Griffin, pp. 117–127. *University of Michigan Museum of Anthropology, Anthropological Papers* No. 8.

BRAY, WARWICK

1973   The Biological Basis of Culture. In *The Explanation of Culture Change: Models in Prehistory,* edited by Colin Renfrew, pp. 73–92. Duckworth, London.

BRETERNITZ, DAVID A.

1966   An Appraisal of Tree-ring Dated Pottery in the Southwest. *University of Arizona Anthropological Papers* No. 10.

BREW, JOHN O.

1942   Review of "Southwestern Archaeology" by John C. McGregor. *American Antiquity* 8:191–196.

1946   Archaeology of Alkali Ridge, Southeastern Utah. *Peabody Museum of American Archaeology and Ethnology, Papers* 21. Cambridge, Massachusetts.

BROOKS, ROBERT L.

1982   Events in the Archaeological Context and Archaeological Explanation. *Current Anthropology* 23:67–75.

BROWMAN, DAVID L., AND DOUGLAS R. GIVENS

1996   Stratigraphic Excavation: The First "New Archaeology." *American Anthropologist* 98:80–95.

CALDWELL, JOSEPH R.

1958   Trend and Tradition in the Prehistory of the Eastern United States. *American Anthropological Association, Memoir* No. 88.

1959   The New American Archaeology. *Science* 129:303–307.

CALDWELL, JOSEPH R., AND A. J. WARING, JR.

1939   Pottery Type Descriptions. *Southeastern Archaeological Conference Newsletter* 1(6).

CAROTHERS, STEVEN W.

1978   Biology. *Plateau* 50(4):24–32.

CHANG, K. C.

1967   *Rethinking Archaeology.* Random House, New York.

COLE, FAY-COOPER
1943   Chronology in the Middle West. *American Philosophical Society, Proceedings* 86:299–303.
COLE, FAY-COOPER, AND THORNE DEUEL
1937   *Rediscovering Illinois: Archaeological Explorations in and around Fulton County.* University of Chicago Press, Chicago.
COLLINS, HENRY B., JR.
1926   Anthropological and Anthropometric Work in Mississippi. *Smithsonian Miscellaneous Collections* 78(1):89–95.
1927a   Potsherds from Choctaw Village Sites in Mississippi. *Washington Academy of Sciences, Journal* 17:259–263.
1927b   Archaeological Work in Louisiana and Mississippi. *Explorations and Field-work of the Smithsonian Institution in 1931,* Smithsonian Institution, Washington, D.C., pp. 200–207.
1932   Archaeology of Mississippi. In *Conference on Southern Pre-History,* pp. 37–42. National Research Council, Washington, D.C.
COLTON, HAROLD S.
1932   A Survey of Prehistoric Sites in the Region of Flagstaff, Arizona. *Bureau of American Ethnology, Bulletin* 104.
1936   The Rise and Fall of the Prehistoric Population of Northern Arizona. *Science* 84:337–343.
1939   Prehistoric Culture Units and Their Relationships in Northern Arizona. *Museum of Northern Arizona, Bulletin* 17.
1942   Archaeology and the Reconstruction of History. *American Antiquity* 8:33–40.
1943   Reconstruction of Anasazi History. *American Philosophical Society, Proceedings* 86:264–269.
1946   The Sinagua: A Summary of the Archaeology of the Region of Flagstaff, Arizona. *Museum of Northern Arizona, Bulletin* 22.
1965   Check List of Southwestern Pottery Types. *Museum of Northern Arizona Ceramic Series* No. 2 (revised).
COLTON, HAROLD S., AND LYNDON L. HARGRAVE
1937   Handbook of Northern Arizona Pottery Wares. *Museum of Northern Arizona, Bulletin* 11.
CORLISS, DAVID W.
1980   Arrowpoint or Dartpoint: An Uninteresting Answer to a Tiresome Question. *American Antiquity* 45:351–352.
COWGILL, GEORGE L.
1963   Review of "A Quantitative Method for Deriving Cultural Chronology" by James A. Ford. *American Anthropologist* 65:696–699.
CRABTREE, D. E.
1939   Mastodon Bone with Artifacts in California. *American Antiquity* 5:148.
CRACRAFT, JOEL
1989   Species as Entities in Biological Theory. In *What the Philosophy of Biology Is,* edited by Michael Ruse, pp. 31–52. Kluwer, Dordrecht, Netherlands.
CRESSMAN, LUTHER S.
1951   Western Prehistory in the Light of Carbon 14 Dating. *Southwestern Journal of Anthropology* 7:289–313.
CUSHING, FRANK H.
1886   A Study of Pueblo Pottery as Illustrative of Zuni Culture Growth. *Bureau of Ethnology, Annual Report* 4:467–521.

DAIFUKU, HIROSHI
1952   A New Conceptual Scheme for Prehistoric Cultures in the Southwestern United States. *American Anthropologist* 54:191–200.

DALL, WILLIAM H.
1877   On Succession in the Shell-Heaps of the Aleutian Isands. *Contributions to North American Ethnology* 1:41–91.

DE BOOY, THEODOOR
1913   Certain Kitchen-Middens in Jamaica. *American Anthropologist* 15:425–434.

DEETZ, JAMES
1965   The Dynamics of Stylistic Change in Arikara Ceramics. *Illinois Studies in Anthropology* No. 4. University of Illinois Press, Urbana.
1970   Archeology as Social Science. In Current Directions in Anthropology: A Special Issue, edited by Ann Fischer, pp. 115–125. *American Anthropological Association, Bulletin* 3(3).

DEETZ, JAMES, AND EDWIN DETHLEFSEN
1965   The Doppler Effect and Archaeology: A Consideration of the Spatial Aspects of Seriation. *Southwestern Journal of Anthropology* 21:196–206.

DE LAGUNA, FREDERICA
1934   *The Archaeology of Cook Inlet, Alaska.* University of Pennsylvania Press, Philadelphia.

DETHLEFSEN, EDWIN, AND JAMES DEETZ
1966   Death's Heads, Cherubs, and Willow Trees: Experimental Archaeology in Colonial Cemeteries. *American Antiquity* 31:502–510.

DEUEL, THORNE
1935   Basic Cultures of the Mississippi Valley. *American Anthropologist* 37:429–445.

DIXON, ROLAND B.
1913   Some Aspects of North American Archeology. *American Anthropologist* 15:549–577.
1928   *The Building of Cultures.* Scribner, New York.

DOUGLASS, A. E.
1919   *Climate Cycles and Tree Growth,* Vol. 1. Carnegie Institution, Washington, D.C.
1921   Dating Our Prehistoric Ruins. *Natural History* 21:27–30.

DRIER, ROY WARD
1939   A New Method of Sherd Classification. *American Antiquity* 5:31–35.

DRUCKER, PHILIP
1972   Stratigraphy in Archaeology: An Introduction. *Addison-Wesley Module in Anthropology* 30.

DUNNELL, ROBERT C.
1970   Seriation Method and Its Evaluation. *American Antiquity* 35:305–319.
1971a   Sabloff and Smith's "The Importance of Both Analytic and Taxonomic Classification in the Type-Variety System." *American Antiquity* 36:115–118.
1971b   *Systematics in Prehistory.* Free Press, New York.
1978   Style and Function: A Fundamental Dichotomy. *American Antiquity* 43:192–202.
1980   Evolutionary Theory and Archaeology. In *Advances in Archaeological Method and Theory* Vol. 3, edited by Michael B. Schiffer, pp. 35–99. Academic Press, New York.
1981   Seriation, Groups, and Measurements. In *Manejo de Datos y Metodos Matematicos de Arqueologia,* compiled by George L. Cowgill, Robert Whallon, and Barbara S. Ottaway, pp. 67–90. Union Internacional de Ciendias Prehistoricas y Protohistoricas, Mexico D.F.

1982   Science, Social Science, and Common Sense: The Agonizing Dilemma of Modern Archaeology. *Journal of Anthropological Research* 38:1–25.

1985   Archaeological Survey in the Lower Mississippi Alluvial Valley, 1940–1947: A Landmark Study in American Archaeology. *American Antiquity* 50:297–300.

1986a   Five Decades of American Archaeology. In *American Archaeology: Past and Future,* edited by David J. Meltzer, Don D. Fowler, and Jeremy A. Sabloff, pp. 23–49. Smithsonian Institution Press, Washington, D.C.

1986b   Methodological Issues in Americanist Artifact Classification. In *Advances in Archaeological Method and Theory* Vol. 9, edited by Michael B. Schiffer, pp. 149–207. Academic Press, Orlando.

1989   Philosophy of Science and Archaeology. In *Critical Traditions in Contemporary Archaeology,* edited by Valerie Pinsky and Alison Wylie, pp. 5–9. Cambridge University Press, Cambridge.

1990   The Role of the Southeast in American Archaeology. *Southeastern Archaeology* 9(1):11–22.

1992   Is a Scientific Archaeology Possible? In *Metaarchaeology,* edited by Lester Embree, pp. 75–97. Kluwer, Amsterdam.

1995   What Is It That Actually Evolves? In *Evolutionary Archaeology: Methodological Issues,* edited by Patrice A. Teltser, pp. 33–50. University of Arizona Press, Tucson.

DUNNELL, ROBERT C., AND WILLIAM S. DANCEY
1983   The Siteless Survey: A Regional Scale Data Collection Strategy. In *Advances in Archaeological Method and Theory* Vol. 6, edited by Michael B. Schiffer, pp. 267–287. Academic Press, New York.

DUTTON, BERTHA P.
1938   Leyit Kin, A Small House Ruin, Chaco Canyon, New Mexico. *University of New Mexico Bulletin, Monograph Series* 1(6).

EGGAN, FRED R.
1952   The Ethnological Cultures and Their Archeological Backgrounds. In *Archeology of Eastern United States,* edited by James B. Griffin, pp. 35–45. University of Chicago Press, Chicago.

EGGLETON, PAUL, AND RICHARD I. VANE-WRIGHT (editors)
1994   *Phylogenetics and Ecology.* Academic Press, London.

EHRICH, ROBERT W.
1950   Some Reflections on Archaeological Interpretation. *American Anthropologist* 52:468–482.

1963   Further Reflections on Archeological Interpretation. *American Anthropologist* 65:16–31.

1965   Ceramics and Man: A Cultural Perspective. In Ceramics and Man, edited by Frederick R. Matson, pp. 1–19. *Viking Fund Publications in Anthropology* No. 41.

ELLIOTT, MELINDA
1995   *Great Excavations: Tales of Early Southwestern Archaeology, 1888–1939.* School of American Research Press, Santa Fe.

ERASMUS, CHARLES J.
1968   Thoughts on Upward Collapse: An Essay on Explanation in Anthropology. *Southwestern Journal of Anthropology* 24:170–194.

EVANS, CLIFFORD, JR.
1951   Review of "Surface Survey of the Virú Valley, Peru" by James A. Ford and Gordon R. Willey. *American Antiquity* 16:270–272.

1954   Spaulding's Review of Ford. *American Anthropologist* 56:114.

EVANS, JOHN
1850   On the Date of British Coins. *The Numismatic Chronicle and Journal of the Numismatic Society* 12(4):127–137.
1875   On the Coinage of the Ancient Britons and Natural Selection. *Royal Institution of Great Britain, Proceedings* 7:24–32.

FAGAN, BRIAN M.
1991   *Ancient North America: The Archaeology of a Continent.* Thames and Hudson, New York.

FEWKES, J. WALTER
1914   Prehistoric Objects from a Shell-Heap at Erin Bay, Trinidad. *American Anthropologist* 16:200–220.

FINKELSTEIN, J. JOE
1937   A Suggested Projectile Point Classification. *American Antiquity* 2:197–203.

FITTING, JAMES E. (editor)
1973   *The Development of North American Archaeology.* Anchor Press, Garden City, New York.

FLANNERY, KENT V.
1967   Culture History v. Cultural Process: A Debate in American Archaeology. *Scientific American* 217(2):119–122.

FLENNIKEN, J. JEFFREY, AND ANAN W. RAYMOND
1986   Morphological Projectile Point Typology: Replication Experimentation and Technological Analysis. *American Antiquity* 51:603–614.

FLENNIKEN, J. JEFFREY, AND PHILIP J. WILKE
1989   Typology, Technology, and Chronology of Great Basin Dart Points. *American Anthropologist* 91:149–158.

FORD, JAMES A.
1935a   An Introduction to Louisiana Archaeology. *Louisiana Conservation Review* 4(5): 8–11.
1935b   Ceramic Decoration Sequence at an Old Indian Village Site, Near Sicily Island, Louisiana. *Louisiana State Geological Survey, Department of Conservation, Anthropological Study* No. 1.
1936a   Analysis of Village Site Collections from Louisiana and Mississippi. *Louisiana State Geological Survey, Department of Conservation, Anthropological Study* No. 2.
1936b   Archaeological Methods Applicable to Louisiana. *Proceedings of the Louisiana Academy of Sciences* 3:102–105.
1938   A Chronological Method Applicable to the Southeast. *American Antiquity* 3:260–264.
1940   Review of "Handbook of Northern Arizona Pottery Wares" by Harold S. Colton and Lyndon L. Hargrave. *American Antiquity* 5:263–266.
1949   Cultural Dating of Prehistoric Sites in Virú Valley, Peru. *American Museum of Natural History, Anthropological Papers* 43(1):29–89.
1951   Greenhouse: A Troyville-Coles Creek Period Site in Avoyelles Parish, Louisiana. *American Museum of Natural History, Anthropological Papers* 44(1):1–132.
1952   Measurements of Some Prehistoric Design Developments in the Southeastern States. *American Museum of Natural History, Anthropological Papers* 44(3):313–384.
1954a   Comment on A. C. Spaulding's "Statistical Techniques for the Discovery of Artifact Types." *American Antiquity* 19:390–391.
1954b   Spaulding's Review of Ford. *American Anthropologist* 56:109–112.

1954c   On the Concept of Types: The Type Concept Revisited. *American Anthropologist*
         56:42–53.
1961   In Favor of Simple Typology. *American Antiquity* 27:113–114.
1962   A Quantitative Method for Deriving Cultural Chronology. *Pan American Union,*
         Technical Bulletin No. 1.
FORD, JAMES A., AND JAMES B. GRIFFIN
1937   [A proposal for a] Conference on Pottery Nomenclature for the Southeastern
         United States. Mimeographed. [Reprinted in *Newsletter of the Southeastern*
         Archaeological Conference 7(1):5–9]
1938   Report of the Conference on Southeastern Pottery Typology. Mimeographed.
         [Reprinted in *Newsletter of the Southeastern Archaeological Conference* 7(1):10–
         22]
FORD, JAMES A., AND GEORGE I. QUIMBY, JR.
1945   The Tchefuncte Culture, An Early Occupation of the Lower Mississippi Valley.
         Society for American Archaeology, Memoirs No. 2.
FORD, JAMES A., AND GORDON R. WILLEY
1939a   Lower Mississippi Pottery Types: I. *Southeastern Archaeological Conference*
         Newsletter 1(3):1–12.
1939b   Lower Mississippi Pottery Types: II. *Southeastern Archaeological Conference*
         Newsletter 1(4):1–8.
1940   Crooks Site, a Marksville Period Burial Mound in La Salle Parish, Louisiana.
         Louisiana State Geological Survey, Department of Conservation, Anthropological
         Study No. 3.
1941   An Interpretation of the Prehistory of the Eastern United States. *American An-*
         thropologist 43:325–363.
FOREY, P. L.
1990   Cladistics. In *Palaeobiology: A Synthesis,* edited by Derek E. G. Briggs and Peter
         R. Crowther, pp. 430–434. Blackwell Scientific Publications, Oxford.
FOWKE, GERARD
1896   Stone Art. *Bureau of American Ethnology, Annual Report* 13:57–178.
1922   Archaeological Investigations. *Bureau of American Ethnology, Bulletin* 76.
FOX, GREGORY L.
1992   *A Critical Evaluation of the Interpretive Framework of the Mississippi Period in*
         Southeast Missouri. Ph.D. dissertation, Department of Anthropology, University
         of Missouri–Columbia.
FREEMAN, DEREK
1974   The Evolutionary Theories of Charles Darwin and Herbert Spencer. *Current*
         Anthropology 15:211–237.
FRITZ, JOHN M., AND FRED T. PLOG
1970   The Nature of Archaeological Explanation. *American Antiquity* 35:405–412.
GALLAGHER, MARSHA
1978   Anthropology. *Plateau* 50(4):18–23.
GAMIO, MANUEL
1909   Restos de la Cultura Tepaneca. *Anales del Museo Nacionál de Arqueologia, His-*
         toria y Etnología 1(6):241–253.
1913   Arqueologia de Atzcapotzalco, D.F., Mexico. *Eighteenth International Congress*
         of Americanists, Proceedings, pp. 180–187.
1917   Investigaciones Arqueológicas en México. *Nineteenth International Congress of*
         Americanists, Proceedings, pp. 125-133.

1924   The Sequence of Cultures in Mexico. *American Anthropologist* 26:307–322.

1959   Boas sobre Cerámica y Estratigrafía. In The Anthropology of Franz Boas, edited by Walter Goldschmidt, pp. 117–118. *American Anthropological Association, Memoirs* 89.

GAYTON, ANNA H.

1927   The Uhle Collections from Nieveria. *University of California, Publications in American Archaeology and Ethnology* 21:305–329.

GAYTON, ANNA H., AND ALFRED L. KROEBER

1927   The Uhle Pottery Collections from Nazca. *University of California, Publications in American Archaeology and Ethnology* 24:1–21.

GIFFORD, JAMES C.

1960   The Type–Variety Method of Ceramic Classification as an Indicator of Cultural Phenomena. *American Antiquity* 25:341–347.

GILLIN, JOHN

1938   A Method of Notation for the Description and Comparison of Southwestern Pottery by Formula. *American Antiquity* 4:22–29.

GIVENS, DOUGLAS R.

1992   *Alfred Vincent Kidder and the Development of Americanist Archaeology.* University of New Mexico Press, Albuquerque.

GLADWIN, HAROLD S.

1936   Editorials: Methodology in the Southwest. *American Antiquity* 1:256–259.

1937   Conclusions. In Excavations at Snaketown, I: Material Culture, by Harold S. Gladwin, Emil W. Haury, E. B. Sayles, and Nora Gladwin, pp. 247–269. *Medallion Papers* No. 25.

1943   A Review and Analysis of the Flagstaff Culture. *Medallion Papers* No. 31.

GLADWIN, WINIFRED, AND HAROLD S. GLADWIN

1928   The Use of Potsherds in an Archaeological Survey of the Southwest. *Medallion Papers* No. 2.

1929   The Red-on-Buff Culture of the Gila Basin. *Medallion Papers* No. 3.

1930a   A Method for the Designation of Southwestern Pottery Types. *Medallion Papers* No. 7.

1930b   Some Southwestern Pottery Types, Series I. *Medallion Papers* No. 8.

1931   Some Southwestern Pottery Types, Series II. *Medallion Papers* No. 10.

1933   Some Southwestern Pottery Types, Series III. *Medallion Papers* No. 13.

1934   A Method for the Designation of Cultures and Their Variations. *Medallion Papers* No. 15.

1935   The Eastern Range of the Red-on-Buff Culture. *Medallion Papers* No. 16.

GLEASON, H. A.

1923   Review of "Age and Area, a Study in Geographical Distribution and Origin of Species" by J. C. Willis. *Ecology* 4:196–201.

GOULD, STEPHEN J.

1986   Evolution and the Triumph of Homology, or Why History Matters. *American Scientist* 74:96–118.

GOULD, STEPHEN J., DAVID M. RAUP, J. JOHN SEPKOSKI, JR., THOMAS J. M. SCHOPF, AND DANIEL S. SIMBERLOFF

1977   The Shape of Evolution: A Comparison of Real and Random Clades. *Paleobiology* 3:23–40.

GRAYSON, DONALD K.

1983   *The Establishment of Human Antiquity.* Academic Press, New York.

GRIFFIN, JAMES B.
  1938   The Ceramic Remains from Norris Basin, Tennessee. In An Archaeological Sur-
          vey of the Norris Basin in Eastern Tennessee, edited by W. S. Webb. *Bureau
          of American Ethnology, Annual Report* 118:253–259.
  1939   Report on the Ceramics of Wheeler Basin. In An Archaeological Survey of
          Wheeler Basin on the Tennessee River in Northern Alabama, edited by W. S.
          Webb. *Bureau of American Ethnology, Annual Report* 122:127–165.
  1943   The Fort Ancient Aspect: Its Cultural and Chronological Position in Mississippi
          Valley Archaeology. *University of Michigan Museum of Anthropology, Anthropo-
          logical Papers* No. 28.
  1946   Cultural Change and Continuity in Eastern United States Archaeology. In Man
          in Northeastern North America, edited by Frederick Johnson, pp. 37–95. *Papers
          of the Robert S. Peabody Foundation for Archaeology*, Vol. 3. Phillips Academy,
          Andover.
  1952   Culture Periods in Eastern United States Archeology. In *Archeology of Eastern
          United States,* edited by James B. Griffin, pp. 352–364. University of Chicago
          Press, Chicago.
  1976   A Commentary on Some Archaeological Activities in the Mid-Continent 1925–
          1975. *Midcontinental Journal of Archaeology* 1:5–38.
  1985   The Formation of the Society for American Archaeology. *American Antiquity*
          50:261–271.
GUTHE, CARL E.
  1927   A Method for Ceramic Description. *Michigan Academy of Science, Arts, and Let-
          ters, Papers* 8:23–29.
  1934   A Method of Ceramic Description. In Standards of Pottery Description, by Ben-
          jamin March, pp. 1–6. *Occasional Contributions from the Museum of Anthropology
          of the University of Michigan* No. 3. Ann Arbor.
  1936   Review of "Basic Cultures of the Mississippi Valley" by Thorne Deuel. *American
          Antiquity* 1:249–250.
  1952   Twenty-Five Years of Archeology in the Eastern United States. In *Archeology
          of Eastern United States,* edited by James B. Griffin, pp. 1–12. University of Chi-
          cago Press, Chicago.
  1967   Reflections on the Founding of the Society for American Archaeology. *American
          Antiquity* 32:433–440.
HAAG, WILLIAM G.
  1939   Pottery Type Descriptions. *Southeastern Archaeological Conference Newsletter*
          1(1).
  1942   Early Horizons in the Southeast. *American Antiquity* 7:209–222.
  1959   The Status of Evolutionary Theory in American History. In *Evolution and
          Anthropology: A Centennial Appraisal,* edited by Betty J. Meggers, pp. 90–105.
          Anthropological Society of Washington, Washington, D.C.
  1961   Twenty-Five Years of Eastern Archaeology. *American Antiquity* 27:16–23.
  1985   Federal Aid to Archaeology in the Southeast, 1933–1942. *American Antiquity*
          50:272–280.
  1986   Field Methods in Archaeology. In *American Archaeology: Past and Future,* edited
          by David J. Meltzer, Don D. Fowler, and Jeremy A. Sabloff, pp. 63–76. Smith-
          sonian Institution Press, Washington, D.C.
HAEBERLIN, HERMAN K.
  1917   Some Archaeological Work in Porto Rico. *American Anthropologist* 19:214–238.

1919 Types of Ceramic Art in the Valley of Mexico. *American Anthropologist* 21:61–70.

HANCOCK, J. M.

1977 The Historic Develoment of Concepts of Biostratigraphic Correlation. In *Concepts and Methods of Biostratigraphy*, edited by Erle G. Kauffman and Joseph E. Hazel, pp. 3–22. Dowden, Hutchinson & Ross, Stroudsburg, Pennsylvania.

HARGRAVE, LYNDON LANE

1932 Guide to Forty Pottery Types from the Hopi Country and the San Francisco Mountains, Arizona. *Museum of Northern Arizona Bulletin* 1.

HARGRAVE, LYNDON LANE AND WATSON SMITH

1936 A Method for Determining the Texture of Pottery. *American Antiquity* 2:32–36.

HARRINGTON, MARK R.

1909a Ancient Shell Heaps near New York City. In The Indians of Greater New York and the Lower Hudson, edited by Clark Wissler. *American Museum of Natural History, Anthropological Papers* 3:167–179.

1909b The Rock-Shelters of Armonk, New York. In The Indians of Greater New York and the Lower Hudson, edited by Clark Wissler. *American Museum of Natural History, Anthropological Papers* 3:123–138.

1924a An Ancient Village Site of the Shinnecock Indians. *American Museum of Natural History, Anthropological Papers* 22(5):227–283.

1924b The Ozark Bluff-Dwellers. *American Anthropologist* 26:1–21.

HAURY, EMIL W.

1936a Some Southwestern Pottery Types, Series IV. *Medallion Papers* No. 19.

1936b The Mogollon Culture of Southwestern New Mexico. *Medallion Papers* No. 20.

1937a Pottery Types at Snaketown. In Excavations at Snaketown: I. Material Culture, by Harold S. Gladwin, Emil W. Haury, E. B. Sayles, and Nora Gladwin, pp. 169–229. *Medallion Papers* No. 25.

1937b Stratigraphy. In Excavations at Snaketown: I. Material Culture, by Harold S. Gladwin, Emil W. Haury, E. B. Sayles, and Nora Gladwin, pp. 19–35. *Medallion Papers* No. 25.

HAWKES, E. W., AND RALPH LINTON

1916 A Pre-Lenape Site in New Jersey. *University of Pennsylvania Museum, Anthropological Publications* 6(3):47–77.

1917 A Pre-Lenape Culture in New Jersey. *American Anthropologist* 19:487–494.

HAWLEY, FLORENCE M.

1934 The Significance of the Dated Prehistory of Chetro Ketl. *University of New Mexico Bulletin, Monograph Series* 1(1).

1936 Field Manual of Prehistoric Southwestern Pottery Types. *University of New Mexico Bulletin* 291.

1937 Reversed Stratigraphy. *American Antiquity* 2:297–299.

HEIZER, ROBERT F. (editor)

1949 *A Manual of Archaeological Field Methods*. National Press, Palo Alto, California.

1950 *A Manual of Archaeological Field Methods*, revised edition. National Press, Palo Alto, California.

HEWETT, EDGAR L.

1916 Latest Work of the School of American Archaeology at Quirigua. In *Holmes Anniversary Volume: Anthropological Essays*, pp. 157–162. Washington, D.C.

HEYE, GEORGE C.

1916 Certain Mounds in Haywood County, North Carolina. In *Holmes Anniversary Volume: Anthropological Essays*, pp. 180–186. Washington, D.C.

HILL, JAMES N.
  1966   A Prehistoric Community in Eastern Arizona. *Southwestern Journal of Anthro-
            pology* 22:9–30.
HOFFMEISTER, DONALD F.
  1964   Mammals and Life Zones: Time for Re-Evaluation. *Plateau* 37:46–55.
HOLMES, WILLIAM H.
  1886a   Pottery of the Ancient Pueblos. *Bureau of Ethnology, Annual Report* 4:257–360.
  1886b   Ancient Pottery of the Mississippi Valley. *Bureau of Ethnology, Annual Report*
            4:361–436.
  1886c   Origin and Development of Form and Ornamentation in Ceramic Art. *Bureau
            of Ethnology, Annual Report* 4:437–465.
  1888   A Study of the Textile Art in Its Relation to the Development of Form and
            Ornament. *Bureau of Ethnology, Annual Report* 6:189–252.
  1892   Modern Quarry Refuse and the Paleolithic Theory. *Science* 20:295–297.
  1897   Stone Implements of the Potomac–Chesapeake Tidewater Province. *Bureau of
            American Ethnology, Annual Report* 15:13–152.
  1903   Aboriginal Pottery of the Eastern United States. *Bureau of American Ethnology,
            Annual Report* 20:1–201.
  1914   Areas of American Culture Characterization Tentatively Outlined as an Aid in
            the Study of Antiquities. *American Anthropologist* 16:413–446.
  1919   Handbook of Aboriginal American Antiquities: Introductory, The Lithic Indus-
            tries. *Bureau of American Ethnology, Bulletin* 60.
HUGHES, RICHARD E.
  1992   California Archaeology and Linguistic Prehistory. *Journal of Anthropological Re-
            search* 48:317–338.
HULL, DAVID L.
  1965   The Effect of Essentialism on Taxonomy: 2000 Years of Stasis. *British Journal
            for the Philosophy of Science* 15:314–316; 16:1–18.
  1970   Contemporary Systematic Philosophies. *Annual Review of Ecology and Systemat-
            ics* 1:19–54.
  1988   *Science as a Process.* University of Chicago Press, Chicago.
JEFFERSON, THOMAS
  1801   *Notes on the State of Virginia.* Furman and Loudan, New York.
JENNINGS, JESSE D.
  1947   Review of "Hiwassee Island" by Thomas M. N. Lewis and Madeline Kneberg.
            American Antiquity 12:191–193.
  1985   River Basin Surveys: Origins, Operations, and Results, 1945–1969. *American
            Antiquity* 50:281–296.
  1989   *Prehistory of North America,* 3rd ed. Mayfield, Mountain View, California.
JENNINGS, JESSE D., AND CHARLES H. FAIRBANKS
  1939   Type Descriptions of Pottery. *Southeastern Archaeological Conference Newsletter*
            1(2).
JOCHELSON, WALDEMAR
  1925   Archaeological Investigations in the Aleutian Islands. *Carnegie Institution of
            Washington, Publication* 367. Washington, D.C.
JOHNSON, FREDERICK
  1951   (assembler) Radiocarbon Dating. *Society for American Archaeology, Memoirs*
            No. 8.

1961   A Quarter Century of Growth in American Archaeology. *American Antiquity* 27:1–6.

1967   Radiocarbon Dating and Archeology in North America. *Science* 155:165–169.

JUDD, NEIL M.

1929   The Present Status of Archaeology in the United States. *American Anthropologist* 31:401–418.

1954   The Material Culture of Pueblo Bonito. *Smithsonian Miscellaneous Collections* 124.

KEHOE, ALICE B.

1990   The Monumental Midwestern Taxonomic Method. In The Woodland Tradition in the Western Great Lakes: Papers Presented to Elden Johnson, edited by Guy E. Gibbon, pp. 31–36. *University of Minnesota, Publications in Anthropology* No. 4.

KIDDER, ALFRED V.

1915   Pottery of the Pajarito Plateau and of Some Adjacent Regions in New Mexico. *American Anthropological Association, Memoir* 2:407–462.

1916   Archeological Explorations at Pecos, New Mexico. *National Academy of Sciences, Proceedings* 2:119–123.

1917a   A Design-Sequence from New Mexico. *National Academy of Sciences, Proceedings* 3:369–370.

1917b   Prehistoric Cultures of the San Juan Drainage. *Nineteenth International Congress of Americanists, Proceedings,* pp. 108–113.

1919   Review of "An Outline for a Chronology of Zuñi Ruins; Notes on Some Little Colorado Ruins; Ruins in the White Mountains, Arizona" by Leslie Spier. *American Anthropologist* 21:296–301.

1924   An Introduction to the Study of Southwestern Archaeology, with a Preliminary Account of the Excavations at Pecos. *Papers of the Southwestern Expedition, Phillips Academy,* No. 1. Yale University Press, New Haven, Connecticut.

1927   Southwestern Archaeological Conference. *Science* 66:489–491.

1931   The Pottery of Pecos, Vol. 1. *Papers of the Southwestern Expedition, Phillips Academy* No. 5. Yale University Press, New Haven, Connecticut.

1932   The Artifacts of Pecos. *Papers of the Southwestern Expedition, Phillips Academy* No. 6. Yale University Press, New Haven, Connecticut.

1936a   Discussion. In *The Pottery of Pecos* Vol. II, by Alfred Vincent Kidder and Anna O. Shepard, pp. 589–628. Yale University Press, New Haven, Connecticut.

1936b   Introduction. In *The Pottery of Pecos* Vol. II, by Alfred Vincent Kidder and Anna O. Shepard, pp. xvii–xxxi. Yale University Press, New Haven, Connecticut.

KIDDER, MADELEINE A., AND ALFRED V. KIDDER

1917   Notes on the Pottery of Pecos. *American Anthropologist* 19:325–360.

KIDDER, ALFRED V., JESSE D. JENNINGS, AND EDWIN M. SHOOK

1946   Excavations at Kaminaljuyu, Guatemala. *Carnegie Institution of Washington, Publication* 561. Washington, D.C.

KIDWELL, SUSAN M.

1986   Models for Fossil Concentration: Paleobiologic Implications. *Paleobiology* 12:6–24.

KLUCKHOHN, CLYDE

1939a   Discussion. In Preliminary Report on the 1937 Excavations, Bc 50–51, Chaco Canyon, New Mexico, edited by Clyde Kluckhohn and Paul Reiter, pp. 151–162. *University of New Mexico, Bulletin* 345.

1939b   The Place of Theory in Anthropological Studies. *Philosophy of Science* 6:328–344.

1960   The Use of Typology in Anthropological Theory. In *Selected Papers of the Fifth International Congress of Anthropological and Ethnological Sciences,* edited by Anthony F. C. Wallace, pp. 134–140. University of Pennsylvania Press, Philadelphia.

KNIFFEN, FRED B.

1938   The Indian Mounds of Iberville Parish. In Reports on the Geology of Iberville and Ascension Parishes, edited by Henry V. Howe, pp. 189–207. *Louisiana Geological Survey, Geological Bulletin* No. 13.

KRIEGER, ALEX D.

1944   The Typological Concept. *American Antiquity* 9:271–288.

1960   Archeological Typology in Theory and Practice. In *Selected Papers of the Fifth International Congress of Anthropology and Ethnological Sciences,* edited by A. F. C. Wallace, pp. 141–151. University of Pennsylvania Press, Philadelphia.

1964   New World Lithic Typology Project: Part II. *American Antiquity* 29:489–493.

KROEBER, ALFRED L.

1909   The Archaeology of California. In *Putnam Anniversary Volume,* edited by Franz Boas, pp. 1–42. Stechert, New York.

1916a   Zuñi Culture Sequences. *National Academy of Sciences, Proceedings* 2:42–45.

1916b   Zuñi Potsherds. *American Museum of Natural History, Anthropological Papers* 18(1):1–37.

1919   On the Principle of Order in Civilization as Exemplified by Changes of Fashion. *American Anthropologist* 21:235–263.

1923a   *Anthropology.* Harcourt, Brace and Company, New York.

1923b   The History of Native Culture in California. *University of California, Publications in American Archaeology and Ethnology* 20:123–142.

1925a   Archaic Culture Horizons in the Valley of Mexico. *University of California, Publications in American Archaeology and Ethnology* 17(7):373–408.

1925b   Handbook of the Indians of California. *Bureau of American Ethnology, Bulletin* 78.

1925c   The Uhle Pottery Collections from Moche. *University of California, Publications in American Archaeology and Ethnology* 21(5):191–234.

1931a   Historical Reconstruction of Culture Growths and Organic Evolution. *American Anthropologist* 33:149–156.

1931b   The Culture-Area and Age–Area Concepts of Clark Wissler. In *Methods in Social Science,* edited by Stuart A. Rice, pp. 248–265. University of Chicago Press, Chicago.

1935   History and Science in Anthropology. *American Anthropologist* 37:539–569.

1936   Prospects in California Prehistory. *American Antiquity* 2:108–116.

1939   Cultural and Natural Areas of Native North America. *University of California, Publications in American Archaeology and Ethnology* 38:1–242.

1940   Statistical Classification. *American Antiquity* 6:29–44.

1942   Tapajó Pottery. *American Antiquity* 7:403–405.

1943   Structure, Function and Pattern in Biology and Anthropology. *Scientific Monthly* 56:105-113.

1944   Peruvian Archaeology in 1942. *Viking Fund Publications in Anthropology* No. 4.

1946   History and Evolution. *Southwestern Journal of Anthropology* 2:1–15.

KROEBER, ALFRED L., AND WILLIAM DUNCAN STRONG
1924a   The Uhle Pottery Collections from Chincha. *University of California, Publications in American Archaeology and Ethnology* 21(1):1–54.
1924b   The Uhle Pottery Collections from Ica. *University of California, Publications in American Archaeology and Ethnology* 21(3):95–133.
LATHRAP, DONALD W. (editor)
1956   An Archaeological Classification of Culture Contact Situations. In Seminars in Archaeology:1955. *Society for American Archaeology, Memoirs* No. 11:1–30.
LEHMANN-HARTLEBEN, KARL
1943   Thomas Jefferson, Archaeologist. *American Journal of Archaeology* 47:161–163.
LEHMER, DONALD J.
1952   The Fort Pierre Branch, Central South Dakota. *American Antiquity* 17:329–336.
LEHMER, DONALD J., AND WARREN W. CALDWELL
1966   Horizon and Tradition in the Northern Plains. *American Antiquity* 31:511–516.
LEONARD, ROBERT D., AND GEORGE T. JONES
1987   Elements of an Inclusive Evolutionary Model for Archaeology. *Journal of Anthropological Archaeology* 6:199–219.
LEWIS, THOMAS M. N., AND MADELINE KNEBERG
1946   *Hiwasee Island: An Archaeological Account of Four Tennessee Indian Peoples.* University of Tennessee Press, Knoxville.
LEWONTIN, RICHARD C.
1974   *The Genetic Basis of Evolutionary Change.* Columbia University Press, New York.
LINTON, RALPH
1944   North American Cooking Pots. *American Antiquity* 9:369–380.
LIPO, CARL, TIM HUNT, MARK MADSEN, AND ROBERT C. DUNNELL
1995   Population Structure, Cultural Transmission, and Frequency Seriation. Unpublished manuscript.
LONGACRE, WILLIAM A.
1964   Archaeology as Anthropology: A Case Study. *Science* 144:1454–1455.
1966   Changing Patterns of Social Integration: A Prehistoric Example from the American Southwest. *American Anthropologist* 68:94–102.
LONGWELL, CHESTER R., RICHARD FOSTER FLINT, AND JOHN E. SANDERS
1969   *Physical Geology.* Wiley, New York.
LOOMIS, FREDERIC B., AND D. B. YOUNG
1912   On the Shell Heaps of Maine. *American Journal of Science* 34:17–42.
LOUD, LLEWELLYN L., AND MARK R. HARRINGTON
1929   Lovelock Cave. *University of California, Publications in American Archaeology and Ethnology* 25:1–183.
LYMAN, R. LEE
1994   *Vertebrate Taphonomy.* Cambridge University Press, Cambridge.
LYMAN, R. LEE, MICHAEL J. O'BRIEN, AND ROBERT C. DUNNELL (editors)
1997   *Americanist Culture History: Fundamentals of Time, Space, and Form.* Plenum Press, New York.
LYON, EDWIN A.
1996   *A New Deal for Southeastern Archaeology.* University of Alabama Press, Tuscaloosa.
MACWHITE, EOIN
1956   On the Interpretation of Archaeological Evidence in Historical and Sociological Terms. *American Anthropologist* 58:3–25.

MALLORY, V. STANDISH
1970   Biostratigraphy—A Major Basis for Paleontologic Correlation. In *Proceedings of the North American Paleontological Convention,* edited by Ellis L. Yochelson, pp. 553–566. Allen Press, Lawrence, Kansas.

MARCH, BENJAMIN
1934   Standards of Pottery Description. *Occasional Contributions from the Museum of Anthropology of the University of Michigan* No. 3. Ann Arbor.

MARLOWE, GREG
1980   W. F. Libby and the Archaeologists, 1946–1948. *Radiocarbon* 22:1005–1014.

MARQUARDT, WILLIAM H.
1978   Advances in Archaeological Seriation. In *Advances in Archaeological Method and Theory* Vol. 1, edited by Michael B. Schiffer, pp. 257–314. Academic Press, New York.

MARTIN, PAUL S.
1936   Lowry Ruin in Southwestern Colorado. *Fieldiana: Anthropology* 23(1):1–216.
1938   Archaeological Work in the Ackmen-Lowry Area, Southwestern Colorado, 1937. *Fieldiana: Anthropology* 23(2):217–304.
1939   Modified Basket Maker Sites, Ackmen-Lowry Area, Southwestern Colorado, 1938. *Fieldiana: Anthropology* 23(3):305–499.
1940   The SU Site, Excavations at a Mogollon Village, Western New Mexico, 1939. *Fieldiana: Anthropology* 32(1):1–97.
1971   The Revolution in Archaeology. *American Antiquity* 36:1–8.

MARTIN, PAUL S., GEORGE I. QUIMBY, AND DONALD COLLIER
1947   *Indians before Columbus.* University of Chicago Press, Chicago.

MARTIN, PAUL S., AND JOHN B. RINALDO
1950a   Sites of the Reserve Phase, Pine Lawn Valley, Western New Mexico. *Fieldiana: Anthropology* 38(3):397–577.
1950b   Turkey Foot Ridge Site: A Mogollon Village, Pine Lawn Valley, Western New Mexico. *Fieldiana: Anthropology* 38(2):233–396.
1951   The Southwestern Co-Tradition. *Southwestern Journal of Anthropology* 7:215–229.

MARTIN, PAUL S., JOHN B. RINALDO, AND ERNST ANTEVS
1949   Cochise and Mogollon Sites, Pine Lawn Valley, Western New Mexico. *Fieldiana: Anthropology* 38(1):1–232.

MARTIN, PAUL S., JOHN B. RINALDO, ELAINE BLUHM, HUGH C. CUTLER, AND ROGER GRANGE, JR.
1952   Mogollon Cultural Continuity and Change: The Stratigraphic Analysis of Tularosa and Cordova Caves. *Fieldiana: Anthropology* 40:1–528.

MASON, J. ALDEN
1943   Franz Boas as an Archeologist. In Franz Boas: 1858–1942, pp. 58–66. *American Anthropological Association, Memoirs* 61.

MASON, OTIS T.
1896   Influence of Environment upon Human Industries or Arts. *Smithsonian Institution, Annual Report* (1894), pp. 639–665.
1905   Environment. In *Handbook of American Indians,* edited by Frederick W. Hodge, pp. 427–430. *Bureau of American Ethnology, Bulletin* 30.

MASON, RONALD J.
1970   Hopewell, Middle Woodland, and the Laurel Culture: A Problem in Archeological Classification. *American Anthropologist* 72:802–815.

MAYR, ERNST
1959   Darwin and the Evolutionary Theory in Biology. In *Evolution and Anthropology: A Centennial Appraisal,* edited by Betty J. Meggers, pp. 1–10. Anthropological Society of Washington, Washington, D.C.
1969   *Principles of Systematic Zoology.* McGraw-Hill, New York.
1972   The Nature of the Darwinian Revolution. *Science* 176:981–989.
1981   Biological Classification: Toward a Synthesis of Opposing Methodologies. *Science* 214:510–516.
1982   *The Growth of Biological Thought: Diversity, Evolution, and Inheritance.* Harvard University Press, Cambridge, Massachusetts.
1987   The Ontological Status of Species: Scientific Progress and Philosophical Terminology. *Biology and Philosophy* 2:145–166.
1988   *Toward a New Philosophy of Biology: Observations of an Evolutionist.* Harvard University Press, Cambridge, Massachusetts.
1995   Systems of Ordering Data. *Biology and Philosophy* 10:419–434.
1996   What is a Species, and What is Not? *Philosophy of Science* 63:262–277.
MCGREGOR, JOHN C.
1941   *Southwestern Archaeology.* Wiley, New York.
MCKERN, WILLIAM C.
1934   *Certain Culture Classification Problems in Middle Western Archaeology.* National Research Council, Committee on State Archaeological Surveys. Washington, D.C.
1937   Certain Culture Classification Problems in Middle Western Archaeology. In The Indianapolis Archaeological Conference, pp. 70–82. *National Research Council, Committee on State Archaeological Surveys, Circular* No. 17.
1938   Review of "Rediscovering Illinois" by Fay-Cooper Cole and Thorne Deuel. *American Antiquity* 3:368–374.
1939   The Midwestern Taxonomic Method as an Aid to Archaeological Culture Study. *American Antiquity* 4:301–313.
1940   Application of the Midwestern Taxonomic Method. *Bulletin of the Archaeological Society of Delaware* 3:18–21.
1942   Taxonomy and the Direct Historical Approach. *American Antiquity* 8:170–172.
1943   Regarding Midwestern Archaeological Taxonomy. *American Anthropologist* 45:313–315.
1944   An Inaccurate Description of Midwestern Taxonomy. *American Antiquity* 9:445–556.
1946   A Cultural Perspective of Northeastern Area Archaeology. In Man in Northeastern North America, edited by Frederick Johnson, pp. 33–36. *Papers of the Robert S. Peabody Foundation for Archaeology* 3. Phillips Academy, Andover.
1956   On Willey and Phillips' "Method and Theory in American Archaeology." *American Anthropologist* 58:360–361.
MEGGERS, BETTY J.
1955   The Coming of Age of American Archaeology. In *New Interpretations of Aboriginal American Culture History,* edited by Betty J. Meggers and Clifford Evans, pp. 116–129. Anthropological Society of Washington, Washington, D.C.
1956   (editor) Functional and Evolutionary Implications of Community Patterning. In Seminars in Archaeology: 1955. *Society for American Archaeology, Memoirs* No. 11:129–157.

1959   (editor) *Evolution and Anthropology: A Centennial Appraisal.* Anthropological
           Society of Washington, Washington, D.C.

MEIGHAN, CLEMENT W.

1966   *Archaeology: An Introduction.* Chandler, San Francisco.

MELTZER, DAVID J.

1979   Paradigms and the Nature of Change in American Archaeology. *American
           Antiquity* 44:644–657.

1983   The Antiquity of Man and the Development of American Archaeology. In
           Advances in Archaeological Method and Theory Vol. 6, edited by Michael B.
           Schiffer, pp. 1–51. Academic Press, New York.

1985   North American Archaeology and Archaeologists, 1879-1934. *American Antiquity*
           50:249–260.

1991   On "Paradigms" and "Paradigm Bias" in Controversies over Human Antiquity
           in America. In *The First Americans: Search and Research,* edited by Tom D.
           Dillehay and David J. Meltzer, pp. 13–49. CRC Press, Boca Raton, Florida.

MELTZER, DAVID J., AND ROBERT C. DUNNELL

1992   Introduction. In *The Archaeology of William Henry Holmes,* edited by David J.
           Meltzer and Robert C. Dunnell, pp. vi–l. Smithsonian Institution Press, Wash-
           ington, D.C.

MERRIAM, C. HART

1892   The Geographic Distribution of Life in North America, with Special Reference
           to the Mammalia. *Biological Society of Washington, Proceedings* 7:1–64.

1898   Life Zones and Crop Zones of the United States. *U.S. Department of Agriculture,
           Division of the Biological Survey, Bulletin* 10.

1927   William Healey Dall. *Science* 65:345–347.

MILLS, WILLIAM C.

1916   Exploration of the Tremper Mound in Scioto County, Ohio. In *Holmes Anni-
           versary Volume: Anthropological Essays,* pp. 334–358. Washington, D.C.

MITCHEM, JEFFREY M.

1990   The Contribution of Nels C. Nelson to Florida Archaeology. *The Florida
           Anthropologist* 43:156–163.

MORGAN, LEWIS HENRY

1877   *Ancient Society.* Holt, New York.

MORRIS, EARL H.

1917   The Place of Coiled Ware in Southwestern Pottery. *American Anthropologist*
           19:24–29.

MURDOCK, GEORGE P.

1948   Clark Wissler, 1870–1947. *American Anthropologist* 50:292–304.

1956   How Culture Changes. In *Man, Culture, and Society,* edited by Harry L. Shapiro,
           pp. 247–260. Oxford University Press, New York.

NEFF, HECTOR

1992   Ceramics and Evolution. In *Archaeological Method and Theory* Vol. 4, edited by
           Michael B. Schiffer, pp. 141–193. University of Arizona Press, Tucson.

1993   Theory, Sampling, and Analytical Techniques in the Archaeological Study of
           Prehistoric Ceramics. *American Antiquity* 58:23–44.

NEIMAN, FRASER D.

1995   Stylistic Variation in Evolutionary Perspective: Inferences from Decorative Di-
           versity and Interassemblage Distance in Illinois Woodland Ceramic Assem-
           blages. *American Antiquity* 60:7–36.

NELSON, NELS C.
  1910   The Ellis Landing Shellmound. *University of California, Publications in American Archaeology and Ethnology* 7(5):357–426.
  1913   Ruins of Prehistoric New Mexico. *American Museum Journal* 13:63–81.
  1914   Pueblo Ruins of the Galisteo Basin, New Mexico. *American Museum of Natural History, Anthropological Papers* 15(1):1–124.
  1915   Ancient Cities of New Mexico. *American Museum Journal* 15:389–394.
  1916   Chronology of the Tano Ruins, New Mexico. *American Anthropologist* 18:159–180.
  1917a   Archeology of the Tano District, New Mexico. *Nineteenth International Congress of Americanists, Proceedings,* pp. 114–118.
  1917b   Contributions to the Archaeology of Mammoth Cave and Vicinity, Kentucky. *American Museum of Natural History, Anthropological Papers* 22(1):1–74.
  1918   Chronology in Florida. *American Museum of Natural History, Anthropological Papers* 22(2):74–103.
  1919a   Human Culture. *Natural History* 19:131–140.
  1919b   The Archaeology of the Southwest: A Preliminary Report. *National Academy of Sciences, Proceedings* 5:114–120.
  1919c   The Southwest Problem. *El Palacio* 6(9):132–135.
  1920   Notes on Pueblo Bonito. *American Museum of Natural History, Anthropological Papers* 27:381–390.
  1932   The Origin and Development of Material Culture. *Sigma Xi Quarterly* 20:102–123.
  1936   The Lure of Archeology. *Scientific Monthly* 42:255–257.
  1937   Prehistoric Archeology, Past, Present and Future. *Science* 85:81–89.
  1938   Prehistoric Archaeology. In *General Anthropology,* edited by Franz Boas, pp. 146–247. Heath, Boston.
  1948   Clark Wissler, 1870–1947. *American Antiquity* 13:244–247.
NUTTALL, ZELIA
  1926   The Aztecs and Their Predecessors in the Valley of Mexico. *American Philosophical Society, Proceedings* 65:245–255.
O'BRIEN, MICHAEL J.
  1996a   (editor) *Evolutionary Archaeology: Theory and Application.* University of Utah Press, Salt Lake City.
  1996b   *Paradigms of the Past: The Story of Missouri Archaeology.* University of Missouri Press, Columbia.
  1996c   The Historical Development of an Evolutionary Archaeology. In *Darwinian Archaeologies,* edited by Herbert D. G. Maschner, pp. 17–32. Plenum Press, New York.
O'BRIEN, MICHAEL J., AND GREGORY L. FOX
  1994   Sorting Artifacts in Space and Time. In *Cat Monsters and Head Pots: The Archaeology of Missouri's Pemiscot Bayou,* by Michael J. O'Brien, pp. 25–60. University of Missouri Press, Columbia.
O'BRIEN, MICHAEL J., AND THOMAS D. HOLLAND
  1990   Variation, Selection, and the Archaeological Record. In *Archaeological Method and Theory* Vol. 2, edited by Michael B. Schiffer, pp. 31–79. University of Arizona Press, Tucson.
  1992   The Role of Adaptation in Archaeological Explanation. *American Antiquity* 57:36–59.

1995a   Behavioral Archaeology and the Extended Phenotype. In *Expanding Archaeology*, edited by James M. Skibo, William H. Walker, and Axel E. Nielsen, pp. 143–161. University of Utah Press, Salt Lake City.

1995b   The Nature and Premise of a Selection-Based Archaeology. In *Evolutionary Archaeology: Methodological Issues*, edited by Patrice A. Teltser, pp. 175–200. University of Arizona Press, Tucson.

O'BRIEN, MICHAEL J., THOMAS D. HOLLAND, ROBERT J. HOARD, AND GREGORY L. FOX

1994   Evolutionary Implications of Design and Performance Characteristics of Prehistoric Pottery. *Journal of Archaeological Method and Theory* 1:259–304.

O'CONNELL, JAMES F., AND CARI M. INOWAY

1994   Surprise Valley Projectile Points and Their Chronological Implications. *Journal of California and Great Basin Anthropology* 16:162–198.

OLSON, ALAN P.

1962   A History of the Phase Concept in the Southwest. *American Antiquity* 27:457–472.

OLSON, RONALD L.

1930   Chumash Prehistory. *University of California, Publications in American Archaeology and Ethnology* 28(1):1–21.

OSGOOD, CORNELIUS

1951   Culture: Its Empirical and Non-empirical Character. *Southwestern Journal of Anthropology* 7:202–214.

PATTERSON, THOMAS C.

1991   Who Did Archaeology in the United States before There Were Archaeologists and Why? Preprofessional Archaeologies of the Nineteenth Century. In *Processual and Postprocessual Archaeologies: Multiple Ways of Knowing the Past*, edited by Robert W. Preucel, pp. 242–250. *Southern Illinois University, Center for Archaeological Investigations, Occasional Paper* No. 10.

PEABODY, CHARLES

1904   Explorations of Mounds, Coahoma Co., Mississippi. *Peabody Museum, Papers* 3(2):23–66.

1908   The Exploration of Bushey Cavern, near Cavetown, Maryland. *Phillips Academy, Department of Archaeology, Bulletin* 4(1).

1910   The Exploration of Mounds in North Carolina. *American Anthropologist* 12:425–433.

1913   Excavation of a Prehistoric Site at Tarrin, Department of the Hautes Alpes, France. *American Anthropologist* 15:257–272.

PEABODY, CHARLES, AND WARREN K. MOOREHEAD

1904   The Exploration of Jacobs Cavern. *Phillips Academy, Department of Archaeology, Bulletin* 1.

PEARL, RICHARD M.

1966   *Geology: An Introduction to Principles of Physical and Historical Geology*, 3rd ed. Barnes and Noble, New York.

PEPPER, GEORGE H.

1916   Yacatas of the Tierra Caliente, Michoacan, Mexico. In *Holmes Anniversary Volume: Anthropological Essays*, pp. 415–420. Washington, D.C.

PETRIE, SIR WILLIAM MATTHEW FLINDERS

1899   Sequences in Prehistoric Remains. *Journal of the Royal Anthropological Institute of Great Britain and Ireland* 29:295–301.

1901   Diospolis Parva. *Egypt Exploration Fund, Memoir* No. 20.

1904   *Methods and Aims in Archaeology*. Macmillan, London.

PHILLIPS, PHILIP
  1942   Review of "An Archaeological Survey of the Pickwick Basin in the Adjacent Portions of the States of Alabama, Mississippi, and Tennessee" by William S. Webb and David L. DeJarnette. *American Antiquity* 8:197–201.
  1955   American Archaeology and General Anthropological Theory. *Southwestern Journal of Anthropology* 11:246–250.
  1958   Application of the Wheat–Gifford–Wasley Taxonomy to Eastern Ceramics. *American Antiquity* 24:117–125.
  1970   Archaeological Survey in the Lower Yazoo Basin, Mississippi, 1949-1955, Part 1. *Peabody Museum of Archaeology and Ethnology, Papers* 60. Cambridge, Massachusetts.

PHILLIPS, PHILIP, JAMES A. FORD, AND JAMES B. GRIFFIN
  1951   Archaeological Survey in the Lower Mississippi Valley, 1940-1947. *Peabody Museum of American Archaeology and Ethnology, Papers* 25. Cambridge, Massachusetts.

PHILLIPS, PHILIP, AND GORDON R. WILLEY
  1953   Method and Theory in American Archaeology: An Operational Basis for Culture-Historical Integration. *American Anthropologist* 55:615–633.

PITT-RIVERS, LT. GEN. A. LANE-FOX
  1875a   On the Principles of Classification Adopted in the Arrangement of His Anthropological Collection, Now Exhibited in the Bethnal Green Museum. *Journal of the Anthropological Institute of Great Britain and Ireland* 4:293–308.
  1875b   The Evolution of Culture. *Royal Institution of Great Britain, Proceedings* 7:496–520.

PRAETZELLIS, ADRIAN
  1993   The Limits of Arbitrary Excavation. In *Practices of Archaeological Stratigraphy*, edited by Edward C. Harris, Marley R. Brown, III, and Gregory J. Brown, pp. 68–86. Academic Press, London.

QUIMBY, GEORGE I.
  1954   Cultural and Natural Areas before Kroeber. *American Antiquity* 19:317–331.

RAMBO, A. TERRY, AND KATHLEEN GILLOGLY (editors)
  1991   Profiles in Cultural Evolution. *University of Michigan Museum of Anthropology, Anthropological Papers* No. 85.

RAU, CHARLES
  1876   The Archaeological Collections of the United States National Museum in Charge of the Smithsonian. *Smithsonian Contributions to Knowledge* 22(4).

REED, ERIK K.
  1940   Review of "Prehistoric Culture Units and Their Relationships in Northern Arizona" by Harold S. Colton. *American Antiquity* 6:189–192.

REITER, PAUL
  1938a   Review of "Handbook of Northern Arizona Pottery Wares" by Harold Sellers Colton and Lyndon Lane Hargrave. *American Anthropologist* 40:489–491.
  1938b   The Jemez Pueblo of Unshagi, New Mexico. *University of New Mexico Bulletin, Monograph Series* 1(5).

RINALDO, JOHN B.
  1950   An Analysis of Culture Change in the Ackmen-Lowry Area. *Fieldiana: Anthropology* 36(5):93–106.

RINDOS, DAVID
  1985   Darwinian Selection, Symbolic Variation, and the Evolution of Culture. *Current Anthropology* 26:65–88.

RITCHIE, WILLIAM A.
1937   Culture Influences from Ohio in New York Archaeology. *American Antiquity*
        2:182–194.
ROBERTS, FRANK H. H., JR.
1927   *The Ceramic Sequence in the Chaco Canyon, New Mexico, and Its Relation to
        the Cultures of the San Juan Basin.* Unpublished Ph.D. dissertation, Harvard Uni-
        versity, Cambridge.
1929   Shabik'eshchee Village, a Late Basketmaker Site in the Chaco Canyon, New
        Mexico. *Bureau of American Ethnology, Bulletin* 92.
1931   The Ruins of Kiatuthlanna, Eastern Arizona. *Bureau of American Ethnology,
        Bulletin* 100.
1935   A Survey of Southwestern Archaeology. *American Anthropologist* 37:1–35.
ROBINSON, W. S.
1951   A Method for Chronologically Ordering Archaeological Deposits. *American
        Antiquity* 16:293–301.
ROUSE, IRVING B.
1939   Prehistory in Haiti: A Study in Method. *Yale University Publications in Anthro-
        pology* No. 21.
1941   Culture of the Ft. Liberté Region, Haiti. *Yale University Publications in Anthro-
        pology* No. 24.
1944   On the Typological Method. *American Antiquity* 10:202–204.
1952   Porto Rican Prehistory: Introduction; Excavations in the West and North. In
        Scientific Survey of Porto Rico and the Virgin Islands, pp. 305–460. *Transactions
        of the New York Academy of Sciences* 18(3).
1953   The Strategy of Culture History. In *Anthropology Today,* edited by Alfred L.
        Kroeber, pp. 57–76. University of Chicago Press, Chicago.
1954   On the Use of the Concept of Area Co-tradition. *American Antiquity* 19:221–225.
1955   On the Correlation of Phases of Culture. *American Anthropologist* 57:713–722.
1960   The Classification of Artifacts in Archaeology. *American Antiquity* 25:313–323.
1965a   Caribbean Ceramics: A Study in Method and in Theory. In Ceramics and Man,
        edited by Frederick R. Matson, pp. 88–103. *Viking Fund Publications in Anthro-
        pology* No. 41.
1965b   The Place of 'Peoples' in Prehistoric Research. *Journal of the Royal Anthropo-
        logical Institute of Great Britain and Ireland* 95:1–15.
1967   Seriation in Archaeology. In *American Historical Anthropology: Essays in Honor
        of Leslie Spier,* edited by Carroll L. Riley and Walter W. Taylor, pp. 153–195.
        Southern Illinois University Press, Carbondale.
1972   *Introduction to Prehistory: A Systematic Approach.* McGraw-Hill, New York.
ROWE, JOHN HOWLAND
1954   Max Uhle, 1856–1944: A Memoir of the Father of Peruvian Archaeology. *Uni-
        versity of California, Publications in American Archaeology and Ethnology* 46(1):1–
        134.
1961   Stratigraphy and Seriation. *American Antiquity* 26:324–330.
1962a   Alfred Louis Kroeber. *American Antiquity* 27:395–415.
1962b   Stages and Periods in Archaeological Interpretations. *Southwestern Journal of
        Anthropology* 18:40–54.
1962c   Worsaae's Law and the Use of Grave Lots for Archaeological Dating. *American
        Antiquity* 28:129–137.
1975   Review of "A History of American Archaeology" by Gordon R. Willey and
        Jeremy A. Sabloff. *Antiquity* 49:156–158.

RUDWICK, MARTIN
1996   Cuvier and Brongniart, William Smith, and the Reconstruction of Geohistory. *Earth Sciences History* 15:25–36.

SABLOFF, JEREMY A., AND ROBERT E. SMITH
1969   The Importance of Both Analytic and Taxonomic Classification in the Type–Variety System. *American Antiquity* 34:278–285.

SABLOFF, JEREMY A., AND GORDON R. WILLEY
1967   The Collapse of Maya Civilization in the Southern Lowlands: A Consideration of History and Process. *Southwestern Journal of Anthropology* 23:311–336.

SAPIR, EDWARD
1916   Time Perspective in Aboriginal American Culture, A Study in Method. *Canada Department of Mines, Geological Survey, Memoir* 90.

SAYLES, E. B.
1937   Stone: Implements and Bowls. In Excavations at Snaketown: I. Material Culture, by Harold S. Gladwin, Emil W. Haury, E. B. Sayles, and Nora Gladwin, pp. 101–120. *Medallion Papers* No. 25.

SCHENCK, WILLIAM E.
1926   The Emeryville Shellmound: Final Report. *University of California, Publications in American Archaeology and Ethnology* 23(3):147–282.

SCHIFFER, MICHAEL B.
1972   Archaeological Context and Systemic Context. *American Antiquity* 37:156–165.
1987   *Formation Processes of the Archaeological Record.* University of New Mexico Press, Albuquerque.

SCHMIDT, ERICH F.
1927   A Stratigraphic Study in the Gila-Salt Region. *National Academy of Sciences, Proceedings* 13(5):291–298.
1928   Time-Relations of Prehistoric Pottery Types in Southern Arizona. *American Museum of Natural History, Anthropological Papers* 30(5):247–302.

SCHRABISCH, MAX
1909   Indian Rock-Shelters in Northern New Jersey and Southern New York. In The Indians of Greater New York and the Lower Hudson, edited by Clark Wissler, pp. 139–165. *American Museum of Natural History, Anthropological Papers* Vol. 3.

SEARS, WILLIAM H.
1961   The Study of Social and Religious Systems in North American Archaeology. *Current Anthropology* 2:223–246.

SERVICE, ELMAN R.
1964   Archaeological Theory and Ethnological Fact. In *Process and Pattern in Culture: Essays in Honor of Julian H. Steward,* edited by Robert A. Manners, pp. 364–375. Aldine, Chicago.

SETZLER, FRANK M.
1933a   Hopewell Type Pottery from Louisiana. *Washington Academy of Sciences, Journal* 23:149–153.
1933b   Pottery of the Hopewell Type from Louisiana. *United States National Museum, Proceedings* 82(22):1–21.
1934   A Phase of Hopewell Mound Builders in Louisiana. *Explorations and Field-work of the Smithsonian Institution in 1933,* pp. 38–40.

SHARER, ROBERT J., AND WENDY ASHMORE
1993   *Archaeology: Discovering Our Past,* 2nd ed. Mayfield, Mountain View, California.

SIMPSON, GEORGE GAYLORD
1943   Criteria for Genera, Species, and Subspecies in Zoology and Paleozoology. *Annals of the New York Academy of Sciences* 44:145–178.
1961   *Principles of Animal Taxonomy*. Columbia University Press, New York.
1975   Recent Advances in Methods of Phylogenetic Inference. In *Phylogeny of Primates: A Multidisciplinary Approach*, edited by W. Patrick Luckett and Frederick S. Szalay, pp. 3–19. Plenum Press, New York.
SKINNER, ALANSON
1917   Chronological Relations of Coastal Algonquian Culture. *Nineteenth International Congress of Americanists, Proceedings*, pp. 52–58.
SMITH, ANDREW B.
1994   *Systematics and the Fossil Record: Decomenting Evolutionary Patterns*. Blackwell, London.
SMITH, ROBERT E., GORDON R. WILLEY, AND JAMES C. GIFFORD
1960   The Type–Variety Concept as a Basis for the Analysis of Maya Pottery. *American Antiquity* 25:330–340.
SOBER, ELLIOTT
1980   Evolution, Population Thinking, and Essentialism. *Philosophy of Science* 47:350–383.
1988   *Reconstructing the Past: Parsimony, Evolution, and Inference*. MIT Press, Cambridge, Massachusetts.
SOKAL, R. R., AND P. H. A. SNEATH
1963   *Principles of Numerical Taxonomy*. Freeman, San Francisco.
SPAULDING, ALBERT C.
1948a   Committee on Nomenclature. *Plains Archaeological Conference Newsletter* 1(3): 37–41.
1948b   Committee on Nomenclature: Pottery (continued). *Plains Archaeological Conference Newsletter* 1(4):73–78.
1949   Cultural and Chronological Classification in the Plains Area. *Plains Archaeological Conference Newsletter* 2(2):3–5.
1951   Recent Advances in Surveying Techniques and Their Application to Archaeology. In Essays on Archaeological Methods, edited by James B. Griffin, pp. 2–16. *University of Michigan Museum of Anthropology, Anthropological Papers* No. 8.
1953a   Review of "Measurements of Some Prehistoric Design Developments in the Southeastern States" by J. A. Ford. *American Anthropologist* 55:588–591.
1953b   Statistical Techniques for the Discovery of Artifact Types. *American Antiquity* 18:305–313.
1954a   Reply (to Ford). *American Anthropologist* 56:112–114.
1954b   Reply to Ford. *American Antiquity* 19:391–393.
1955   Prehistoric Cultural Development in the Eastern United States. In *New Interpretations of Aboriginal American Culture History*, edited by Betty J. Meggers and Clifford Evans, pp. 12–27. Anthropological Society of Washington, Washington, D.C.
1957   Review of "Method and Theory in American Archeology: An Operational Basis for Cultural-Historical Integration" by Philip Phillips and Gordon R. Willey, and "Method and Theory in American Archeology II: Historical-Developmental Interpretation" by Gordon R. Willey and Philip Phillips. *American Antiquity* 23:85–87.

1960a   Statistical Description and Comparison of Artifact Assemblages. In The Application of Quantitative Methods in Archaeology, edited by Robert F. Heizer and Sherburne F. Cook, pp. 60–83. *Viking Fund Publications in Anthropology* No. 28.

1960b   The Dimensions of Archaeology. In *Essays in the Science of Culture in Honor of Leslie A. White,* edited by Gertrude E. Dole and Robert L. Carneiro, pp. 437–456. Crowell, New York.

1978   Artifact Classes, Association and Seriation. In *Archaeological Essays in Honor of Irving B. Rouse,* edited by Robert C. Dunnell and Edwin S. Hall, Jr., pp. 27–40. Mouton, The Hague.

1982   Structure in Archaeological Data: Nominal Variables. In *Essays on Archaeological Typology,* edited by Robert Whallon and James A. Brown, pp. 1–20. Center for American Archeology Press, Evanston, Illinois.

1985   Fifty Years of Theory. *American Antiquity* 50:301–308.

SPIER, LESLIE

1915   Review of "On the Shell Heaps of Maine" by Frederic B. Loomis and D. B. Young. *American Anthropologist* 17:346–347.

1916   New Data on the Trenton Argillite Culture. *American Anthropologist* 18:181–189.

1917a   An Outline for a Chronology of Zuñi Ruins. *American Museum of Natural History, Anthropological Papers* 18(3):207–331.

1917b   Zuñi Chronology. *National Academy of Sciences, Proceedings* 3:280–283.

1918a   Notes on Some Little Colorado Ruins. *American Museum of Natural History, Anthropological Papers* 18(4):333–362.

1918b   The Trenton Argillite Culture. *American Museum of Natural History, Anthropological Papers* 22(4):167–226.

1919   Ruins in the White Mountains, Arizona. *American Museum of Natural History, Anthropological Papers* 18(5):363–388.

1931   N. C. Nelson's Stratigraphic Technique in the Reconstruction of Prehistoric Sequences in Southwestern America. In *Methods in Social Science,* edited by Stuart A. Rice, pp. 275–283. University of Chicago Press, Chicago.

SPINDEN, HERBERT J.

1915   Notes on the Archeology of Salvador. *American Anthropologist* 17:446–487.

1928   Ancient Civilizations of Mexico and Central Mexico. *American Museum of Natural History, Handbook Series* No. 3.

SPINDLER, LOUISE S., AND GEORGE D. SPINDLER

1959   Culture Change. In *Biennial Review of Anthropology 1959,* edited by Bernard J. Siegel, pp. 37–66. Stanford University Press, Stanford.

SQUIER, EPHRAIM G., AND EDWIN H. DAVIS

1848   Ancient Monuments of the Mississippi Valley. *Smithsonian Contributions to Knowledge* 1.

STANISLAWSKI, MICHAEL B.

1973   Review of "Archaeology as Anthropology: A Case Study" by William A. Longacre. *American Antiquity* 38:117–122.

STEIN, JULIE K.

1990   Archaeological Stratigraphy. In *Archaeological Geology of North America,* edited by N. P. Lasca and J. Donahue, pp. 513–523. *Geological Society of America, Centennial Special Volume* 4.

STEPHENSON, ROBERT L.

1954   Taxonomy and Chronology in the Central Plains—Middle Missouri River Area. *Plains Anthropologist* 1:15–21.

1967   Frank H. H. Roberts, Jr., 1897–1966. *American Antiquity* 32:84–94.

STERNS, FRED H.

1915   A Stratification of Cultures in Nebraska. *American Anthropologist* 17:121–127.

STEVENS, S. S.

1946   On the Theory of Scales of Measurement. *Science* 103:677–680.

STEWARD, JULIAN H.

1929   Diffusion and Independent Invention: A Critique of Logic. *American Anthropologist* 31:491–495.

1941   Review of "Prehistoric Culture Units and Their Relationships in Northern Arizona" by Harold S. Colton. *American Antiquity* 6:366–367.

1942   The Direct Historical Approach to Archaeology. *American Antiquity* 7:337–343.

1944   Re: Archaeological Tools and Jobs. *American Antiquity* 10:99–100.

1948   A Functional-Developmental Classification of American High Cultures. In A Reappraisal of Peruvian Archaeology, assembled by Wendell C. Bennett, pp. 103–104. *Society for American Archaeology, Memoirs* No. 4.

1954   Types of Types. *American Anthropologist* 56:54–57.

1955   *Theory of Culture Change.* University of Illinois Press, Urbana.

STEWARD, JULIAN H., AND FRANK M. SETZLER

1938   Function and Configuration in Archaeology. *American Antiquity* 4:4–10.

STIEBING, WILLIAM H., JR.

1993   *Uncovering the Past: A History of Archaeology.* Prometheus Books, Buffalo, New York.

STIRLING, MATTHEW W.

1932   The Pre-Historic Southern Indians. In *Conference on Southern Pre-History,* pp. 20–31. National Research Council, Washington, D.C.

STRONG, WILLIAM D.

1925   The Uhle Pottery Collections from Ancon. *University of California, Publications in American Archaeology and Ethnology* 21(4):135–190.

1935   An Introduction to Nebraska Archaeology. *Smithsonian Miscellaneous Collections* 93(10).

1936   Anthropological Theory and Archaeological Fact. In *Essays in Anthropology Presented to A. L. Kroeber,* edited by Robert H. Lowie, pp. 359–368. University of California Press, Berkeley.

1940   From History to Prehistory in the Northern Great Plains. In Essays in Historical Anthropology of North America, pp. 353–394. *Smithsonian Miscellaneous Collections* 100.

1952   The Value of Archeology in the Training of Professional Anthropologists. *American Anthropologist* 54:318–321.

SWANSON, EARL H., JR.

1959   Theory and Method in American Archaeology. *Southwestern Journal of Anthropology* 15:120–124.

TAX, SOL (editor)

1960   *Evolution After Darwin: The University of Chicago Centennial,* 3 vols. University of Chicago Press, Chicago.

TAYLOR, R. E.

1985   The Beginnings of Radiocarbon Dating in *American Antiquity:* A Historical Perspective. *American Antiquity* 50:309–325.

1987   *Radiocarbon Dating: An Archaeological Perspective.* Academic Press, Orlando.

TAYLOR, WALTER W.

1948   A Study of Archeology. *American Anthropological Association, Memoir* 69.

1954   Southwestern Archaeology, Its History and Theory. *American Anthropologist* 56:561–575.

1969   Archeological Research: Review of "New Perspectives in Archaeology," edited by Sally R. Binford and Lewis R. Binford. *Science* 165:382–384.

1972   Old Wine and New Skins: A Contemporary Parable. In *Contemporary Archaeology,* edited by Mark P. Leone, pp. 28–33. Southern Illinois University Press, Carbondale.

TELTSER, PATRICE A.

1995   Culture History, Evolutionary Theory, and Frequency Seriation. In *Evolutionary Archaeology: Methodological Issues,* edited by Patrice A. Teltser, pp. 51–68. University of Arizona Press, Tucson.

THOMAS, CYRUS

1894   Report of the Mound Explorations of the Bureau of Ethnology. *Bureau of Ethnology, Annual Report* 12:3–742.

THOMAS, DAVID HURST

1978   Arrowheads and Atlatl Darts: How the Stones Got the Shaft. *American Antiquity* 43:461–472.

1981   How to Classify the Projectile Points from Monitor Valley, Nevada. *Journal of California and Great Basin Anthropology* 3:7–43.

1986   Points on Points: A Reply to Flenniken and Raymond. *American Antiquity* 51: 619–627.

1989   *Archaeology,* 2nd ed. Holt, Rinehart and Winston, Fort Worth, Texas.

THOMPSON, RAYMOND H.

1956a   (editor) An Archaeological Approach to the Study of Cultural Stability. In Seminars in Archaeology:1955. *Society for American Archaeology, Memoirs* No. 11:31–57.

1956b   The Subjective Element in Archaeological Inference. *Southwestern Journal of Anthropology* 12:327–332.

1958a   (editor) Migrations in New World Culture History. *University of Arizona, Social Science Bulletin* 27.

1958b   Modern Yucatecan Maya Pottery Making. *Society for American Archaeology, Memoirs* No. 15.

1972   Interpretive Trends and Linear Models in American Archaeology. In *Contemporary Archaeology,* edited by Mark P. Leone, pp. 34–38. Southern Illinois University Press, Carbondale.

TOZZER, ALFRED M.

1937   Mexico, Central and South America [review of George C. Vaillant 1930, 1931, 1935a, 1935b and Suzannah B. Vaillant and George C. Vaillant 1934]. *American Anthropologist* 39:338–340.

TRIGGER, BRUCE G.

1968   *Beyond History: The Methods of Prehistory.* Holt, Rinehart and Winston, New York.

1989   *A History of Archaeological Thought.* Cambridge University Press, Cambridge.

TYLOR, EDWARD B.

1871   *Primitive Culture.* Murray, London.

TSCHAUNER, HARTMUT

1994   Archaeological Systematics and Cultural Evolution: Retrieving the Honour of Culture History. *Man* 29:77–93.

UHLE, (FRIEDRICH) MAX

1903   *Pachacamac.* University of Pennsylvania Press, Philadelphia.

1907   The Emeryville Shellmound. *University of California, Publications in American Archaeology and Ethnology* 7:1–107.

VAILLANT, GEORGE C.
1930   Excavations at Zacatenco. *American Museum of Natural History, Anthropological Papers* 32(1):1–198.
1931   Excavations at Ticoman. *American Museum of Natural History, Anthropological Papers* 32(2):199–432.
1932   Stratigraphical Research in Central Mexico. *National Academy of Sciences, Proceedings* 18:487–490.
1935a   Early Cultures of the Valley of Mexico: Results of the Stratigraphical Project of the American Museum of Natural History in the Valley of Mexico, 1928–1933. *American Museum of Natural History, Anthropological Papers* 35(3):281–328.
1935b   Excavations at El Arbolillo. *American Museum of Natural History, Anthropological Papers* 35(2):137–279.
1936   The History of the Valley of Mexico. *Natural History* 38:324–328.
1937   History and Stratigraphy in the Valley of Mexico. *Scientific Monthly* 44:307–324.

VAILLANT, SUZANNAH, AND GEORGE C. VAILLANT
1934   Excavations at Gualupita. *American Museum of Natural History, Anthropological Papers* 35(1):1–135.

VAN RIPER, A. BOWDOIN
1993   *Men among the Mammoths: Victorian Science and the Discovery of Human Prehistory.* University of Chicago Press, Chicago.

VOLK, ERNEST
1911   The Archaeology of the Delaware Valley. *Peabody Museum of American Archaeology and Ethnology, Papers* 5. Cambridge, Massachusetts.

WALKER, S. T.
1883   The Aborigines of Florida. *Smithsonian Institution, Annual Report* (1881), pp. 677–680.

WALKER, WINSLOW M.
1932   Pre-Historic Cultures of Louisiana. In *Conference on Southern Pre-History*, pp. 42–48. National Research Council, Washington, D.C.
1936   The Troyville Mounds, Catahoula Parish, La. *Bureau of American Ethnology, Bulletin* 113.

WALLIS, WILSON D.
1925   Diffusion as a Criterion of Age. *American Anthropologist* 27:91–99.
1945   Inference of Relative Age of Culture Traits from Magnitude of Distribution. *Southwestern Journal of Anthropology* 1:142–159.

WATSON, PATTY J., STEVEN A. LEBLANC, AND CHARLES L. REDMAN
1971   *Explanation in Archeology: An Explicitly Scientific Approach.* Columbia University Press, New York.

WAUCHOPE, ROBERT
1956   Preface. In Seminars in Archaeology: 1955, edited by Richard B. Woodbury, pp. v–vii. *Society for American Archaeology, Memoirs* No. 11.
1965   Alfred Vincent Kidder, 1885–1963. *American Antiquity* 31:149–171.
1966   Archaeological Survey of Northern Georgia with a Test of Some Cultural Hypotheses. *Society for American Archaeology, Memoirs* No. 21.

WEBB, WILLIAM S., AND DAVID L. DEJARNETTE
1942   An Archaeological Survey of Pickwick Basin in the Adjacent Portions of the States of Alabama, Mississippi, and Tennessee. *Bureau of American Ethnology, Bulletin* 129.

WEDEL, WALDO R.
1938   The Direct-Historical Approach in Pawnee Archaeology. *Smithsonian Miscellaneous Collections* 97(7).
1940   Culture Sequence in the Central Great Plains. In Essays in Historical Anthropology of North America, pp. 291–352. *Smithsonian Miscellaneous Collections* 100.
WHEAT, JOE B., JAMES C. GIFFORD, AND WILLIAM W. WASLEY
1958   Ceramic Variety, Type Cluster, and Ceramic System in Southwestern Pottery Analysis. *American Antiquity* 24:34–47.
WHEELER, MORTIMER
1954   *Archaeology from the Earth*. Penguin Books, Baltimore.
WHITE, LESLIE A.
1938   Science is *Sciencing*. *Philosophy of Science* 5:369–389.
1945   History, Evolutionism, and Functionalism. *Southwestern Journal of Anthropology* 1:221–248.
1949   *The Science of Culture*. Farrar, Straus and Giroux, New York.
WHITEFORD, ANDREW H.
1947   Description for Artifact Analysis. *American Antiquity* 12:226–239.
WILKE, PHILIP J., AND J. JEFFREY FLENNIKEN
1991   Missing the Point: Rebuttal to Bettinger, O'Connell, and Thomas. *American Anthropologist* 93:172–173.
WILL, GEORGE F., AND HERBERT J. SPINDEN
1906   The Mandans: A Study of Their Culture, Archaeology and Language. *Peabody Museum of American Archaeology and Ethnology, Papers* 3(4):79–219. Cambridge, Massachusetts.
WILLEY, GORDON R.
1938   Time Studies: Pottery and Trees in Georgia. *Society for Georgia Archaeology, Proceedings* 1:15–22.
1939   Ceramic Stratigraphy in a Georgia Village Site. *American Antiquity* 5:140–147.
1945   Horizon Styles and Pottery Traditions in Peruvian Archaeology. *American Antiquity* 10:49–56.
1948   A Functional Analysis of "Horizon Styles in Peruvian Archaeology. In A Reappraisal of Peruvian Archaeology, assembled by Wendell C. Bennett, pp. 8–15. *Society for American Archaeology, Memoirs* No. 4.
1949   Archeology of the Florida Gulf Coast. *Smithsonian Miscellaneous Collections* 113.
1951   The Chavín Problem: A Review and Critique. *Southwestern Journal of Anthropology* 7:103–144.
1953a   A Pattern of Diffusion–Acculturation. *Southwestern Journal of Anthropology* 9:369–384.
1953b   Archaeological Theories and Interpretation: New World. In *Anthropology Today*, edited by Alfred L. Kroeber, pp. 361–385. University of Chicago Press, Chicago.
1953c   Prehistoric Settlement Patterns in the Virú Valley, Peru. *Bureau of American Ethnology, Bulletin* 155.
1960   Historical Patterns and Evolution in Native New World Cultures. In *Evolution After Darwin*, Vol. 2: *The Evolution of Man*, edited by Sol Tax, pp. 111–141. University of Chicago Press, Chicago.
1961   Review of "Evolution and Culture" edited by Marshall D. Sahlins and Elman R. Service. *American Antiquity* 26:441–443.

1966   *An Introduction to American Archaeology* Vol. 1: *North and Middle America*. Prentice-Hall, Englewood Cliffs, New Jersey.

1968   One Hundred Years of American Archaeology. In *One Hundred Years of Anthropology*, edited by J. O. Brew, pp. 26–53. Harvard University Press, Cambridge, Massachusetts.

1981   Spinden's Archaic Hypothesis. In *Antiquity and Man: Essays in Honour of Glyn Daniel*, edited by John D. Evans, Barry Cunliffe, and Colin Renfrew, pp. 35–42. Thames and Hudson, London.

1988   *Portraits in American Archaeology: Remembrances of Some Distinguished Americanists*. University of New Mexico Press, Albuquerque.

WILLEY, GORDON R., AND PHILIP PHILLIPS

1955   Method and Theory in American Archaeology, II: Historical-Developmental Interpretation. *American Anthropologist* 57:723–819.

1958   *Method and Theory in American Archaeology*. University of Chicago Press, Chicago.

WILLEY, GORDON R., AND JEREMY A. SABLOFF

1974   *A History of American Archaeology*. Freeman, San Francisco.

1980   *A History of American Archaeology*, 2nd ed. Freeman, San Francisco.

1993   *A History of American Archaeology*, 3rd ed. Freeman, New York.

WILLEY, GORDON R., AND R. B. WOODBURY

1942   A Chronological Outline for the Northwest Florida Coast. *American Antiquity* 7:232–254.

WILLIS, J. C.

1922   *Age and Area, a Study in Geographical Distribution and the Origin of Species*. Cambridge University Press, Cambridge.

WILMSEN, EDWIN N.

1968a   Functional Analysis of Flaked Stone Artifacts. *American Antiquity* 33:156–161.

1968b   Lithic Analysis in Paleoanthropology. *Science* 161:982–987.

WILSON, T.

1899   Arrowheads, Spearheads, and Knives of Prehistoric Times. *United States National Museum, Annual Report* (1897), Part I, pp. 811–988.

WISSLER, CLARK

1909   Introduction. In The Indians of Greater New York and the Lower Hudson, edited by Clark Wissler. *American Museum of Natural History, Anthropological Papers* 3:xiii–xv.

1914   Material Cultures of the North American Indians. *American Anthropologist* 16:447–505.

1915   Explorations in the Southwest by the American Museum. *American Museum Journal* 15:395–398.

1916a   Correlations between Archeological and Culture Areas in the American Continents. In *Holmes Anniversary Volume: Anthropological Essays*, pp. 481–490. Washington, D.C.

1916b   The Application of Statistical Methods to the Data on the Trenton Argillite Culture. *American Anthropologist* 18:190–197.

1916c   The Genetic Relations of Certain Forms in American Aboriginal Art. *National Academy of Sciences, Proceedings* 2:224–226.

1917a   *The American Indian*. McMurtrie, New York.

1917b   The New Archaeology. *American Museum Journal* 17:100–101.

1919   General Introduction. *American Museum of Natural History, Anthropological Papers* 18:iii–ix.

1921   Dating Our Prehistoric Ruins. *Natural History* 21:13–26.

1923   *Man and Culture.* Crowell, New York.

1924   The Relation of Nature to Man as Illustrated by the North American Indian. *Ecology* 5:311–318.

WOODBURY, RICHARD B.

1956   (editor) Seminars in Archaeology: 1955. *Society for American Archaeology, Memoirs* No. 11.

1960a   Nels C. Nelson and Chronological Archaeology. *American Antiquity* 25:400–401.

1960b   Nelson's Stratigraphy. *American Antiquity* 26:98–99.

1973   *Alfred V. Kidder.* Columbia University Press, New York.

WOODS, CARTER A.

1934   A Criticism of Wissler's North American Culture Areas. *American Anthropologist* 36:517–523.

WOODS, CLYDE M.

1975   *Culture Change.* Brown, Dubuque, Iowa.

WRIGHT, G. FREDERICK

1888   On the Age of the Ohio Gravel Beds. *Boston Society of Natural History, Proceedings* 23:427–436.

1892   *Man and the Glacial Period.* Appleton, New York.

WRIGHT, JOHN H., J. D. McGUIRE, FREDERICK W. HODGE, WARREN K. MOOREHEAD, AND CHARLES PEABODY

1909   Report of the Committee on Archeological Nomenclature. *American Anthropologist* 11:114–119.

WYMAN, JEFFRIES

1868   An Account of Some Kjoekkenmoeddings, or Shell-Heaps, in Maine and Massachusetts. *The American Naturalist* 1:561–584.

1875   Fresh-Water Shell Mounds of the St. John's River, Florida. *Peabody Academy of Science, Memoir* 4.

Index